Landlord's Legal Kit

FOR

DUMMIES®

A Wiley Brand

by Laurence Harmon, JD,
and Robert S. Griswold, MBA

FOR

DUMMIES®

A Wiley Brand

Landlord's Legal Kit For Dummies®

Published by: **John Wiley & Sons, Inc.,** 111 River Street, Hoboken, NJ 07030-5774, www.wiley.com

For general information on our other products and services, please contact our Customer Care Department within the U.S. at 877-762-2974, outside the U.S. at 317-572-3993, or fax 317-572-4002. For technical support, please visit www.wiley.com/techsupport.

Wiley publishes in a variety of print and electronic formats and by print-on-demand. Some material included with standard print versions of this book may not be included in e-books or in print-on-demand. If this book refers to media such as a CD or DVD that is not included in the version you purchased, you may download this material at http://booksupport.wiley.com. For more information about Wiley products, visit www.wiley.com.

Library of Congress Control Number: 2013954220

ISBN: 978-1-118-77519-6

ISBN 978-1-118-77519-6 (pbk); ISBN 978-1-118-77511-0 (ebk); ISBN 978-1-118-77518-9 (ebk)

Manufactured in the United States of America

10 9 8 7 6 5 4 3 2 1

Contents at a Glance

Table of Contents

Introduction

Success as a landlord requires more than finding residents, collecting rent, and performing repairs and maintenance. You also need to be familiar with and abide by federal, state, and local laws that govern rental housing. Failure to do business in compliance with those laws can result in severe and very costly consequences.

You need a guide to bring you up to speed in a hurry about the legal aspects of managing residential rental property and provide you with the contracts, forms, and other documents that will help you to comply with those laws. You also need guidance on how to avoid and protect against legal claims commonly filed against landlords. *Landlord's Legal Kit For Dummies* is your guide.

About This Book

In this book, we lead you through the legal minefield of owning and managing residential rental property, from the time you purchase your rental property and market and advertise the property until the rental contract ends and the resident moves out. You steer clear of legal problems in three ways:

- ✔ Understand and comply with all relevant laws — federal, state, and local.
- ✔ Honor your legal obligations as a landlord to your residents, so they're less likely to file a claim against you — and if they do, they're less likely to win a judgment.
- ✔ Document all landlord-resident agreements and communication, so you have evidence that stands up in court.

This book is based on hands-on experience and lessons from our experiences owning and managing residential rental properties and helping other owners comply with federal, state, and local housing laws. To make your life easier, we've included many of the contracts, forms, and other documents — whether you're just starting out with a single-family rental home or condo, you have a handful of rental units, or you possess a whole portfolio of rental properties. To access the forms, go to www.dummies.com/go/landlordlegalkit. We strongly recommend that you have your local legal counsel review them, and then print them out and start putting them to use. You can access this website by using the user name robertgriswold and the password landlord when prompted.

Foolish Assumptions

In order to provide you with the guidance you need, we had to make a few assumptions about who you are. We assumed the following:

- ✔ You own or manage or you plan to own or manage rental property.
- ✔ You're specifically interested in finding out about laws that govern residential rental properties, not commercial properties.
- ✔ You're committed to operating in accordance with all federal, state, and local laws.
- ✔ You want to avoid having legal claims filed against you.
- ✔ When a legal claim is filed against you, you want to win.

Icons Used in This Book

Throughout this book, icons in the margins highlight different types of information that call out for your attention. Here are the icons you'll see and a brief description of each.

This icon points you to files or forms you can use in your day-to-day property management. You'll find them online at www.dummies.com/go/landlordlegalkit. You can access this website by using the user name robertgriswold and the password landlord when prompted.

We want you to remember everything you read in this book, but if you can't quite do that, then remember the important points flagged with this icon.

Tips provide insider insight. When you're looking for a better, faster way to do something, check out these tips.

Focus on this icon for real-life anecdotes from our many years of experience and mistakes. When you've managed more than 60,000 rental units in 35 years, you see some interesting situations. Now, we share them with you.

"Whoa!" This icon appears when you need to be extra vigilant or seek professional help before moving forward.

This icon points out bonus material you can find online.

Beyond the Book

In addition to the material in the print or ebook you're reading right now, this product also comes with some access-anywhere goodies on the web. Go to www.dummies.com/landlordlegalkit for additional information, such as the following:

- ✔ Sample lease agreement, move-in/move-out inspection checklist, eviction notice, and dozens of other essential legal forms and documents

- ✔ Resources for finding state and local statutes and additional legal information

- ✔ References to organizations, government agencies, media, and vendors/ suppliers that provide additional information, training, tools, and services to make you a better landlord

Use robertgriswold for the username and landlord for the password.

Also, check out the free Cheat Sheet at www.dummies.com/cheatsheet/ landlordlegalkit for strategies you can use for screening applicants, establishing security deposits and procedures, meeting your obligations as a landlord, and brushing up on fair housing laws. Be sure to visit www. dummies.com/extras/landlordlegalkit for free articles about retaining good residents, screening residents, complying with your duties to make repairs, and more. You can also read a bonus chapter about establishing competitive, yet profitable rents.

Where to Go from Here

You can approach this book in three ways:

- ✔ **Read it from beginning to end.** Although being a landlord isn't a linear process, we present topics in the order you're most likely to encounter them. We start with setting up your business and taking possession of a rental property; move on to advertising vacancies, screening applicants, and fulfilling your legal obligations to residents; and end with a resident moving out.

- ✔ **Skip around.** Each chapter is a stand-alone lesson on a specific legal aspect of property management. If you want to know about fair housing laws, skip to Chapter 5. Head to Chapter 10 for guidance in developing a security deposit policy. For information regarding your legal obligations to perform maintenance and repairs, flip to Chapter 12.

- ✔ **Use it as a reference book.** Whenever you need information and advice on a specific legal aspect of being a landlord, turn to the index, look it up, and flip to the chapter or the specific page where that topic is covered.

If you just need some quick advice on how to avoid having legal claims filed against you, skip to Chapter 21, where you'll find ten tips for staying out of legal trouble.

The more you use this book, the more confident you'll be that you're complying with federal, state, and local laws and that you'll have the documented evidence you need to take legal action against a resident and defend yourself when a resident or someone else takes legal action against you.

Part I
Getting Started with Landlording Fundamentals

getting started
with
Landlording
Fundamentals

 Visit www.dummies.com/cheatsheet/landlordlegalkit for more informative tidbits about the ins and outs of landlording.

In this part . . .

✔ Get a bird's-eye view of your legal rights and obligations as they relate to owning and managing residential rental property.

✔ Discover the benefits of operating as a legal entity, such as a limited liability company (LLC), instead of as a sole proprietorship.

✔ Understand your tax obligations, so you can plan ahead and have enough money set aside to cover your tax bills.

✔ Find out how to conduct legal research to find out about state statutes and local regulations regarding residential rentals.

✔ Take possession of a rental property the right way, so you get everything you paid for and avoid any legal snags.

✔ Choose and buy the right insurance policy to cover your rental assets in the event of unavoidable mishaps and disasters.

✔ Decide whether you want to outsource some of your landlord chores to a property manager or management firm, weigh the pros and cons of each option, and find the right individual or firm for the job.

Chapter 1

Grasping the Legal Fundamentals of Managing Residential Rentals

In This Chapter

▶ Incorporating for legal protection and income optimization

▶ Stepping into a rental property as its new owner

▶ Getting up to speed on landlord legalities

*W*henever you approach a subject for the first time, you probably try to wrap your brain around it before getting into the specifics. This chapter helps you gain the big-picture perspective by highlighting the key legal aspects of being a landlord and managing residential rentals. Think of this chapter as a framework on which you can hang all the detailed information, guidance, and insights we present throughout this book.

This chapter begins by laying out the legal foundation for your residential rental operation. The first section stresses the importance of running your business as a legal entity in order to protect your personal assets, minimize taxes, and maximize profits. The second section touches on important steps to follow when taking ownership of the property. The third and longest section in this chapter introduces your legal obligations as a landlord; here you find out how to fulfill your obligations while protecting your rights and avoiding legal problems.

Running Your Operation as a Corporation or LLC

Unless you take steps to give your business the status of a corporation or limited liability company (LLC), you're operating as a sole proprietorship and placing your personal assets at risk. If you can't pay what you owe to a creditor, such as a contractor, a utility company, or the bank that holds the mortgage on your property, they can pursue your personal assets to collect what you owe. Operating your business as a corporation or LLC insulates your personal assets from your business assets, thus protecting your personal assets from such claims. In addition, operating your business as a corporation or LLC potentially reduces your taxes, increasing your net profit.

Most landlords choose to operate as an LLC, because it provides the protection of a corporation without the costs and complexities of forming and managing a corporation. Any claims by creditors against the LLC are limited to the LLC's assets, protecting your home, personal financial accounts, and other personal assets from those claims.

 An LLC doesn't provide complete protection. If a court finds that your carelessness or negligence contributed to a resident's injury, for example, you could be held personally liable. We recommend that you purchase a landlord insurance policy that covers such scenarios, as explained in Chapter 3.

Structuring your business and operating it as a corporation is much more complicated and expensive than forming an LLC. You need to register a name for your corporation with your state's Secretary of State, write and file articles of incorporation and bylaws, issue stock (at least one share), have regular corporate meetings, prepare and file minutes from those meetings, and comply with regulations for recording and reporting financial transactions. In addition, to take full advantage of tax savings, you may need to pay a portion of your profits from the rental property to yourself as a salary, which requires payroll processing.

See Chapter 2 for more about the options for structuring your residential rental business.

Taking Ownership of a Rental Property

Assuming you've completed the closing on your rental property, you realize that transferring ownership of any real estate is a fairly complicated endeavor. The process is even more complicated and perilous when transferring ownership of a rental property. When you buy a rental property, make sure you get the following items from the seller:

- ✔ A list of personal property included in the sale
- ✔ All resident files
- ✔ Seller-verified rent roll and list of all security deposits
- ✔ All required governmental licenses and permits

> ✔ Recent utility bills that are due
>
> ✔ Every service agreement or contract
>
> ✔ Copy of the seller's current insurance policy

Chapter 3 contains additional information about these items.

Meet with a reputable insurance provider and purchase a policy for the property prior to taking possession, so there's no lapse in insurance coverage before you take possession. If the property burns down before closing, it's the seller's problem. If an uninsured property burns down after closing, it's your problem. For more about choosing an insurance policy that provides sufficient coverage, see Chapter 3.

After you become the proud owner of the rental property, you have a few tasks to attend to as soon as possible, including the following:

> ✔ Meet with the residents in person, introduce yourself as the new owner, and answer any questions they ask.
>
> ✔ Inspect the outside of the rental property carefully and make a list of any maintenance and repair issues. Address these issues as soon as possible.
>
> ✔ Evaluate the current rent. You can't raise the rent for current residents until their lease expires or the end of the month (for month-to-month renters), but analyze how much rent your residents are paying now, and how much you need to charge new residents to turn a decent profit and how much to raise the rent for existing residents when that time comes.
>
> ✔ Prepare rental contracts (either a fixed-term lease or a month-to-month rental agreement), so they're ready for new residents and for current residents who decide to remain after their rental contract expires.

Avoiding the Legal Pitfalls of Managing Residential Rental Properties

Owning residential rental property comes with legal obligations and risks. You're legally responsible to comply with fair housing laws, keep your property in "habitable" condition, ensure your residents' rights to "quiet enjoyment" of the property, comply with laws for handling and refunding security deposits, take reasonable steps to prevent crime, and eliminate any dangerous or hazardous conditions. If you have employees, you may be liable for their legal actions, as well. And residents can file a claim against you for any number of reasons, regardless of whether those claims have legal merit.

These sections highlight many of the most common legal issues you need to be aware of. We also guide you in best practices that help you avoid legal problems in the first place, such as screening applicants carefully and honoring your residents' legal rights.

Obeying fair housing laws

Fair housing laws prohibit landlords from using certain criteria, such as race or sex, to target residents in advertising or to refuse housing to applicants. When screening applicants, for example, you're permitted to consider only factors that are likely to indicate whether the person will pay her rent on time, take care of the property, get along with the neighbors, and comply with your other policies. You may use criteria such as income, credit history, past evictions, criminal history, and similar factors to determine the prospect's qualifications. You can't use race, skin color, religion, or certain other criteria.

In the following sections, we explain the federal Fair Housing Act and look at how some states expand coverage of that Act. We also stress the importance of considering fair housing laws when advertising your rental property.

Federal law: The Fair Housing Act

The Fair Housing Act prohibits you, as landlord, from discriminating against or giving preferential treatment to people based on a *protected class* — a characteristic that can't be used to discriminate against or in favor of an individual or group. The Fair Housing Act specifies the following seven protected classes:

- ✔ **Race:** Ethnicities or cultures, such as African American, Caucasian, Hispanic, Asian, or American Indian
- ✔ **Religion:** Christianity, Islam, Judaism, Hinduism, and so on
- ✔ **National origin:** The country or area a person was born in, such as Canada, Mexico, the Middle East, or Nigeria
- ✔ **Sex:** Physical sex — male or female
- ✔ **Color:** Skin color or shade, which may seem to be the same thing as race, but people of the same race sometimes discriminate against one another based on lightness or darkness of skin
- ✔ **Handicap:** Physical or mental handicaps or disabilities, including hearing and visual impairments, chronic alcoholism, and HIV/AIDS
- ✔ **Familial status:** Whether a person or couple has children

Consider only those characteristics that reflect the likelihood that the person will pay rent in full on time, treat your rental property with care, and get along with her neighbors. As a landlord, you should consider nothing else.

State and local laws

Some states and municipalities have extended the Fair Housing Act to other protected classes, including the following:

- ✔ Marital status or changes in marital status
- ✔ Sexual orientation or domestic partner/civil union
- ✔ Age
- ✔ Source of income
- ✔ Creed (belief system)

For more about the Fair Housing Act, protected classes, and state additions to the Act, see Chapter 5.

Advertising within the law

Fair housing also comes into play when you're marketing and advertising your property. To comply with fair housing laws in advertising, follow these four general guidelines:

- ✔ Avoid any obviously discriminating words and phrases that state or imply that certain protected classes are unwelcome or that you prefer a certain type of clientele, such as singles, married couples, or affluent individuals.
- ✔ If you use photographs or pictures of people in your advertisements, make sure they convey diversity in race, sex, familial status, and so on.
- ✔ Don't use location, place names, directions, and so on that may suggest exclusion or preference for a certain protected class. For example, stating that the property is near a certain country club or religious facility may be construed as a preference for some prospects while discriminating against others.
- ✔ Include the US Department of Housing and Urban Development's (HUD's) Equal Housing Opportunity logo or statement on all advertising to invite people of all protected classes to apply.

Most landlords avoid blatantly discriminatory language and images in their advertisements. They're more likely to inadvertently commit a violation by showing a picture of a young white couple, for example, or mentioning that the property is "perfect" for certain classes of prospects.

Have someone who's well versed in federal, state, and local fair housing laws review all of your advertisements before you start running them. For more about complying with fair housing and other laws in your advertising, see Chapter 6.

Setting rents and payment policies

Sometime prior to renting out a property, you need to set your rents and payment policies to address the following aspects of rent payments:

- ✔ **Amount:** You want to charge enough rent to cover your operating expenses, earn a decent profit, and remain competitive. In a few cities in a handful of states, you also may need to consider rental rate regulation or *rent control* as well. Visit www.dummies.com/extras/landlordlegalkit and click on the bonus chapter for guidance on setting rents.

- ✔ **Due date:** We recommend having all residents pay the rent in full on the first of the month. If the resident moves in on a day other than the first, then you collect the first month's rent in full and then prorate the second rent payment. This way you collect more money up-front and minimize your risk that your tenant will gain possession of your rental property by just paying you a nominal amount of rent.

- ✔ **Payment form:** This may be cash, check, money order, cashier's check, or online/electronic payment, depending on what you're willing to accept.

- ✔ **Late payments and penalties:** Specify when payments are considered late; for example, "Payments received more than five (5) days after the first of the month are considered late payments." Also specify a penalty, perhaps a 5 percent late fee when the payment is past due.

- ✔ **Penalties for bounced checks:** Penalties may include a flat fee to cover the fee your bank charges you plus a little extra for your time, inconvenience, and aggravation. You may also want to specify that if a certain number of checks bounce, the resident loses the privilege to pay with a personal check.

- ✔ **Penalties for missed payments:** The penalty for missed payments is usually that the resident is required to move out for breach of contract, but you need to specify what a missed payment is; for example, if you haven't received it within 15 days of the due date.

For more about legal issues regarding rent collection and rent control, see Chapter 7.

Screening applicants

Carefully screening applicants is essential to keep your rental units occupied with residents who pay on time, take care of the property, and get along with their neighbors. Careful screening can help you avoid legal issues, because you have less need to take legal action against good residents, and they're less likely to file legal claims against you. To screen applicants, take the following steps:

1. **Have the person complete and submit an application that includes her name, current address, Social Security number, employment history, rental history, income, and so on.**

   Visit www.dummies.com/go/landlordlegalkit and click on the Leasing folder for a sample application.

2. **Order a credit and background check for the prospective resident.**

   You can find several services online that perform credit and background checks. Your application should include language stating that the applicant agrees to a credit and background check.

3. **Contact the applicant's employer to verify the applicant's employment and income and find out how long the applicant has been employed there.**

   You may also want to require copies of pay stubs, recent W-2s and 1099s, the previous year's tax return, and a recent bank statement.

4. **Contact the applicant's personal references.**

5. **Contact any landlords the applicant rented from in the past and ask about payment history, the condition the applicant left the property in, and whether the applicant caused problems with her neighbors.**

6. **Interview the applicant in person.**

   Ask why the person is moving and why she chose this area. Ask questions related to information you gathered in previous steps to determine whether what the applicant tells you matches up with what you already know. Inconsistencies can be a red flag.

When screening prospective renters, you must comply with fair housing laws, so certain questions are off-limits. You can gather information about a prospect's employment status, income, credit history, housing history, and criminal past, but you're prohibited from asking an applicant whether she has children, what country she's from, her religion, and so forth. For additional details on how to screen applicants, see Chapter 8.

Drafting a lease or rental agreement

Your rental contract (either the lease or month-to-month rental agreement) establishes the terms that you and your resident agree to, including who's going to be living in the unit and paying rent and for how long, the rent amount and when it's due, the security deposit amount and what it can be used for, your obligations, the resident's obligations, whether pets are allowed and under what conditions, and so on.

We recommend that you start with an existing lease and then modify it to suit your specific needs. You can obtain a sample lease by doing any of the following:

- Visit `www.dummies.com/go/landlordlegalkit` and click on the Rental Contract folder. In Chapter 9, we explain the terms of this lease and modifications you may want to consider.

- Search the web for your state followed by "lease" or "rental agreement." Sometimes attorneys or property management companies post the lease or rental agreement they use.

- Ask a reputable local attorney who specializes in landlord-tenant law or real estate for a copy of a residential lease and a residential rental agreement. You may be able to obtain the lease for free or for a modest fee.

- Use an online legal service, such as `www.rocketlawyer.com` to obtain a state-specific lease or rental agreement. (Many of these services advertise "free lease." The hook is that they lead you through a long process of creating a rental contract and then require that you sign up for the service and provide credit card information. You may be able to sign up for a free week or month of the service to get the contracts you need and then cancel the service.)

- Contact your local affiliate of the National Apartment Association (NAA) or a similar rental industry group about membership. They often have comprehensive, up-to-date legal forms that comply with all applicable laws for your area available for their members at a reasonable cost.

Managing security deposits

Prior to when a resident moves in, you need to collect the first month's rent (or prorated rent) along with a *security deposit* — a lump sum that you hold until the resident moves out in order to cover the cost of any unpaid rent and damages (beyond ordinary wear and tear). As we explain in Chapter 10, you should have a security deposit policy in place that specifies the following:

- **Amount:** Usually no more than the equivalent of one- or two-month's rent. Some states and municipalities have specific limits.

- **Due date:** Usually due at the signing of the rental contract.

- **Allowed uses:** State and local laws usually allow landlords to use security deposits only to cover unpaid rent, damages to the unit beyond ordinary wear and tear, cleaning expenses (only to make the unit as clean as it was when the resident moved in), and to restore or replace damaged or missing property, including keys and appliances furnished with the unit.

✔ **Where the deposit will be held:** We recommend depositing all security deposits in a separate interest-bearing account and passing along any interest earned (unless nominal) to the resident when you return any unused portion of the deposit.

✔ **Return of the unused portion:** Specify the maximum number of days you're allowed to hold any unused portion of the security deposit before returning it to the former resident. State law may establish a limitation.

Moving residents in and out

Two very important days in the course of a resident's stay are the first and the last — the day she moves in and the day she moves out. In the following section, we cover the essential tasks you need to perform on these two days.

Moving a resident in

How well you manage the process of getting a new resident moved in can affect your relationship over the entire term of her occupancy. Get started on the right foot by performing the following steps leading up to and including move-in day:

1. **Agree on a move-in date with the resident.**

2. **Make sure any utilities the resident is responsible for paying are transferred to the resident's name and are turned on no later than the move-in date.**

3. **Review important terms of your rental contract and any addenda to the contract and answer any questions the resident asks.**

4. **Collect the rent and security deposit, if you haven't done so already.**

5. **Inspect the property with the resident, complete a checklist to record the property's condition, and make sure you and the resident sign the checklist.**

   We recommend taking photos or a video, so you have a visual record of the property's condition, as well.

6. **Orient the resident to the rental unit and any appliances in the unit, utility shut-offs, and common areas, such as workout facilities, pool, and hot tub.**

7. **Present a move-in letter and a copy of your rules and regulations.**

   These documents may include instructions for requesting maintenance and repairs, taking on a roommate, replacing lost keys, paying rent, and so on. You may also include policies for guests, parking, wall hangings, ceiling hooks, pets, and so on.

8. **Give the resident time to read the move-in letter and the rules and regulations and then have her sign and date two copies of each document — one for her records and one for yours.**

9. **Give the resident keys to the rental unit and her mailbox.**

For details on moving a new resident in, see Chapter 11.

Moving the resident out

To avoid disputes and litigation after a resident moves out, manage the process the right way. Here's how:

1. **Require that residents notify you in writing a certain number of days (30 days is common) prior to the date they intend to move out.**

2. **Present the resident with a move-out letter with instructions on how to prepare the unit for the move-out inspection and a reminder of your policy for returning the security deposit after any deductions for unpaid rent or damages beyond ordinary wear and tear.**

   See Chapter 9 for more about what *ordinary wear and tear* means.

3. **Sign and have the resident sign a termination agreement, so you have documentation that the resident officially moved out.**

4. **Inspect the unit carefully for any damages or missing items that were furnished with the rental unit, and record your observations on a move-out checklist.**

   Take photos or video of any damages.

5. **As soon as possible, perform the repairs, maintenance, and cleaning required to bring the rental unit back to the condition it was in before the departing resident lived in it.**

   Keep receipts for all materials and labor.

6. **Deduct the costs of any repairs, maintenance, or cleaning that qualify as beyond ordinary wear and tear, and return the remainder of the security deposit (with interest, if required by state or local law) and along with an itemized list of expenses deducted.**

   Some jurisdictions require you to provide the former resident with receipts for work done upon request.

Of course, not all residents move out this smoothly. Sometimes, residents simply skip town, abandoning the property without notifying you. In other situations, in which a resident fails to pay rent or breaks the contract in other ways, you may need to either get the resident to leave voluntarily or evict the resident. These exceptions to the standard move-out scenario have special legal procedures you must follow according to state or local law. See Chapter 20 for details about moving residents out and Chapter 19 for more about evictions.

Fulfilling your maintenance and safety obligations

Your rights as a landlord are based upon your rental contract and your state's landlord-tenant laws. Your obligations, however, are primarily in the form of written laws or implied warranties and *covenants* (agreements). In the following sections, we bring you up to speed on your legal obligations to your residents, whether they're in writing or not.

Recognizing your duty to maintain habitable living conditions

According to the *implied warranty of habitability*, you must provide residents with dwellings that are fit to live in. For example, the unit's plumbing and electrical must be in working condition, residents must have running water and reasonable amounts of hot water, the unit must be heated in the winter, common areas must be clean and sanitary, and you must exterminate in response to infestations of rodents and vermin.

If you fail to maintain habitable living conditions, residents may be permitted by law to withhold rent, have the repairs done and bill you for them, sue for damages, take legal action to force you to solve the problems, or move and terminate the lease. See Chapter 12 for details about your obligation to honor the implied warranty of habitability.

Addressing potentially dangerous conditions

Accidents happen regardless of how careful people are, but if anyone is injured on your property as a result of something you did or neglected to do, you could be held liable for the person's medical bills and lost pay and may even be subject to punitive damages (for any reckless or intentional acts that cause injury). Here are a few areas to consider focusing your safety program on:

- ✓ **Fire safety:** Educate residents on the most common fire hazards, provide and maintain fire extinguishers and smoke detectors, and provide residents with a copy of your evacuation procedures. Your local fire department can help you comply with the fire-safety codes in your area. Carbon monoxide detectors are also important if you have gas appliances and are now required in some jurisdictions.

- ✓ **Pool and hot tub safety:** If you have a pool or hot tub, enclose it with fencing and gates that comply with your local building codes, and post required signage to inform residents and their guests of your rules, such as no diving allowed and adult supervision required for children.

- ✓ **Exterior lighting:** Make sure parking lots, stairways, walkways, and entryways have adequate lighting to keep people from tripping or bumping into things.

✔ **Safety within units:** Use safety or tempered glass in shower stalls or tub surrounds, use window coverings that have safe cords, make sure all windows have working locks and screens, use outlets with ground fault protection near water (in bathrooms and near the kitchen sink).

✔ **General maintenance issues:** Fix any loose railings, stairs, or handrails; repair uneven pavement in sidewalks and parking lots; replace burnt-out exterior lights; and so on. Shovel and de-ice walkways in the winter. Make sure that you immediately mop up any spills and that you place signs to warn residents when floors are wet/slippery.

✔ **Set and enforce pet policies:** If you allow pets, make sure your residents comply with local leash laws, at the very least.

✔ **Construction site safety:** Make sure contractors secure their construction sites to prevent injuries to curious children and adults.

Team up with residents to improve safety. Encourage them to report any safety concerns to you, respond immediately to their concerns, and thank them for their efforts. For more about improving safety, see Chapter 13.

Disclosing and responding to environmental hazards

We define *environmental hazard* as anything that may adversely affect a person's health, including the following:

✔ Asbestos

✔ Carbon monoxide

✔ Formaldehyde

✔ Radon

✔ Lead paint

✔ Toxic mold

✔ Hazardous wastes, including chemical residue from meth labs

✔ Pests, including rats, mice, roaches, and bedbugs

Each of these hazards has specific laws regarding the landlord's obligation to disclose and address.

The best course of action isn't always to remove an environmental hazard. In fact, attempts to remove harmful substances, such as asbestos, lead paint, and toxic mold, may increase the danger. If you notice an environmental hazard, head to Chapter 14 to find out how to proceed.

Protecting residents and workers from criminal activity

Landlords are legally obligated to take reasonable steps to prevent crime on their property, which is a job that's more challenging than most landlords realize. If a crime occurs on your property and the courts find that you could have, should have, and didn't take measures to prevent it, you may be held liable for any injuries or property losses that result. Here are several of your primary responsibilities for protecting residents and workers from criminal acts:

- **Provide and maintain basic security features,** including doors with deadbolt locks and peepholes for rental units, key locks, or keyless (smart key) for external doors, windows with working latches and insect screens (and in some jurisdictions, locking devices), and sufficient security lighting.

- **Report suspected criminal activity to local law enforcement** and inform residents of any significant criminal activity in the area that comes to your attention.

- **Evict residents who commit crimes,** within a certain number of days of being notified by local law enforcement.

- **Safeguard sensitive resident information** to prevent identity theft and other crimes.

- **Secure master and duplicate keys** to prevent unauthorized entry to rental units. This also applies to common areas if they're access controlled and to the extent that it's reasonably feasible.

- **Conduct criminal background checks on prospective employees** and monitor employee activity for any signs of criminal activity.

Team up with local law enforcement agencies. Many law enforcement agencies have pamphlets or booklets (some available online), with valuable guidance on how to secure rental properties. Refer to Chapter 15 for more information.

Knowing the limitations on your right to enter the premises

Landlords frequently believe that because they own the rental property, they can enter rental units whenever they want. You do have a right to enter rental units you own, but your right of entry is balanced against the *covenant of quiet enjoyment* that gives a resident the right to undisturbed use of the property. In most states, a landlord can enter a residence only under certain conditions, some of which require the landlord to give reasonable advanced notice, and some that don't:

- You can legally enter a rental unit without notice to respond to an emergency that threatens life or property, when a resident has abandoned the property, when responding to a court order, or when you ask for and a resident gives you permission to enter.

> ✔ You can legally enter a rental unit with reasonable notice to check smoke detectors and carbon monoxide detectors, inspect for and make necessary repairs, check for problems during a resident's extended absence, or show the property to a prospective renter, buyer, or lender.

For more about your right to enter the premises and a resident's right to quiet enjoyment, see Chapter 16.

Dealing with cotenants, sublets, and assignments

Every landlord recognizes the importance of screening applicants before permitting them to move into a unit. Unfortunately, residents often try to move others into their unit without your permission by taking on a roommate, subletting the unit to someone else, or assigning their lease to someone you don't know. Such practices significantly increase your exposure to risk, because it opens your doors to people who have no contractual obligation to you. You're not given the opportunity to screen the person, and you don't have the power of a legal contract to enforce your rules.

Screen everyone prior to allowing them to live in one of your rental units. Have the person complete an application, and then follow your standard screening procedure, including performing background checks. If you give approval, make sure the person signs a rental contract. A roommate may simply sign the existing rental contract. Instead of subletting and assignments, we recommend terminating the previous resident's lease and creating a new one for the new resident. For additional details about roommates, sublets, and leases, see Chapter 18.

Terminating rental contracts

All good things (and bad things) must come to an end, and the same is true of rental contracts. The process differs depending on whether you're terminating a lease or a rental agreement and on the circumstances surrounding the termination:

> ✔ **Lease:** A *lease* is a rental contract for a fixed-term, usually one or two years. You can terminate a lease in any of the following three ways:
>
> • Let it expire and don't renew it. In this case, you should serve your resident a Notice of Nonrenewal 30 or 60 days prior to the date on which the lease expires.

- Mutually agree with your resident to end the lease, in which case you should both sign a Mutual Termination of Lease Agreement.

- Require that the resident move out for breach of contract. In this situation, you must serve the resident a termination notice giving her a certain number of days to move out.

✔ **Rental agreement:** A *rental agreement* is a month-to-month contract. You typically can terminate a rental agreement with or without cause:

- **With cause:** If the resident breaches the contract, you may be able to require that the resident move out in as little as a few days.

- **Without cause:** In most states, you can end a rental agreement without cause, as long as you give the resident sufficient notice, typically 30 to 60 days prior to the termination date.

For more about terminating rental contracts and obtaining the required notices and forms, see Chapter 19.

Chapter 2

Protecting Your Legal Assets

. . . .

In This Chapter

▶ Reducing personal liability through incorporation

▶ Brushing up on the laws that govern residential rentals

▶ Having an attorney cover your back

▶ Dealing with taxes

. . . .

As a landlord, you have a lot to lose and many ways to lose it. You have the same concerns as a homeowner, including damage or loss from fires, natural disasters, theft, and vandalism, plus the added risk of being sued over accidents and crimes committed at your property, alleged housing discrimination, breach of contract, and a host of other issues. If you're not careful, lawsuits may even imperil your personal assets, including the home you live in.

In this chapter, we explain how to protect your personal and business assets from the perils of rental property ownership. Here, you find out how to incorporate in order to protect your personal assets from claims against your business and how to keep abreast of the laws that govern residential rentals so you're less likely to commit a violation that imperils your business and personal assets. We also discuss how an attorney can help you and what you also need to know about taxes associated with your rental property.

Forming Your Business

You can own and manage your rental property as an individual or as a business entity. However, if you take ownership of a rental property personally, you expose your personal assets to increased risk and lose out on some of the tax advantages available to business entities. We recommend that you keep your personal and business assets separate.

Here we compare five forms of real estate ownership, each of which provides benefits and limitations that impact your profitability and personal liability. None of these forms of ownership are ideal; depending on the property itself and your investment goals, one form may be better than the others. You should make this decision only after consulting with your legal and tax advisors.

Choosing a legal structure

How you choose to structure your business depends in part upon your willingness to share its future and yours with others, in part upon your personal appetite for taking or avoiding risks, and in part upon your long-term perspective about the future of residential real estate as a desirable investment.

The various forms of real estate ownership can accommodate any or all of these considerations, giving you options that range from sole proprietorships, which facilitate your willingness to take personal responsibility for the performance of the business, to partnerships and corporations that pool the capital and experience of people of vastly different backgrounds. Table 2-1 provides an overview of the various forms of real estate ownership along with each form's taxation status, owner liability, and management structure and the sections that follow for details.

Table 2-1	Forms of Real Estate Ownership		
Ownership Form	*Taxation Status*	*Owner Liability*	*Management*
Sole Proprietorship	Single	Unlimited	Personal
General Partnership	Single	Unlimited	All partners
Limited Partnership	Single	Limited	General partner(s)
Limited Liability Company	Single	Limited	Manager(s) or member(s)
Corporation	Single or double	Limited	Officers
REIT	Modified single	Limited	Trustees

Sole proprietorships

Some landlords operate as sole proprietors, which enable them to conduct business without the constraints and complexities of partnerships, corporations, and other, more formal, business types. The sole proprietor can be likened to the gunslinger in the Wild West, trusting his instincts and risking everything.

As sole proprietor, you're personally responsible for the consequences of every business decision. You have total control of the property and are entitled to all the proceeds that the property generates. You're free to close its doors whenever you choose, and you may sell it, give it away, or transfer it to your heirs after your death. Perhaps best of all is the sole proprietorship's simplicity — you don't have to comply with complex filing requirements associated with other business entities.

Owning a rental property as a sole proprietor has one main disadvantage that generally outweighs the benefits of simplicity and freedom: As sole proprietor, you're personally liable for debts incurred by the business, which means that unpaid creditors can pursue all of your personal assets, including those wholly unrelated to the sole proprietorship, to cover your debts. You'll also have more difficulty getting a business loan, because of the frequency of defaults by sole proprietors.

Two or more investors may choose to own real estate in *joint tenancy* or *tenancy in common*, both of which are well suited to smaller portfolios. The joint tenancy form transfers ownership to the other joint tenant(s) when one of the joint tenants dies, based upon the legal principle of *right of survivorship*. Each owner ("tenant") in the tenancy in common has an undivided interest in the property; upon the tenant's death, this interest passes to his heirs.

Partnerships

Partnership is similar to sole proprietorship, but with more than one owner. Profits and losses generated by the property are distributed to the individual partners as specified in their partnership agreement or according to how much money each partner has invested in the property. While the partnership must report its annual income, gains, and losses, it doesn't pay income tax. The income or loss passes through to the partners, each of whom is required to report his share as income.

Like a sole proprietorship, a partnership doesn't protect the partners from liability. When a partnership is sued and found liable, the general partners are individually and collectively liable for damages, according to the principle of *joint and several liability*. (See Chapter 9 for more about joint and several liability.)

If you chose to operate as a sole proprietor or act as the general partner of a general partnership, you want to be sure that you have consulted with your insurance advisor or agent and have adequate insurance (including an umbrella policy) to protect your insurable interests and assets. (See Chapter 3 for more information on insurance.)

Partner liability to other partners

In some states, limited liability partnerships protect every partner's personal assets from claims filed by creditors, residents, and others outside the partnership, but they make partners personally liable to one another.

For example, a Minnesota statute, enacted in 1994, insulates limited liability partners from claims against the partnership. However, a partner could be liable to the partnership and his copartners for breaches of duty, such as failure to fulfill legal, moral, or ethical obligations owed to the other partners or the partnership.

Partnerships vary in form:

✔ A *general partnership* comprises two or more owners or investors who associate for business purposes. Title to the property is taken in the name of the partnership, and all partners are legally entitled to participate in the rights, duties, obligations, and financial rewards of the partnership. A general partnership has two potential drawbacks:

  • Partners are individually and collectively liable for all of the partnership's debts and tort liabilities.

  • Any partner can commit the others to a financial obligation, even if the other partners are unaware or don't consent to it.

✔ A *limited liability partnership* is similar to a general partnership, except that the individual partners are protected against personal liability for some partnership liabilities, depending upon the laws of the state in which the partnership does business. Some states protect the limited liability partners against *tort claims* — legal claims based upon an alleged wrongful act not involving a breach of contract — but not claims of a partner's negligence or incompetence. Other states provide much more extensive protection, including immunity from contractual claims brought by the partnership's creditors.

✔ A *limited partnership* is an especially popular ownership form, consisting of one or more general partners who supervise the investment, together with a number of limited partners. The general partners are exposed to unlimited liability, while the liability of the limited partners is fixed at the amount of their capital investment.

✔ In a *limited liability limited partnership*, the general partners' liability is fixed at the amount of their individual investment.

Corporations

A corporation is a business owned by one or more than one persons. A corporation

- Is an independent legal entity that can sue or be sued
- Shields owner(s) from personal liability
- May be required to pay federal, state, and local taxes
- Is prohibited from transferring its tax deductions to its owners
- Is managed by a board of directors elected by the corporation's owners (its shareholders)
- May continue to exist after the departure of one or more of its owners
- Can require legal and accounting advice to establish as well as to operate
- Has strict rules that must be complied with exactly or the owner could be found to be personally liable

You can choose to organize your business as one of two types of corporations:

- **C Corporation:** C Corps pay income taxes, resulting in *double-taxation* the corporation pays taxes on its profits, and its owners pay income taxes on the money they receive from the corporation. (Unlike S Corps, C Corps aren't restricted in the number of shareholders they have or the types of stock they can issue.)

- **S Corporation:** An S Corp doesn't pay federal income tax. As with a partnership, profits pass through the corporation to its owners, usually in the form of a salary, distributions, or both.

    The S Corp classification is strict. The number of shareholders is limited to 100, and only one class of stock can be issued. Shareholders must be individuals or estates; other types of entities can't own stock in an S Corp.

Attorneys and accountants often recommend structuring a small business as an S Corp because this status can be used to reduce the amount of self-employment tax you're required to pay in compliance with the Federal Insurance Contributions Act (FICA). When you work for an employer, the employer pays half of FICA, and you pay the other half. When you work for yourself, you pay both halves (what's referred to as the *self-employment tax*). To reduce the self-employment tax, the S Corp pays you a portion in salary and a portion in distributions. For the salary portion, the S Corp pays half of FICA and you pay the other half, but neither you nor the corporation pays FICA on the amount of money you receive in the form of distributions. However, taking too much of your S Corp's profits in distributions is likely to trigger an audit.

Considering joint ventures

The *joint venture* is a business that combines different forms of ownership to leverage the knowledge, skills, and assets of the investors while sharing the risks and rewards of all. For example, one member may invest money while another member invests time and expertise.

The advantages, disadvantages, and tax consequences of the joint venture depend upon the type of business entity that the members select. Common joint ventures couple the abilities of developers and institutional investors, the latter contributing capital, land, or both, whereas the developer provides the necessary skills to deliver a quality product. Foreign capital is often a component of joint ventures.

Limited liability company (LLC)

A limited liability company (LLC) is a hybrid legal structure intended to combine the benefits of a corporation and a partnership. Specifically, the LLC offers limited liability protection for its member(s) (owner(s) and investor(s)) together with the tax efficiencies and operational flexibility of a partnership. (Members may be individuals, two or more people, corporations, or other LLCs, depending upon the state in which the LLC is formed.) Note, however, that limited liability doesn't always protect members from wrongful acts, such as those committed by the LLC's employees.

Members of an LLC are considered self-employed and must pay self-employment tax. The entire net income of the LLC is subject to this tax.

There are distinct advantages to LLCs but there are also added costs. The cost to form and maintain an LLC in the form of legal and professional accounting expenses should be evaluated as part of the cost/benefit analysis. Although the single taxation of S Corps and LLCs is attractive, be sure to inquire if your state has minimum taxes or fees as well as other specific requirements such as annual filings.

Exploring ways to incorporate

Forming a corporation is a fairly complex legal endeavor that involves the following steps:

1. **Choose and register a name for your corporation that complies with state requirements.**

2. **Write and file your articles of incorporation.**

3. **Write bylaws to govern corporate operations.**

4. **Issue stock certificates to your corporation's owners and investors.**

5. **Obtain any business licenses and permits required by your state and local governing bodies.**

You can take any of the following three approaches to form your corporation:

✔ Do it yourself. If you're the sole owner of the business and don't intend to add owners, seek outside capital, or do business in multiple locations, you may be able to incorporate without expert assistance. Check out *Incorporating Your Business For Dummies* by The Company Corporation (John Wiley & Sons, Inc.).

✔ Use a third-party service, as explained in the next section.

✔ Hire a reputable, local attorney. (See "Hiring an attorney," later in this chapter.)

In the following sections, we explore the options of using a third-party service and hiring an attorney and provide some guidance on how to run your business as a corporation.

Outsourcing to a business-formation service

Numerous firms offer services to help you form a business entity. Three of the best known are Legal Zoom (www.legalzoom.com), Rocket Attorney (www.rocketattorney.com), and The Company Corporation (www.incorporate.com). Others include www.infile.com, www.mynewcompany.com, www.incforfree.com, and www.directincorporation.com.

Before using a service, check with others who've used it, and expand your search to include LinkedIn (www.linkedin.com), Facebook (www.facebook.com), and Twitter (twitter.com). Find out how they're regarded by the Better Business Bureau (www.bbb.org) and local consumer protection organizations to determine whether any complaints have been filed against them.

Keep in mind that these firms are ordinary retailers who tend to advertise low prices "Starting at . . ." for only a few of the services you need. Comparison shop. Find out what's included and what's not. Get a price quote from a reputable local attorney, as well, for comparison purposes. Make sure you get a price quote that covers everything you need to form your corporation.

Hiring an attorney and accountant

We recommend that you hire a reputable, local attorney to guide you through the process of incorporating your business and an accountant to manage the corporation's payroll, taxes, and financial reporting for several reasons, including the following:

✔ Your attorney can help evaluate your specific needs for the area where you're setting up shop and recommend the best business structure to meet those needs.

✔ Choosing the wrong business structure may imperil your personal assets and limit your tax benefits.

✔ Your attorney makes sure all documents are filed properly with the right government agencies and in a timely manner.

✔ Your attorney can refer you to experts in accounting, banking, financial planning, insurance, and web design.

✔ A good business attorney will have an ongoing professional interest in your success.

✔ Your accountant keeps the books and creates and files financial reports in compliance with federal, state, and local laws.

Running your operation as a corporation

As complicated as forming a corporation is, running it requires even more attention to detail. You must fulfill the obligations of corporate governance, which include:

✔ Paying yourself and other owners and investors salaries or distributions

✔ Holding at least one director and shareholder meeting annually

✔ Typing up and filing minutes from those meetings

✔ Updating the bylaws

✔ Practicing generally accepted accounting principles (GAAP) — standards and procedures for recording financial transactions and producing financial reports

✔ Producing and filing an annual report with your Secretary of State

✔ Preparing the corporation's annual tax return

Knowing the Law or Consulting Someone Who Does

Landlords often become the targets of lawsuits simply because they don't know the federal, state, and local laws that govern the residential rental industry. To avoid getting blindsided by a lawsuit, do your own research or consult a reputable attorney who has experience with residential rental property in the location where you operate.

In the following sections, we provide guidance on how to find federal, state, and local laws that govern residential rentals and the landlord-resident relationship. We also shed some light on how to find and work with a qualified attorney.

Conducting your own legal research

You don't have to graduate from law school or even attend a single class to be able to do your own legal research. Many legal resources, indeed all of the legal resources you're likely to need, are available on the Internet. These include secondary sources and primary law:

- ✔ *Secondary sources* are legal encyclopedias and treatises (books, textbooks, and texts) that present, explain, analyze, and critique laws. Another secondary source can be rental housing industry organizations such as IREM or NAA or their state and local affiliates. Also, governmental agencies, such as your state real estate bureau or agency or the department that oversees the real estate industry and/or assists tenants, may be great resources. Secondary sources enable you to familiarize yourself with a particular legal subject and either answer your question or direct you to a primary legal authority, such as a court decision, that contains the answer.

- ✔ *Primary law* comprises cases (judicial opinions decided by federal, local, and state courts, as well the United States Supreme Court); statutes (the US Constitution and laws passed by legislatures); regulations; local ordinances; and general government information.

In the following sections, we explain how to start with secondary sources and find primary laws. We cover the process of finding primary laws in two sections — one on digging up federal and state statutes and local ordinances, and the other on tracking down court decisions.

Getting started with secondary sources

Useful legal research starts with a precise identification of the legal issues you want to explore. One way to do this is to write down a description of the legal issue you're dealing with. Here's an example:

> My apartment property is nonsmoking. The lease and the rules and regulations as well as notices posted in the leasing office and in the entries to every building include the nonsmoking policy. The leasing agents require every resident to sign a separate agreement to comply with the policy. I advertise the policy in all of my newspaper, guidebook, and Internet postings, and I have found that the residents appreciate that smoking is prohibited. It's a benefit that separates this property from the competition, and it's an important reason for our high occupancy rates.

> With the arrival of very cold weather recently, the staff has received complaints from many of the residents about secondhand smoke in their apartments. Are there any legal remedies available? What are they? Do they apply to apartments in Nevada?

However you phrase the question, you're actually asking if any laws might apply to the situation. At this point, you want to identify the facts that are directly relevant to your question and eliminate those that are unnecessary.

Extract keywords or phrases from your description that are likely to appear in a relevant court decision, such as the following:

- ✔ Apartment
- ✔ Nonsmoking
- ✔ Secondhand smoke
- ✔ Legal remedies
- ✔ Nevada

Type the keywords into your favorite Internet search engine and click the Search button. The search results include links to a variety of relevant legal resources. Our search for these terms revealed links to a variety of secondary sources, including several treatises that address the subject generally, but with specific reference to secondhand smoke infiltration in residences; an article that considers the application of the Fair Housing Act to secondhand smoke in apartments; a PDF authored by the Centers for Disease Control that specifically considers "Smoke-Free Policies in Multifamily Housing"; an article composed by "tobacco.org" that not only describes the legal remedies for smoke infiltration in apartments but also references Nevada law; and the "List of Smoking Bans in the United States," again referencing Nevada.

There's more — much more, in fact — but these references provide enough information for an apartment owner to consider the legal options available in Nevada.

Tracking down federal and state statutes and local ordinances

Statutes are laws enacted by legislatures. The US Congress enacts federal statutes that are law in all states. Each state legislature enacts statutes that are law only in that state. Statutes are published in several formats:

- ✔ *Session laws* are official texts of laws passed during a legislative session; session laws of the Congress are compiled in a set (Statutes at Large, commonly shortened to *stat*).
- ✔ *Statutory codes* arrange laws that are currently in force; the US Code organizes these laws into subject areas (titles) and numbers them in sections in each title.
- ✔ *Annotated codes* include the history of the law, the legislative *intent* of those who passed it, citations to case law, and regulations that apply to the law, along with secondary sources that discuss the various ways the statute has been applied. Searching annotated codes is a good way to determine whether a statute applies to a legal issue.

Statutes can be difficult to find. Some annotated codes include a Popular Name Table volume at the end of the Index, which helps you find statutes according to the names that people may use for them, such as the "Fair Housing Act" (42 U.S.C. 3601-3619). The Popular Name Table directs you to the appropriate title and section number of the US Code.

You can find *ordinances*, which are local statutes enacted by city councils and county supervisors, in addition to other information, such as minutes of meetings and calendars of events, on municipality websites.

Finding court decisions

Case law is comprised of written decisions made by judges of appellate courts. It's an important subject for legal researchers because the legal system in the United States is based on precedent; that is, applying the law decided in a prior case to a current issue. *Precedent* means that courts are required to follow case law when deciding lawsuits, particularly when the facts of the current case are very similar to those of the prior case.

One of the best ways to research case law on the Internet is to use Google Scholar:

1. **Research secondary sources, federal and state statutes, and local ordinances, as explained in the previous two sections, and gather a list of keywords that are relevant to your current legal issue.**

2. **Go to Google Scholar at** `scholar.google.com`.

3. **Click Case law (below the Search box).**

4. **Click Federal courts or click Select courts, click the courts you want to search, and click Done.**

5. **Click in the search box and type the keywords that describe your current legal issue.**

6. **Click the Search button (the button with the magnifying glass on it).**

   Google Scholar displays links to relevant case law enacted by the court(s) you chose to search.

Below the description of each case law resource are additional options, including Cited by, How cited, and Related articles. You can click these links to find related information.

All federal and state appellate courts make their opinions available online, and you can find decisions by case name; many of these websites also have a search capability by topic. You can access United States Supreme Court cases at `www.findlaw.com/casecode/supreme.html`.

Turning to an attorney

Some landlords make an attorney an integral part of their operation, allowing the attorney to handle legalities so the landlord can focus more on property management. Others consult an attorney only when absolutely necessary — when they can't handle a legal situation on their own and have exhausted other options.

However you choose to employ an attorney in your operations, you need to know when to consult an attorney, how to find an attorney that best meets your needs, how to hold legal fees to a minimum, and how to resolve issues when you and your attorney disagree. In the following sections, we address each of these issues in turn.

Knowing when to seek legal assistance

When you're deciding whether to consult an attorney, consider the following three questions:

- ✔ Is this situation something I feel comfortable handling on my own, perhaps after talking with other landlords or others who have experience with problems like this? If you're not comfortable handling an issue, perhaps with input from others, consult an attorney.

- ✔ Would it be a good idea to consult with an attorney who has experience with landlord-tenant matters? If you think hiring an attorney is likely to result in a better outcome or less expense, consult an attorney.

- ✔ Just to be safe, should I just find an attorney who specializes in complicated problems like this one and turn the whole thing over to him? In a complicated, high-stakes case that's likely to require a great deal of attention to detail, consider hiring an attorney.

The issues you most likely encounter as a landlord vary in terms of consequences and complexities. Here are a few legal issues you can probably handle on your own:

- ✔ Terminating a lease. As we explain in Chapter 19, you and your resident simply sign and date the termination notice.

- ✔ Evictions are generally straightforward legal matters that don't require an attorney in many jurisdictions. But in some states, especially California and other states with active tenants-rights legal advisors or pro-tenant laws, you should consult with an attorney to process an eviction or accompany you to court appearances.

- ✔ Drafting routine documents, such as notices to residents. You can find all the documents you need at www.dummies.com/go/landlordlegalkit or by searching the Internet.

On the other hand, if someone files a lawsuit alleging that you violated a fair-housing provision, you probably want to hire an attorney. Cases such as these are complicated legal matters that could result in steep fines and other penalties. Situations that are outside your expertise and the expertise of other landlords and can have serious short- and long-term consequences require the expertise of legal professionals.

Finding the right attorney for you

The right attorney is the attorney who has the necessary experience and expertise in the rental housing industry to handle the kind of problem you're facing. If the matter involves a court proceeding, you want an attorney who has had litigation success and who feels comfortable in the courtroom. On the other hand, if the matter requires expertise in corporate taxation, look for a business attorney who perhaps has a specialization in tax law.

Several resources can help you find the right attorney. Local apartment associations often can provide referrals, and bar associations frequently maintain lists of specialists in various specialties and can make referrals. Other landlords are also good resources.

Find a few attorneys who specialize in your legal area of need and then meet with them to discuss the legal issue you're dealing with. Hire the attorney who makes you feel most confident in his abilities and his dedication to meeting your needs and who's candid when you ask about fees.

You should make a few calls, and you may find an attorney with a policy of an initial free consultation meeting with potential clients to discuss a legal matter. They may even provide you with a do-it-yourself solution, but remember the old adage that "Free legal advice is worth what you pay for it."

Keeping attorney fees in check

The best way to keep attorney fees in check is to negotiate your fee agreement when you hire the attorney, and then finalize it in a written document. Remember that the fee arrangement you choose is subject to negotiation. You're doing the hiring, and the amount you pay for these services has to make sense financially for you and your business. When negotiating a fee agreement, consider the following options:

- ✔ **Retainer:** A *retainer* is a flat fee you pay in monthly installments for routine legal services, such as ensuring that you are complying with the record-keeping and reporting requirements of your corporation. If an unexpected, complex legal issue arises, you're likely to be charged an additional fee.

- ✔ **Flat fee:** Some attorneys may charge a *flat fee* to resolve specific legal issues. The flat fee is likely to be lower overall than paying an hourly rate.

- ✔ **Contingency:** An attorney may collect his fee only if he's successful in resolving your legal issue. An attorney is often willing to work on a *contingency* basis if a client is seeking damages and the attorney is confident he can win the case or negotiate a settlement. In such instances, the fee is typically a percentage of the amount of money collected or recovered by the client.

- ✔ **Hourly rate:** An *hourly* rate is likely to be the most expensive option unless your particular legal issue has a quick fix.

Resolving disagreements between you and your attorney

You can settle disagreements with legal counsel in several ways, but the best way to avoid them is to keep in mind that you're the employer and the attorney's your employee. You're the boss! In the event of a disagreement, however, you may fire your attorney, as is your prerogative with any employee. You may need outside assistance, however, if the subject of the disagreement is a violation of legal ethics or incompetent representation. In such cases, contact your state's attorney licensing authority or the local bar association.

Preparing for and Paying Taxes

Taxation laws regarding investment real estate are unique and far more complex than those regarding homeownership. If you're just starting out in landlording and you're confused by tax laws, you're not alone. Because tax laws can work for or against real estate investors, you need to have a general understanding of the basic concepts, which is why, in the following sections, we paint a clear picture of some tax-related issues you're likely to face.

Tax laws change frequently, and the call for a new federal taxation system seems to become louder every election cycle. And most states have their own income tax system that may or may not mirror the federal laws for income-producing rental properties. So be sure to check with your tax advisor before taking any action. We strongly suggest that you use a Certified Public Accountant (CPA) or tax specialist to prepare your tax returns if you own investment real estate.

Making sense of income taxes

To get a firm grasp on paying Uncle Sam, you first need to understand all about income taxes. Taxpayers generally have two types of income:

- ✔ **Ordinary income:** This type includes wages, bonuses and commissions, rents, dividends, and interest. It's taxed at various rates, depending on your net taxable income. The higher the reportable net income, the higher the *marginal tax rate* (the amount of additional tax paid by the taxpayer on each dollar of additional reportable income), with the top rate currently at 39.6 percent.

- ✔ **Capital gains:** You generate this type of income when you sell possessions, including real estate and stock, for a profit. Capital gains are classified as

  - **Short-term:** Currently, short-term gains (applies to investments that are sold within 12 months of acquisition) are taxed at the same rate as ordinary income.

  - **Long-term:** Currently, long-term gains are taxed at lower rates than ordinary income, with a maximum of 20 percent.

The income you receive from your rental property is subject to taxation as ordinary income. The positive cash flow is determined by deducting all operating expenses, including the following:

- ✔ Advertising costs
- ✔ Auto and travel expenses
- ✔ Cleaning and janitorial
- ✔ Damages
- ✔ Depreciation from rental income
- ✔ Equipment rental
- ✔ Gardening or landscape maintenance
- ✔ Homeowner association dues

- ✔ Insurance premiums
- ✔ Interest paid on mortgage debt
- ✔ Leasing commissions
- ✔ Maintenance and repair costs
- ✔ Management fees
- ✔ Payroll
- ✔ Professional fees
- ✔ Property taxes
- ✔ Supplies
- ✔ Theft
- ✔ Utilities and waste removal

You don't have to pay taxes on security deposits until they become income. When you receive them, security deposits are a liability that you must pay back to residents at a later time. However, after a resident vacates and you withhold a portion of the security deposit, it may become classified as income. Essentially, the deposit isn't taxable as long as you have an expense for the same amount as the deduction. For example, if you deduct $300 from a resident's security deposit to paint and you actually hire a painter for $300, then you don't owe any taxes on that $300 you retained. But if you deduct $300 and then do the work yourself for $100, you owe taxes on the $200 difference, which is classified as income.

Understanding passive and active activity

Landlords often start out with their real estate activities serving as a second income. They typically generate the majority of their income from professions and sources unrelated to real estate. The taxation rules that apply to these part-time real estate investors are different from the ones that apply to real estate pros. Unless you qualify as a real estate professional, the IRS classifies all real estate activities as *passive* and limits your ability to claim real estate loss deductions.

The IRS defines a *real estate professional* as a person who performs at least 50 percent of his personal services in businesses related to real estate or spends at least 750 hours per year in these endeavors. These individuals are considered *active investors* and are allowed to claim all their real estate loss deductions in the year incurred. All others are considered *passive investors,* and they're subject to limitations on the real estate losses they can deduct. However, if you're a passive investor, you may still be able to use rental property losses to shelter ordinary income if you own a minimum of 10 percent of the assets and you're actively involved in the management of your property.

This allowance doesn't mean, however, that you can't hire a property management company to handle the day-to-day activities while you oversee its efforts. According to the IRS, you're *actively involved* if you oversee or approve the setting of rent, approval of residents, and decisions about repairs and capital improvements.

If you meet the IRS standard of being actively involved, you can take a rental property loss deduction of up to $25,000 against other income in the current tax year, as long as your adjusted gross income doesn't exceed $100,000. If it does, you'll be denied 50 cents of the loss allowance for every dollar over $100,000, which means the entire $25,000 loss allowance disappears at an adjusted gross income of $150,000. You can save any losses disallowed in one year and apply them to reduce rental or other passive income in future years. If you can't use the losses in this manner, you can use them when you sell your property to effectively reduce the taxable gain. Thus, the losses ultimately benefit you.

Taking advantage of depreciation

Depreciation is one expense that allows you to shelter positive cash flow from taxation. *Depreciation* is an accounting concept that allows you the right to claim as a deduction a certain portion of the value of a rental property just because you own it, with no relationship to whether it's actually wearing out or losing value. Depreciation lowers your income taxes in the current year by essentially providing a governmental, interest-free loan until the property sells.

Under current tax laws, recently acquired rental properties can only use *straight-line depreciation,* which reduces the property's value by set equal amounts each year over its established economic life. The period during which depreciation is taken is called the *recovery period.* Currently, the IRS mandates that residential rental property has a recovery period of 27.5 years, and owners are required to use straight-line depreciation and deduct a depreciation loss of $\frac{1}{27.5}$, or about 3.64 percent each year. Depreciation is prorated for the first or last year of ownership.

Depreciation is only allowed for the value of the buildings; land isn't depreciable. Often, you can use the property tax assessor's allocation ratio between the value of your buildings and land to determine the appropriate basis amount for calculating depreciation.

Using tax-deferred exchanges to your benefit

A *tax-deferred exchange* is an important tool if you're looking to increase the size of your real estate holdings. You can defer taxation of capital gains by effectively exchanging one property for another. Therefore, you can keep exchanging upward in value, adding to your assets without ever having to pay any capital gains tax.

Section 1031 of the Internal Revenue Code allows exchanges, sometimes called *Starker exchanges,* that permit the postponement of a capital gains tax payment when you purchase another property of like kind within a specified period. The tax is deferred, not eliminated. For real estate purposes, the IRS defines *like-kind property* as any property held for business, trade, or investment purposes. This broad definition allows real estate investors to use a Section 1031 exchange to defer taxes when they sell an apartment building and buy raw land, or vice versa. Check out www.irs.gov for the basic rules for the Section 1031 exchange.

The IRS also allows a reverse Section 1031 exchange. This regulation permits a real estate investor to purchase a new investment property first, before following the 1031 guidelines to close on the sale property within the 180-day limitation while deferring any capital gains taxes.

Grasping (and appealing) property taxes

Local municipal and governmental agencies generally receive a major portion of their operating funds by taxing real estate within their jurisdictions. Typically, property taxes are an *ad valorem* (based on the property's value) tax, but sometimes, other factors or mathematical formulas are used to reach the final value upon which the tax rate is applied. Contact your county tax assessor to find out exactly how your county determines your property taxes.

In certain areas of the country, improvement districts have been established with special assessments in addition to the property tax obligations. These taxes are usually flat fees or amounts based on square footage, as opposed to the property's value.

Naturally, problems can arise in determining the value to place on a property. Governmental tax assessors or appraisers value or *assess* real estate for real estate taxation purposes. These public employees are responsible for determining a market value for each property in a jurisdiction. A property's *market value* is the price the property would most likely sell for in a competitive market.

The building and land are appraised separately, and most states have laws that require the property to be periodically reassessed or revalued. A tax or mill rate is then applied to the assessed value to determine the actual tax billed to the property owner. The higher the assessed value of your property, the higher your property tax bill. Property taxes are typically due in two semiannual installments, and unpaid taxes or special assessments become liens on the property. A *lien* is a claim or attachment against property as security for payment of an obligation.

You may feel helpless against the property tax bureaucracy in your area, but remember that tax assessors have been known to make clerical errors or fail to take all pertinent factors into account when placing a value on your property. If you feel that your property assessment is too high, contact your local tax assessor. The assessor may be willing to make an adjustment if you can back up your opinion with careful research and a good presentation. Or you may need to make a formal property tax protest. Tax protests are often first heard within the tax assessor's office or a local board of appeal. If a dispute still exists, appeals may be taken to court in many states.

Contact your assessor and inquire about a reassessment if real estate values decline in your area. A lower assessment leads to a direct reduction in your property tax bill and a corresponding increase in your cash flow. Some jurisdictions even temporarily lower the valuation based on broad declines in real estate, but most of these programs call for an annual reassessment, and your value can quickly increase to the previous or even higher assessed valuation.

Many municipalities have implemented business license or rental unit taxes for rental property owners. Sometimes these resources are used to finance code enforcement or mandatory inspections of some or all rental properties. But these special taxes may just generate revenue for the general fund. Contact your local government to ensure you're meeting all its specific requirements. The licensing or rental taxes are high enough, but the fines and penalties can be extreme.

Chapter 3

Taking Possession of a Rental Property

*A*cquiring a rental property, especially one that has existing residents, is not only a financial transaction but also a legal one. As the property transfers from the previous owner to you, you need to perform the necessary due diligence to obtain the required documentation, insure the property, and notify residents about the change in ownership and any changes you plan to implement that may affect them.

Transferring the property to you from the previous owner while protecting yourself legally and financially helps you avoid legal issues and deal more effectively with any unavoidable issues or unforeseen expenses. In this chapter, we provide guidance to help ease the transition.

For more information on rental property acquisitions, proper due diligence steps, and property inspections, plus ideas on how to hold title to your rental properties, check out the latest edition of *Real Estate Investing For Dummies* by Eric Tyson and Robert Griswold (John Wiley & Sons, Inc.).

Knowing What to Get Up-Front

If you're thinking about buying a rental property, you need to start by researching the property and its current residents, if any, and finding out exactly what's included in the sale. After all, no one is going to represent your interests as well as you. During the *due diligence period,* which is when your escrow and purchase are pending, ask lots of questions.

(*Escrow* is an account for funds and documents held by a neutral third party in a real estate transfer until all the conditions have been met, per the written instructions of the seller and buyer.) Don't be shy. Talk to the residents, the neighbors, the local government officials, and the property's contractors or suppliers to be sure you know what you're getting. Search the web for public information such as code violations, police reports, and sexual predator residents. Your goal: *No surprises.*

Most sellers are honest and don't intentionally withhold information or fail to disclose important facts. However, the old adage *buyer beware* applies to purchasing rental real estate. Resolving questions and issues now through regular communication with your seller and others eliminates some very unpleasant and possibly contentious disagreements with your residents in the future.

The due diligence period is probably your only opportunity to discover whether the seller has misrepresented any important issues. When you sign your name on the dotted line, the deal is done. You can't go back and ask the seller where a resident's security deposit is. So even though taking over your new property can be chaotic, don't just verbally verify the facts. Confirm all information in writing and begin setting up a detailed filing system for your new property.

In the following sections, we cover some items you must have in writing *before* the deal is final. Visit www.dummies.com/go/landlordlegalkit and click on the Miscellaneous folder to obtain a Property Takeover Checklist for both small and large properties.

A list of the property included in the sale

Inventory all the personal property included in the sale. This list may include appliances, equipment, and supplies owned by the seller.

Don't assume anything is included in the sale unless you have it in writing. Verify that all items indicated are actually physically at the property before you close the deal. It's your responsibility to avoid any misunderstandings about who owns the appliances in the rental unit. For example, if the seller says all the refrigerators belong to the property owner (as opposed to the residents), you want to verify that fact in writing with each resident. Otherwise, you run the risk of a serious dispute or loss in future years as residents take appliances when they leave, claiming that the new refrigerator or washer-dryer combo belongs to them.

A copy of all resident files

Make sure you have all the appropriate paperwork in the resident files. These documents include rental applications, current and past rental contracts, move-in inspection checklists, full payment history, any rent increase documents, all legal notices, maintenance work orders, current contact information, a resident complaint or communication log, and correspondence sent to or received from each resident.

A seller-verified rent roll and list of all security deposits

A *rent roll* is a listing of all rental units with the residents' names, move-in dates, current and market rents, and security deposits. Be sure you get a written seller statement that no undisclosed verbal agreements or concessions have been made with any resident regarding any aspect of the tenancy, including rent or security deposits. Ensure that where interest must be paid on security deposit balances, you collect the deposits (plus all accrued interest to date) at closing.

When acquiring an occupied rental property, follow state or local laws about handling the resident's security deposit. Most state laws require the seller and/or purchaser of a rental property to advise the residents *in writing* of the status of their security deposit. These laws usually give the seller the right to return the deposit to the resident or transfer the deposit to the new owner. Here's why you want the latter to happen:

- ✔ If the seller refunds the security deposits, you have to collect them from residents already in possession of the rental units. Avoid this scenario by strongly urging the seller to give you a credit for the full amount of the security deposits on hand in escrow along with any accrued interest owed to the residents, and have each resident agree *in writing* to the amount of the security deposit transferred during the sale. Close the loop by sending each resident a letter confirming her security deposit amount.

- ✔ If the seller transfers the security deposits to you — rather than returning the deposits to the residents — make sure you receive in cash (or as a credit in escrow) an amount equal to all the security deposits held (plus all accrued interest owed to the residents, if any). Of course, remember that if you just get a credit in escrow, you must be able to refund the remaining balances (after taking proper deductions) of any resident security deposits when the individuals move out.

See Chapter 10 for more about managing and accounting for security deposits.

Without written proof to the contrary, dishonest residents may later claim they had a verbal agreement with the former owner or manager for a monthly rent credit or discount for maintaining the grounds, or that they were promised new carpeting or another significant unit upgrade. If this scenario happens to you, offer to get the former owner or manager on the phone to verify the resident's story. When you offer to verify a made-up story, the resident typically begins to backpedal, and the truth comes out. But to avoid any surprises, obtain a written statement from each resident proving that no such verbal agreements exist.

A copy of all required governmental licenses and permits

Rental property owners in many areas are now required to have business licenses or permits. Contact the appropriate government entity in writing and notify it of the change in ownership and/or billing address.

These governmental entities often impose stiff penalties if you fail to indicate the change in ownership in a timely manner. They inevitably find out about the change because they monitor the local recording of deeds and receive notification of changes in billing responsibility from local utility companies.

Make sure you have current copies of all state and local rental laws and ordinances that affect your rental property. For access to resources for state landlord-resident laws, visit www.dummies.com/go/landlordlegalkit and click on the Legal Resources folder.

A copy of all the latest utility bills

Get copies of all account information and verification that all payments are current for every utility that provides services to the rental property. These utilities may include electricity, natural gas, water/sewer, trash collection, telephone, cable, and Internet access. Prior to the close of escrow, contact each utility company and arrange for the transfer of utilities or change in billing responsibility as of the estimated escrow closing date. If provided with sufficient advance notice, many utility companies can arrange for the final meter reading and/or billing cutoff to coincide with the close of escrow, which prevents the need to prorate any of the utility billings between the owners.

A copy of every service agreement or contract

Make sure you obtain copies of all service agreements and/or contracts. These documents may include agreements with landscapers or gardeners; pest control services; heating, ventilating, and air conditioning (HVAC) companies; boiler maintenance services; laundry services; elevator, swimming pool, or spa servicing; and other providers. Review all current contracts and meet with service providers that the current owner uses. If contracts bind you to continue service, ensure such provisions are legal and in your best interest.

An expensive lesson

Verifying the accuracy of all utility bills is extremely important. One case involved a water utility improperly charging a property owner for sewer charges related to a water meter used only for irrigation. (Some water utilities allow for irrigation-only meters that are exempt from sewer charges because the water never enters the sewer system.)

In this case, the water company had been collecting sewer fees for many years until the discrepancy was brought to its attention. The property owner did receive lower billings in the future, but state law protected the company from refunding any overcharges beyond the previous 12 months. The owner paid thousands of dollars in overpayments for a very expensive management lesson.

If you plan to terminate the services of a particular contractor or service provider, the seller may be willing to voluntarily send a written conditional notice of termination indicating that, should the property sell as planned, the provider's services will no longer be needed as of the close of escrow. You're then free to make your own plans for services and can even renegotiate with the current company for better terms. Of course, if you find the seller already had favorable pricing from the provider, you may be able to negotiate the same terms.

A copy of the seller's current insurance policy

One of the most important things you do when taking over your new rental property is to secure insurance coverage. You need the proper insurance policy in place at the time that you legally become the new owner. Although the seller's policy won't protect you in any way, request a copy of his existing policy or declaration of coverage, because this information can be very helpful to your insurance agent when analyzing the property to determine the proper coverage you need.

When you receive the current insurance information, take steps to verify the accuracy of all records. If certain representations about the types and amounts of coverage are made verbally but not in writing, you need to protect yourself by sending documentation to the seller and all agents to confirm any information you've received. This step can be important in preventing future disputes about the representations made by the seller or any of the agents.

A final walk-through can save you headaches

Before you close escrow, take a final walk-through to make sure the property hasn't been damaged prior to closing. The new buyers of a rental property learned this lesson the hard way because they didn't visit the rental home before closing.

After the sale was complete, the new buyers excitedly went to see their new property, which had sat vacant for nearly a week during escrow. They were shocked to find the home completely flooded and severely contaminated with mold. The buyers sued the seller, claiming that someone had intentionally or inadvertently left the water supply line valve to the refrigerator ice maker open, allowing water to cover the entire first floor. The buyers were unable to prove that the damage occurred while the seller still owned the property, so the seller's insurance company denied the claim.

Ultimately, the buyers' insurance company agreed to pay for some of the damage but only after an extended period of litigation while the property sat vacant. The buyers could've avoided this mess if they had simply inspected the property just before the close of escrow and stopped the sale until the damage was addressed.

To avoid the unpleasant surprise of very high premiums, have your agent run a *loss history* on your new property before you close escrow to determine whether any losses have been claimed. You may find that the property has had significant claims in the past, which affect your ability to find reasonably priced insurance coverage. The loss history can also reveal problems that have occurred at the property, including those that may indicate a larger problem (such as plumbing leaks). Finally, make sure that the current insurer hasn't paid any claims for repair or replacement work that hasn't been done.

Although you may trust your insurance agent implicitly, don't allow your escrow to close until you have documentation confirming that your insurance coverage is in force.

Insuring Your New Property

Some insurance companies want to sell you coverage against any conceivable danger or loss. To make sure you're covered at a reasonable cost, you need to decide which type and amount of coverage is right for you.

Your goal is to pay only for coverage for events and losses that are most likely to occur at your property and that you're responsible for paying. For example, buying hurricane insurance in Minnesota may not make a ton of sense. In addition, assuming you take reasonable steps to secure rental units, you shouldn't be held liable for a resident's losses from theft.

You also need to be concerned about lawsuits and having the proper insurance coverage to defend yourself and protect your assets. Why? Landlords and property managers tend to be sued quite frequently. The good news: You'll likely be okay if you have sound ownership and management policies combined with insurance that's customized for your specific needs. In the following sections, we help you determine what those needs are.

Your best defense against losses is to properly manage your rentals and assertively avoid, control, or transfer the inherent risks of owning and managing rental property. Seek the feedback and advice of your insurance agent or company, many of which routinely inspect your property to help you identify and mitigate risks. Some companies even offer discounts if you implement some of their recommendations and lower premiums for no or few claims in a certain period of time.

Finding the right insurance company

The coverage you can get as a rental property owner varies from company to company, so do the following when selecting an insurance company or agent:

- ✔ **Interview and choose a qualified insurance broker or agent who understands your unique needs.** Have an in-depth discussion with several insurance agents about the types and amounts of coverage, costs, deductible amounts, and exclusions. Make a chart that allows you to compare several companies side by side.

- ✔ **Look at each company's ratings and its reputation for quickly and fairly handling and paying claims.** Although several rating firms exist, the most widely known is A. M. Best Company. It uses an *A* through *F* rating scale, just like in grade school. The top companies have an *A* or *A*– but preferably an *A+* or *A++* rating (as high as the scale goes). You can visit A. M. Best online at www.ambest.com and search for its Financial Strength Ratings on insurance companies you're considering. Remember to add a rating column to your comparison chart.

Insurance professionals are either independent brokers or exclusive agents who write policies for only one company. Talk with an insurance broker and a couple of company agents to ensure you're receiving the insurance coverage you need at the best value. Keep in mind that the lowest premium often isn't the best policy for your needs. Ask a lot of questions and insist on evidence that the company provides coverage with a *written binder,* a document issued by an agent to the insured prior to the formal issuance of the insurance policy. Always make sure that communications regarding insurance coverage and policies are in writing, and remember that your best proof of coverage (besides the actual policy) is a formal certificate of insurance that outlines who and what the policy covers.

Telling the difference among the types of insurance coverage

The first step in getting the right insurance is to understand the different types of insurance available. Of course, building insurance is essential to protect against losses from fire, storms, burglary, vandalism, and so on, but you also want general liability insurance and other coverage to protect against losses from personal injury lawsuits and other misfortunes. Here we describe various types of insurance that are essential as well as additional types that you may want to consider.

Knowing the different full-building coverage available

Three types of full-building insurance coverage exist:

- ✔ **Basic:** Most insurance companies offer *basic* building coverage packages that insure your property against loss from fire, lightning, explosion, windstorm or hail, smoke, aircraft or vehicles, riot or civil commotion, vandalism, sprinkler leakage, and even volcanic activity. This coverage often doesn't include protection against claims alleging property damage or personal injury from mold or protection for certain contents, such as boilers, equipment, and machinery, unless specifically added as an endorsement. (Fair housing discrimination claims aren't typically covered either, but recently, limited policies have become available but not for intentional acts, which still aren't covered.)

- ✔ **Broad form:** With *broad form* coverage, you get the entire basic package plus protection against losses due to glass breakage, falling objects, weight of snow or ice, water damage associated with plumbing, and collapse from certain specific causes.

- ✔ **Special form:** The broadest coverage available is *special form,* which covers your property against all losses, except those specifically excluded from the policy. This coverage offers the highest level of protection and is typically more expensive. However, many insurance companies offer competitive packages specially designed to meet the needs of rental owners, so shop around. Insurance agents often market their policies at favorable terms through National Apartment Association (NAA) affiliates or to Institute of Real Estate Management (IREM) members, so be sure to check these sources as well.

If you own multiple rental units, you may receive discounts (and better coverage!) if you have a single insurance policy that covers all properties. For example, if you currently own three properties, each with a $1 million policy, you can get a single policy with a $3 million limit at a more competitive rate. Doing so provides up to $3 million in coverage for each property. You can also benefit if you have an *aggregate deductible,* which is the portion of your loss that you essentially self-insure. The losses at any of your properties can be used toward meeting the aggregate deductible. Extremely competitive rates on group package policies are also sometimes available for the clients of professional property management firms.

Eyeing supplemental coverage

Flood, hurricane, and earthquake insurance are examples of *supplemental* coverage available for a separate cost. This coverage can be critical in the event of a natural disaster. However, these policies are often expensive and have extremely high deductibles, making them uneconomical for the average small rental property owner. Get quotes nonetheless and see whether supplemental coverage is something you think you can afford or can't afford to do without.

Seriously consider replacement cost coverage. An insurance company pays owners for losses in two ways:

- *Actual cash value* pays the cost of replacing property after subtracting for physical depreciation.

- *Replacement cost* pays the cost of replacing the property without subtracting for physical depreciation.

The standard policies most insurance companies offer provide for actual cash value coverage only; you must specifically have an endorsement and pay extra for replacement cost coverage. The extra cost is often well worth it.

If you decide to rent out your personal residence, immediately contact your insurance agent and have your homeowner's policy converted to a landlord's policy. A landlord's policy contains special coverage riders that aren't in the typical homeowner's policy. Because of the increased liability risk for rental properties, your insurance company may not even offer this coverage, whereas certain companies specialize in this business. Either way, make sure you have proper landlord's coverage for your rental property or any claim may be denied. A single uncovered lawsuit can cost you dearly, whether or not you're ultimately found to be at fault, because the cost of litigation is so high. Plus, in some states, if you're found to be even 1 percent responsible for the plaintiff's claims, you could be required to pay all the plaintiff's legal fees, which could be greater than the damages awarded.

Grasping general liability insurance

Besides building coverage, a *comprehensive general liability* policy covers injuries or losses suffered by others as a result of defective conditions on the property. General liability insurance also covers the legal costs of defending personal injury lawsuits. Because legal defense costs are commonly much greater than the ultimate award of damages, if any, liability insurance is a valuable feature.

Considering umbrella coverage

Umbrella coverage, which is designed to supplement other policies, can be a very cost-effective way to increase your coverage, which is another way to decrease your exposure to a financially devastating lawsuit. Your primary policy may have liability limits of $1 million, but an umbrella policy can provide an additional $1 or $2 million in vital coverage at a reasonable cost. Depending on the value of your property and assets, buying an umbrella liability policy with higher limits makes sense. The proper policy limits are always your decision as the owner, but seek and listen carefully to the advice of an experienced insurance agent.

We suggest you purchase your umbrella policy from the same company that handles your underlying liability insurance. Otherwise, you may find yourself dealing with conflicting strategies on how best to defend yourself in litigation.

Looking at other insurance coverage

A variety of other insurance options make sense for certain rental property owners. You may want to consider the following nonstandard options:

- ✔ **Non-owned auto liability coverage:** If you plan to have any maintenance or management employees assisting you with your rental activities, consider buying this type of coverage. It protects you from liability for accidents and injuries caused by your employees while working and using their own vehicles.

- ✔ **Fidelity bond:** This type provides reimbursement if a dishonest employee steals your rents. An *endorsement for money and securities* can protect you from losses occasioned by the dishonest acts of nonemployees.

- ✔ **Building ordinance:** This type protects you in the event your rental property is partially or fully destroyed. It covers the costs of demolition and cleanup, plus the increased costs to rebuild if the property needs to meet new or stricter building code requirements, or the loss of value if the property can't be rebuilt to its prior condition.

- ✔ **Loss of rents or income insurance:** Loss of rents or income insurance can come in handy to keep up with the mortgage payments and other costs of ownership in the event of a loss that interrupts your income stream, such as a fire or natural disaster.

Paying attention to coinsurance clauses

Some insurance companies have a *coinsurance clause,* which is the joint assumption of risk between the insurer and the insured and requires rental property owners to carry a minimum amount of coverage. If you carry less than the minimum amount, the company imposes a coinsurance penalty that comes out of your recovery. These penalties reduce the payment on the loss by the same percentage as the insurance shortfall.

If you carry only $1.6 million in coverage when you should have $2 million, you're only carrying 80 percent of the minimum required insured value. If the building suffers a loss, the insurance company will pay only 80 percent of that loss.

Determining the right deductible

A *deductible* is the amount of money you must pay out of pocket before your insurance coverage kicks in. Deductibles can be expressed as a percentage (such as 10 percent) but usually can be purchased as a fixed dollar amount or cap that generally ranges from $250 to $500, or sometimes $1,000 for small rental properties. The larger the property, the higher the customary deductible will be, but also, the higher the deductible, the lower your insurance premium.

Evaluate the possibility of having a higher deductible and using your savings to purchase other important coverage. Contact your insurance agent for quotes on the premium reduction based on each level of deductible. To score a lower insurance premium, you must be willing and able to absorb the amount of a much higher deductible. And because you always want to minimize the number of claims, remember that you're unlikely to submit any claim for an amount that's just higher than your deductible. For example, if you decide you can increase your deductible from $500 to $2,500, you're realistically agreeing that you aren't going to submit any claim for less than $3,000 to $4,000, because making a claim for a small amount beyond the deductible doesn't make sense. Always contact your insurance agent to discuss any potential claims because not all claims negatively impact your future coverage or premium charges.

Letting your tenants know about renters insurance

Renters insurance is something your tenants obtain and pay for themselves; it covers losses to their personal property as a result of fire, theft, water damage, and so on. Residents often think they don't need renters insurance because they possess few valuables, but renters insurance covers much more than just their personal possessions. It also provides protection against claims made by injured guests or visitors and offers supplemental living expenses if the rental unit becomes uninhabitable because of fire or smoke damage. And it protects the resident in the event that she causes damage to another tenant's property.

Although the number of residents with renters insurance has increased significantly, the most recent Insurance Research Council study showed that only 43 percent of renters have a renters insurance policy compared to 96 percent of homeowners.

As a landlord, you benefit from renters insurance because it covers any claims in the event that residents start a fire or flood. Their premiums go up instead of yours. So to protect your property, be sure to place a clause in your rental contract that clearly states that every resident must have renters insurance. Depending on the policy limits, renter's policies typically cost from $150 to $300 per year, with deductible amounts of $250 or $500. As with car insurance, the insurance company only pays for losses over and above the deductible amount. If you're going to require your tenant have renters insurance, be sure to include this requirement in your lease and be sure you're named as an additional insured under the tenant's renters insurance policy. You should also insist that the tenant provide you with a copy as proof of coverage and the insurance company notify you if the policy expires, is canceled, or lapses for nonpayment or any other reason. You can contractually require your tenant to carry this insurance, but you shouldn't insist that the tenant use a specific insurance carrier.

A *renters insurance addendum* is a document that informs renters about insurance coverage so they can protect against loss. This document helps prevent misunderstandings about the owner's and resident's insurance coverage and also allows you the option of requiring the tenant to obtain renters insurance. To access a sample Renters Insurance Addendum from the California Apartment Association, visit www.dummies.com/go/landlordlegalkit and click on the Legal Resources folder.

Handling potential claims

Immediately document all facts when an incident occurs on your property, particularly if it involves injury. Use an Incident Report to record all the facts. Be sure to immediately get in touch with your insurance company or agent. Follow up with a written letter to ensure your contact was notified and has the information on file. Failure to do so in a timely manner could result in the denial of a claim.

Refer to www.dummies.com/go/landlordlegalkit and click on the Legal Resources folder for an Incident Report.

Renters insurance is no laughing matter

The importance of renters insurance was reinforced to me early in my management career when a bad fire occurred at one of the properties that I (Robert) managed. Apparently, a new tenant was getting help from *six-pack movers* — friends who assist with a move in exchange for a six-pack of their favorite beverage. The fire started when one of the tenant's friends negligently placed a box of paper goods right on top of the gas-stove pilot light.

Luckily, no one was seriously injured, but 12 of 16 rental units in the building were completely destroyed. None of the tenants had renters insurance, and even the innocent neighbors lost everything they owned. I was covered legally because all the tenants had initialed the rental contract clause indicating they should have renters insurance. But facing tenants who had just lost everything because they didn't get around to buying renters insurance was still difficult.

Notifying Residents of a Change in Ownership

If you're like most rental property owners and you're acquiring property that's already occupied, the residents are probably well aware of the pending ownership change, but they may be apprehensive when their rental unit changes ownership because of the uncertainty of change. So begin your relationship with your residents on a positive note by following the steps we outline in the next sections.

Meeting with the residents in person

When you first acquire your new property, contact your residents in person and reassure them that you intend to treat them with respect and have a cordial yet businesslike relationship. Respond to your residents' questions and concerns honestly and directly. Often, the first question they ask is whether they'll be allowed to stay. Other common concerns are the potential for a rent increase, the status of their security deposit, the proper maintenance or condition of their rental unit, and the continuation of certain policies, such as allowing pets. Anticipate these concerns and prepare your responses. You'll lose credibility and damage your relationship with your residents if you later decide to implement changes that you didn't acknowledge up-front.

Give your residents a letter of introduction during this brief in-person meeting. This letter should provide your contact information and explain your rent collection policies, the status of residents' security deposits, and the proper procedures for requesting maintenance and repairs.

Inspecting the rental unit

Although you likely had a brief chance to view the unit's interior during the due diligence period before escrow closed, walking through again with the resident can be helpful. However, know your state laws. In most states, residents don't have to let you enter their units unless you have a legal reason and have given proper advance notice. If you set a voluntary appointment, the resident knows you're coming and can prepare. If conducting a periodic unit interior inspection (perhaps annually) is legal in your state, set that expectation with your residents at the outset and include it as a provision in their lease.

Don't just knock on the door and expect to walk through your resident's rental unit. But if you're already at the property delivering your letter of introduction (see the preceding section for more on this), you can schedule a mutually convenient time to meet. Some residents are glad to meet with you right then, but don't necessarily count on that. Giving your residents time to think about any issues they'd like to discuss benefits you both.

The former owner of the property may have had a policy of documenting the unit's condition at the time the resident took possession. If so, you may want to compare those notes to the notes you make when you walk through the unit. If proper documentation of the unit's move-in condition wasn't made, consider preparing such information during your walk-through. This info allows you to establish some sort of baseline for the unit's condition to use when the resident moves out, which then helps you determine the proper amount of the security deposit to return. (See Chapter 11 for more about completing a move-in checklist, but change the name of the checklist to something more along the lines of "Current Condition Checklist.")

Using a new rental contract

When you take over an occupied rental property, you'll want to transfer the residents to your own rental contract eventually. The sooner you begin to convert your new property to your rental contracts, the better. If your policies are markedly stricter, you may find the transition period difficult. For a single-family rental or a small rental property, implementing your own rental contract as soon as legally allowed is relatively easy. However, with larger rental properties, you may want to gradually transition to a new rental contract upon resident turnover. Regardless, establish uniform policies for all your residents to avoid any possible fair housing violations (find out more about fair housing in Chapter 5).

Your residents already have one of the following:

- ✔ A valid written lease
- ✔ An expired written lease that has become a month-to-month rental agreement
- ✔ A written month-to-month rental agreement
- ✔ A written rental agreement for a period of less than a month
- ✔ A verbal agreement

Although you may want to make some changes in the terms or policies of your residents' current leases or rental agreements, when you acquire an occupied rental property, your legal and business relationship is already established by whatever agreement the residents had with the former owner. Wait until the expiration of the leases or rental agreements to change the terms — or provide the resident with proper legal notice of any proposed changes.

Consider the potential impact of making significant changes in the rental rates or policies immediately after you acquire the property. For example, although you may have strong feelings against allowing pets on the property, your residents may have pets already. Although you legally have the right to implement your no-pet policy upon lease renewal or upon giving proper legal notice, you're almost guaranteed a vacant rental unit if you do so. Impose your policies over a reasonable period of time, remaining aware of the potential financial consequences in the short run.

The resident information the seller provided you during escrow may be outdated. One quick way to update your records is to have the residents voluntarily complete your rental application form. In many states, you may not have a strong legal argument for requiring existing residents to provide this information; however, many residents will understand your reasoning and not mind. Other residents may be reluctant to complete an entirely new rental application. Even if you receive initial resistance, seek this updated information prior to renewing any lease. You need to be able to properly determine the financial qualifications of your residents, particularly if you anticipate future rent increases.

Evaluating the current rent

When you acquire a rental property, a significant part of your research should be to establish its fair market rental value. This accurate calculation should play a role in your decision to buy. If a resident's current rent is below market value, one of your toughest decisions is how to handle rent increases.

For more about determining fair market rents, visit `www.dummies.com/extras/landlordlegalkit` for the bonus chapter. You also can find it online at `www.dummies.com/go/landlordlegalkit`.

Do unto others' pets

One of the most common and emotional complaints when transitioning a rental property to a new owner involves a new owner implementing a no-pets policy in a rental property that previously allowed pets. Though exceptions exist for service animals under the Americans with Disabilities Act and fair housing laws, the elimination of pets affects a lot of residents. Nothing fosters resentment and animosity as much as telling dedicated pet owners that they need to get rid of a member of their family.

Though in most circumstances a new owner can implement a no-pets policy as the leases expire,

implementing such a policy on existing residents is inherently unreasonable. Better to apply such a policy to new residents only and grandfather any existing pets for the greater of as long as the resident owns them or the remainder of their life. Doing so is a good way to implement other new policy changes — about parking, late charges, and so on. As a rental property owner and manager, you really need to have empathy for your residents and practice the golden rule.

As the new owner, you often have higher mortgage payments and expenses to make necessary repairs and upgrades to the property than the last owner did. Some residents get very upset and antagonistic about any rent increase, however, and you won't be able to appease them. If residents simply can't afford an increase, work with them and give them ample time to relocate. Other residents often welcome the improvements that accompany the purchase of their building by a new owner and will accept the necessary increase.

Fortunately, the majority of residents just expect to be treated fairly and honestly. They understand you may have higher expenses and will reluctantly accept a rent increase as long as two basic conditions are met:

- ✔ **You don't raise the rent beyond the current market rent for a comparable rental unit in the area.** Give residents documented information on comparable rentals in your area to show them you're not asking for an unreasonable rent.

- ✔ **You're willing to make basic repairs to the rental unit.** Don't ask residents to shell out extra cash without proving you're committed to maintaining and even improving the property. But residents don't appreciate all improvements equally. A new roof may not mean much if their unit didn't leak, but a new boiler or water heater could mean better water pressure or more consistent hot water, which all residents will notice and appreciate.

Buying unoccupied rental property

The takeover procedure for an unoccupied rental property or one that has some vacant rental units isn't much different from the procedure for taking over an occupied property. You may actually prefer a vacant property so you can quickly implement a plan to upgrade and get the property rent-ready as soon as possible. If you want an occupied rental property vacant upon the change of ownership, make the vacancy of the unit a condition for the close of escrow. *Remember:* After you own the property, every day a unit sits vacant is lost income you'll never recoup, so work diligently during the escrow time frame to make as much progress as possible.

Begin your marketing and advertising of the rental property near the close of escrow and the completion of renovation. Time is of the essence if you want to minimize any lost rent.

Most residents just want to be sure they're receiving some benefit of paying higher rent. So if you ask for more rent, be willing to reinvest a portion of the rent increase into the property with cost-effective improvements that conserve energy and/or increase resident satisfaction. Clean the carpet, repaint the unit's interior, or send in a maintenance person for a few hours to repair the miscellaneous items that need attention.

Although tempting, be wary of making significant renovation or repairs to the property before the close of escrow. If the sale of the property doesn't go through as planned, you may have spent considerable sums to upgrade the seller's property without any recourse.

Chapter 4

Hiring a Property Manager

In This Chapter

▶ Deciding whether to hire a company or an individual to manage your property

▶ Choosing the right property management firm and negotiating a good contract

▶ Dealing with the legalities of employing a resident property manager

▶ Keeping residents posted of any change in management

Success as a landlord depends on how well your property is managed, either by you, someone else, or a property management firm. If you're just getting started, you may try to manage your rental property, particularly if you have a single-family rental home or condo or even a small, multifamily rental property such as a duplex, triplex, or fourplex. If you're like most owners, though, at some point you'll consider hiring a property manager or management firm. In this chapter, we compare the options of hiring a property management firm or an individual and help you limit your legal liability and exposure to other risks for whichever option you choose to pursue.

Recognizing Your Property Management Options

When using someone to handle your property management tasks, you have three options:

✔ **Negotiate a service contract with a property management firm.** Contracting with a professional property management firm avoids most of the complexities of hiring an individual. The firm is typically qualified to handle all property management work, including finding and screening new residents. You simply pay the firm a fee instead of a salary, so you're not on the hook as an employer. The firm carries liability insurance to cover any damages resulting from improper or illegal property management activities. The primary drawback of contracting with a firm is the generally higher cost, but that may not be true if you accurately consider the value of your own time.

Of these three choices, we lean toward hiring a management firm, for the following reasons:

- A good firm has skilled staff members who are specialized in several key areas, including law, marketing, human resources, accounting, and maintenance. They have established procedures and contacts for most situations and can be more efficient than you might be as a novice.

- The firm sticks with you. It's not going to leave you to take another job — especially without notice just before the first of the month.

- The firm always has you covered. If an employee becomes ill or goes on vacation, the firm has someone who can step in temporarily to fill his shoes.

Refer to the next section, "Hiring a Professional Property Management Firm" for more information about the legal issues if you go this route.

✔ **Hire an individual.** Landlords frequently hire an individual (often one of their residents) to handle some property management tasks, including collecting rent, cleaning and light maintenance of the common areas, performing minor repairs in rental units, and responding to certain resident concerns. Hiring an individual, however, comes with some additional risks and responsibilities. You may be held liable for any actions the individual takes on your behalf (as your *agent*) and any injuries the person suffers in providing services on your behalf. You must also provide oversight to make sure your employee is responsive to your residents' needs. Furthermore, you take on additional responsibilities as an employer (see "Going with an Individual to Manage Your Property," later in this chapter, for details).

The primary benefit of hiring an individual is that the person can focus exclusively on your rental properties and can be more responsive than a firm to problems that arise. An individual may even live on-site, which enables him to monitor the property more closely and establish positive relationships with residents. If you find a well-qualified candidate, we don't want to discourage you from hiring the person, especially if he has experience and a good track record of managing rental properties.

✔ **Do it yourself.** If you choose to manage the property yourself, consider taking on the tasks that you're most qualified to perform and that you're likely to enjoy and outsourcing the rest. For example, you may want to handle the money yourself — collecting and depositing rent payments, security deposits, and other fees and paying the bills — and hiring other individuals or companies to handle other tasks, including the following:

- Maintenance and repairs (for example, you may want to hire a maintenance person who lives in one of your rental units to serve as building superintendent)

- Accounting (hire an accountant or an accounting firm)

- Applicant screening (hire a real estate broker or a rental locator to find and screen applicants)

- Legal issues (hire an attorney to draft agreements and make sure you're following all applicable housing laws)

If you decide to hire an individual or a professional property management firm, doing so is a matter of personal preference, but also a matter of good business practice. In certain states and municipalities, you actually may be required to have a *resident property manager* — a person who lives in the apartment complex — if it has more than a certain number of rental units. For example, in California a *responsible party* is required to live on-site if you have 16 or more contiguous rental units. You should contact your local affiliate of the National Apartment Association (NAA) or a landlord-tenant legal expert to see if your area has any such requirements.

If you have a rental property with more than four units, we suggest that your best option is to hire a professional management company and also have an on-site person who can be the eyes and ears of the property for a reasonable rent credit or small cash payment.

Hiring a Professional Property Management Firm

Many rental property owners who are just starting out drift blindly into self-management by default because they assume they can't afford a management company. Others simply don't want to give up part of their profit — "Why pay someone to manage my rental property when I can keep the money myself?" is a common refrain. Other owners would really prefer to hire a professional management company, but they've heard so many horror stories that they don't know whom to trust. Many of their concerns are real; some property managers mismanage properties and lack any semblance of ethics.

Luckily, you can avoid hiring the wrong management company by following our advice on how to choose a good property manager. The following sections touch on some important points for you to consider if you're contemplating using a professional management company.

Although we usually recommend full-service management, you can pay for just the services you use instead of shelling out for the complete package. For example, maybe you just need help with the rental of your property and are willing to pay a leasing fee. Or perhaps you want a property manager who charges only a small fee to cover the basic service and not much more.

Finding the right company for you

You want to find a property management company that suits you. Find property managers who are active in the area and specialize in your kind of rental unit, which can range from home rentals and apartment complexes with only a few units up to mega-complexes.

Keep the following in mind to help you select the management company that best fits you and your property:

- ✔ **Hire a firm that manages property exclusively.** This guideline is particularly important when selecting a management company for a single-family home, condo, or very small rental property. Many traditional real estate sales offices (as opposed to property management firms) offer property management services; however, property management is often a *loss leader* (meaning it costs more for the real estate office to manage your property than it's charging you for that service because it's hoping to get your business later on, when you're ready to sell the property). Most property managers in real estate sales offices don't have the same credentials, experience, and expertise as employees of property management firms. The skills required to represent clients in *selling* property are entirely different from the skills required to *manage* property. You can always hire a firm that sells only real estate when the time comes to sell your rental property.

- ✔ **Verify that the property manager and the management company have current licenses that are in good standing.** You can call or use the Internet to double-check. Most states require property managers to have a real estate license and/or a property manager's license. Simply holding a license doesn't ensure exceptional services, but it does show that the property manager is motivated enough to comply with state law. You may also have some recourse in the event that you have problems with your management company because the potential of losing its license can be a serious concern for the company.

Always make sure the property manager you're considering has a current license, designations/certifications, and proper insurance coverage. The recent significant rise in unemployment has led to increases in the number of unlicensed individuals offering their services as property managers. Often, they may be managing properties that they partially own themselves and are exempt from state licensing laws, but they're breaking the law in most states if they manage a rental property they don't own. Working with one of these people can lead to serious liability for you if a problem arises and the authorities find out you used an unlicensed property manager.

✔ **Examine the property manager's credentials.** The Institute of Real Estate Management (IREM) provides professional designations and certifications, including the Certified Property Manager (CPM) designation and the Accredited Residential Manager (ARM) certification. A very select group of management firms have earned the Accredited Management Organization (AMO) accreditation. These designations and certifications signify excellence and dedication.

For more information along with details on NAA designations, visit www.dummies.com/go/landlordlegalkit and click on the Property Management folder.

✔ **Confirm that the company is properly insured.** The company should carry insurance for general liability, automobile liability, workers' compensation, and professional liability. The company is your agent and will collect your rents and security deposits, so it should also have a fidelity bond to protect you in case an employee embezzles or mishandles your money. Look for a company that has separate bank accounts for each property managed.

Many property managers use a single master trust bank account for all properties where they combine the funds of multiple clients into a single bank account. Although doing so is legal in most states, avoid this practice because, typically, the primary violation encountered during audits of property managers by state oversight agencies is related to shortages and other misuse of the master trust bank account.

✔ **Check references, particularly the company's other clients.** Don't sign a management contract until you feel confident that the company you hire has a sound track record. Checking with the company's chosen referrals isn't enough. Ask for a list of all its current and past clients, and contact the ones with rental properties similar in size and type to your own. Make certain the rental owners you contact have been with the company long enough to have a meaningful opinion on the quality of the service and are truly unbiased.

Business rating or reference sites can be deceiving. Some very good companies may have a few disgruntled former residents, or a few planted recommendations can lead you to a false sense of confidence that you've found the best management company or disqualify a good one.

Keep an eye on the repair bills

Most management contracts contain clauses that allow property management companies to perform emergency repairs up to a specified dollar amount without advance approval from the owner. Of course, this clause allows the company to take care of problems that occur unexpectedly. When you're in the early stages of working with a new management company, make sure you closely monitor its expenses. Even though it may have the legal right to use funds up to a certain amount, the company should always keep you informed as the owner. "No surprises" is one of our favorite sayings.

Repairs serve as a profit center for many management companies. They may offer very low property management fees, knowing that they'll make it up through markups on repairs, and often the repairs aren't even necessary. Look for a property management firm that doesn't mark up materials, supplies, or maintenance labor or one whose costs for such work you consider fair and equitable.

Knowing what to ask a prospective management company

The quality of your property management company directly affects the success of your real estate investments and your peace of mind. Visit the company's office armed with the following questions:

- ✔ Can you give me a list of exactly what management services you provide and a breakdown of management fees/costs?
- ✔ Is your firm an Accredited Management Organization (AMO) recognized by IREM?
- ✔ Is your firm an active member in good standing with a local affiliate of the NAA, and does it hold any NAA designations?
- ✔ Are your legally required state and/or local licenses current and without any history of violations?
- ✔ Do you carry errors and omissions coverage of at least $500,000, plus general liability coverage of at least $2 million?
- ✔ Do you have a $500,000 fidelity bond and a forgery and alterations policy of at least $25,000 for all employees?
- ✔ Do you have separate bank trust accounts for each client rather than a single master trust bank account containing multiple owners' funds?
- ✔ Can you communicate via email with your clients, your contractors/suppliers, and your residents to be responsive and efficient, providing excellent customer service?

✔ Can you explain your methods of advertising or generating interest in my rental property and of selecting residents in compliance with all fair housing laws?

✔ How do you screen prospective residents? Do you use an outside firm? Who pays for the service and how much is it?

✔ Do all funds that you collect from applicant screening fees, resident late charges, and other administrative charges go directly to the owner and not the manager?

✔ Do you provide 24/7 on-call maintenance services with a live person answering the calls who also has email capability?

✔ Whether you provide maintenance in-house or use an affiliated firm, do you only charge the actual cost of labor and materials, without any surcharges, markups, administrative fees, or other such add-ons?

✔ Do you pass along any volume-purchasing discounts fully and directly to clients for appliances, flooring, and other items, without any markups?

✔ If allowed by law, do you give all employees pre-employment screenings that include thorough background checks by an independent employment screening consultant, plus drug and alcohol testing by a certified lab?

✔ Can I contact several of your current and former clients with rental properties that are similar in type, size, and location to mine?

If at all possible, also try to secure a meeting with the person who would have control of the hands-on management of your property so you can ask these questions:

✔ How many years have you been in the property management business? Do you exclusively manage real estate?

✔ What are your qualifications? Do you hold IREM's distinguished CPM designation or ARM certification? Do you hold National Association of Residential Property Managers (NARPM) designations such as Residential Management Professional (RMP) or Master Property Manager (MPM)?

✔ How many other properties do you manage? Where are these properties located?

When you hire outside property managers, treat them as valued members of your management team, but be sure they know that you're the team leader and they understand your long-term goals. If you're looking for appreciation and preservation of your rental property's value, make sure the company keeps your property in great condition and looks for stable, long-term residents rather than just premium rent from short-term rentals. Of course, the manager should ask before spending significant amounts of your money, and he should keep you informed.

Sidestepping pitfalls

The *management agreement* is a pivotal document because it spells out the obligations of the property management company to you, the client. Study the fine print; doing so is tedious but necessary in order to avoid unpleasant surprises. Even the management agreements available through state and national real estate organizations may contain clauses that are clearly one-sided in favor of the management company.

For example, many management agreements call for the property manager to collect and keep all the income from applicant screening fees, late charges, or returned check charges. Of course, property managers justify this policy on the basis that they incur additional time and costs when handling such situations. But these fees should belong to you because you want to give the property manager a financial incentive to fill your unit with a resident who pays rent on time and cares for the property. A management fee based on actual rents collected is a better arrangement.

Read on to find out what other nuggets may be hidden in the fine print of your management agreement and how to protect your investment:

- ✔ **The "no management fee charged when the unit is vacant between residents" line:** Although this seems like an arrangement that saves you money, especially when rental revenues aren't coming in, the property manager can rush to fill the vacancy without properly screening residents — and a destructive resident can be worse than no resident in the long run.

- ✔ **The "hold harmless" clause:** This clause protects the property manager from liability for his own errors in judgment or the mistakes of the workers the firm sends to your rental unit. One solution is to include a "reasonable care" provision so the property manager is motivated to be diligent in his management and avoid workers that he knows have had problems in the past. Your agreement should also mention such obvious requirements as informing you of what's happening with your rental property.

- ✔ **The long-term management contract request:** Some property management companies request long-term management contracts that can't be canceled or can only be canceled for cause. Avoid signing any contract that can't be canceled by either party with or without cause upon a 30-day written notice. A company that knows it's only as good as its most recent month's performance will stay motivated to treat your property with the time and attention needed to get top results. But the company can make a reasonable argument that it needs a minimum term in order to amortize the significant time and cost of taking over a property. So, rather than agree to a long-term, non-cancelable agreement, we suggest you negotiate an early termination fee that's waived after a certain number of months.

If the property manager won't agree to reasonable clarifications of the contract language or a complete list of the services provided for his fee, he may not go out of his way to help you later. Consider this refusal a warning sign and find a property management company willing to accept your reasonable terms.

✔ **The "I'll use my own agreement that suits my best interests" maneuver:** Many property managers use their own proprietary agreements written strictly in the best interests of the property management company. Be sure to have your attorney review this agreement very early in the discussions with your prospective property manager.

Make sure that the management agreement addresses all your concerns. You need to know how much the manager can spend without your authorization, what weekly or monthly reporting the company provides, when your property expenses will be paid, and who is responsible for payment of critical items, such as mortgages, insurance premiums, and property taxes. Leave nothing to chance.

For a sample Residential Management Agreement from IREM, visit www. dummies.com/go/landlordlegalkit and click on the Property Management folder. Use the agreement to familiarize yourself with such contracts. And remember, ultimately you can propose that your property manager sign *your* agreement — after your attorney reviews it, of course.

Going with an Individual to Manage Your Property

If you choose to hire an individual to manage one or more of your properties, you take on the role of employer with the accompanying risks and obligations. You need to screen candidates carefully to make sure you hire someone competent and responsible; spell out the person's job responsibilities; agree on compensation that complies with minimum wage and overtime laws; and establish an arrangement that makes it easier to fire and perhaps evict the individual later, if necessary.

In the following sections, we explain how to hire an individual to manage or maintain your property and how to fulfill your obligations as an employer in a way that decreases your exposure to lawsuits and other risks.

Screening candidates

The best way to avoid lawsuits and other problems with a property manager or other employee is to hire someone who is well qualified and has a clean record. These sections provide guidance on how to do your due diligence in screening candidates and choosing the best person for the job.

When advertising and screening candidates for any position, comply with all federal, state, and local antidiscrimination laws. Don't discriminate on the basis of race, color, religion, sex, national origin, age, or handicap. Technically, Title VII of the Civil Rights Act, which prohibits such discrimination, applies only to employers who have 15 or more employees, but we recommend that you comply with all antidiscrimination laws to avoid any possible lawsuit and protect yourself if you're taken to court.

Detailing your property manager's job responsibilities

To enable candidates to screen themselves, provide them with a list of property manager job responsibilities, which may include the following:

- Perform rental market surveys and advise on setting the rental rate
- Prepare, advertise, and show rental units to prospective renters
- Screen and select applicants
- Prepare leases and rental agreements and all legal forms
- Process new residents upon move-in
- Perform property inspections as required
- Collect and deposit rent payments and security deposits and pay bills (including the mortgage, property taxes, and insurance, if you don't pay directly)
- Prepare regular accounting reports
- Maintain and repair rental units and common areas
- Respond in a timely manner to resident requests and complaints
- Enforce lease terms consistently and fairly
- Understand and comply with federal, state, and local laws that govern rental properties

Evaluating skills and experience

As you read through applications, cover letters, and resumes and interview candidates of a position as property manager, look for the following traits:

- Experienced (ideally at least two years' experience in managing rental properties)
- Computer literate

✔ Able to handle basic accounting

✔ Skilled in marketing and sales

✔ Handy — able to perform light janitorial and basic repairs and maintenance

✔ Personable

✔ Firm but patient

✔ Articulate (speaking and writing)

✔ Skilled at solving problems

✔ Organized and efficient

✔ Knowledgeable of federal, state, and local housing laws

Checking work history

The best indication of a candidate's ability to manage rental properties is a work history showing that the person effectively managed rental properties in the past or held positions that required many of the same skills you're looking for in a property manager.

Check the person's self-reported work history, giving priority to candidates who've managed rental properties in the past. Call past employers and supervisors to verify past employment and gather insight into the candidate's job performance in those positions. Here are some questions you may want to ask a candidate's past employers and supervisors:

✔ How long did this person work for you?

✔ Why did the person leave?

✔ Was the person reliable? Did he show up for work on time?

✔ Was this person honest and trustworthy?

✔ Would you recommend that I hire this person? Why?

Performing a credit check

If your state permits using credit checks to screen job candidates, obtain a copy of the candidate's credit report and review it for any serious issues, including a high level of debt, unpaid bills, and late payments. A poor credit history may indicate that the candidate is

✔ Irresponsible

✔ Unable to handle basic accounting tasks

✔ In a desperate financial situation, which may be a motivation for theft

Chapter 8 discusses credit checks in greater depth in the context of screening residents.

Performing a criminal background check

As a condition of employment, require that all candidates consent to a criminal background check, and then order a criminal background check for any candidate under serious consideration. Screening out candidates who've been convicted of crimes protects you and your residents. See Chapter 8 for more about ordering a criminal background check.

Search the national sex offender registry at www.nsopr.gov to determine whether the applicant has been convicted of a sex offense. Hiring someone who's listed on the national sex offender registry to be your resident property manager not only exposes your residents and perhaps their children to a potential risk, but it also likely will hurt your business.

Researching the person's driving record

Prior to hiring a property manager, check the candidate's driving record with the bureau of motor vehicles in whichever states the person has recently held a driver's license. A candidate who has few or no accidents and traffic violations poses less of a safety risk to your residents and exposes you to less risk, particularly if the person will be driving a vehicle you own.

You can access driving records on most state bureau of motor vehicles websites for free or for a small fee. Consider having the candidate access his driving record online in your office, so you can review it.

Signing an employment agreement

To avoid future disputes regarding job responsibilities and compensation, you and the candidate you decide to hire should review and sign an employment agreement that details the following:

✔ Property manager's responsibilities (see the earlier section "Detailing your property manager's job responsibilities")

✔ Schedule and hours

✔ Payment terms (see the next section, "Compensating your property manager")

✔ Your right to terminate employment

For a sample employment agreement, visit www.dummies.com/go/landlordlegalkit and click on the Property Management folder.

Compensating your property manager

You may compensate your property manager by paying an hourly rate, reducing the person's rent, or both, but whatever form the compensation takes, it must comply with minimum wage and overtime laws. For example, the federal minimum wage at the time we're writing this is $7.25 per hour. If the property manager works 30 hours per week, his total compensation must be at least $217.50 per week. If compensation includes a $500 per month rent reduction, that represents less than $125 per week. You'd have to pay an additional $92.50 per week to reach the minimum of $217.50.

When hiring a property manager who's also a resident, be careful with the rental agreement and any rent reduction. We recommend the following arrangement:

✔ Keep your employment agreement and rental agreement separate to simplify terminating and evicting the property manager if you need to do so later.

✔ Charge full rent. Don't include rent deduction as part of the compensation. Rent reduction complicates the process of calculating hourly pay and may cause problems later if you terminate the property manager's employment, which would require him to start paying full rent.

✔ Specify a maximum number of hours per day and per week that your property manager is allowed to work unless he has prior authorization from you. You probably don't want to pay time and a half (or even double time) to a property manager who claims to have worked 80 hours in a given week.

States and municipalities may have statutes that extend the federal minimum wage and overtime laws. For example, some states have a minimum wage that's higher than that required by federal law. Consult an attorney who specializes in employment law in your area to find out more about state and local requirements.

Complying with employment laws and accounting requirements

If you hire an individual to manage one or more properties for you, you become an employer (if you aren't one already) and subject to a host of additional laws and accounting tasks, including the following:

✔ **Verifying employment eligibility:** The Immigration Reform and Control Act (IRCA) requires that you verify any new employee's identity and complete and submit a United States Citizen and Immigration Services (USCIS) Form I-9 Employment Eligibility Verification form. (Visit www.uscis.gov for more info.)

✔ **Reporting your newly hired employee:** Shortly after hiring a property manager (or anyone else to work for you), you must report your new hire to a designated state agency. The Office of Child Support Enforcement (OCSE) and state agencies use this information to track down parents who owe child support. (Visit www.acf.hhs.gov for more info.)

✔ **Paying minimum wage and overtime:** As an employer, you must comply with the Fair Labor Standards Act (FLSA), which establishes standards for minimum wages and overtime pay and recordkeeping, and with the Equal Pay Act, which requires that you pay men and women equally for doing the same work. (Visit the US Department of Labor website at www.dol.gov for more about the FLSA and other labor laws.)

Minimum wage and overtime requirements generally apply only to blue-collar workers (generally people who perform manual labor for an hourly wage), which the FLSA refers to as *non-exempt employees*. White-collar workers (executives, administrators, professionals, and some computer specialists who typically are paid a salary) are *exempt* from minimum wage and overtime pay, if they meet specific criteria.

✔ **Paying unemployment taxes and worker's compensation:** You must pay the federal unemployment tax and perhaps pay into any state unemployment fund. You may also be required to purchase worker's compensation insurance to cover medical expenses and a portion of an employee's pay if the employee gets injured on the job.

✔ **Withholding taxes and paying FICA:** Have your property manager complete IRS Form W-4: Employee Withholding Allowance Certificate. When you pay your property manager, you must withhold income tax (federal and usually state and local) and your employee's portion of any Federal Insurance Contributions Act (FICA) payments and turn these amounts, along with your (employer's) share of FICA payments, over to the various taxing authorities on a quarterly basis.

Don't try to dodge your responsibilities for withholding taxes, paying FICA, and providing worker's compensation insurance for employees by declaring an employee an independent contractor. To qualify as an *independent contractor*, the person must:

- Be truly independent

- Decide when, where, and how to perform their work

- Work for several clients

- Set his hours, pay, and schedule

If you include rent reduction as compensation to a property manager, you're not required to withhold or pay any federal payroll taxes (income tax or FICA) on rent reduction, as long as the following three conditions are met:

✔ The property manager's employment is conditional upon him living onsite.

✔ The rent or rent reduction is for a unit that's part of your rental property.

✔ You're furnishing the lodging as a matter of your convenience.

Firing and evicting an employee

If a resident property manager, maintenance person, or other employee doesn't work out, you need to terminate the person's employment. You may also need to evict the person. Proper preparation leading up to the termination and possible eviction is key in protecting yourself from any legal fallout. We recommend that you take the following precautions to prepare for the possible necessity of terminating their employment and evicting the person:

✔ Negotiate separate employment and month-to-month rental agreements, so you can terminate employment immediately and terminate the rental agreement soon thereafter.

✔ Include in your employment agreement a clause that gives you the right to terminate employment at any time for any reason or no reason whatsoever.

✔ Conduct regular performance reviews, put your reviews in writing, and file them. You may want to conduct performance reviews once a month for the first three months and then once every six months or so. Having a documented history of an employee's poor performance makes you less of a target for a wrongful termination lawsuit.

✔ Request that any complaints from residents about your property manager or other employee be presented in writing and file them with your performance reviews.

✔ Whenever you have an issue with an employee, put it in writing and discuss it with him. Issuing written warnings confirms that your employee is aware of performance issues and prepares your employee in advance to expect termination. An employee is less likely to claim wrongful termination if he knows that you're dissatisfied with his performance.

✔ Have a good reason to fire your property manager or other employee. If your property manager or other employee is performing poorly, stealing from you or from residents, being insubordinate to you or rude to residents, engaging in criminal activity, or doing anything else that's likely to hurt your business, you have a good reason to fire the person.

Don't terminate a whistleblower out of retaliation. If an employee reports you to authorities for breaking a law, for example, you're prohibited from firing that person just to get even.

Notifying Residents of a Change in Management

Whenever you experience a change in management, you must notify all residents in order to comply with the law and keep your business running smoothly. Residents need to be aware of who's currently in charge, so they know:

✔ Who has their security deposit (and that it's in safe hands)

✔ Where to send future rent payments

✔ Who to contact for repair and maintenance requests and other issues

✔ Who has the authority to act on your behalf

In some states, you're legally obligated to inform residents, within a certain period of time, of any change in management and supply them with the name, address, and contact information for the new manager. But even if your state doesn't legally require you to do so, we recommend that you keep your residents posted as a matter of courtesy and good business sense.

Refer to www.dummies.com/go/landlordlegalkit for a sample change in management notification letter.

Part II

Advertising and Taking on New Residents Legally

Rental Application

ADDRESS_____ APARTMENT NO._____ DATE:_____

Apartment Occupants

Name (Head of Household)	Birth Date	1. ☐ Male 2. ☐ Female	Marital Status	1. ☐ Married 2. ☐ Separated	3. ☐ Divorced 4. ☐ Widowed	5. ☐ Single	S.S. No.

Name A		1. ☐ Male 2. ☐ Female	Birth Date	Relationship	1. ☐ Spouse 2. ☐ Child	3. ☐ Roommate 4. ☐ Other
Name B		1. ☐ Male 2. ☐ Female	Birth Date	Relationship	1. ☐ Spouse 2. ☐ Child	3. ☐ Roommate 4. ☐ Other
Name C		1. ☐ Male 2. ☐ Female	Birth Date	Relationship	1. ☐ Spouse 2. ☐ Child	3. ☐ Roommate 4. ☐ Other

Present Address _____ How long at present address?: _____

Street	City	State	Phone	Landlord

Previous Address _____ How long at previous address?. _____

Street	City	State	Phone	Landlord

IN CASE OF EMERGENCY – NOTIFY:

Name	Address	City/State	Phone	Relationship

PRIMARY OCCUPATION OF HEAD OF HOUSEHOLD (check one)

1 ☐ Professional (Charges fees, i.e., Doctor, Lawyer, etc.)	3 ☐ White Collar	7 ☐ Unskilled laborer
2 ☐ Semi-Professional (Salaried technicians, etc.)	4 ☐ Sales representative	8 ☐ Retired
	5 ☐ Skilled laborer (plumber, electrician, etc.)	9 ☐ Not employed
	6 ☐ Semi-skilled laborer (job requires some training)	10 ☐ Student

TOTAL ANNUAL INCOME OF HEAD OF HOUSEHOLD:

1. ☐ 5,999 – 7,488	3. ☐ 10,000 – 12,499	5. ☐ 15,000 – 17,499	7. ☐ 20,000 – 29,999
2. ☐ 7,500 – 9,999	4. ☐ 12,500 – 14,999	6. ☐ 17,500 – 19,999	8. ☐ Above 30,000

EMPLOYMENT

Name of Company	Address	How Long?	Bus. Phone
Former Employer	Address	How Long?	Bus. Phone
Spouse employed? Yes No	Occupation	Address	How Long?	Bus. Phone

TOTAL ANNUAL INCOME OF HOUSEHOLD:

1. ☐ 5999 - 7488	3. ☐ 10,000 – 12,499	5. ☐ 15,000 – 17,499	7. ☐ 20,000 – 30,000
2. ☐ 7500 – 9999	4. ☐ 12,500 – 14,999	6. ☐ 17,500 – 19,999	8. ☐ Above 30,000

Head to www.dummies.com/extras/landlordlegalkit for criteria you *can* use to weed out less desirable applicants.

In this part . . .

- ✔ Understand the federal Fair Housing Act and any state statutes and local ordinances that extend fair housing protections.

- ✔ Purge your advertising of any fair-housing or truth-in-advertising violations before presenting your ads to the public.

- ✔ Establish and enforce your rent payment policy and deal effectively and equally with any rent collection problems that arise.

- ✔ Comprehend and comply with any state or local rent regulations in the few areas of the country where rent is regulated.

- ✔ Carefully screen applicants within the confines of fair housing laws and choose applicants who are less likely to cause legal problems.

- ✔ Start with a sample lease or month-to-month rental agreement and customize it to meet your specific needs.

- ✔ Develop a security deposit policy that's clear and fair in order to avoid future disputes over the use and return of security deposits.

- ✔ Attend to the details of moving in a new resident, so your residents have the information they need and you have the documentation you need.

Chapter 5

Getting the Lowdown on Fair Housing

Fair housing law prohibits you, a landlord, from discriminating against or playing favorites based on the protected class to which the prospect or resident belongs. These laws apply to every stage of the rental process starting with how you market and advertise your rental property, through the screening process and the signing of the rental contract, and throughout your renters' occupancy until the lease ultimately ends and they move out.

Sure, as landlord, you need to be selective. In fact, in Chapter 8, we encourage you to carefully screen applicants and weed out people who probably can't or won't pay the rent or who have a record of damaging rental property or stirring up trouble in other ways. Legally and ethically, however, you and everyone in your organization are obligated by federal and state law to operate without regard to a prospect's or renter's status as a member of a protected group. Complying with fair housing laws is a wise business decision. Not only does compliance steer you clear of huge penalties and legal fees, but it also helps you build a solid reputation in your community and in the local housing industry as a landlord who's fair and ethical.

In this chapter, we introduce the concept of fair housing; explore the ins and outs of fair housing laws at the federal, state, and local levels; describe types of discriminatory conduct that are illegal along with the penalties that you may face for fair housing violations; and highlight a few exceptions to the law.

Examining the Fair Housing Act

The Civil Rights Act of 1968 (also known as the *Fair Housing Act*), including amendments to the act that were added in 1974 and 1988, is intended to give everyone, regardless of their race, color, religion, national origin, sex, handicap, or familial status equal access to available housing. The Act prohibits you, as landlord, from discriminating against or giving preferential treatment to these groups of people, which are referred to as *protected classes*.

At this point, you may be saying, "Well, duh! Everyone knows that housing discrimination is illegal!" However, some of the nuances of the law may surprise you, and you'll save a lot of time and money by being surprised *now* than being surprised *after* you commit a violation and find yourself staring at significant fines along with attorney fees and other court costs.

These sections examine the Fair Housing Act, define a few key terms, and clarify your understanding of the Fair Housing Act and how it applies to various landlord-related activities.

Recognizing the seven protected classes

The Fair Housing Act prohibits discrimination or favoritism based on the following seven protected classes (a *protected class* is a personal quality that shouldn't be used as a basis for making housing decisions):

- **Race:** Ethnicities or cultures, including African American, Caucasian, Hispanic, and Asian. Some interpretations may include designations that would seem to belong to other protected classes, such as Polish or Jewish.

- **Religion:** System of belief, such as Christian, Muslim, Wiccan, or atheist.

- **National origin:** The country or area a person was born in, such as Canada, Mexico, the Middle East, Nigeria, and even the United States.

- **Sex:** Physical sex — male or female. Sexual harassment is recognized to be an element of sex discrimination.

- **Color:** Skin color or shade, which may seem to be the same thing as race, but whether or not someone knows another person's race, they may discriminate based on lightness or darkness of skin.

- **Handicap:** Physical or mental handicaps or disabilities, including hearing and visual impairments, chronic alcoholism, HIV/AIDS, depression, hoarding, allergies, and more.

- **Familial status:** Whether a household includes minors. Pregnancy is also protected. An exception does apply to bona fide senior housing (refer to the later section, "Noting exceptions" for more information).

Expanding the protected classes

The original Fair Housing Act designated the protected classes based on a person's race, religion, national origin, and sex (male/female). Familial status (households with minor children) and handicap (disability) were added in 1988.

To expand fair housing protections even further, some state and local governments have added their own protected classes to the list. See "Identifying How Local and State Governments Expand Fair Housing" later in this chapter for more information.

Keep in mind that everyone is a member of more than one protected class. For example, everyone is of a certain sex, race, skin color, and national origin. As a result, the Fair Housing Act is intended to ensure equal opportunity housing for *everyone*.

Identifying conduct that constitutes discrimination

By federal law, *discrimination* is the unfair treatment of people based on characteristics defined in the seven protected classes. Here's how the current Fair Housing Act addresses the subjects of discrimination and protected class:

> In General. It shall be unlawful for any person or other entity whose business includes engaging in residential real estate-related transactions to discriminate against any person in making available such a transaction, or in the terms or conditions of such a transaction, because of race, color, religion, sex, handicap, familial status, or national origin.

Here are a few examples of conduct that's considered discriminatory under the Fair Housing Act:

- Posting a rental ad stating that "no children" are allowed
- Not showing a second-floor apartment to someone in a wheelchair
- Rejecting an applicant for no other reason than that the person is in one of the protected classes
- Telling someone who is of a certain race or nationality that you have no apartments available when you actually do
- Arbitrarily charging people of a certain race or nationality higher rent or a higher security deposit
- Using different eviction criteria for men and women
- Delaying maintenance or repairs (or not performing them at all) for residents in a particular protected class

Is discrimination ever legal?

Although discrimination is always unethical and immoral, it's not always illegal. Antidiscrimination laws generally protect people only in their public and professional interactions, not in their private dealings. Acts of discrimination fall into two categories:

✔ **Public discrimination:** Laws prohibit you from discriminating in public matters. You can't reject an applicant based solely on race or religion, for example. If you hire people to work for you, you're not allowed to discriminate against people of specific groups (for example, women or Italians).

✔ **Private discrimination:** Discrimination is not legally prohibited in your private life. For example, you can choose not to socialize with members of any of the protected classes. Everyone, including a landlord, has a private life, and you can discriminate in private without breaking the law.

We discourage discrimination in private or public for a couple of reasons. If you discriminate in private, certain conduct is likely to creep into your public dealings with people. In addition, you're likely to miss out on golden opportunities to experience diversity in both in your professional and personal life.

Identifying conduct that constitutes preferential treatment

Landlords typically have no trouble grasping the concept of discrimination and how antidiscrimination laws apply to their daily activities. They tend to have more trouble avoiding conduct (specifically in advertising their rental units) that shows a preference for renters based on one or more of the protected classes. Specifically, the Fair Housing Act states that "it shall be unlawful . . ."

> To make, print, or publish, or cause to be made, printed, or published any notice, statement, or advertisement, with respect to the sale or rental of a dwelling that indicates any preference, limitation, or discrimination based on race, color, religion, sex, handicap, familial status, or national origin, or an intention to make any such preference, limitation, or discrimination.

Expressing a preference for a certain type of resident based on protected class, includes the following illegal practices:

✔ Posting an ad on Craigslist that states "Couples preferred" or "English-speaking preferred"

✔ Including pictures in your rental office that show only fit, white, young adults

✔ Advertising the location of your rental property as being close to a certain country club that caters primarily to the upper class

✔ Advertising a unit as a "bachelor apartment" or perfect for "empty nesters"

For more about how the Fair Housing Act applies to advertising, see Chapter 6.

Meeting the three conditions of a violation

Not all discriminatory conduct rises to the level of committing a Fair Housing Act violation. The conduct (or alleged conduct) must meet the following three conditions to qualify as a violation:

✔ People are treated differently.

✔ The treatment has a negative impact.

✔ Differences in treatment are based on factors related to a protected class.

Different treatment alone isn't sufficient to be considered illegal discrimination for fair housing purposes. The treatment must have a negative impact on one or more people and be related to at least membership in a protected class.

Including principals and agents

The Fair Housing Act applies to both principals and agents:

✔ **Principals:** As landlord, you're the *principal.*

✔ **Agents:** An *agent* is anyone who acts on your behalf, such as a property manager. The principal-agent relationship gives legal authority for the agent to act as principal, which is essential to the rental housing industry. Without it, all landlords, not just apartment owners, would have to lease their apartments *personally.*

The flip side means that an agent's actions are considered to be the principal's actions as well. If the agent discriminates against prospective renter or residents at (the landlord's) property, for example, the law considers the principal to have committed the violation. The financial consequences of fair housing violations are substantial, so you, as landlord and principal, need to be very careful that your agents — property managers, leasing personnel, caretakers, porters, and even groundskeepers — are aware of, and fully understand, the risks of housing discrimination. Check out "Paying the price for infractions," later in this chapter, where we discuss the possible consequences.

How an agent's actions can be destructive

The owner of ABC Apartments, David, hired Donna to manage his company's main office, including all hiring. Donna hired DEF Contractors to plow ABC's parking lot and do grounds maintenance. Donna later became general manager for all of David's apartment buildings and hired DEF to do this work at all of David's apartment buildings.

Unfortunately, DEF experienced financial problems and had to cancel its insurance coverage. One late afternoon, George, a DEF employee, was planting flowers at one of David's properties. He started a conversation with a renter, but a misunderstanding arose between them. The conflict escalated. George called the renter a "stupid Mexican, who ought to get deported" and punched the renter, breaking his jaw. The renter sued DEF Contractors, David, David's company (ABC), and Donna, claiming that George was their agent and his actions were discriminatory. The resulting damages forced DEF Contractors into bankruptcy.

What about the consequences for David, his company, George, and Donna? All were found equally responsible for George's actions and fined heavily. Donna and George had to declare bankruptcy, and David's company was required to hire several well-paid fair housing specialists to oversee daily operations at David's apartment buildings.

Knowing what you're allowed to do under the law

The Fair Housing Act doesn't require you to accept all applicants. You can and should carefully screen applicants based on information that predicts how likely the resident is to pay the rent, care for the premises, and get along with the neighbors. You can screen out applicants based on criteria gathered from several sources, including:

- ✔ Credit history
- ✔ References from previous landlords
- ✔ Employment history
- ✔ Criminal history
- ✔ Income

For more about screening applicants, see Chapter 8.

Noting exceptions to the law

The Fair Housing Act does have a couple of exclusions that may apply to you, depending on the type of property you're renting. Here they are:

- ✔ In owner-occupied apartments with four (or fewer) units, owners may discriminate against members of protected classes — for example, by not renting to families with children. But they may never *advertise* a discriminatory preference. This type of housing is often referred to as a "Mrs. Murphy" Exemption. "Mrs. Murphy" is the hypothetical elderly widow who uses a portion of her residence as a rooming house to supplement her income. Although the landlord of a "Mrs. Murphy" apartment building may not advertise in a discriminatory way, the building is otherwise exempt from coverage by the Fair Housing Act.

- ✔ A single-family rental home rented by the owner without the assistance of an agent as well as rentals operated for a noncommercial purpose by a religious organization or a private club. However, in such situations there is still a prohibition against discriminatory advertising.

- ✔ If the housing meets the criteria for *housing for older persons* — residential properties that can be marketed as "55+" or "age restricted," as long as it is either occupied only by persons who are 62 or older, or it houses at least one person who is 55 or older in at least 80 percent of the occupied units. Advertising may specifically target senior prospects who would qualify under the property's age restrictions. Take care not to advertise for "Adults Only." There is no exception for adults, only for seniors. Also don't designate specific areas of a non-senior property for adults or families, as that could lead to a familial status violation.

Paying the price for infractions

Violations of the Fair Housing Act are often costly. Applicants or residents who believe they've suffered some loss from illegal acts of discrimination can seek legal recourse in any of the following ways:

- ✔ **File a private lawsuit against you in federal, state, or local court.** There's no limit on the amount of damages the court can award the plaintiff.

The statute of limitations for a discriminatory housing lawsuit varies from state to state. In California, it's two years from the alleged action but can be extended if the case was first brought with a government agency and wasn't handled in a timely fashion.

✔ **File a claim with the US Department of Housing and Urban Development (HUD).** HUD has the authority to order the landlord to pay damages, civil penalties, and attorney fees. The statute of limitations for HUD is one year. As of the writing of this book, civil penalties for Fair Housing Act violations are up to

- $16,000 for a first offense

- $37,500 for a second offense committed within five years from the previous offense

- $65,000 if the alleged violator committed two or more offenses within a seven-year period prior to the current offense

✔ **File a claim with the state or local housing authority.** The state or local housing authority may have the same power as HUD to order the landlord to pay damages, civil penalties, and attorney fees. Additional damages or penalties may be assessed based on state and local statutes.

✔ **File a claim with the US Department of Justice (DOJ or Attorney General).** Cases can be filed directly with this federal agency, but often they handle large cases that cross state lines and/or reflect a "pattern or practice" of discrimination. Be aware that the statute of limitations for the federal US DOJ is 18 months.

Digging Deeper into the Sex, Familial, and Handicap Protected Classes

Of the protected classes, race, color, religion, and national origin are more straightforward than sex, familial status, and handicap. Those last three demand special attention, because the violations aren't always so obvious. In fact, some actions by housing providers that are meant to be helpful to prospective owners and renters, or that are neutral and not based upon protected class status, may be considered illegal. In the following sections, we help you navigate these trickier classes and provide guidance on conduct that's likely to result in a violation.

Sex

At first glance, sex discrimination is obvious: Men and women should have equal access to housing. This protected class becomes a little tricky, however, when you start to consider segregation by sex in student dormitories and when the law is applied to sexual orientation and gender identity or gender expression issues when renting to members of the lesbian, gay, bisexual, or transgender (LGBT) community.

Segregation by sex is a fair housing violation regardless of the circumstances. Male-only and female-only dormitories, for example, are diminishing in popularity. Such housing is increasingly being targeted by the Department of Housing and Urban Development (HUD) for this discriminatory practice. However, in some states (even progressive California) there are exceptions for shared living, which is usually renting rooms in your home. Also, sororities and fraternities have been allowed to show a preference based on membership. Always consult with local fair housing experts for any unique situations.

The Fair Housing Act doesn't specifically protect individuals who are lesbian, gay, bisexual, or transgender. Here's how HUD addresses these special cases:

> "The Fair Housing Act does not specifically include sexual orientation and gender identity as prohibited bases. However, a lesbian, gay, bisexual, or transgender (LGBT) person's experience with sexual orientation or gender identity housing discrimination may still be covered by the Fair Housing Act. In addition, housing providers that receive HUD funding, have loans insured by the Federal Housing Administration (FHA), as well as lenders insured by FHA, may be subject to HUD program regulations intended to ensure equal access of LGBT persons."

The Fair Housing Act may provide protection for such individuals based on one or more of the protected classes. For example, a transgender person may qualify under sex. Additional protection for members of the LGBT community may come into play in state and local fair housing laws. See the later "Exploring Additional Protected Classes at the State and Local Levels" section for details.

Familial status

Familial status became a protected class in 1988 when Congress recognized that families with children under the age of 18 and pregnant women were increasingly becoming the victims of housing discrimination. The familial protected class includes the following:

✔ Families with children under age 18

✔ Pregnant women

✔ Persons in the process of securing legal custody of children under age 18

The purpose is to protect family members from landlords and leasing personnel who attempt to maintain a no children policy or steer families with children to particular areas of an apartment property. (For more about steering, see the later "Steering Clear of Steering" section.) In the following sections, we explain how to comply with the law regarding families with children.

Avoiding violations

Many landlords who violate the Fair Housing Act as it applies to families with children do so with no ill will and may not even realize they're discriminating, so you need to be even more careful than usual. Here are some examples of questions or statements that constitute violations of the Fair Housing Act:

- ✔ Asking applicants whether they have a disability that requires an accommodation. This appears to be a reasonable question to ask a prospect, but HUD considers it objectionable. The reason? Unless the landlord, or the leasing agent, asks this question of *every* prospect, asking it of *any* prospect is discriminatory.

- ✔ Making statements that suggest a preference for adults, such as "We don't have places for kids to play," or "This building is too dangerous for children."

- ✔ Lying about the availability of housing, or refusing to lease because the applicant has (one or more) children.

- ✔ Attempting to evict a family because children move into the apartment or a baby is born into the family, depending on the facts of the situation such as if the occupants are within or lower than the maximum occupancy standards (see "Using occupancy guidelines" below).

- ✔ Charging families a higher security deposit based upon the presence or number of children.

- ✔ Segregating families (for example, in ground-floor units only or in apartments close to other families or children-friendly amenities).

- ✔ Creating or enforcing unfair rules targeted against children (for example, establishing restrictive hours for the use of common area facilities such as swimming pools, based on age).

- ✔ Threatening or harassing family members, including children.

You may legally impose reasonable health and safety rules to protect children from harm or to control disruptive behavior. For example, adult supervision can be required for children to use swimming pools and other potentially dangerous activities. State health and safety laws often set forth such restrictions. Compliance with fair housing laws doesn't require rental property owners and managers to ignore conditions that are obviously dangerous to residents or their families. However, landlords must be prepared to defend age-related restrictions by citing local law or providing statistical evidence of the reasonableness of a specific restriction. Remember that there are exceptions for qualified senior housing.

Using occupancy guidelines

The familial status protected class affects the subject of occupancy guidelines, which place reasonable limits on the number of residents who can occupy apartments. At the federal level, occupancy guidelines were published in a memo from HUD based on the commonsense reason that large numbers of residents who occupy a studio apartment, for example, can overwhelm such building systems as utilities and waste removal.

HUD's standard for the intake of cases based on discrimination has been two persons per bedroom, although if state or local occupancy standards are different, HUD accepts them if they're reasonable. HUD's occupancy standards consider the following factors:

- ✔ The size of the apartment
- ✔ The number and sizes of bedrooms
- ✔ The capacity of building systems and other physical limitations
- ✔ Other relevant factors, such as the unavailability of similarly sized apartment types in the neighborhood.

Imposing strict occupancy standards is potentially risky, because the limitations can adversely affect families. For example, the two "per bedroom" standard is used as a tool to look at occupancy in general, not as a directive to control how a household actually assigns sleeping areas. HUD is likely to closely review standards that limit the number of people who can legally occupy an individual bedroom, rather than limit the number of occupants per apartment unit. Unfortunately, studio units haven't been addressed in the memo, but citing square footage restrictions in local health and safety laws may be helpful in justifying a housing provider's standard.

This family-friendly focus typically requires a justification by the landlord that the negative effect would be reasonable under the circumstances. For example, a legitimate business reason, such as limiting the number of renters for an unusually small, 600-square foot, two-bedroom unit, may be a justification that HUD will approve.

Handicap

The Fair Housing Act prohibits discrimination against any individual who has a handicap that substantially hinders the person's ability to perform certain functions. In the following sections, we analyze this protected class and explain the reasonable accommodations you're obligated to make under certain conditions.

Be careful with even well-intentioned statements suggesting that the property is "not suitable" for someone with an impairment. Even if you're genuinely concerned that a certain property lacks the necessary amenities, has potential safety hazards, or provides limited access, hold your tongue. Regardless of your intentions, such statements are unlawful. Let the individual decide whether she can live with or overcome any obstacles to living in the unit.

Recognizing what "handicap" covers

According to the Fair Housing Act a *handicap* is any "physical or mental impairment which substantially limits one or more major life activities, a record of such an impairment, or a person being regarded as having such an impairment." To fully grasp the meaning of this clause, you need to understand what qualifies as a *physical or mental impairment* and as a *major life activity*:

- **Physical or mental impairments** include the following, some of which may surprise you:

  - Epilepsy

  - Cancer

  - Heart disease

  - Diabetes

  - Mental illnesses, such as major depressive disorder, bipolar disorder, schizophrenia, and post-traumatic stress disorder

  - Developmental disabilities

  - HIV/AIDS

  - Chronic alcoholism and those recovering from drug addiction (as long as they're not currently using illegal drugs)

  - Chemical sensitivities and allergies

- **Major life activities** covered by this clause include the following:

  - Self-care

  - Manual tasks

  - Walking

  - Breathing

  - Seeing and hearing

  - Speaking

  - Learning

  - Working

The Fair Housing Act's definition of handicap opens this protected class to broad interpretation. "Being regarded as having an impairment" suggests that even if a person has no documented proof of an impairment or disability, a person's physical appearance may make her a member of the handicap class. In addition, "a record of such an impairment" indicates that even if the person shows no signs of having a given impairment, if she's had the impairment in the past, she qualifies for protection in this class. Some state definitions further expand the coverage by removing the word substantial, adding "medical conditions" and so on.

The 1988 amendments to the Fair Housing Act extend coverage to common areas and facilities. For example, any rules denying the use of the swimming pool to children or the use of facilities to individuals with HIV/AIDS are violations of the law.

The one exception here is that you're not obligated to make housing available to anyone who poses a direct threat to the health or safety of others or is currently using illegal drugs.

Determining whether someone has a handicap

Avoid initiating any conversations about a person's handicap or perceived handicap. Such questions could be viewed as a means of screening out applicants with handicaps. Generally speaking, the Fair Housing Act prohibits housing providers from asking questions with respect to the existence, nature, or severity of a handicap, unless they participate in a federal subsidy program that requires such an inquiry.

However, if an applicant or resident brings up the topic and requests help, you can ask clarifying questions about what they need from you to more effectively respond to the person's unique needs. Suppose a resident tells the landlord that because she frequently works late at her office, she needs to have access to the property's exercise room after hours in order to perform doctor-prescribed therapy on her injured legs. In this case, because the *resident* has made a request for an accommodation (due to an impairment), the landlord may ask for proof of the disability-related need if the disability and the related need aren't apparent.

Making reasonable accommodations

You, as landlord, and your agents are obligated by law to make "reasonable accommodations in rules, policies, practices, or services," when doing so would be necessary to provide someone with a handicap an "equal opportunity to use and enjoy" the apartment. *Reasonable* means that the accommodation doesn't place an undue burden on you or your business in terms of finances or administration or constitute a fundamental change in the nature of your business. *Accommodation* means you make exceptions to certain rules. Common reasonable accommodations include the following:

- Allowing service animals when you have a no-pet policy
- Reserving a parking space for a resident when the other spaces on the property are available on a first-come, first-served basis
- Extending the maximum visitor stay for someone who requires a live-in aide

Determining what makes an accommodation unreasonable is the tricky part, because what constitutes "undue" hardship is tough to define. Suppose the resident of an apartment has a severe respiratory illness. She notifies the landlord of the illness, and if the handicap isn't apparent, provides verification of the disability-related need and requests that certain cleaning compounds and pesticides not be used within 1,000 feet of her apartment.

Whether this request is reasonable depends upon whether similarly priced substitute products are readily available. Each request should be evaluated on a case-by-case basis. In a fair housing matter, reasonableness would be determined based on whether there is any undue financial or administrative burden and no fundamental change in the nature of the business. If one is deemed to be unreasonable, the parties are expected to become involved in an interactive process to attempt to reach a reasonable alternative.

You can make reasonable accommodations conditional. For example, if you allow a resident after-hours access to a workout facility, you may want to make the accommodation conditional upon the resident's not disturbing other residents and agreeing not to give anyone else access to the facility.

Allowing reasonable modifications

You're also obligated under the Fair Housing Act to allow residents with handicaps to make "reasonable modifications" of existing premises if doing so is necessary for the person with a handicap to have "full use and enjoyment" of the premises. *Modifications,* which can be done by either the resident or the landlord, are changes to the property, such as installing grab bars in the bathroom or a ramp outside the entry door to the unit to improve access.

Addressing the issue of service animals

Apartment rules and regulations often contain restrictions prohibiting animals, especially dogs or certain animals based on their size or weight. However, none of these regarding pets can be enforced to prohibit the use of service animals.

Handicapped residents have the right to be accompanied by a service animal, as long as the following three tests are met:

- ✔ The person must have a handicap as defined by the Act.
- ✔ The service animal must serve a function that is directly related to the handicap and necessary to their equal use and enjoyment of the premises.
- ✔ The request to have the service animal must be reasonable.

The Act, unfortunately, doesn't define service animal, nor does it distinguish service animals that provide psychological support from those that guide the blind or hearing impaired or service animals in training that live with the handicapped renters for whom they will work.

Clearly, however, a service animal can't be subjected to the rules applied to pets. For example, housing providers may not:

- ✔ Enforce pet weight, size, or breed restrictions on service animals
- ✔ Exclude service animals from common areas
- ✔ Require special tags, equipment, or identification of service animals

Perhaps because the Act doesn't interpret the term, and because the definition of handicap is so inclusive, what qualifies as a service animal is controversial. Healthcare professionals increasingly recognize that people with physical or mental disabilities — and those in nursing homes — tend to respond favorably to the companionship of animals.

Making new buildings handicap-accessible

The Fair Housing Act also contains requirements for new buildings that have four or more units:

- ✔ Public and common areas must be accessible to individuals with disabilities.
- ✔ Doors and hallways must be wide enough to accommodate wheelchairs.

If the building also has an elevator, all units are required to have the following (in buildings without elevators, only the ground floor units require these):

- ✔ Accessibility into and through the unit
- ✔ Accessible light switches, electrical outlets, and thermostats
- ✔ Reinforced bathroom walls that support the later installation of grab bars
- ✔ Kitchens and bathrooms that people in wheelchairs can use

Exploring Additional Protected Classes at the State and Local Levels

State legislatures and local city and county councils are prohibited from removing or modifying any of the federally protected classes from the Fair Housing Act, but states and local municipalities are permitted to expand fair housing coverage by adding protected classes. And many states and cities have done just that. Knowing whether your state or city has added protected classes and what those classes are is essential to protecting yourself and your business from claims of housing discrimination.

For the current list of your state's protected classes, search the web for "protected classes" followed by the name of your state. Conduct similar searches to track down protected classes in the county and the city or town where you own rental property. Be careful with information from nongovernmental websites or alleged fair housing experts because some private websites may not have current and/or accurate information.

A few of the more common protected classes that state, county, and city legislators have added include the following:

- **Sexual orientation/gender identity/gender expression:** Members of the LGBT community are protected from housing discrimination.

- **Source of income:** A person who has any lawful source of income, including government assistance, alimony, child support, or other compensation or benefit, including Section 8 housing subsidies, is protected.

- **Political affiliation:** In states that have a protected class for political affiliation, landlords are prohibited from discriminating based on whether a person is a registered Democrat or Republican or a staunch libertarian.

Steering Clear of Steering

Steering is a subtle form of discrimination that occurs when a landlord or leasing agent tries to limit or influence a prospective resident's choice of apartments. To avoid this unlawful practice, follow these three guidelines:

- **Present prospective renters with all available options.** Limiting a person's options to only the units you want the person to consider is a form of steering.

- **Stick to facts.** Describe each unit objectively, focusing on size, number of rooms, amenities, rent amounts, and so on. Present all available options and let the prospect decide what's best based on location, rent, and other factors.

- **Keep your opinions to yourself.** Let prospective residents choose what they deem suitable for them and which available apartments they would like to see. Don't make assumptions about what they may prefer.

Here are a couple of examples that illustrate steering conduct that may be unintentional, or even intended to be helpful, but are nonetheless a violation of the Fair Housing Act:

Leasing agent #1 to prospect: "Ms. Rockwell, I see from your rental application that you'll be living alone in your apartment. We have three different buildings here at The Highlands. Most of the families with small children live in the two buildings next to the playground and swimming pool, and they're quite noisy. Let's start by looking at a couple of one-bedrooms in the building next to the parking lot, shall we? I live over there myself, and it's really quiet, even during the daytime."

Leasing agent #2 to prospect: "Mr. Stevens, I think it would be easiest for you to maneuver your wheelchair from the parking area into the town-home right along the lakefront. That's a perfect unit for you, and we have quite a few retired professionals in that area. Shall we go over there and see it?"

These examples illustrate that illegal discrimination may occur even when the discrimination doesn't appear to involve intentionally exclusionary behavior. In these examples, because the agents are trying to influence each prospect's decision by subtly limiting the range of their choices, the leasing agent has violated the Fair Housing Act.

Here's an example of a leasing agent taking the right approach:

Leasing agent #3 to prospect: "Mrs. Farnsworth, I see from your rental application that you'll be housing four persons in your apartment. We have a lovely two-bedroom apartment next to the playground; it rents for $430, and it has brand new carpeting and new appliances. There are two others over in building two—that's the one nearest the clubhouse and the pool area—and they're both $450. There's also a big three-bedroom for $520 that overlooks the lake. We've just painted and re-carpeted it. Which one would you like to see first?

In this example, the leasing agent presents the prospective resident with all available options, provides concrete details about each apartment, doesn't express her opinion of which would be best for the prospect, and lets the prospect take the lead in deciding which apartment she would like to see first.

Safeguarding from Claims of Housing Discrimination

Protecting yourself against claims of discrimination is essential. We recommend that you take a two-pronged approach: Proactive/preventive (to avoid violations) and reactive/corrective (to defend against or resolve any claims that you committed a violation). In the following sections, we explain each approach and provide additional guidance to help keep you out of legal trouble.

Taking a proactive/preventive approach

The best way to avoid potentially costly fines and legal fees is to take preventive measures that reduce the chances that you or one of your agents will violate a fair housing law or engage in other conduct that could be perceived as a violation. In the following sections, we present three ways to steer clear of trouble.

Avoiding illegal conduct

The single best thing you can do to try to avoid being accused of violating fair housing laws is the most obvious: Don't violate fair housing laws. See the previous sections in this chapter for detailed coverage of fair housing laws and what constitutes violations of those laws. Here are some additional examples of the kinds of conduct that HUD considers to be illegal discrimination:

- ✔ Refusing to rent to a member of a protected class

- ✔ Discriminating against a member of a protected class regarding the terms, conditions, or privileges of a lease or in providing services or facilities

- ✔ Limiting families to ground floor units, which is steering (check out the earlier "Steering Clear of Steering" section)

- ✔ Advertising or making any statement that indicates a limitation or preference based upon protected class membership (see Chapter 6 for more about avoiding discrimination in advertising)

- ✔ Evicting a white tenant from her apartment because her black friends visit her there

- ✔ Charging Hispanic tenants larger security deposits or higher rent than you're charging white tenants

Here are a few more detailed scenarios to give you a better feel for the type of conduct that violates the Fair Housing Act and other such laws:

Scenario: A landlord checks the credit records of all minority applicants and uses minor credit problems as an excuse to reject their applications. The landlord doesn't always check white applicants' credit records or overlooks minor credit problems with their records.

Commentary: Had this landlord performed credit checks for all applicants and done so using the same standards for approving them, his conduct would be legal. Consequently, if the landlord chooses to use credit checks as a means of qualifying prospective tenants, he or she must do so for all prospects and use the same criteria uniformly for everyone.

Scenario: A black person answers a newspaper ad for an apartment. The landlord falsely tells him that the unit has been rented and later leases it to a white person who responds to the same ad.

Commentary: Here, the landlord's "refusal to rent housing" to a black person but then renting to a white person is a blatant violation of the Fair Housing Act. The landlord's decision is obviously based on the applicant's color, which is a protected class.

Scenario: A landlord turns away a prospect in a wheelchair because the only vacant units are accessible only by stairway.

Commentary: The wheelchair qualifies the prospect for membership in the handicap protected class, so turning away the applicant is a fair housing violation. To comply with the law, the landlord should show the prospect the available apartments and let the prospect decide whether she wants to deal with the stairs.

Scenario: A newspaper advertisement offers rental housing in a good Christian community.

Commentary: Religion is a protected class. This ad conveys a preference for Christians and subtly discriminates against Jews, Muslims, Buddhists, and so on.

In each of these situations, the landlord treats individuals differently, and negatively, because of their protected class status, which means that the landlord's actions violate the Fair Housing Act. These examples illustrate conduct that is illegal and wrong — the type of intentional behavior that fair-minded people would consider discriminatory.

Documenting policies and enforcing them consistently

Having fair housing policies in place and enforcing them consistently regardless of protected class (and making any necessary exceptions for handicaps) is one of the best ways to stay out of trouble. With the assistance of an attorney who specializes in fair housing law in your area, document the following policies and procedures:

✔ **Application:** Craft an application to collect only the information you need to make a well-informed decision about whether to consider an applicant. Don't include questions that enable you to draw distinctions based on any of the protected classes. Stick to questions regarding prior evictions, why the resident is leaving her current residence, employment history, and credit history, for example. (See Chapter 8 for guidance in creating a rental application.)

In some areas, source of income is a protected class, so be careful when asking about employment history or source of income.

✔ **Screening:** List the criteria you use to determine whether applicants qualify to live in the property, and make sure the criteria don't exclude applicants based on any of the seven protected classes. Criteria may include employment history, monthly income, credit history, and so on. (See Chapter 8 for more about screening applicants.)

✔ **Occupancy standards:** In general, limiting occupancy to two persons per bedroom is acceptable, but this can vary depending on the overall size of the rental unit, whether the unit has any unusually large bedrooms or living areas, and whether any of the residents is a child or infant. Check state and local housing agencies because some jurisdictions allow a distinction based on age and some also have suggested guidelines such as the "2+1 minimum occupancy standard guideline," which means that a landlord or property manager must allow at least two individuals per bedroom, plus an additional occupant for the unit.

✔ **House rules:** Write a list of rules that you expect *all* residents to abide by, regardless of any of the protected classes. Making the rules applicable to "all residents and guests" should keep you on the right track. Remember to make any reasonable accommodations for anyone in the handicap protected class.

✔ **Eviction:** Carefully document your eviction policy, specifying the grounds for eviction and the procedure and time line that you will follow. Consider drafting templates for warning letters and eviction notices to ensure uniformity in communicating notices. Be consistent in enforcing evictions; don't evict someone for a violation and then let someone else who commits the same violation slide, or you may have to prove that you didn't base the decision on a differing protected class status.

✔ **Antidiscrimination policy:** If you have employees or other agents acting on your behalf, compose an antidiscrimination policy, to ensure that everyone is on the same page. See the later "Training your agents and holding them accountable" section for details.

Keeping impeccable records

If you ever end up on the wrong side of a housing discrimination lawsuit, having documentation to back up your side of the story is essential, assuming of course, that you haven't committed a violation. Here's a list of the types of information you should gather and store:

✔ Advertisements, including dates of placement

✔ All completed resident applications, both approved and denied

✔ Names, dates, and times of prospective resident visits, including the properties they visited

✔ Tentative and actual move-in dates

✔ All communication with prospective residents, including phone call records, email, and texts

✔ Payment ledgers

✔ History of rental unit availability

Training your agents and holding them accountable

As explained in the earlier "Including principals and agents" section, you're legally responsible not only for your conduct but also for the conduct of your *agents* — leasing agents, employees, and anyone else who represents your business or operates on your behalf. Make sure you provide fair housing training and resources to your agents.

To protect yourself against claims of housing discrimination, you must protect them, as well. Take the following steps to keep your agents on the right track:

1. **Write detailed policies and procedures to significantly reduce the chance that your agent will commit a fair housing violation.**

2. **Carefully review your antidiscrimination policy with all of your agents and encourage them to ask questions.**

3. **Convey the seriousness of fair housing laws and penalties.**

    Confirm that agents should check with supervisors before making a fair housing decision.

4. **Let your agents know the possible consequences that may follow if you discover that an agent has committed a fair housing violation, including the possibility of termination.**

Defending yourself against claims of housing discrimination

Full compliance with fair housing laws doesn't give you immunity from prosecution. Anyone can file a claim of housing discrimination against you, and you can be hauled into court over even frivolous lawsuits. In the following sections, we clarify the legal process, so you know what to expect if someone files a housing discrimination claim against you. We also tell you what to do and not do if someone threatens to file a claim or you're notified that someone has already filed a claim.

Knowing what to expect: Brushing up on the legal process

When someone files a fair housing complaint with HUD, HUD notifies the alleged perpetrator of the complaint and gives that person the opportunity to respond. (See the next section for guidance on how to respond.) When HUD has the complaint and the landlord's response (or failure to respond within the specified period), it does one of the following:

✔ Conducts an investigation to determine whether there's reasonable cause to believe that the landlord committed a Fair Housing Act violation.

✔ Refers the complaint to a state or local agency (if there is one in the area and HUD determines that the agency has the same fair housing powers as HUD) and notifies both parties of the referral. HUD may take the case back if the state or local agency doesn't begin to work on it within 30 days.

If HUD or the state or local agency decides that there's reasonable cause to believe that the landlord committed a violation, HUD or the agency attempts to negotiate an agreement between the complainant (person who filed the complaint) and the respondent (the landlord). If a breach of the conciliation agreement occurs, HUD turns the case over to the Attorney General.

Knowing how to respond to a complaint or threat of complaint

Whether someone files a claim or threatens to do so, try your best to remain calm. Impulsive action is only likely to get you into more trouble.

If someone claims that you violated the Fair Housing Act, don't try in any way to discourage that person from exercising his right. The Fair Housing Act prohibits you from threatening, coercing, intimidating, or interfering with anyone exercising a fair housing right or helping someone else exercise their right.

If you receive a notice from HUD or any other agency that someone has filed a housing discrimination complaint against you or one of your agents, read the complaint closely and follow the instructions in the notice to respond to the accusation. Also note any deadlines for responding, so you don't miss important dates. Carefully prepare your response and include as much documentation as possible to clarify and support your side of the story. We recommend that you consult an attorney who specializes in fair housing law to assist you.

Chapter 6

Exploring the Legal Aspects of Advertising

In This Chapter

▶ Complying with fair housing laws in advertising

▶ Recognizing the importance of being honest

▶ Staying legal when advertising online

*R*etail advertising is usually judged by how effective it is at building a brand and boosting sales. As long as any claims made in an advertisement are true and the ad generates the targeted sales numbers, it's considered a success. You don't need to worry about the advertising police showing up at your door to hand you a citation or a summons. Advertising for most products and services doesn't carry much legal risk.

Advertising rental property, however, is fraught with legal land mines. What constitutes a violation can be so subtle that you're likely to miss it if you don't know the laws and what to look for. In this chapter, we bring you up to speed on the laws that govern the advertising of rental properties. We explain how fair housing laws come into play, the importance of accurately representing the property, and how to avoid legal trouble when advertising online.

Applying the Fair Housing Act to Apartment Advertising

A constant challenge for landlords is maintaining high occupancies. Occupancy levels generate rent payments, and that revenue pays your bills and produces income, which is why effective marketing and advertising are essential.

You always have a need to advertise, because your occupancies can change monthly (depending on how many rental units you own), and you need replacement tenants who are likely to pay their rent promptly and be good residents and neighbors. You can advertise in several ways — email, print, social media, billboards, websites, radio, cable TV, flyers, and the like, as we explain in Chapter 5. However you choose to advertise, you must keep in mind fair housing law.

In the following sections, we help you steer clear of legal trouble by explaining the fair housing law and how you can comply with the law when advertising in any medium including online.

Understanding the law

The purpose of the Fair Housing Act (see Chapter 7 for the ins and outs of the law) is to prevent discrimination in residential real estate sales and rental housing. The section of the Fair Housing Act that applies specifically to residential renting advertising provides in part as follows:

> "Section 804(c) of the Fair Housing Act, 42 U.S.C. 3604(c), as amended, makes it unlawful to make, print, or publish, or cause to be made, printed, or published, any notice, statement, or advertisement, with respect to the sale or rental of a dwelling, that indicates any preference, limitation, or discrimination because of race, color, religion, sex, handicap, familial status, or national origin, or an intention to make any such preference, limitation, or discrimination."

This brief paragraph contains a few key bits of information. First, it prohibits advertising that indicates any "preference, limitation, or discrimination" — three terms you need to understand:

- ✔ **Preference:** The goal of attracting members of certain protected classes as prospective residents, such as white, single professionals

- ✔ **Limitation:** The goal of restricting or discouraging residency for members of certain protected classes, such as families or racial minorities

- ✔ **Discrimination:** Treating residents or prospects differently, and negatively, because they're members of a protected class, such as refusing to advertise rental vacancies in minority publications

Second, it identifies seven *classes* (classifications used to characterize people) that the federal Fair Housing Act advertising laws apply to, which we discuss in Chapter 5.

As you prepare your advertisement, scrutinize its message for any language, image, or logo that could be interpreted as a preference, limitation, or discrimination against a member of any of the seven protected classes (race, color, religion, national origin, sex, handicap, or familial status).

In order to help advertisers and the people who hire advertisers avoid the most common pitfalls, the Department of Housing and Urban Development (HUD) enumerates the criteria it uses to determine whether advertising is preferential, discriminatory, or limiting:

"§ 109.20 Use of words, phrases, symbols, and visual aids.

"(HUD) will normally consider the use of (certain) words, phrases, symbols, and forms to indicate a possible violation of the act and to establish a need for further proceedings on the complaint, if it is apparent from the context of the usage that discrimination within the meaning of the act is likely to result.

"(a) *Words descriptive of dwelling, landlord, and residents*. White private home, Colored home, Jewish home, Hispanic residence, adult building.

"(b) *Words indicative of race, color, religion, sex, handicap, familial status, or national origin—*

"(1) *Race*—Negro, Black, Caucasian, Oriental, American Indian.

"(2) *Color*—White, Black, Colored.

"(3) *Religion*—Protestant, Christian, Catholic, Jew.

"(4) *National origin*—Mexican American, Puerto Rican, Philippine, Polish, Hungarian, Irish, Italian, Chicano, African, Hispanic, Chinese, Indian, Latino.

"(5) *Sex*—the exclusive use of words in advertisements, including those involving the rental of separate units in a single or multi-family dwelling, stating or tending to imply that the housing being advertised is available to persons of only one sex and not the other, except where the sharing of living areas is involved (see Chapter 5 for a more detailed discussion of the narrow exemptions). Nothing in this part restricts advertisements of dwellings used exclusively for dormitory facilities by educational institutions.

"(6) *Handicap*—crippled, blind, deaf, mentally ill, retarded, impaired, handicapped, physically fit. Nothing in this part restricts the inclusion of information about the availability of accessible housing in advertising of dwellings.

"(7) *Familial status*—adults, children, singles, mature persons. Nothing in this part restricts advertisements of dwellings which are intended and operated for occupancy by older persons and which constitute *housing for older persons*. . . .

"(8) *Catch words*—Words and phrases used in a discriminatory context should be avoided, e.g., *restricted, exclusive, private, integrated, traditional, board approval or membership approval.*

"(c) *Symbols or logotypes.* Symbols or logotypes (that) imply or suggest race, color, religion, sex, handicap, familial status, or national origin.

"(d) *Colloquialisms.* Words or phrases used regionally or locally which imply or suggest race, color, religion, sex, handicap, familial status, or national origin.

"(e) *Directions to real estate for sale or rent (use of maps or written instructions).* Directions can imply a discriminatory preference, limitation, or exclusion. For example, references to [a] real estate location made in terms of racial or national origin [or] significant landmarks, such as an existing black development (signal to blacks) or an existing development known for its exclusion of minorities (signal to whites). Specific directions (that) make reference to a racial or national origin significant area may indicate a preference. References to a synagogue, congregation or parish may also indicate a religious preference."

Complying with the law

After reading the actual statute (refer to the previous section for the specific wording), you may have a better understanding of the law, but what constitutes a violation of the law may surprise you.

Whether you're the owner of a single rental unit or a large apartment complex, you're subject to fair housing laws whenever you advertise. Here's what the law provides:

"*Persons placing advertisements.* A failure by persons placing advertisements to use the criteria contained in this part, when found in connection with the investigation of a complaint alleging the making or use of discriminatory advertisements, will be considered . . . (to determine whether) a discriminatory housing practice has occurred or is about to occur."

Any discrimination in rental housing advertising is illegal and can result in severe penalties. We guide you through this in more detail in the following sections.

Showing no preference

Everyone who owns residential rental property has a mental image of the perfect residents — they pay their rent on time, care for the property as if they owned it, and get along with their neighbors. Such preferences are perfectly understandable, but fair housing laws prohibits any advertising that shows a preference for certain groups that have a higher concentration of members who have the desired characteristics; for example, younger, more affluent individuals who are less likely to have children.

Deciding whether words or images convey a "preference" depends upon how a "reasonable person" is likely to interpret them. Names of places that could suggest a preference for members of one or more protected classes — "one block from Avon Country Club" or "private golf course nearby" or "exclusive neighborhood," for example — convey a message that some residents may not be welcome. Here's the law on this subject:

> "(f) *Area (location) description.* Names of facilities (that) cater to a particular racial, national origin or religious group, such as country club or private school designations, or names of facilities which are used exclusively by one sex may indicate a preference."

Instead of devising, and then communicating, a profile of the "perfect" resident, just describe the physical aspects of the rental property. Spotlight the number of bedrooms and bathrooms. Talk about the great room, if you have one, or the spacious office fitted with bookshelves and Internet access. Does it have an eat-in kitchen? What about granite countertops? And how about the terrific amenities — the world-class exercise facility, the tricked-out clubhouse, and all the rest? If you limit yourself to the features and amenities you have to offer and stay away from the type of resident you're trying to lure to your property, you should be fine.

Recognizing exceptions to the "preference" rules

Of course, you'll find exceptions to the rules. Advertisements that use descriptive terms or images that *encourage* members of two protected classes — Familial Status and Handicap — are acceptable, because families and disabled persons historically have been especially subjected to housing discrimination. Thus, ads containing language such as "children welcome," "family friendly," or "handicapped/wheelchair accessible" are okay.

Here's the specific statutory language that authorizes preferential advertising:

> "(b) *Affirmative advertising efforts.* Nothing in this part shall be construed to restrict advertising efforts designed to attract persons to dwellings who would not ordinarily be expected to apply, when such efforts are pursuant to an affirmative marketing program or undertaken to remedy the effects of prior discrimination in connection with the advertising or marketing of dwellings."

Steering clear of limitations

Advertising that expresses limitations about desired renters may be blatant, such as "graduate students preferred," or more subtle, such as "no international students," but in both cases, such advertising violates fair housing laws. The risk is much greater when human models appear in the ad. Showing white families enjoying the property amenities, for example, suggests that minorities might not be welcome. If you choose to show people in your advertisements, make sure that, at a minimum, you include human models that are representative of the demographic makeup of your community.

Meet "Mrs. Murphy"

The Fair Housing Act includes an important exemption involving a fictitious Irish lady who, according to the story, owned a rooming house and needed to rent out individual rooms in her home when her finances required.

The Act exempts rooming houses as long as (1) the facility has four rooms or fewer, and (2) the owner of the place actually *lives* in one of the units. The exemption permits the owner of a Mrs. Murphy dwelling to refuse to rent to minorities because of their race — otherwise, a clear violation of the Act — as well as impose discriminatory terms and conditions upon these residents, such as charging higher rents or security deposits, which of course would be another violation of the law.

The Fair Housing Act includes two significant restrictions for Mrs. Murphy owners.

- They must actually live in the property, not merely rent a room there or lease units and collect rents from the boarders.

- They can't advertise discriminatory preferences.

Apparently, members of Congress believed strongly that the American public shouldn't be subjected to discriminatory housing advertising, even if, in the case of "Mrs. Murphy," one very limited kind of discrimination is legal in practice.

Avoiding discriminatory advertising

The days when landlords could use blatantly discriminatory language in their advertising messages — "no Negroes," "no Irish," "adults only" — are, fortunately, long past. However, there are more subtle ways to suggest that a prospect of a certain group is unwelcome, and these subtle messages are equally unethical and illegal.

Fortunately, HUD has put together a list of commonly used advertising words and expressions that have been found to be discriminatory. You can access the list at www.proassoc.org/adguide.html. Although this list isn't comprehensive, it can help you focus on the most common examples of what's right and wrong, legal and illegal.

The Fair Housing Act also highlights any selective use of advertising media, content, or, as noted above, human models as discriminatory:

- **Selective use of advertising media or content:** Using particular media or language can be suspect. The law specifically mentions that using English exclusively as a means of advertising to the majority population in the metropolitan area, when media are available that use other languages, can be discriminatory. The law notes that selectively using billboards, brochures, the equal opportunity slogan or logo, or other advertising that is limited to certain geographic areas as a means of reaching only a segment of the population is also illegal.

✔ **Selective use of human models:** This is an obvious example of possible discrimination, one that critics have labeled the "Barbie factor." Depicting persons of only one color, or one sex, or of adults only, without a complementary advertising campaign directed at members of other protected classes, is illegal. If you use human models, make sure that they also are representative of the demographic makeup of your community so there is no inference that some protected classes are subservient to others.

Using the Equal Housing Opportunity logo, statement, or slogan

The Fair Housing Act also requires that advertisements contain the Equal Opportunity Housing logo, statement, or slogan to communicate inclusiveness (that your establishment doesn't discriminate against anyone based on any of the seven protected classes). The following explains these three:

✔ **Logo:** Figure 6-1 shows the Equal Housing Opportunity logo.

✔ **Statement:** "We are pledged to the letter and spirit of US policy for the achievement of equal housing opportunity throughout the Nation. We encourage and support an affirmative advertising and marketing program in which there are no barriers to obtaining housing because of race, color, religion, sex, handicap, familial status, or national origin."

✔ **Slogan:** "Equal Housing Opportunity."

Figure 6-1:
The Equal Housing Opportunity logo.

Illustration courtesy of Equal Housing Opportunity

The law reads as follows:

> "All advertising of residential real estate for sale, rent, or financing should contain an equal housing opportunity logotype, statement, or slogan as a means of educating the home-seeking public that the property is available to all persons."

Recognizing the most likely targets of discrimination

Studies of residential rental advertising have found that families are the most likely targets of discriminatory advertising. Families, after all, are considered to be the most likely to damage apartment units and common areas, and younger family members can certainly be the noisiest and most disruptive residents. There are always exceptions to generalizations, however, and gone are the days when owners can designate "family" buildings, or restrict families to ground floor apartments in an effort to cut down on the noise from children playing on upper floors.

Be particularly careful when creating or reviewing advertisements to make sure they're not discriminating against families with children or suggesting a preference for residents without children. As much as you may want to rent exclusively to adults, fair housing law prohibits any efforts to exclude families with children.

The law also states that, where the Equal Housing Opportunity statement is used, "the advertisement may also include a statement regarding the coverage of any local fair housing or human rights ordinance prohibiting discrimination in the sale, rental or financing of dwellings."

To access the Equal Housing Opportunity logo, statement, and slogan along with guidelines for using them in your advertising, visit `www.fairhousing.com/index.cfm?method=page.display&pagename=regs_fhr_109apx`.

Adhering to Truth in Advertising Laws

The Federal Trade Commission (FTC) Act (also known as the Federal Truth in Advertising Law) directs all advertisers to meet specific requirements in all advertisements. Here are the conditions of the Act:

- ✔ **Deception:** All advertisement must be truthful, fair, and free of misleading misrepresentations. Claims must be supported with solid proof. The Commission's Deception Policy Statement describes *deception* as a misleading feature of the ad that convinces a customer to purchase or use the product or service.

- ✔ **Fairness:** The FTC describes an unfair advertisement as an ad that causes harm that overrides any beneficial features that appeal to consumers.

- ✔ **Supporting evidence:** If a product or service is being advertised that deals with health or safety, documented scientific evidence must support the claims.

✔ **Specific products and services:** Federal truth-in-advertising laws include specific regulations for certain products (for example, alcoholic beverages, automobiles, clothing, consumer credit, and real estate). For rental housing, the FTC mandates that advertisements must follow the requirements provided in the Fair Housing Act.

In the following sections, we provide guidance on how to develop advertisements that comply with truth-in-advertising guidelines.

Accurately describing the rental units

Regardless of where and how you choose to advertise, make sure your advertisements accurately describe the rental property. Here are some specific suggestions for producing accurate ads:

✔ Use photos of actual rental units in their current condition. Avoid using photos that feature a model apartment, outfitted with upscale furnishings and decorating, if the model doesn't represent what you're really offering.

✔ If you include the rent amount or range, make sure the dollar amounts accurately represent what you customarily charge residents.

✔ Indicate any up-front fees, such as "application fee required."

✔ Stick to the facts, such as the overall square footage of units, number of rooms, and whether the units are furnished.

✔ Avoid expressing value judgments with words such as "quiet," "convenient," "luxurious," and "exceptional," because other people may have different ideas of what those words mean.

✔ Be careful not to make any implied claims that could mislead someone; for example, including a photo of someone carrying a tennis racket when your property has no tennis court.

Misleading advertising hurts you in two ways:

✔ Exposes you to possible claims of false advertising. If you're found guilty of false advertising, the FTC may issue a cease-and-desist order to stop running the ad and fine you for every day a future ad violates truth-in-advertising laws. Courts may also award damages to consumers for any harm caused.

✔ Wastes a lot of your time when interested parties show up to check out the rental units, are disappointed, and leave.

Disclosing any important policies

Indicate any rental policies that are likely to turn away certain prospects to dissuade people who are unqualified or unlikely to be interested in renting from you. (Just make sure the reason you're turning away these prospects doesn't constitute illegal discrimination.) Here are a few policies a landlord may want to include in advertisements:

✔ No pets

✔ No smoking

✔ Credit check required

Think twice about establishing a no-pet policy. According to a recent renter survey conducted by http://www.apartments.com, a leading Internet apartment listing service, 75 percent of renters are pet owners. Do you really want to exclude 75 percent of your market? In addition, if you do decide to have a no-pets policy, be sure to make exceptions for service animals, as explained in Chapter 5.

Presenting rents and amenities accurately

Prospective renters need to know what their rental payment includes. If residents are responsible for paying their own utilities and you charge extra for additional services, be sure to mention those charges in your advertising. Here are a few examples:

✔ Utilities (many landlords separately meter utilities and pass the costs directly to the resident)

✔ Water and sewer

✔ Parking

✔ Pet rent

✔ Storage

Consider using an absence of a fee as a selling point in your advertising. For example, you may advertise "all utilities included" or "pets welcome at no extra charge" or "free Wi-Fi!"

Avoiding bait-and-switch advertising

Bait-and-switch advertising misleads consumers into thinking that something is much better than it really is. The most common bait-and-switch tactic in the residential rental business is to advertise a spacious unit along with the price of one of the smaller units.

To avoid technically committing the bait-and-switch, some landlords include in tiny print just before the big, bold low price the words "Starting at." Well, that may help you avoid any trouble with the FTC, but it's still misleading and defeats your purpose of turning away anyone who's probably not interested or qualified in the units you're trying to lease.

Advertising on the Internet

The Internet is an exceptionally popular and productive medium for residential advertising, because many people begin their search for apartments online. However, posting advertisements and listings online is so easy that you need to be particularly vigilant in complying with fair housing law in all of your online advertising.

Many online services, such as Craigslist, require compliance with fair housing laws and may provide guidelines similar to those listed above that identify words and phrases that may be considered discriminatory. These sections explain the essentials for Internet advertising.

Understanding the Communications Decency Act of 1996

The Communications Decency Act of 1996 was an attempt by Congress to regulate the use of pornographic material on the Internet. The following year, however, the anti-indecency provisions of the CDA were found to be unconstitutional.

What remains of the Act is an amendment that's been interpreted to mean that operators of Internet services aren't considered to be publishers of the contents of their advertising and therefore aren't legally liable for the words and phrases of the advertising that appears in their Internet postings. Any liability for using discriminatory language, therefore, applies only to the advertisement's originator. In other words, if you post an ad online, you're responsible for making sure it complies with all federal, state, and local laws.

A still unsettled law

The first lawsuit involving a discriminatory housing ad, not surprisingly perhaps, involved Craigslist ads. Craigslist is a virtual bulletin board, a place where any registered user can post classified advertisements for all to see.

A group of Chicago civil rights attorneys, citing more than a hundred discriminatory housing ads that had been posted on Craigslist, filed a lawsuit claiming that the advertising violated the Fair Housing Law, which, of course, it did. The District Court found, however, that Craigslist advertisers, and not the website itself, were the publishers of the ads, and therefore that Craigslist wasn't responsible for the illegal advertising.

Subsequent cases have produced different results. In a recent Massachusetts lawsuit, a landlord and a property manager were ordered to pay more than $38,000 in a housing discrimination case based upon a Craigslist advertisement stating that an apartment "is not deleaded, therefore it cannot be rented to families with children under six years old."

Another case, this one in Ohio, applied the Fair Housing Act and state law to a Craigslist advertisement for a one-bedroom apartment in Dayton, Ohio, advertising a "great bachelor pad for any single man looking to hook up." This case went to trial, and surprisingly the jury found that the ad didn't violate either statute even though ads showing a gender preference is prohibited.

The law regarding Internet apartment advertising is unsettled. Future cases will clarify the uncertainty. Until then, play it safe.

Applying the Communications Decency Act to apartment advertising

Although website owners may be immune from prosecution regarding content posted on their sites, you may still be held accountable as an individual or a business for any discriminatory advertising content that you post or have posted anywhere online. The safest course is to strictly follow the provisions of the Fair Housing Act and make absolutely certain that your advertising — wherever you post it — doesn't discriminate against anyone.

Chapter 7

Addressing the Legalities of Rent Collection and Rent Control

Rent collection is essential to a successful residential rental business. Ideally, residents pay their rent in full on or before the date it's due. The reality, however, is that most residents don't have significant cash resources, and many live from paycheck to paycheck. So if a resident's paycheck is delayed, her car breaks down, or she has an unexpected major expense, then her ability to pay the rent in full and on time is in jeopardy. And because her funds are so tightly budgeted, when she falls even one month behind on rent, catching up again is even more difficult. Fortunately, you can take steps to increase the likelihood that you'll get all your rent money, all the time.

You can begin laying the foundation for successful rent collection before you rent your property. The best preventive measures include targeting your advertising to responsible residents and establishing a thorough and careful resident screening and selection process. (See Chapter 8 for more about screening residents.)

In this chapter, we explain how to write a rent collection policy that spells out your expectations for when, where, and how residents pay rent; outline ways to handle rent collection issues, including late- and nonpayment; and fill you in on how to deal with any rent-control statutes in your area.

Creating a Written Rent Collection Policy

The keys to rent collection success are establishing policies and procedures and firmly enforcing your payment requirements. Setting up a rent collection policy, putting it in writing in your rental contract (either in your lease or rental agreement), and repeating it to your residents in the resident handbook or information letter are effective strategies to reinforce your payment expectations. No single rent collection policy works for *all* property owners, but every policy should cover when rent is due, where it's paid, and how it's paid. We offer considerations for each of these key issues in the following sections.

Be sure to point out that each resident is jointly and severally responsible for the full payment of rent. *Jointly* means all residents on the lease, as a group, are responsible to pay the rent. *Severally* means each resident is responsible to pay the rent. Regardless of any agreement between co-occupants or room-mates, every resident can be legally required to pay the entire rent, not just her share. Use this phrase on the lease immediately after the insertion of the residents' names and note the meaning when you sign the lease agreement with the residents. (See Chapter 9 for more about leases.)

Review your rent collection procedures with each adult occupant of your rental unit before accepting her rental application, so that everyone under-stands the importance of prompt and full payment of rent. Then make rent collection a featured topic before your move-in orientation meeting with resi-dents, when they review and sign the lease or rental agreement.

When rent is due

We recommend that you require that the rent be received in full in advance, on or before the first day of each month. This method is the most common, and many state laws require it unless the rental contract specifies otherwise.

That said, you and your resident can determine that the rent is due on any mutually agreeable date during the month. This approach may make sense if your resident receives income or financial assistance payments on certain dates. For example, you may have a resident who receives a check on the tenth of each month, so you set the rent due date for the 15th of each month.

Some owners make the rent payable on the date the resident moves in. For example, if the resident moves in on the 25th of the month, then her rent is due on the 25th of each future month. This practice is legal and may be acceptable if you have only a few residents and are willing to keep track of each due date, but making all your rents due on the first of the month makes life simpler and avoids confusion.

If your rent due date falls on a weekend or a legal holiday, most states allow the resident to pay by the next business day. This policy may not be mandatory in your state, but adopting it is a good idea.

Although rent is traditionally paid in full at one time, you may agree to let your resident divide up the rent and pay twice a month, every week, or in some other time frame. Try to avoid accepting more frequent payments, because your goal is efficiency, and handling the rent collection process as few times as possible is definitely more efficient. (Also, if you accept partial payments, you may not be able to serve a legal notice seeking the full amount on the due date, but may be limited to only seeking each partial payment amount as it becomes past due.)

Be careful to document that any differences in rental collection terms are based on legitimate business decisions or else your actions may be seen as favoring one resident over another. Of course, you may have a resident who formally requests an accommodation in payment terms under fair housing laws. In this case, seek advice from local landlord-resident legal counsel. (See Chapter 5 for more about fair housing laws.)

In addition to fair housing concerns, think about the ramifications of accepting rent based on the resident's scheduled receipt of income rather than your usual rent due date. By accommodating the resident, you're tacitly acknowledging that she needs that payment plan to afford the rent. But one of the fundamental tenets in rental housing management is to avoid residents who can't afford the rent. If your resident needs that income to pay her rent that month, you have no safety net if the resident's check is lost in the mail, her car breaks down, or she's temporarily laid off from work.

To avoid surprises and delinquent rent, you don't want your residents' finances to be so tight that they need this month's income to pay this month's rent. Check out Chapter 8 for tips on selecting residents with enough financial resources to pay every month's rent with cash on hand.

Prorating rent

Life would be simpler if all your residents moved in and out on the first day of the month, but they don't. If your resident's occupancy begins in the middle of the month, and your rent collection policy states that all rents are due on the first of each month, then you need to prorate the resident's rent at move-in. Following are two basic ways to prorate the rent at the beginning of your new resident's occupancy:

- ✔ **If your resident moves in toward the end of a month, collect a full month's rent (for the next month), plus the rent due for the prorated portion of the current month.** For example, if your resident takes occupancy on June 25, then upon move-in, collect six days' rent for the period of June 25 to June 30, plus a full month's rent for July. A new resident is usually glad to oblige if just a few days are prorated.

- ✔ **If your resident moves in early in a month, collect a full month's rent prior to move-in and then collect the balance due for the prorated rent on the first day of the next month.** For example, if your resident moves in on May 10, then before she takes occupancy, collect a full month's rent that covers the period of May 10 through June 9. Then on June 1, collect the balance due for June 10 through June 30 (21 days' worth). By July 1, the resident is on track to pay her full rent on the first day of each month.

Don't let your new resident move in without making at least a full month's rent payment. Though the resident may want you to accept just the prorated rent for that month, you don't want to risk turning over your rental unit for a payment of only several days' rent.

Unless otherwise agreed, you normally uniformly apportion rent from day to day using a 30-day month. Divide your monthly rental rate by 30 to determine the daily rate and multiply your answer by the number of days in the partial rental period. (This formula applies to February as well.)

Providing a grace period

Many rent collection policies allow for a *grace period* that gives residents a few extra days to pay their rent in full after the due date but before incurring late charges. Most residents incorrectly believe that if they pay rent within the grace period, their payment is legally on time. However, the rent is due on or before the due date. If paid after the due date, but before the end of the grace period, a late fee may not accrue, but the payment is still considered legally delinquent.

Make sure your rental contract and the resident information letter are very clear about the fact that the rent is due on or before the due date and that it's technically late if paid during the grace period.

Grace periods are optional in most states and can be any number of days in length. However, a few states (including Connecticut, Delaware, Maine, Oregon, and Rhode Island) have mandatory grace periods or restrictions on serving a *notice to pay rent or quit* (a legal notice demanding rent payment), so be sure to check your local and state laws. Unless restricted by law, we recommend you set up your grace period to expire on the third of the month and allow an extra day or two if the third falls on a weekend or holiday.

In most states, you don't have to wait until the grace period expires to begin your collection efforts with residents who show a pattern of being late. You can even serve legal notices demanding the rent payment. Your rental contract should contain a specific provision that you have the right to refuse payment after the expiration of your legal demand notice so you aren't obligated to accept an offer of rent from the resident and can move forward with eviction, if necessary.

Getting real about rent

My (Laurry's) consulting practice includes working with owners of very low and low-income properties. For all of my owners, rent is due on the first of the month, no excuses! Real-life situations, however, are challenging, posing problems that are more difficult than they first seem. Here are a few examples:

✔ The long-time renter (we'll call her Janet) depends upon Social Security payments for rent, and of necessity lives month to month. But Janet gets these checks during the middle of the month, and then pays her rent immediately, at least a week after her landlord files evictions. What about her? Should Janet be evicted?

✔ A low-income renter, Adam, has unexpected car problems that prevent him, for the first time, from paying rent on the first of the month. Should he be evicted as well?

✔ How about Carolina, a resident whose daughter has had emergency surgery. Carolina is faced with paying her rent while waiting for a medical insurance issue to be resolved. Should she be evicted?

Making exceptions is fine. After all, even a great renter can experience an occasional financial squeeze. Just be sure that you're making exceptions and not rewriting the rules. Allowing Adam, with a history of on-time rent payments, to pay late because of this one-time emergency situation, makes sense, because it gives him a break while enabling you to retain a quality resident.

However, when the landlord requires rent to be paid on the first, yet routinely accepts Janet's late payments, her rent is no longer legally due on the first of the month. The landlord, in effect, has modified the due date for her rent payment until midmonth and can't claim that rent is due on the first and late on the second day of the month.

The problem is further complicated by the possibility of a fair housing claim (see Chapter 5). If the landlord evicts Adam, who's Jewish, and doesn't evict Janet, a Christian, Adam may claim discrimination based on religion (a protected class). Even if the landlord contends that he didn't base his decision on religion, he may lose.

Where rent is paid

You can collect your rent in several ways, including the following:

- ✔ **You can collect the rent payment in person.** Unless otherwise agreed, many states require that you collect the rent on the premises. Although stopping by the unit allows you the opportunity to see your property, it isn't time-efficient unless you live on or very close to your property, especially if you have to make multiple trips. The benefits of in-person collection also depend on your residents' expectations. Residents in low-rent properties often expect you to come by and collect the rent in person, whereas renters in middle- to higher-rent properties tend to think you're too nosy if you personally come by for the rent.

- ✔ **Residents can mail the rent payment to you.** For most rental property owners and residents, the most popular way to remit the rent payment is to have the residents mail it. Because collecting rent by mail is only effective if your residents pay on time, be sure to inform your residents that they need to allow extra time for the delivery of the mail because you require payment to be received by the due date. We strongly suggest you make doing so extremely simple for your residents by providing them with stamped, preaddressed envelopes.

    If you and your residents agree that the rent will be mailed, you may run into a major question: Is the rent considered paid when it's postmarked, or when you receive it? Check your local laws and have a clear, written agreement in your rent collection policy. Absent any legal requirements, we recommend you consider the rent paid when the payment is received.

- ✔ **You can accept electronic payments or transfers.** Having the resident transfer money from her account to yours is very efficient and effective. See the next section for details.

- ✔ **Residents can bring the rent to your home or office.** Although this method may be very convenient for you, many residents object to the added burden of having to personally deliver their monthly rent. We discourage this practice, but do suggest you have a secure mail drop box or slot to make it more convenient as long as you also have a sign warning that the risk of loss is on the resident.

How rent is paid

Your rental contract should clearly indicate how residents should pay rent: by electronic payment, personal check, cashier's check, money order, or cash. Regardless of the method, give your residents a receipt for all money received.

Accepting electronic payments

Technology is making the rent collection process much more efficient and timely. Rental owners and property managers can now benefit from their financial institution's ability to process hundreds of rent payments in a matter of minutes. Due to improvements in software automation and *security encryption,* which prevents the theft of confidential information, electronic payments are actually more secure than the conventional check payment method.

Several companies now offer technology for the electronic transfer of funds to allow residents to pay their rent. The computer software enables you to download the details on all payments processed each month. You're automatically notified if a resident has insufficient funds to cover the transfer so you can enforce your regular rent collection policies. Check with your local Institute of Real Estate Management (IREM) chapter or National Apartment Association (NAA) affiliate for more info on these companies.

Most residents are comfortable paying electronically rather than writing out and mailing a check each month. This method of payment is becoming increasingly popular with tenants and rental property owners. With electronic payments, a resident simply fills out a form one time, and the preauthorized amount is deducted on a designated day (usually between the first and fifth of each month) from his bank account and deposited directly into your account.

If you want to set up your residents to pay electronically, visit www.dummies. com/go/landlordlegalkit and click on the Rent Collection forms folder for the Tenant Automatic Clearing House (ACH) Debit Authorization Form. Consult with your financial institution for the necessary banking information to ensure payments are properly credited to your rental property account. Another caveat with ACH payments by your residents is that you need the ability to stop the electronic payment under certain conditions. A good reason: if you're in process of evicting your tenant and you don't want to accept rent payments beyond the eviction date.

Going old school with checks and money orders

For many rental property owners, accepting checks (personal, cashier's, or money order) is routine. Most residents have a personal checking account, and paying by check is easy for them. Check processing has also improved greatly with new federal regulations for the banking industry that allow checks to be scanned and converted to an electronic funds transfer. Check with your financial institution to see whether you can use this technology to simplify your rent collection, provide immediate access to the funds, and eliminate trips to the bank.

Some landlords request postdated checks in advance from their residents with the idea that they'll already have the rent payment in hand, and the residents just need to make the funds available to cover the check. We strongly advise against accepting postdated checks. Often these checks aren't good, and many state laws consider a postdated check a promissory note. You may be unable to file an eviction action for nonpayment of rent while the note is pending.

Payment by check is conditional. If the check isn't honored for any reason, it's as if the resident never paid, and late charges and returned check charges should apply. Check scanning can give you immediate notice that funds aren't available, allowing you to contact the resident and promptly begin collection efforts.

Never accept second-party checks, such as payroll or government checks. Instead, institute a policy that all rent payments made after the grace period must be in the form of a cashier's check or money order. The only exception might be if you're making a reasonable accommodation based on a disability. Then you can accept a third-party check directly from a disability assistance agency, if requested by your resident.

Refusing cash payments, when possible

Although some residents may want to pay rent with cash, avoid accepting it whenever possible. Turning down cash is always difficult, and your residents may remind you that cash is legal tender. However, according to the US Department of the Treasury, you have the legal right to refuse cash because accepting cash

- **Can make you a target for robbery:** Even if you use a safe, your risk is increased.

- **Can add the risk of employee theft, if you have employees:** Plus, you're potentially putting your employees in danger.

- **Attracts residents who may be involved in illegal businesses that deal primarily in cash:** Although many employees in legitimate businesses derive income, at least partially, from cash tips (wait staff and beauticians, for example), so do drug dealers. Criminal residents don't want to have their activities tracked and prefer properties where cash payments are allowed. Don't make your rental property more attractive to the criminally inclined.

Clearly state in your rental contract that you don't accept cash under any circumstances. Reinforce this policy early in the relationship and don't accept even small amounts of cash for rental application fees or late charges. However, if a resident is facing eviction and offers full payment in cash, you may want to accept the funds at a place where you feel safe (your home or office) because you may find that the eviction court isn't inclined to allow you to terminate the tenancy if you refuse the proposed cash payment for the entire amount due.

Managing multiple rent payments

When you have multiple residents in one of your units, you'll probably receive several payments for portions of the total rent due. And you may not receive all the payments at the same time or for the proper amount. When you call the residents, some of them may say that they paid their share and that you need to track down one of the other residents.

How your residents choose to divide the rent between them isn't your problem, and accommodating your residents by accepting multiple payments can cause administrative nightmares. It can also lead roommates to erroneously believe that they're not responsible for the entire rent. You're better off having a firm written policy of requiring one payment source (either check, money order, or electronic payment) for the entire month's rent. This practice offers more than just administrative convenience. Legally, each roommate in your rental property is *jointly and severally* liable for all rental contract obligations, meaning that if one skips out, the others owe you the entire amount.

Encourage your residents to let the delinquent roommate know that, although they've all paid a portion of the rent, they're on the hook until the balance is paid. After all, your residents are in a better position to track down their elusive roommate than you are.

Good accounting practices suggest that you clearly document all your income and expenses. The IRS may consider auditing your rental housing if it finds out about frequent cash transactions at your property.

Dealing with Rent Collection Problems

Residents don't always pay rent on time and in full, which is why you need to have policies in place for the most common problems you'll encounter in rent collection. These rules should outline the specific penalties for late payments, bounced checks, insufficient funds, and failure to pay in full. We cover some of these key issues in the following sections.

Apply your rent collection policies — including charges for late payments, dishonored payments, and partial payments — consistently with all residents. If you don't, you can be accused of discrimination by simply allowing some residents to pay late or by accepting multiple payments from some roommates and not from others.

Collecting late rent

One of the most difficult challenges for a rental property owner is dealing with late rent payments. You don't want to overreact and begin serving threatening legal rent-demand notices because doing so creates tension and hostility if the resident has a legitimate reason for the delay. Then again, late rent can be a very serious issue.

Communication is the key to keeping your response appropriate to the magnitude of the problem. Remain calm and businesslike, and focus on determining why the rent is late before taking any action. If you're having trouble collecting rent on time, consider these options:

- ✔ **Email or mail your residents monthly payment reminders or invoices.** Although electronic payments are the best approach, some owners find that a rent coupon book (just like a mortgage payment coupon book) can be helpful in improving their rental collections.

- ✔ **Call slow rent payers routinely.** Landlords and property managers seeking payment of delinquent rent aren't subject to the regulations set by the Fair Debt Collection Practices Act, so you can call residents at home *and* at their places of business. (Although you may not want to bother your residents at work, don't feel bad calling there as long as you're respectful and professional. You do have a right to know when to expect your rent.) When you call, remind these slow payers that the rent is due on or before the first of the month. You can also remind them that you expect your rent to be a top priority among their various financial obligations.

- ✔ **Go to the rental unit and speak directly with residents.** Don't be shy, or else paying the rent will quickly become a low priority for your residents. But remember to document your visit with a written notice to the resident. You may need to show it to a judge at some point in the collection process.

The most effective way to collect rents and determine whether you should exercise patience is to contact your residents directly. Simply mailing a rent reminder or hanging a late notice on the front door can be effective with residents who just need a reminder, but these tactics typically don't get the job done with residents who are financially strapped and likely to respond only to direct personal contact.

When contacting residents, your goal isn't to harass them but to remind them about rent payments. Be solution-oriented and work out an agreement to get your rent. Whatever agreement you reach, make sure that it's in writing and that the residents sign it.

If you're having trouble locating a resident, check with her neighbors or call the emergency contact listed on her rental application. Check to see whether the utility company has been told to cancel the utilities; maybe the resident has skipped town without notifying you. (For advice on how to reclaim an abandoned unit, turn to Chapter 20.)

Be firm in your rent collections. The most common mistake landlords and managers make is breaking their own rent collection rules. They allow rents to be paid late, accept excuses, fail to send timely collection or legal notices, and find themselves housing residents who are weeks — even months — behind in rent payments. Keep in mind that you're running a business.

Charging late fees

More than a dozen states have laws addressing restrictions on late charges for rent payments, so be sure to check with your local NAA affiliate before establishing a late fee policy, and read your state statutes for late fee guidelines and restrictions. Generally speaking, though, implementing and enforcing a late charge policy makes sense, as long as it's reasonable and relates to your actual out-of-pocket costs or expenses incurred by the late payment.

Don't allow residents to form the impression that your late charge policy approves of late rent payments as long as you collect the late charges. Your late charge should be high enough to discourage habitual lateness but not so high as to be unreasonable or illegal. Send written warnings to residents who regularly pay late (even if they pay the late charges), clearly indicating that their late payments are unacceptable and are a legal violation of the terms.

You can assess late charges in one of several ways:

- **Daily late fee:** Set a daily late charge with a reasonable cap or maximum fee. A late charge of $5 per day, with a maximum of $50, works very well. A resident who is only one day late pays a nominal $5 late fee. A resident who is eight days late pays a heftier $40. The purpose of the cap is to keep the late charge reasonable and within legal limits. By the time you get to the cap (at ten days late), you'll have already sent the proper legal rent-demand notices.

- **Flat fee:** The most common late charge is a *flat fee,* which can be any set amount (within legal limits), due immediately after the grace period. Typical flat fees range from $30 to $100 and are usually set at 4 to 6 percent of the monthly rental rate. One problem is that many residents are only one or two days late, making the flat late charge unreasonable. Property owners in this situation often end up waiving the flat fee, especially if it's at the higher end of the range. If the matter ever goes to court, the resident usually challenges the fee, and the court may throw it out.

✔ **Percentage late fee:** A *percentage late fee* is calculated as a percentage of the rent payment and ranges from 4 to 8 percent of the monthly rental rate. The customary late fee percentage for late rent payments is either 5 or 6 percent, but be aware that some states have legal limits on late charges expressed as a percentage of the rent. ***Note:*** Although we prefer the daily late fee, some courts may be more willing to accept and enforce this method because the percentage late fee is customarily the method used by lenders who receive an owner's late mortgage payment.

The flat fee and the percentage late fee methods both fail to provide an incentive for the resident to pay rent promptly. After the late charge has been incurred, the resident often finds other financial obligations more important than your rent. Assessing a daily fee, on the other hand, offers the incentive some residents need to get their rent in sooner rather than later.

Waiving the late charge excuses late payment of rent and can send the wrong message to your residents. If you routinely accept late payments and waive the late charges, you can't suddenly change your attitude and begin eviction proceedings the next time a resident pays late. Instead, you need to provide a written notice that you're once again actively enforcing the strict rent collection terms of your rental contract. You also need to be consistent in applying your late charge policy to all residents equally — or risk facing claims of discrimination. Making exceptions also causes issues in court. Judges often rule that if you break your own rules, they're no longer rules that can be enforced against your residents. As difficult as it is to be firm at times, you must show consistency.

If you receive a late payment by mail, always keep the envelope with the postmark and the date received clearly indicated in writing just in case the resident wants to dispute the late charge.

Except where restricted by law, you need to evaluate your own increase in costs as a result of late rent payments to determine what a reasonable late charge should be for your property. Put this amount in writing and be prepared to explain your policy if challenged in court. Additional costs may include phone calls and in-person meetings with the resident, the preparation and sending of warning letters and required legal rent-demand notices, time and costs spent preparing delinquency lists, and additional accounting and bank deposits when you receive the funds.

Handling returned rent payments

Dishonored rent checks or electronic payments can cause major problems for your rent collection efforts, so you should be able to charge residents a fee when you incur expenses because you're unable to collect payments as required by your rent collection policy.

Giving early-payment rent discounts: Yes or no?

Some landlords have tried to get around late charge problems by using early-payment rent discounts to entice their residents to pay rent on time. These landlords set the rent in the rental contract slightly higher than the market rent and then offer residents a reduced rent if it's paid in full and on time. For example, if a landlord wants $900 in rent and a $75 late charge, she sets the contracted rent at $975 with a $75 discount if the resident pays on or before the third of the month.

Although this tactic may be creative, the US legal system has consistently determined that the actual rent is the discounted amount. The courts view giving a large discount for an on-time payment the same as charging an excessive late fee.

Don't play the early-payment rent discount game. If you're challenged, your case will be thrown out of court. At least two large class-action lawsuits on this specific practice have been ruled in favor of the residents, and the landlords were levied with major legal costs and severe financial penalties. If you want more rent money, raise your rent amount. If you want residents who pay on time, carefully screen your prospects. Establish a reasonable and fair late charge policy and apply it uniformly to all residents.

Often, when you contact your resident, she'll have some excuse for the returned item and tell you that her payment is now good. Check with your bank about its policy for handling dishonored electronic payments. For old-fashioned paper checks, we recommend you go to the resident's bank and cash the check immediately instead of depositing it again. Or you can get the check *certified,* which means the bank reserves the funds for payment when you deposit it in your bank. (Unless you receive payment before the end of your grace period, your resident is also responsible for late charges.)

Demand that your resident immediately replace a returned check with a cashier's check or money order. After a resident's check is returned a second time, regardless of her excuse, your lease (or at least your rules) should provide that the resident is required to make all future payments electronically or with a cashier's check or money order (both of which are guaranteed to have sufficient funds). Residents can still cancel their electronic payments or request a stop payment on a cashier's check or money order, so be sure to process the transaction right away.

Like late charges (covered in the preceding section), dishonored electronic payment and returned check charges should be reasonable. Try setting the fee at $25 to $35 per returned item, or slightly higher than the amount your bank charges you, to cover the time devoted to getting the required payment. A late fee may also be appropriate if you don't receive payment in a timely manner.

Dealing with partial rent payments

Occasionally, you'll encounter a resident who isn't able to pay the full rent on time. She may offer to pay a portion of the rent with a promise to catch up as the month proceeds. Your written rent collection policy shouldn't allow partial payments of rent, and deviating from this standard generally isn't a good idea.

In some instances, however, allowing for partial rent payments may make sense. If your resident has an excellent rental payment history and you can verify that this partial payment is a one-time situation, then you're probably safe in accepting a partial rent payment. Of course, you need to be careful and watch for the resident who's delaying the inevitable and stalling you from pursuing your legal options.

If you do accept a partial payment, prepare the proper legal notice for nonpayment of rent or draw up a written notice outlining the terms of your one-time acceptance of the partial rent payment, and a notice to perform covenant or quit for late charges. Then present the resident with the legal rent-demand notice or written agreement when she gives you the partial payment. This way, you can be sure she understands your terms.

In most areas, the acceptance of a partial payment voids any prior legal notices for nonpayment of rent. If your resident is causing trouble besides the delinquent rent (breaching any other terms of the lease), don't accept any partial payments or you'll have to begin your eviction proceedings from scratch. In most states, after you begin the legal process for an eviction, you may demand full rent plus all late fees and other penalties, including legal and court costs. Should you accept any partial payment before the court hearing, the legal notice is voided, and in some cases you must refile the eviction action.

Always apply rental payments to the oldest outstanding past-due rent amount, even if the resident tries to indicate the payment is for a different time period. However, be aware that in at least one state (California), the law says that if the landlord accepts a check with a notation that the payment is for "July rent," it can only be applied as indicated.

Serving legal notices

If you're having trouble collecting rent from one of your residents, you may need to pursue legal action. In most states, you don't need to wait until the end of the grace period to serve a legal rent-demand notice, but you should serve it personally whenever possible. But be aware that some states forbid the service of legal documents by the plaintiff (in this case, the plaintiff being you, in a legal action against your residents). So check your state statutes because you may need to have the resident served by another employee or a contracted process server. Contact your local NAA affiliate for the process-serving requirements in your area.

Rewarding timely payments

Because timely rent collection can make or break your career as a rental property owner, you may want to offer your residents incentives to pay on time. If you have several rental units, one good way to motivate your residents to pay the rent is to offer a monthly prize drawing for everyone who pays rent in full by your due date. Of course, you need to carefully outline your rules in writing and make sure you don't violate any local or state laws.

The drawing should be simple and easy for your residents to understand. Limit eligibility to residents who are current with their rent, and automatically enter residents when you receive their full rent on or before the due date. Inform residents of the time and place for the drawing and try to hold it in a common area at one of your properties. You can also give a second entry to residents who pay early, but be sure your rules disqualify a winner whose rent payment is later returned for any reason.

The prize can be a gift certificate to a local store or restaurant. (Often, the merchant is willing to discount or donate the prize if it gets some good publicity from your drawing.) Consider sending out a written announcement congratulating your monthly drawing winner.

 Legal notices for nonpayment of rent and similar breaches of the rental contract vary widely from state to state. The generic forms available from office supply stores may be ineffective or even invalid in your region. Contact your local NAA affiliate or the National Association of Realtors member board in your area for current and legally correct forms.

Raising the Rent

Increasing the rent is one of the most difficult challenges rental property owners face. You may be wondering how to raise the rent, worrying that residents will leave or questioning how rent control ordinances may affect your efforts. We help clear up these murky waters in the following sections.

 The best way to establish your rent increase is to regularly review the local rental market to determine the current market rental rate for *comparable properties* — ones that are of similar size and condition and that have the same features and amenities. To find out more about strategies for setting rent, visit www.dummies.com/extras/landlordlegalkit to read this bonus chapter.

Recognizing restrictions on rent increases

If a resident is on a month-to-month lease and you're not operating in a rent-controlled area, you can increase the rent of a month-to-month or periodic resident — with proper legal notice (as we explain in the next section). Otherwise, you may have to deal with the following restrictions on rent increases:

- **Rent-control statutes:** In a rent-controlled area, you may be limited on how frequently and how much you can raise the rent. See "Dealing with Potential Rent Regulation Issues," later in this chapter, for details.

- **Lease restrictions:** You must comply with any language in the lease that limits the frequency and amount of rent increases. Also, unless your lease specifies otherwise, you can't raise the rent until the lease expires.

- **Consistency:** To discourage any claims of retaliatory rent increases or violations of fair housing laws, be consistently fair and equitable with all your residents when raising rents and keep good records.

Be careful when raising the rent so that you're not accused of retaliatory rent increases. An increase immediately after a resident complains to the local health department or building code enforcement agency is likely to lead to problems, especially if you have nothing to prove that the rent increase is fair and equitable.

Giving residents advanced notice

One step to take to avoid objections or lawsuits over rent increases is to give your residents advanced written notice of your plans to increase the rent. Make sure your written notice contains the following information:

- **Explanation of why you're raising the rent:** Residents are more likely to accept a rent increase if they know why the extra money is needed. Perhaps your operating costs have increased, you're building a new clubhouse that all residents will enjoy, or you're upgrading the resident's apartment. Whatever the reason(s), lay them out for your residents.

- **Amount of the rent increase:** State the amount of the rent increase or show the current and future rent the resident is paying, so she can do the math.

   If you're raising the rent in response to rent increases in your area, you may want to provide information on rent increases in nearby rental properties, especially if your rent increase is lower in terms of a percentage increase in rent.

- **The date on which the resident's rent payment will increase:** Let your resident's know when they need to start making the higher rent payments. (You'll probably need to remind them when the next payment date nears or when a resident forgets and continues paying the previous amount.)

A sample Notice of Rental Rate Change form is shown in Figure 7-1. To obtain a copy of the form, visit `www.dummies.com/go/landlordlegalkit` and click on the Rent folder.

Many states require that landlords provide residents with a 30-day notice of a rent increase, but we recommend a minimum notice of 45 days. If the rent increase is significant (10 percent or more), a 60-day written notice is advisable, and sometimes required. Some owners fear that giving their residents notice also gives them plenty of time to find another rental. However, if you set your increased rent properly and treat your residents fairly, you want your residents to have the opportunity to compare the new rental rate to the market conditions, as well as taking into account the effort and cost of moving.

Notice of Rental Rate Change

Date:_____

_____

_____, Apt No._____
_____, {State} _____
AND ALL OTHER OCCUPANTS OF THE PREMISES

You are hereby notified that effective _____("Effective Date") your total monthly rent for the premises you now occupy including our amenities that you presently have in your possession will be increased to the following month-to-month rate. (You may instead select lease renewal of six or twelve months, but not any other duration):

	Prior Rent	New Rent Month-to-Month	Anticipated 6-month lease renewal rate*	Anticipated 12-month lease renewal rate*
1) Apartment Rent..........	$	$	$	$
2) Other:_____	$	$	$	$
3) Other:_____	$	$	$	$
Total Rent...............	$	$	$	$

* A Lease Renewal signed by both parties supersedes this notice. If you do not renew your lease prior to the effective date of your month- to- month tenancy, you may elect to renew at a future date at the then existing lease renewal rates. Lease renewal is subject to management approval. Lease renewal is not available if: 1) a lease violation exists; 2) an accounts receivable balance is due; or 3) an eviction is pending. If prior lease violations occurred, lease renewal may not be available. If lease renewal is available, and you desire to renew your lease, please advise us and we will prepare the necessary documents.

Change of Lease Terms. Attached to the Notice of Rental Rate Change is an Apartment Lease Contract ("New Lease Contract"). If you execute the attached contract, commencing on the Effective Date, the terms of your Lease Contract are modified to include the terms of the attached New Lease Contract and Addenda. To the extent there is any inconsistency between your current Lease Contract and the attached New Lease Contract and Addenda, the terms of the New Lease Contract and Addenda shall prevail.

_____   Date:____ / ____ / ____   _____
SIGNATURE OF OWNER'S REPRESENTATIVE   MONTH DAY   YEAR   RESIDENT'S SIGNATURE, IF REQUIRED

_____   Date:____ / ____ / ____   _____
PROPERTY NAME   MONTH DAY   YEAR   RESIDENT'S SIGNATURE, IF REQUIRED

_____   Date:____ / ____ / ____   _____
PROPERTY ADDRESS   MONTH DAY   YEAR   RESIDENT'S SIGNATURE, IF REQUIRED

_____   Date:____ / ____ / ____   _____
PROPERTY ADDRESS   MONTH DAY   YEAR   RESIDENT'S SIGNATURE, IF REQUIRED

_____

Date notice was ☐ hand delivered or ☐ mailed by certified mail

To: ☐ Resident or ☐ the leased premises

Figure 7-1: Sample Notice of Rental Rate Change form.

Form courtesy of IREM

If possible, inform each resident personally of the pending rent increase and be sure to follow up by legally serving a formal written notice of the increase and keeping a copy in each resident's file. The letter doesn't have to be a literary work, but you may consider attaching any market information obtained from your market survey (see more about market surveys in Chapter 6) so your residents can see you've made an informed decision.

Dealing with Potential Rent Regulation Issues

In most areas of the United States, landlords can set the rent to any amount they want with the expectation that market forces will keep rents reasonable. In certain cities and counties in a handful of states, rent regulations limit the amount and frequency of rent increases for existing residents living in certain residential rental properties.

The purpose of rent regulation is to ensure that a city has a sufficient supply of affordable housing for lower- and middle-class residents. Without such regulation, proponents argue, landlords would be able to raise rents beyond what their current residents can afford, essentially driving all but the wealthiest residents out of the neighborhood.

In the following sections, we guide you in determining whether your rental property is subject to rent regulation, explain restrictions on rent setting and increases, and help you navigate other legal issues that you may encounter if you're operating in a rent-regulated area.

Rent control by any other name . . .

In some circles, rent control is often called *rent stabilization* or *rent regulation.* In other circles, these three terms have distinct meanings. New York, for example, draws the following distinctions:

✔ *Rent control* "applies to residential buildings constructed before February 1947 in municipalities that have not declared an end to the postwar rental housing emergency."

✔ *Rent stabilization* applies to apartments in buildings of six or more units built between February 1, 1947 and January 1, 1974.

✔ *Rent regulation* is the umbrella term that covers both rent control and rent stabilization.

If you operate in an area that distinguishes between rent control and rent stabilization, obtain a copy of the ordinance for each and read them carefully, because the laws, exemptions, and governing boards are likely to differ depending on the category in which your property is placed.

Determining whether your rental property is subject to rent regulation

You may be able to save yourself a lot of time getting up to speed on rent regulation statutes by first determining whether your property is subject to such regulation. These sections identify areas in the United States where rents for certain properties are regulated and, if you're operating in a regulated area, whether your property is exempt from such regulation.

Finding out whether you're operating in a rent-regulated area

Rent regulation currently applies only to residential rental properties in Washington, DC, and specific cities or counties in California, Maryland, New Jersey, and New York. Most states *preempt* rent control, meaning they prohibit municipalities from enacting rent-control statutes. The remaining states have no rent-control statutes and no preemption. However, regardless of where you operate, you need to check with your state or local housing authority or rental association to determine whether your area is subject to rent regulation, because laws change.

Determining whether your property is exempt

Even if your rental property is in a rent-regulated area, it may not be subject to regulation. Common exemptions include the following:

- ✔ The building was built after a specific year. For example, in San Francisco, buildings constructed after June of 1979 are exempt from rent control.

- ✔ The building has been substantially renovated. What qualifies as *substantial* is usually tied to the cost of renovations; for example, in Oakland, California, the amount spent on renovating the property must be at least 50 percent of the cost of constructing a similar building that's new.

- ✔ You're providing subsidized housing.

- ✔ You own the property as a *natural person* (personally, not through a corporation), and it has no more than a certain number of units (for example, four rental units in Washington, DC).

- ✔ You own the property and live in one of the units, and the property has no more than a certain number of units.

- ✔ The property was vacant when the statute took effect or for a specific period of time after the statute took effect.

In rent-regulated areas, a regulation board (often referred to as a rent control board or rent stabilization board) is usually in charge of enforcing regulations. Contact the board to find out what the exemptions are. You may also find exemptions online. Search for your state and municipality followed by "rent control" or "rent stabilization."

Even if your property qualifies as exempt, you may need to file paperwork to obtain an exemption number before you can increase the rent.

Registering your property

If your property is subject to rent regulation of any kind, you probably need to register the property with the agency in charge of regulating the rent. This may be the local housing authority or rent control board. Failure to register your property could lead to hefty fines.

Increasing rents

If you own a rent-regulated property, obtain a copy of the current ordinance and read it carefully before increasing rents. In most cases, rent regulations give you greater flexibility in increasing rent when a property is vacant or when a resident moves out.

If you're limited to only nominal future rent increases, make sure you get the maximum rent possible for a new resident, because this base rent will be a factor in your rental income for the entire duration of the tenancy. In other words, if you lower your rent by $100 to quickly rent your property, you'll likely be negatively affecting your income stream for as long as the resident continues living in the unit.

Finding out about allowed annual increases

In most rent-regulated areas, the rent control board allows annual rent increases or adjustments to help cover the rising costs of operations. Regulations typically limit both the amount and frequency of rent increases:

- **Rent increase amount:** The board usually sets a maximum percentage or amount that owners are allowed to increase their rents. When setting this amount or percentage, boards often consider any changes in the Consumer Price Index (CPI).

- **Rent increase frequency:** In many rent-regulated areas, landlords are permitted to increase the rent only once a year, and the increase can't take effect prior to the anniversary of the resident's move-in date.

In some areas, you can *bank* your allowable increases; that is, you can carry over any unused allowable increase from previous years the resident lived in the unit to the current year. For example, if you were allowed to increase the rent 2 percent last year and 3 percent this year, and you didn't increase the rent last year, this year you can raise it 5 percent.

Check with your local rent control board to find out what this year's rent increase allowance is.

Getting a resident's okay to raise the rent

Depending on the regulations in your area, you may be permitted to raise the rent beyond the regulated limit if your resident consents to the increase. Of course, most residents aren't eager to have their rent increased, but if you plan to improve the property in ways that provide significant benefits to the resident, she may be willing to go along with a rent increase to pay for them.

If a resident consents to a rent increase, put your agreement in writing and have the resident sign and date it.

Petitioning for a rent increase

One way around rent increase limitations is to petition the rent control board for a rent increase. Rent-regulated areas usually provide some flexibility in raising rents to enable landlords to earn a fair return on their rental property. If you can show that your net operating income for a property is lower than it should be, you may be able to convince the board to permit the rent increase. The board usually bases its decision on the following factors:

- ✔ **The base year net operating income for the property:** You need to pull records from whatever is considered the base year in your area and calculate the net operating income for the property in that year.

- ✔ **The cumulative CPI increase from the base year to now:** Add up the annual CPI percentage increases from the base year until now. (Your rent control board should have a chart that shows CPI increases for all years back to the base year.)

- ✔ **Operating expenses excluding property taxes and management expenses for both the base year and the current year:** Again, you need to pull records from whatever year is considered the base year in your area. You also need to calculate your operating expenses over the past 12 months. The board may also consider whether the increases in operating expenses are reasonable.

- ✔ **Capital expenditures to improve the property:** If you invested a significant amount of money to renovate the building or the resident's unit, the board may take this into consideration.

- ✔ **Your performance in maintaining the premises and the services offered:** A resident can petition the board to have the rent increase reduced or even petition for a rent reduction for failure to maintain habitable premises or for a reduction in services provided.

Consult your rent control board or visit its website to obtain the form you need to file to petition the board for a rent increase.

Bumping up the rent when a resident moves or sublets her unit

Limitations on rent increases typically apply only to current residents. When a resident moves out or sublets her unit, you're usually permitted to increase the rent as much as you want. Some exceptions may apply, so read the rent-regulation ordinance carefully for regulations that govern setting the initial rent for new residents.

If no restrictions apply to rent setting for new residents, take the opportunity to increase the rent as high as the market will bear, because as soon as you fill that vacant unit, the restrictions on rent increases are reactivated.

Notifying residents and the board in advance of rent increases

Regardless of whether your property is rent-regulated, you must notify residents in advance of any rent increase. See the earlier section, "Giving residents advanced notice," for details.

If the property is rent-regulated, you may also need to notify the rent control board of your intent to increase the rent. Contact your rent control board or visit its website to find out about rent-increase notification requirements and obtain the required notification forms.

Being extra careful when evicting a resident

To discourage landlords from evicting a resident just because they want to raise the rent, most rent-regulation ordinances contain strict guidelines for evictions. Contact the rent control board or visit its website to obtain a list of just causes for evicting a resident and other requirements for evicting residents from a rent-regulated property.

When writing an eviction notice for a resident in a rent-regulated property, give specific details of the incidents that provide just cause for the eviction, including dates, times, and places in which the incidents occurred.

You may be required to pay the resident a relocation fee for eviction for certain allowable reasons (not based on just cause), such as demolishing the building.

Closing down a rent-regulated property

To discourage landlords from closing down a rental property temporarily to get rid of rent-control residents and then re-opening with higher rents, most ordinances contain rules and regulations that govern the closing of rent-regulated properties. Regulations may require that you:

✔ Obtain a permit for the removal of any rent-regulated units from the market

✔ Provide proof that you can't earn a fair return by keeping the unit or that an uninhabitable unit can't be made habitable in an affordable way

✔ Notify residents well in advance of when they need to move out

✔ Give existing residents right of first refusal to rent any newly renovated, converted, or constructed units

✔ Offer a certain number or percentage of newly renovated, converted, or constructed units at rents affordable to low-income residents

✔ Pay residents who are forced to move out a relocation fee

Complying with Housing Choice Voucher (HCV) Rules and Regulations

The Housing Choice Voucher (HCV) program, a major component of what is commonly known as *Section 8*, is the federal government's primary program to assist very low income families, the elderly, and the disabled in renting decent, safe, and sanitary housing in the private market. Established in 1974 and administered by local public housing authorities (PHAs), the tenant-based voucher component of Section 8 is the country's largest rent subsidy program, which pays a large portion of the rent and utilities for more than 2 million tenants.

HCV is available to qualified low-income residents and requires each resident to pay a percentage of her monthly income toward rent, with the balance paid by the local PHA. You can find complete details of the program in the HCV Guidebook, located at www.hud.gov/offices/pih/programs/hcv/forms/guidebook.cfm. In the meantime, the next few sections give you an overview on what you need to know about and comply with the HCV program.

Understanding how HCV works

The HCV program has two goals:

✔ To allow low-income households more choice in housing

✔ To reduce the concentration of low-income households in particular buildings and neighborhoods

Various kinds of rental housing qualify for HCV certification, including single-family homes, condos, duplexes, apartments, and mobile homes. The rental unit must comply with HUD occupancy standards guidelines, which generally allow two occupants per bedroom.

HUD allows you to establish your own occupancy standards for your property, which can be higher or lower than the federal standards. But be cautious about establishing standards that are more restrictive (fewer residents in your rental unit) because they must be based on legitimate business reasons or be required to protect your residents' health and safety. Of course, you must abide by more stringent state or local restrictions if they exist.

The HCV program provides resident-based Housing Assistance Payments (HAP), which are rental subsidies or vouchers that residents can use to rent privately owned rental housing. Residents with household incomes that are less than the published PHA maximum annual income by family size for a local area are eligible for HCV assistance. The overall income caps for families admitted to the HCV program are usually set between 50 percent and 80 percent of the local median income.

After qualifying, residents receive HCV vouchers or certificates and have up to 60 days to locate rental units. In certain tight rental markets, residents have up to 120 days to find suitable rental units. The local PHA makes inspections to ensure that the rental unit meets the HUD Minimum Housing Quality Standards (HQS) at the beginning of the tenancy, upon annual renewal, and upon request if the resident believes the condition of the unit is unacceptable.

The PHA pays the rental subsidy directly to the rental property on behalf of the program participant. Under this program, the resident must pay whichever amount is greater — the PHA minimum rent (usually $25 to $50) or the Total Tenant Payment (TTP), which is based on either 30 percent of a resident family's monthly adjusted income or 10 percent of a resident family's monthly gross income. Another possibility is if the family receives payments for welfare assistance from a public agency and part of the payments are specifically designated to meet housing costs. Usually the calculation — based on 30 percent of the adjusted monthly income — is the basis for setting the minimum resident portion of the rent. If the resident selects a unit with rent higher than the PHA limits, the program also provides for a maximum initial rental burden limit so that the resident's share of the rent doesn't exceed 40 percent of her monthly adjusted household income.

The HCV rental subsidy is based on the HUD Fair Market Rent. At least annually, the PHA surveys the local rental housing market and determines the median rents and utility allowance for each unit type based on the number of bedrooms. The amount of rent that owners can charge is limited to amounts set by the local PHA that don't exceed a maximum of the HUD Fair Market

Rent level for the particular county. HCV residents may choose rental units with higher rents than the PHA maximums and then pay the difference or choose lower-cost units and keep the difference for themselves.

In some areas of the country, the maximum allowable rents are reasonable. But in many areas, the maximum rents set by the local PHA rule out many of the local rental units because they're too low. In these locations, HCV participants and rental property owners are effectively unable to work together to achieve decent affordable housing. The PHAs have been allowed to adjust the maximum HCV rents up to 10 percent higher than the HUD Fair Market Rent to be consistent with actual rents in the area and allow residents more alternatives.

The maximum rents vary based on whether the owner or the residents pay the utilities. In general, you're better off having the residents pay their own utilities because the HUD utility allowances are typically insufficient, and owner-paid utilities don't encourage your residents to conserve energy.

Knowing what to do if you rent to HCV residents

If you participate in HCV, you're required to enter into a one-year lease with a participating resident using a standardized, HUD-approved lease form or a combination of your lease with a HUD addendum. You're locked into the one-year lease agreement except for nonpayment of rent or another serious breach. You must also sign a Housing Assistance Payments (HAP) lease (provided by your local public housing authority) authorizing the payment of rent, which can be deposited directly into your bank account.

Use your own standard rental application, rental contract, and all other forms and procedures. Attach the PHA lease and HAP contract to your paperwork. If your HCV resident doesn't pay her share of the rent or you have another problem, immediately notify your contact person at the local PHA. Although the PHA is limited in what it can do, it *can* be helpful in resolving issues.

The greatest benefit to rental owners is that the local PHA pays the majority of the resident's monthly rent like clockwork, and the resident's portion is low enough that she usually doesn't have any problem meeting this financial obligation. Also, if the resident fails to pay her portion of the rent, you have the right to evict her and apply the security deposit to any unpaid rent or rental unit damage. Some PHAs may have formal or informal requirements to contact them to resolve any issues before beginning an eviction action.

Process an HCV resident's move-out just like any other resident, but be sure to notify the local PHA. The availability of HCV assistance is limited, with long waiting lists. This fact can be very helpful in motivating your residents to be responsible, because the termination of their leases for nonpayment or other breaches often results in a loss of their rental assistance.

For most landlords, participating in the HCV program is very easy. Contact the PHA in your city or county for more info or to be sure your rental rates are within their maximum guidelines. If they are, your local PHA will refer eligible applicants to you and prepare the necessary documents should you decide to rent to an eligible applicant. Obtain a copy of the HCV rules and procedures from HUD before determining whether the HCV rental program will work for you.

You can't charge higher rent for an HCV rental unit than you would if you were renting the same unit to a private, unassisted resident. Make sure you regularly conduct market surveys of rents for comparable properties in your area so that you know your rents are reasonable. Most PHAs conduct periodic audits, so be prepared to provide your local PHA with documentation that supports the fact that you're collecting the same or a higher rental rate for a comparable non–Section 8 unit.

Chapter 8

Screening Applicants: Knowing When to Approve or Reject Them

. . . .

In This Chapter

▶ Establishing a nondiscriminatory screening policy

▶ Knowing what to ask and not ask on a rental application

▶ Performing a thorough background check

▶ Taking on or turning down an applicant

▶ Keeping a history of approved and unapproved applicants

. . . .

*T*aking on a new renter is a little like hiring a new employee. You wouldn't hire someone without interviewing the person, checking work history and references, and performing a criminal background check. In the process, you may discover serious issues; for example, the person may have been fired from his last three jobs, convicted of a felony, and owe so much money that he may be tempted to steal or embezzle money to cover his debt. You want to know what you're getting yourself into before you get into it.

The same is true for taking on a new renter. You want to screen anyone who's likely to cause trouble — individuals who can't afford the rent or have a poor track record as renters. However, when screening prospective renters, you're legally limited to asking only certain types of questions and digging into only certain aspects of a person's past, often only if you have his permission to do so.

In this chapter, we offer guidance to help you develop your screening program, one that incorporates written rental applications, credit reports, background searches, reporting requirements, and more. We also explain how to screen applicants *legally*. That's right: The Fair Housing Law and the Fair Credit Reporting Act establish the legal guidelines for tenant screening. In addition, we show you how to operate within the confines of the law to choose residents who are more likely to pay their rent, take care of your property, and be good neighbors.

Establishing solid resident selection criteria and performing a thorough screening process doesn't guarantee that you'll find a good resident, but it certainly improves the odds.

Preparing a Legal Screening Policy and Letter of Consent to Background Checks

Fair housing laws (see Chapter 5 for more information about these laws) prohibit discrimination based on any of the seven protected classes: race, color, national origin, sex, religion, handicap, or familial status. Nowhere are these laws more applicable than in the screening process. Rejecting an applicant for any reason other than a reason related to the likelihood that the person will pay the rent, take care of the property, and get along with the neighbors constitutes illegal discrimination.

Your screening program must demonstrate and *prove* that everyone, including members of protected classes, is evaluated equally as prospective residents, using a process that asks all applicants the same questions and evaluates them using the same criteria. For example, you're not allowed to require work history from one applicant and not from another. Nor are you allowed to set different minimum income levels for different applicants.

These sections show you how to set up an unbiased screening policy that complies with fair housing and credit reporting laws. Here we also provide a sample letter of consent that you should have residents sign to give you written permission to perform background and credit checks.

Setting criteria for acceptance

The first step in developing a legal screening policy is to establish a set of criteria to use for evaluating each applicant's suitability. You may want to start with a list that describes the characteristics you're looking for in an acceptable applicant. Here are a few characteristics you may want to consider:

- Pays rent on time and is financially responsible
- Treats your property respectfully as is it were his own
- Lives peacefully with his neighbors
- Complies with apartment rules and regulations regarding quiet enjoyment of the apartment premises
- Recognizes the reasonable obligation to leave the premises in a condition that's the same or better than he found them at the time of move-in (not including normal wear and tear)

That list is a good start, but these characteristics aren't exactly measurable. You need verifiable criteria that if used determine whether any given applicant measures up. Here are some examples:

- ✔ At least 18 years of age
- ✔ Legal right to residency
- ✔ Currently employed with at least two years of consistent employment

    (It's the landlord's determination about the length of time that the applicant must be employed. Two years, in some circumstances, is unreasonably long.)

- ✔ If not employed, sufficient verifiable income or resources to pay the rent
- ✔ Monthly income of not less than 30 percent of the monthly rent
- ✔ Positive credit history
- ✔ Positive housing history
- ✔ No convictions for serious bodily-injury or life endangerment criminal offenses

Starting with a boilerplate screening policy and making adjustments

One of the best ways to get started with your screening policy is to use an existing screening policy, and then modify it for your specific needs.

For a copy of the sample Resident Screening Policy, visit www.dummies.com/go/landlordlegalkit and click on the Resident Screening folder.

The following sections discuss certain items in the sample Resident Screening Policy and changes you may want to make to them to fit the specific tenant screening criteria that you would like to use.

Application fee

The first item below the "Application Requirements" section on the form specifies that applicants must pay a nonrefundable application fee. In most cases, landlords limit the application fee to the out-of-pocket expense of processing the application and performing background checks. If you outsource the processing and background checks, all you do is pass those charges from the third-party screening service along to the applicant. If you do use such a company for background checks, refer to the later section, "Disclosure of screening service" for what information to include in your policy.

More and more jurisdictions are setting limits on the amounts that landlords can charge in application fees. You may be limited to a specific dollar amount or to your actual out-of-pocket expense. Check your state and local laws for restrictions.

Minimum age and photo ID

The third item under the "Application Requirements" section specifies a minimum age of 18 and requires that applicants provide a government-issued photo ID to verify age and identity. Although unusual, you may encounter an applicant that is an emancipated minor who has the legal capacity and competency to enter into an agreement and authorize a pre-tenancy applicant background screening.

Strongly consider setting a minimum age requirement of 18 years or older, because screening agencies are able to provide very little information for younger applicants. With insufficient information, you may be more likely to accept an unqualified applicant, and trying to enforce the lease in the event of default could be more legally complicated.

Requiring *government-issued identification* is extremely important and prudent as you always want to know the identity of who is in possession of your rental unit. Several types of photo IDs are acceptable, including the following:

- ✔ Driver's license
- ✔ State or federal identification card
- ✔ Military ID
- ✔ Passport (US or other recognized governmental entity)

Don't accept library cards, check-cashing cards, school identification, or other non-governmental documentation.

Minimum income

Minimum income is a tough criterion to set, because so many factors contribute to a resident's ability to pay the rent, including whether the person has children to support (and how many), credit card balances, car loans, student loans, and monthly bills for everything from groceries and insurance premiums to cellular phone service. Because there are so many variables, most landlords don't try to calculate net income, but rather focus on a multiple of gross income.

Minimum income is only one criterion that enables you to quickly eliminate certain applicants. Don't focus exclusively on minimum income when evaluating whether an applicant is likely to be a stable and reliable resident that consistently pays the rent in a timely manner.

Positive housing history

A positive housing history is crucial in determining an applicant's acceptability. The first two items in the "Housing References" section of the sample screening policy help ensure you receive the information you need to check the applicant's housing history, regardless of whether the person owned or rented over the course of the past three years. The third item allows you to make exceptions, but provides you with a way to protect yourself financially for taking a chance with the applicant.

Occupancy limits

Federal occupancy guidelines require that you allow at least two people per bedroom. State and local occupancy standards may allow even more people per bedroom and may require properties that have large living areas that aren't bedrooms accommodate even more people. Contact your state and local housing authorities to determine what the acceptable occupancy limits are in your areas. State and local health and safety departments may also specify maximum occupancy.

Be careful when setting occupancy limits. Setting the number of persons who can live in a residence too low may constitute a violation of fair housing laws on the grounds that the limitation discriminates against families.

Credit and eviction

Poor credit and any prior evictions are serious red flags. Make sure your screening policy provides a way for you to deny applicants who have a blemished credit history or any record of being evicted from a rental property.

Denial of an application for reasons related to credit history triggers the requirement to provide the Notice of Adverse Action (See the later section, "Notifying Unqualified or Less-Qualified Applicants of Adverse Action") of the Federal Credit Reporting Act. If you receive a consumer report that was a factor in rejecting an application, the prospect must receive the notice.

How strict you are in evaluating applicants may depend on how badly you need residents. If you're having trouble keeping your rentals occupied, you may want to become more flexible in approving applications. However, for any exception you make, you need to adjust your acceptance criteria to reflect the exception. Making an exception for one applicant while rejecting another based on the same criteria exposes you to claims of discrimination.

Criminal history

The sample screening policy shown in Figure 8-1 states that every applicant must consent to and undergo a criminal background check and that an applicant may be rejected if he has a felony conviction.

Background Investigation Information And Authorization

THIS IS AN IMPORTANT DOCUMENT THAT REQUIRES YOUR ATTENTION. PLEASE REVIEW IT CAREFULLY.

As part of a tenant background check, [INSERT PROPERTY NAME] may obtain a report about you from a consumer reporting agency for the purpose of evaluating you as a prospective tenant. Please provide the following information about yourself.

Applicant Name:_____
        First   Middle   Last

Social Security #:_____Date of Birth:_____(For Identification Purposes Only)

Current Address:_____

How long at current address:_____

Previous address:_____

Have you been known by other names in the past five years?   YES   NO

If yes, please list those names here:_____

Have you plead or been adjudged guilty of a criminal offense in a court of law within the last seven (7) year period?   YES   NO

If yes, please provide details here:_____

_____

_____

_____

_____

1.   Criminal History Check

Please list previous addresses (last 5 years). (List current address first.)

Street Address	City/State/Zip	County (If known)
_____	_____	_____
_____	_____	_____
_____	_____	_____
_____	_____	_____

IF YOU WISH TO BE CONSIDERED FOR TENANCY AT [INSERT PROPERTY NAME], YOU MUST SIGN THIS AUTHORIZATION. PLEASE READ THOROUGHLY.

I, _____, hereby consent and authorize [INSERT PROPERTY NAME] and/or its agents to prepare and obtain a consumer report including, but not limited to, information as to my criminal history, employment experience and/or credit history. This report may contain information bearing on my criminal history (if any), creditworthiness, credit standing, credit capacity, character, general reputation, personal characteristics, or mode of living. Public records may be used in this reports, such as civil and court records.

By signing below, I certify that I have read this document carefully, understand it, and agree to it voluntarily and without duress.

I agree that withholding any of the information requested in this document or submitting false information in connection with this document constitutes valid grounds for rejecting the rental application or the termination of tenancy.

Authorization Signature of Applicant:_____ Date:_____

DISCLAIMER: These sample forms and agreements are not endorsed by the Institute of Real Estate Management. They are presented for informational purposes only and should not be relied upon for accuracy, completeness or consistency with applicable law. The user is advised to check all applicable state and federal law before using these forms, agreements, or parts thereof. Because certain forms have legal implications (e.g., management agreements, rental applications), it is recommended that downloaded versions of such forms should be reviewed with legal counsel prior to their use and that any modifications made by the user should also be reviewed by legal counsel.

Figure 8-1:
Background
check
consent
form.

Form courtesy of IREM

You may want to consider any criminal conviction as a disqualifying event. Although certain crimes, such as prostitution and possession of marijuana, are misdemeanors in most states, they probably justify denial, if only because such activities certainly aren't activities you want on your property. On the other hand, you may consider mitigating circumstance, including the possibility that the conviction could be expunged from the prospect's record.

When considering criminal convictions, use your best judgment. For instance, a marijuana possession from ten years ago isn't as serious as a residential burglary conviction or some other felony.

Fair housing statement

Near the end of your screening policy, include a statement indicating your commitment to being a fair housing provider. This statement reminds you and any prospective residents of the criteria you're prohibited from using to evaluate applicants during the screening process.

Make sure your fair housing statement covers not only the protected classes specified in the federal Fair Housing Act, but also any extensions of those protections established by state or local statutes. See Chapter 5 for more about fair housing laws.

Disclosure of screening service

If you use a third-party screening service to process applications and perform credit and background checks on applicants, include information about the screening service you use. This disclosure is required by law.

Using a reputable rental applicant screening service is often a good idea, even though it's an added expense. A good screening service knows what it can and can't discriminate against and may be more skilled than you in weeding out unqualified applicants. Be sure that they're familiar with any unique requirements under state law.

Getting consent for a background check

To perform a credit check or criminal background check, you must have the applicant's consent. For a sample consent form, refer to Figure 8-1.

You can also access this form online at www.dummies.com/go/landlord legalkit in the Resident Screening folder.

If you're going to perform a background check, you must do so for all applicants. Performing background checks on some applicants and not others exposes you to charges of discrimination.

Developing Your Rental Application

Your rental application represents the initial step in the process of screening applicants. It allows you to gather essential information that's valuable in the following three ways:

- Provides information about the applicant
- Gives you the information you need (name, Social Security number, and driver's license number) to identify the applicant and dig deeper for information, such as credit and criminal history
- Helps you assess the applicant's honesty by giving you applicant-supplied information that you can check against facts you dig up later

Your rental application is a fill-in-the-blanks form that may include some or all of the following information:

- Compete legal name
- Social Security number (SSN) or individual tax identification number (ITIN)
- Contact information (phone numbers and an email address)
- Current and previous addresses
- Date of birth
- Banking information
- Personal references
- Vehicles
- Pets (if any)
- Other occupants of the apartment (of any age)
- Driver's license number
- Recent employment history (unless your state prohibits discrimination based on source of income)
- Current income
- Names and contact information of previous landlords
- Past evictions
- Bankruptcies
- Any information that may be discovered in a criminal history search, if you decide to do a search

Consider starting with a sample Rental Application, such as the one shown in Figure 8-2 and then tweak it, if necessary, to meet your needs.

Rental Application

ADDRESS_____ APARTMENT NO._____ DATE:_____

Apartment Occupants

Name (Head of Household)	Birth Date	1. ☐ Male 2. ☐ Female	Marital Status	1. ☐ Married 2. ☐ Separated	3. ☐ Divorced 4. ☐ Widowed	5. ☐ Single	S.S. No.

Name A		1. ☐ Male 2. ☐ Female	Birth Date	Relationship	1. ☐ Spouse 2. ☐ Child	3. ☐ Roommate 4. ☐ Other
Name B		1. ☐ Male 2. ☐ Female	Birth Date	Relationship	1. ☐ Spouse 2. ☐ Child	3. ☐ Roommate 4. ☐ Other
Name C		1. ☐ Male 2. ☐ Female	Birth Date	Relationship	1. ☐ Spouse 2. ☐ Child	3. ☐ Roommate 4. ☐ Other

Present Address_____ How long at present address?:_____

Street	City	State	Phone	Landlord

Previous Address_____ How long at previous address?:_____

Street	City	State	Phone	Landlord

IN CASE OF EMERGENCY – NOTIFY:

Name	Address	City/State	Phone	Relationship

PRIMARY OCCUPATION OF HEAD OF HOUSEHOLD (check one)

1 ☐	Professional (Charges fees, i.e., Doctor, Lawyer, etc.)	3 ☐	White Collar	7 ☐	Unskilled laborer
2 ☐	Semi-Professional (Salaried technicians, etc.)	4 ☐	Sales representative	8 ☐	Retired
		5 ☐	Skilled laborer (plumber, electrician, etc.)	9 ☐	Not employed
		6 ☐	Semi-skilled laborer (job requires some training)	10 ☐	Student

TOTAL ANNUAL INCOME OF HEAD OF HOUSEHOLD:

1. ☐ 5,999 – 7,488	3. ☐ 10,000 – 12,499	5. ☐ 15,000 – 17,499	7. ☐ 20,000 – 29,999
2. ☐ 7,500 – 9,999	4. ☐ 12,500 – 14,999	6. ☐ 17,500 – 19,999	8. ☐ Above 30,000

EMPLOYMENT

Name of Company	Address	How Long?	Bus. Phone
Former Employer	Address	How Long?	Bus. Phone

Spouse employed? Yes No	Occupation	Address	How Long?	Bus. Phone

TOTAL ANNUAL INCOME OF HOUSEHOLD:

1. ☐ 5999 – 7488	3. ☐ 10,000 – 12,499	5. ☐ 15,000 – 17,499	7. ☐ 20,000 – 30,000
2. ☐ 7500 – 9999	4. ☐ 12,500 – 14,999	6. ☐ 17,500 – 19,999	8. ☐ Above 30,000

REFERENCES

BANK(S)		Name	Address	City	Type of Account(s) 1 Checking 2 Savings 3 Loan
	A				
	B	Name	Address	City	Type of Account(s) 1 Checking 2 Savings 3 Loan
CREDIT	A	Name	Address	City	Type of Business
	B	Name	Address	City	Type of Business
PERSONAL	A	Name	Address	City	Relationship
	B	Name	Address	City	Relationship

CHECK ONE OPTION IN EACH OF THE FOLLOWING AREAS

Former Residence location:	Former Residence Description:		If Former Residence Was an Apartment. Why did you move?
1 ☐ Out of State	1 ☐ Apt community	5 ☐ Owned home/duplex	1 ☐ Job Transfer 5 ☐ Parking
2 ☐ Out of town (in state)	2 ☐ Rented a duplex	6 ☐ Mobile home	2 ☐ Better Location 6 ☐ Management
3 ☐ Local	3 ☐ Rented a house	7 ☐ Other _____	3 ☐ Price 7 ☐ Noise
	4 ☐ Condominium	8 ☐ Establishing new household	4 ☐ Maintenance 8 ☐ Other _____

Vehicles:

AUTOS:	OTHER:
0 ☐ None	1 ☐ Boat
1 ☐ One Year_____ Make_____ License_____	2 ☐ Camper
2 ☐ Two Year_____ Make_____ License_____	3 ☐ Motorcycle Dr. Lic. No_____ State_____ Exp._____
3 ☐ More than two	4 ☐ Bicycle
	5 ☐ Other _____

CREDIT: A credit report on applicant may be obtained by Agent on behalf of Owner prior to execution of a lease. Applicant consents to obtaining of such credit report.

INSURANCE: Owner and Agent carry no insurance on the personal property of tenants. **It is recommended that you obtain insurance.**

ENTIRE AGREEMENT: The foregoing constitutes the entire agreement between the parties and may be modified only by written notice signed by both parties. This agreement is predicated upon all of the information which has been furnished by applicant being accurate; and if the facts provided are not accurate, this lease agreement may be voided at the option of the Owner. Execution of this agreement by other parties to this agreement constitutes acceptance thereof.

_____   _____
Applicant   Date

_____   _____   _____
Applicant   Date   Agent

DISCLAIMER: These sample forms and agreements are not endorsed by the Institute of Real Estate Management. They are presented for informational purposes only and should not be relied upon for accuracy, completeness or consistency with applicable law. The user is advised to check all applicable state and federal law before using these forms, agreements, or parts thereof. Because certain forms have legal implications (e.g., management agreements, rental applications), it is recommended that downloaded versions of such forms should be reviewed with legal counsel prior to their use and that any modifications made by the user should also be reviewed by legal counsel.

Figure 8-2:
A sample Rental Application.

Form courtesy of IREM

To obtain a copy of the sample Rental Application, visit www.dummies.com/go/landlordlegalkit and look in the Resident Screening folder.

If you decide to outsource applicant screening to a third-party service, check with the service to determine the information it needs in order to perform background and credit checks, and then include spaces for that information on your rental application. Check out the later section, "Outsourcing to a screening service" for more information.

Knowing Your Options When Screening

You have the legal right to verify an applicant's source of income, bank accounts, and similar sources. You can also legally reject applicants who have bad credit histories, income that you reasonably believe is insufficient to support rent payments, negative rental histories, which can include a history of late rental payments, negative references from previous landlords, and criminal histories that reasonably indicate that the prospect could be a resident who may fail to meet required behavioral requirements or increase your liability by creating a dangerous environment for your residents. As long as you make consistent inquiries about all of your prospects, you're entitled to reject those applicants that you have logically determined are too risky for business.

To screen applicants, you have the option of outsourcing the task to an online tenant screening service, as explained in "Outsourcing to a screening service," later in this chapter, or doing it yourself, as explained next.

Taking the do-it-yourself approach

If you choose to check an applicant's credit history and background yourself, take the following steps:

1. **Contact the applicant's previous landlords and ask for strictly factual (verifiable) information.**

   This info can include whether the tenant paid rent on time, whether the tenant was evicted, whether the rental unit was in acceptable condition when the resident moved out, and so on.

Out of fear of legal action, some landlords may not be willing to release information. If you have a signed consent from the applicant, offer to fax or scan and email it to the previous landlord(s). They may be more willing to open up if the applicant signed a consent form.

2. **Order a credit report.**

   The three major credit reporting agencies — Equifax (`www.equifax.com`), Experian (`www.experian.com`), and TransUnion (`www.transunion.com`) — can provide credit reports, assuming the applicant consents. Often these services can perform the entire screening process for you, including completing a criminal background check.

3. **Contact the applicant's current employer to verify employment and reported income.**

   Employers may not be able to provide you with an income amount, but they can tell you whether the amount the applicant reported is correct. If the applicant isn't employed, check other legal, verifiable sources of income or assets.

4. **Contact the applicant's current and former counties of residence to determine whether the person has been evicted.**

   Evictions are court proceedings that are recorded and become a matter of public record. In some counties, you can search eviction records online. Often this information will be available through a credit reporting agency as previously mentioned, or you can contact the county clerk's office.

5. **Conduct a criminal background check for information on convictions.**

   The easiest way to collect this information will be through your credit reporting agency and is an option as part of your credit screening when you obtain a credit report. If your applicant has a criminal conviction record, you may want to consult with your attorney to confirm that the specific conviction is grounds for denial of tenancy.

6. **Search the national sex offender registry at `www.nsopr.gov` to determine whether the applicant has been convicted of a sex offense.**

   The fact that an applicant may be on the registry may or may not be a basis for denial of housing. We suggest that you contact your attorney to discuss the specific information that is available and what is the appropriate response, which may be to accept the applicant or deny the applicant.

Screening out "professional residents"

Establishing and implementing legal resident screening criteria is particularly important if you own only a single apartment or a small, multi-unit rental property. *Professional residents* (people who go from property to property, damaging the units and/or not paying rent) are experienced and shrewd.

Unfortunately, professional residents are a reality in most rental community markets, and they tend to target mom-and-pop operations. They know that the large, professionally managed rental properties have detailed and thorough screening procedures that attempt to verify every single item on their rental applications. If certain items don't check out, property managers for these large operations don't just trust their impressions about the prospective resident. Professional residents know that small landlords are easier targets because the novice rental property owner probably won't scrutinize them as closely.

If you own and run a small operation, screening applicants is even more important. Sometimes the mere mention of the screening process is enough to make the prospect fidget and shift into the classic "I'm just looking" mode. And if that's not enough to drive off professional residents, then your actual screening process should be able to weed them out.

Don't rush a prospect or allow one to hurry you through the resident screening and selection process. Keep your needs in check. If the rental unit is sitting empty or half-full, your mortgage payment is due, and you haven't had any prospects for a while, you may be inclined to accept any applicant. Resist the temptation.

Outsourcing to a screening service

You can save yourself a great deal of time and aggravation, as well as lessen your exposure to a lawsuit, by outsourcing the screening process to a company that specializes in screening applicants for residential rental properties. These providers are required by law to "follow reasonable procedures to assure maximum possible accuracy of the information concerning the individual about whom the report relates." In other words, it's their responsibility to do business legally on your behalf.

We don't recommend any specific companies, but here are a few you may want to look into:

- ✔ Tenant Verification Services, Inc. (www.tenantverification.com)
- ✔ Experian Screening Services (www.experian.com/screening-services)
- ✔ TransUnion SmartMove (www.mysmartmove.com)
- ✔ LeaseRunner (leaserunner.com)

Charging a fee to cover your costs

If you order and pay for a credit check or pay for a complete background check for an applicant, you can usually recoup those costs by charging an application fee. However, most states frown upon the practice of charging residential rental application fees as a source of profit. To operate on the up-and-up, here's what you need to do:

- ✔ **Check state and local law to determine any restrictions on applications fees.** Some areas limit the fees to actual costs incurred for ordering credit reports and background checks. Other jurisdictions may limit the fees to a maximum amount. For example, Wisconsin prohibits landlords from charging a screening fee if the applicant can produce a credit report that's less than 30 days old.

- ✔ **Record the actual costs you incur and provide the applicant with an itemized receipt for the screening fees.** Keep a copy of the receipt for your own records. Check out the later section, "Keeping Essential Records," for what else you need to save.

 Don't rely solely on a credit report that the applicant provides. Credit reports can be doctored. Understandably, applicants may be reluctant to pay for a credit report every time they fill out an application. However, at least one of the major credit reporting agencies (Experian) allows a consumer to pay for his credit report and then give access to the landlords who need it.

Notifying Unqualified or Less-Qualified Applicants of "Adverse Action"

As you screen residents, you basically have three choices:

- ✔ Accept the applicant unconditionally
- ✔ Accept the applicant with conditions
- ✔ Reject the applicant

The first option is easy. You send the applicant an acceptance letter, and everyone's happy. The second two options, however, are considered adverse actions; that is, they run counter to the applicant's interests and to the interests of any co-signer. *Adverse actions* include the following:

- ✔ Rejecting the applicant
- ✔ Requiring a co-signer to guarantee rent payments
- ✔ Charging a deposit you don't normally charge new residents

- ✔ Charging a larger deposit than you typically charge
- ✔ Charging higher rent to cover the increased risk

If you take adverse action against an applicant based solely or partially (even insignificantly) on the applicant's credit score or on information provided in a credit report, the Fair Credit Reporting Act (FCRA) requires that you provide the applicant with a Notice of Adverse Action. If you reject an applicant based on the credit information or score of a co-signer, you must supply that co-signer with a Notice of Adverse Action as well. However, don't share anyone's credit score or information with anyone else. Refer to www.dummies.com/go/landlordlegalkit for a sample form in the Resident Screening folder.

Even if you use a third-party service to screen applicants, you're solely responsible for notifying the applicant that you decided not to rent the unit to the applicant. However, the service you use may be able to provide you with a Notice of Adverse Action form that you may use.

The Notice of Adverse Action must contain the following details:

- ✔ The name, address, and telephone number of the consumer-reporting agent — the screening firm — that provided the report
- ✔ The prospect's right to a free copy of the report
- ✔ The prospect's right to dispute the report's accuracy and completeness
- ✔ The adverse action you're taking; for example, rejecting the applicant or requiring a co-signer

The FCRA requires that you provide oral, written, or electronic notice of the adverse action. We strongly recommend that you provide your notice in writing and keep a copy for your records.

Keeping Essential Records

Your resident screening process is a potential target for a discrimination lawsuit. To protect yourself, keep a paper trail that documents the procedure you use to screen every prospect's rental application along with any paperwork that process generates.

As a result, you must save records for both approved and rejected applicants. Keep them on file for the minimum length of time required by your state.

The following sections describe the records you should keep for both rejected and approved applicants and discusses your legal obligation to secure each individual's personal information.

Keeping records for rejected applicants

For each rejected applicant, set up a separate folder that contains the following:

- ✔ The rental application
- ✔ Credit report and any other reports you obtained
- ✔ Notes on conversations with previous employers, prior landlords, and personal references
- ✔ Notes on your conversations at the showing
- ✔ Criteria you used in deciding to reject the applicant
- ✔ A record and receipts of any application fees charged, collected, and refunded (if any)

Organize the folders by year and then alphabetically by last name for easy reference. To reduce the paper storage and to make your records easier to search, consider scanning and storing documents electronically. Again, create a separate folder for every year and include a subfolder for every applicant. Just be sure to back up your records regularly and store the backups offsite to prevent loss.

Maintaining residents' files

For each applicant you accept, set up a separate folder that contains all of the items listed in the previous section plus the following items as they become available:

- ✔ The original signed lease or rental agreement and any riders (see Chapter 9)
- ✔ The lease package your tenant received upon moving in (see Chapter 11)
- ✔ The move-in and move-out inspection checklists and any before and after photos that pertain to those lists (refer to Chapters 11 and 21)
- ✔ Any other documentation generated over the course of the individual's residency

Keep folders for approved applicants separate from those for rejected applicants. Again, organize them by year first and then alphabetically by last name.

Securing sensitive information

Rental applications, credit reports, leases, and rental agreements contain a lot of personal information about applicants and tenants. Although you need to store these records to defend yourself in the event of a lawsuit, you must also safeguard these records to prevent identity theft and any unauthorized access to someone's personal information.

The first order of business is to find out how long you need to store the records. By destroying them as soon as you possibly can, you have less information to protect. Contact your state and local housing authorities and ask what the statute of limitations is in your state for filing fair housing discrimination complaints. Generally, as soon as that time has passed, you can safely destroy the records regarding denied applications. When an applicant becomes a resident, the statute of limitations for a written contract is four years.

According to the Disposal Rule of the Fair and Accurate Credit Transaction Act (the FACT Act, a federal law passed in 2003), old records must be burned or shredded. Tossing them in the dumpster is prohibited.

Next, decide how to secure the files you have on hand most effectively. Keeping the files in a locked filing cabinet in a secure office location is sufficient. If you store data electronically, take proper precautions, including operating behind a firewall and using anti-virus and anti-spyware software. Use encryption features on your computer or special encryption software to password-protect the contents of folders that store sensitive resident information.

However you choose to store applicant and resident information, limit access to that information to only one or two other people. Property managers and other workers have been known to steal resident IDs for their own use or to sell to others online. You may not entirely be able to prevent such theft, but you can limit it by restricting access to only a couple of necessary individuals.

If you discover a security breach, immediately notify anyone whose personal information may have been compromised, including rejected applicants. Many states require prompt notification; visit www.consumeraction.gov to find out details that apply to your state.

Chapter 9

Composing Your Rental Contract

A rental contract is the most important legal document in any residential rental business, because it establishes the legal relationships that landlords have with their residents. To ensure that the rental contract protects your legal rights as a landlord and clearly communicates your residents' obligations, invest some time understanding the legal and practical options a rental contract provides and considering what you want to include in it.

We begin with an overview of the different types of rental contracts, then consider some general provisions that you should keep in mind as you draft your own rental contracts. Finally, we examine an actual model lease to see whether you may want to use some of its provisions in yours.

Eyeing the Need for a Rental Contract

Before you begin advertising your rental property, you need to determine if you're going to offer your prospective residents a lease or a rental agreement. Or you may want to offer the option of both a lease and a rental agreement so that you broaden your target market.

Whichever rental contract you use, remember that it's the primary document that specifies the terms and conditions of the tenancy and binds both you as the landlord and the rental property owner, your property manager (if you have one), and the tenant.

Distinguishing a gift from a contract

Many courtroom judgments depend upon whether the litigants truly formed a contract. If you tell your Uncle Leo that he can live in your rental property, and Uncle Leo says, "Wow, that's great! I'll move in next week!" the two of you haven't formed a contract, because Uncle Leo promised nothing in return for your offer. In this situation, your promise is a *gift*.

With a gift, neither party is legally obligated to do anything for the other party. You have no legal obligation to follow through on your promise to let Uncle Leo live in your rental property. Nor is Uncle Leo legally obligated to pay you anything for letting him live there. If you and Uncle Leo have a falling out later, no judge is going to order Uncle Leo to pay rent for time he lived in the unit.

Without a written agreement, a judge has to try to figure out exactly what the two parties agreed to, if anything. A written lease or agreement doesn't guarantee to keep you out of the courtroom, but it certainly limits your exposure to lawsuits, and it provides a written record of your arrangement that a judge can read and interpret in order to resolve any disputes — without having to rely on any potentially harmful guesswork.

The following sections take a look at the differences between leases and rental agreements and provide additional detail on why written agreements are superior to their oral counterparts.

Comparing leases and rental agreements

As a landlord, you can choose to document your arrangement with renters using a lease or a rental agreement. In the following sections, we describe each and provide guidance on which is best for any given situation.

All enforceable contracts, including leases and rental agreements, have three requirements:

- ✔ **Offer:** One party offers the other something in return for receiving something else. In the case of a rental arrangement, the landlord offers a resident a place to live in exchange for rent payments.

- ✔ **Acceptance:** The person who's offered something must accept the offer. Acceptance may be in the form of a written or oral agreement.

- ✔ **Consideration:** Whatever each party gives up is called *consideration*. For example, the landlord agrees to transfer property rights to the resident for a period of time in exchange for regular rent payments from the resident.

For more about contracts, check out *Contract Law For Dummies*, by Scott J. Burnham (John Wiley & Sons, Inc.).

Looking at leases

A *lease* is a contract that specifies the legal obligations between the landlord and the resident for a particular period of time — often one year — and prevents the landlord from raising the rent or modifying any of the other lease terms until the lease expires or a term of the lease allows for such changes.

During the term of the lease, the landlord may not evict the resident unless the resident fails to pay rent on time or violates one or more of its other provisions. At the end of the lease term, the landlord may end the tenancy, renew the lease on the same or different terms, or allow the resident to continue her tenancy under a month-to-month rental agreement.

Understanding how a rental agreement differs from a lease

A *rental agreement* sets up a contract between the landlord and the resident for a short period of time, usually one month. Such a month-to-month rental agreement is automatically renewed each month unless either the landlord or the resident gives the other proper notice — usually 30 days.

Realizing the importance of putting the agreement in writing

A lease may be oral — such as a *handshake* lease — or written, although most states require that a lease of one year or more be in writing. Whether the laws of your state limit the use of an oral lease in any way, the best practice is to make sure that your leases are *in writing*. In the following sections, we explain why.

Understanding the benefits of written contracts

Except for rare exceptions, any agreements involving real estate must be in writing, and for several good reasons, including the following:

- ✔ **The terms of the agreement are documented in writing for future reference.** You don't have to remember the details of what you and the other party agreed to, because the agreement is in writing. If a dispute arises, examining the terms of the contract is usually sufficient to resolve the dispute. If the dispute ends up in court, both parties have written proof of what they agreed to.

- ✔ **A written agreement makes uncomfortable issues easier to discuss.** If you're like most landlords, you feel awkward telling a prospective resident how much rent to pay, when rent is due, and your expectations for how the resident will behave and care for the property.

✔ **You don't have to remember to state all the details.** Oral agreements are usually empty of detail, because the parties can't possibly remember to tell one another everything they expect. Having the details in writing ensures that you inadvertently won't forget to mention a certain expectation.

✔ **Written terms are usually clearer.** The process of writing down terms of an agreement gives you the opportunity to use clear, precise language.

A well-drafted written lease must include anything that could be an issue at any time during the lease term — when rent is due, how often it must be paid, and how and when your resident is responsible to pay it are just some obvious examples. These subjects have to be crystal clear — *and written down* — at the beginning of the lease term.

Beginning with your rental application right through to your rental contract, document your interactions with your residents in writing so that you and each of them knows exactly what's expected and required. All rent increases, maintenance requests, and other communications to and from your residents throughout their entire tenancy should be in writing as well. Be sure to keep copies in each resident's folder and store these records in a secure location that's fireproof, if possible.

Avoiding the train wreck of oral agreements

An oral agreement or handshake lease guarantees trouble, because you have no way to prove that you and your resident ever agreed to *anything*. If a dispute arises, you're most likely to end up in court and sacrifice some money unnecessarily. The burden of proof is often placed on the landlord, and courts generally give renters the benefit of the doubt. Courts expect landlords to provide well-documented evidence.

Playing telephone

There's an old party game called telephone. If you've never played it, here's how it goes: One person in a group makes up a sentence: "The handsome Norwegian tennis player lives in a small town in Nebraska and drives an old Volkswagen," for example. She whispers it to the next player in the circle, who in turn whispers it to the next one, until the sentence is repeated to everyone. The last person in the group repeats the sentence as she just heard it. The differences between the first whispered sentence and the last spoken one are almost always amazing.

Telephone illustrates the importance of making sure your leases are in writing and that your lease specifically prevents any oral changes to its terms. If a single sentence can't be accurately conveyed among a group of people within a minute or two, the specifics of an oral lease are certainly impossible for a landlord and a resident to recall when a dispute arises, especially because both of them are understandably motivated to remember the terms differently.

If you rely solely on an oral agreement, what seemed so clear the day your resident moved in can likely become a source of tension and even conflict as selective memories recall the agreement differently. Your resident may claim you told her you'd never raise the rent or that she can play music as loud as she wants.

Starting with a State-Specific Template

One of the best ways to draft a lease is to start with a sample lease drafted specifically for your state from a reliable source, such as a reputable apartment association in your state.

Visit www.dummies.com/go/landlordlegalkit and click on the Rental Contract folder to obtain a sample lease agreement developed specifically for California by the California Apartment Association (CAA). Keep reading for a discussion of this lease's terms and suggestions on how to customize it.

If you operate in a state other than California, you can still start with the CAA lease, but look at one or two leases developed specifically for use in your state and perhaps even in the city where you operate. Search the Internet for the name of your state (or state and city) followed by the words *residential lease*. The search results are likely to include links to both free and commercial templates for residential rental properties. Click through some of the links to find out what's available. Track down a free template from a state or local government or legal organization or a reputable apartment or landlord association.

Standardized leases, such as those you can find in stationery stores, are unlikely to be state-specific. They're useful in a very general way but often omit state-specific or other important provisions, such as those that govern security deposits.

Customizing the Lease Template

When you have a lease template, you're ready to tweak it for your own use. In the following sections, we lead you clause-by-clause through a sample lease developed by CAA, highlight key words and phrases and explain them, and offer guidance, when relevant, on changes you may want to consider depending on special circumstances.

Introductory language

All rental property agreements begin with language that specifies the date on which the agreement is made and the names of the parties to the agreement. Here's an example (<u>underlined items</u> represent specific information that you must add to the lease):

> THIS AGREEMENT is made and entered into this <u>DAY</u> of <u>MONTH</u>, <u>YEAR</u> between <u>OWNER/AGENT NAME</u> "Owner/Agent", whose address and phone number are <u>ADDRESS</u> & <u>PHONE NUMBER</u>, and <u>RESIDENT NAME(S)</u> "Resident."

This first paragraph establishes the following:

- ✔ The date the parties enter into the agreement
- ✔ The names of the parties to this agreement — the property owner (or her agent, for example, a property manager) and the resident(s)
- ✔ The owner's or agent's address and phone number

List the name of every resident on the lease for two reasons:

- ✔ Any approved resident whose name isn't included in the list of "Residents" isn't a party to the lease, and therefore isn't legally obligated to fulfill its terms.
- ✔ Only people whose names appear on the lease are entitled to live in the unit. If someone on the lease allows others to live in the unit, that can be addressed as a breach of the agreement.

Following the first paragraph, many leases have a short paragraph that establishes the lease to be a binding contract:

> For the valuable consideration described in this Lease Agreement, the sufficiency of which is hereby acknowledged, Owner/Agent and Resident covenant, contract, and agree as follows:

The words and phrases "valuable consideration," "sufficiency," and "covenant, contract, and agree" make clear that you and the resident agree to enter a legally binding *contract*.

Rental unit

Sometimes referred to as *grant of lease*, this provision transfers property rights to the resident and specifies the location of the property:

Subject to the terms and conditions of this Agreement, Owner/Agent rents to Resident and Resident rents from Owner, for residential use only, the premises located at: <u>STREET ADDRESS</u>, <u>UNIT # (if applicable)</u>, <u>CITY</u>, <u>STATE</u>, <u>ZIP</u>.

When drafting your lease, make sure this paragraph contains the following three key elements:

✔ **Statement of the contractual nature of the relationship between the owner and resident:** The owner agrees to rent the property to the resident, and the resident agrees to rent the property from the owner.

✔ **Stipulation that only residential uses are permissible:** Restricting rental units to residential (non-business) use prevents increased traffic, burdens on available parking, and liability for potential injuries by business visitors.

✔ **The address of the rental property:** The address of the property (usually referred to as the *premises*) must include the unit number (if applicable), together with specific identification of any separate garage, parking stall, storage unit, and other amenities included in the lease.

To strengthen the provision that the property is to be used only for residential purposes, you may add something like "excluding all other uses, specifically excluding use of the premises for any and all business purposes." As an alternative, consider deleting "for residential use only" and adding, at the end, the following provision:

The apartment is leased for residential use only. Resident shall not operate any business on the premises. Resident's use of the premises for any business or illegal purpose is grounds for termination.

Some states, including California, specifically allow family day care centers to be operated on apartment properties, even if the lease disallows commercial or business purposes. Check your own state laws to see whether these centers are allowed, even if disallowed by the lease. Turn to Chapter 2 for more about researching state laws.

Rent

Every lease specifies the amount of monthly rent, when, where, and how it's to be paid, and a statement about late fees — when they're assessed and in what amounts:

Rent is due in advance on the <u>DAY</u> of each and every month, at $<u>AMOUNT</u> per month, beginning on <u>DATE</u>, payable to Owner/Agent at <u>ADDRESS</u>.

Payments made in person may be delivered to Owner/Agent between the hours of <u>TIME</u> and <u>TIME</u> on the following days of the week:

❑ Monday ❑ Tuesday ❑ Wednesday ❑ Thursday ❑ Friday ❑ Saturday ❑ Sunday ❑ Other _____

Acceptable methods of payment:

❑ Personal check ❑ Cashier's check ❑ Money order ❑ EFT/Credit ❑ Cash

If rent is paid after the <u>DAY</u> of the month, there will be a late charge of $<u>AMOUNT</u> assessed. The parties agree that this late fee is presumed to be the amount of damage sustained by late payment of rent. It would be impracticable or extremely difficult to fix the actual damage. This sum represents a reasonable endeavor by the Owner/Agent to estimate fair average compensation for any loss that may be sustained as a result of late payment of rent. Pursuant to <u>STATE</u> law, if Resident passes a check on insufficient funds, Resident will be liable to Owner/Agent for the amount of the check and a service charge of $<u>AMOUNT</u>, not to exceed $25 for the first check passed on insufficient funds, and $35 for each subsequent check passed on insufficient funds. The Owner/Agent may refuse a personal check as the form of rent payment to cure a Three-Day Notice to Pay Rent or Quit.

Owner may apply any payment made by Resident to any obligation of Resident to Owner notwithstanding any dates or other direction from Resident that accompanies any such payment. Any attempt by Resident to allocate a payment in any other way shall be null and void, including the use or application of a restrictive endorsement on the face of any check.

You may want to add to your lease the following provisions:

✔ **Prorated rent, for instances when the resident moves in after the first of the month:**

If the commencement date of this Lease is other than the first day of the month, then the rent for the fractional month shall be pro-rated on the basis of the number of days in that month, with that pro-rated rent in the amount of $<u>AMOUNT</u> due on the commencement date.

✔ **When rent is considered paid:**

Resident agrees that rent will not be considered paid until Owner/Agent receives the rent payment.

✔ **Residents are collectively and individually ("jointly and severally") responsible for paying rent in full:**

All Residents signed to this lease are jointly and severally liable for paying the rent in full by or before the agreed-upon due date.

✔ **Security deposit and first month's rent to be paid prior to moving in:**

Security deposit and first month's rent (or prorated portion thereof) must be paid in full, and previous Resident must have vacated the premises, before Resident is entitled to possession of the premises.

Security deposit

The security deposit provision of the lease establishes the amount of the security deposit, when the resident must pay it, how either party can use the deposit, and when the owner will return it to the resident in part or whole or ever:

> Resident shall deposit with Owner/Agent, as a security deposit, the sum of $<u>AMOUNT</u>
>
> ❏ prior to taking possession of the unit or ☐ no later than _____
> _____ (check one).
>
> Resident shall not use the security deposit to pay any month's rent. Owner/Agent may withhold from the security deposit only such amounts as are reasonably necessary to remedy Resident defaults including, but not limited to, the following:
>
> (a) defaults in the payment of rent,
>
> (b) to repair damages to the premises caused by Resident, exclusive of ordinary wear and tear, and/or
>
> (c) to clean the premises, if necessary, upon termination of the tenancy in order to return the unit to the same level of cleanliness it was in at the inception of the tenancy, and/or
>
> (d) to restore, replace, or return personal property or appurtenances, exclusive of ordinary wear and tear.
>
> No later than 21 calendar days after Owner/Agent has regained possession of the premises, Owner/Agent shall return any remaining portion of such security deposit to Resident. Any remaining portion of the security deposit shall be returned in the form of a single check made out to all Residents listed above.

Revise this clause, if necessary, to comply with your state law, which governs the payment, management, and return of security deposits. (For more about researching federal, state, and local laws and codes, see Chapter 2.) Also, consider adding the following provisions to the security deposit clause:

✔ **Transfer of security deposit upon sale of property:**

Upon sale or assignment of the leased premises, Owner/Agent has the right to transfer Resident's security deposit to the new owner to hold according to the terms of this Lease Agreement and after doing so shall be released from all liability for return of security deposit to Resident.

✔ **Resident's forfeiture of security deposit:**

Owner should but may not be obligated to return security deposit or give the Resident a written description of damages and charges until the Resident gives the Owner a written statement of the Resident's forwarding address for the purpose of refunding the security deposit. However, we suggest that in order to meet your legal obligations concerning the disposition of the security deposit, you should always complete the written statement of security deposit and mail it to the rental unit address because the resident may have a mail forwarding address on file with the US Postal Service.

Never make security deposits nonrefundable or use them as another source of income. By law, the security deposit is the resident's money to be used only to cover unpaid rent, damage to the premises beyond ordinary wear and tear, damaged or missing items furnished with the unit, and cleaning only to the extent of making the premises as clean as they were when the resident moved in. For more about creating a security deposit policy and the rules and acceptable uses of security deposits, see Chapter 10.

Term

The term clause of the lease specifies its length (typically one year), start and end dates, and a provision for continuation of the rental arrangement after the lease term expires:

> The term of this Agreement is for <u>TERM</u>, beginning on <u>DATE</u> and ending on <u>DATE</u>, at which time this Lease shall terminate without further notice. Any holding over thereafter shall result in Resident being liable to Owner/Agent for daily rental damages equal to the current market value of the unit, divided by 30. A "month-to-month" tenancy subject to the terms and conditions of this agreement shall be created only if Owner/Agent accepts rent from Resident thereafter, and if so accepted, tenancy may be terminated by Resident after service upon the Owner/Agent of a written 30-day Notice of Termination. Except as prohibited by law, that month-to-month tenancy may be terminated by the Owner/Agent by service upon the Resident of a written 60-day notice of termination of tenancy. However, Civil Code Section 1946.1 provides that "if any tenant or resident has resided in the dwelling for less than one year," the Owner/Agent may terminate the tenancy by service upon the Resident of a written 30-day notice.

The term clause differentiates a lease from a rental agreement. A *lease* is for a fixed length of time. A *rental agreement* is for a month-to-month tenancy.

Utilities

The utilities provision specifies which utilities (water, sewer, electricity, gas, trash collection, cable TV, and Internet access, for example) the resident is responsible for paying and states that the resident is responsible for contacting the utility companies to have service turned on or off:

> Resident shall pay for all utilities, services and charges, if any, made payable by or predicated upon occupancy of Resident, except: _____
> _____.
>
> Resident shall have the following utilities connected at all times during the tenancy (check as applicable):
>
> ❏ Gas ❏ Electric ❏ Water ❏ Trash ❏ Sewer ❏ Other: _____
>
> Disconnection of utilities due to nonpayment is a material violation of this Agreement.
>
> Resident shall not use common area utilities (such as water or electricity) for the Resident's personal use, without prior written permission from the Owner/Agent.

In almost every state, the resident is responsible to pay for telephone and electricity usage. If your rental property has shared utilities (usually the electricity or natural gas being shared by one or more rental units and/or the common areas), you must clearly disclose this fact in the rental contract and clearly state the method of allocating the utility expense. The allocation method could be equally dividing the expense or splitting the cost based on unit size (square footage or number of bedrooms).

The statement "Disconnection of utilities due to nonpayment is a material violation of this Agreement" advises the tenant of the importance of keeping the utilities on to prevent damage to the property. But it also prohibits you from disconnecting utilities for nonpayment of rent. Doing so constitutes *constructive eviction* — making the rental unit uninhabitable in order to compel a resident to leave. Constructive eviction constitutes a breach of contract, which gives the resident the right to terminate the lease and seek additional damages.

Cash payment

The cash payment provision gives you the right to require cash payments in the event that a resident's rent or security deposit check, draft, or money order has bounced due to insufficient funds or stopped payment:

> The Owner/Agent may demand or require cash as the exclusive form of payment of rent or security deposit if the Resident has previously attempted to pay the Owner/Agent with a check drawn on insufficient funds or the Resident has stopped payment on a check, draft, or money order. If the Owner/Agent chooses to demand or require cash payment under these circumstances, the Owner/Agent shall give the Resident a written notice stating that the payment instrument was dishonored and informing the Resident that the Resident shall pay in cash for a period determined by Owner/Agent, not to exceed three months, and attach a copy of the dishonored instrument to the notice.

Occupants

Include the names and birthdates of all residents that are party to this agreement and any other persons who will occupy the premises:

Premises shall be occupied only by the following named person(s):

Name   *Birthdate*

_____   _____

_____   _____

_____   _____

_____   _____

Prohibitions

Prohibitions exclude specific items or behaviors on the rental property. These exclusions may prohibit waterbeds, plants on wood floors, bikes in the hallway, or certain types of window coverings, such as Confederate flags. Here's an example:

> Without Owner/Agent's prior written permission as an addendum to this Agreement, no pets, waterbeds, charcoal burners or other open-flame cooking devices, or liquefied petroleum gas fueled cooking devices ("grills") or
>
> 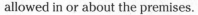 _____ shall be kept or allowed in or about the premises.

You may establish any prohibitions, as long as they're not discriminatory and don't violate state laws or local ordinances.

Smoking prohibition

You may be required by state law or local ordinances to establish and enforce a no-smoking policy, or you may decide for yourself that you don't want anyone smoking tobacco on your property. If your rental property is smoke-free, include a smoking provision stating that smoking is not allowed and specifying the resident's responsibility to comply with and help to enforce this policy:

> Without Owner/Agent's prior written permission as an addendum to this Agreement, smoking of tobacco products is not permitted anywhere on the premises, including in individual units and interior and exterior common areas.

❑ This property's policy with respect to smoking is in the attached addendum.

❑ This property is subject to a local non-smoking ordinance. The policy for this property is in the attached addendum.

Resident shall inform his or her guest(s) of this Smoking Prohibition. Resident shall promptly notify Owner/Agent in writing of any incident where tobacco smoke is migrating into Resident's unit from sources outside of Resident's unit. Resident acknowledges that Owner/Agent's adoption of this policy, does not make the Owner/Agent the guarantor of the Resident's health or of the smoke-free condition of the areas listed above. However, Owner/Agent shall take reasonable steps to enforce this provision. Owner/Agent shall not be required to take steps in response to smoking unless Owner/Agent has actual knowledge or has been provided written notice. Owner/Agent and Resident agree that the other residents of the property are the third-party beneficiaries of this provision. A resident may sue another resident to enforce this provision but does not have the right to evict another resident. Any lawsuit between residents regarding this provision shall not create a presumption that the Owner/Agent has breached this Agreement. A breach of this provision by the Resident shall be deemed a material breach of the Rental/Lease Agreement and grounds for immediate termination of the Rental/Lease Agreement by the Owner/Agent.

Quiet enjoyment

The *mutual covenant of quiet enjoyment* guarantees all residents the right to the undisturbed use and enjoyment of the rental property, even if the lease doesn't include the term or specific language about what it means. (A *covenant* is an agreement between two parties.) You should include the Quiet Enjoyment provision in your contract to remind residents of their obligation to their neighbors. Here's the quiet enjoyment provision in the sample contract:

> Resident and Resident's guest(s) shall not violate any criminal or civil law, ordinance or statute in the use and occupancy of the premises, commit waste or nuisance, annoy, molest or interfere with any other person on the property, or neighbor. Any such action may result in the immediate termination of this Agreement as provided herein and by law.

The mutual covenant of quiet enjoyment enables you to set limits on residents' illegal and unacceptable behaviors, such as the possession, use, or sale of illegal drugs; vandalizing property; and having loud parties. This covenant can be a very useful means of giving cause to evict undesirable residents.

This covenant is *mutual*, meaning you're not allowed to disturb the resident's quiet enjoyment of the property except under certain conditions. For example, you may not enter a resident's premises whenever you like. See "Entry," later in this chapter, and Chapter 16 for details on balancing your right to enter the premises with the resident's right of quiet enjoyment.

Fines and penalties

The fines and penalties provision makes the resident responsible for paying any fines or penalties levied against you for violations committed by the resident or one of her family members or guests:

> Resident is responsible for any fines or other costs occasioned by violations of the law by Resident or Resident's guests on the premises or property while Resident is in possession. If any such fines or costs are levied against Owner/Agent, Resident agrees to pay such fines or costs attributed to Resident's tenancy or the conduct of Resident, Resident's guests or others at the premises, upon receipt of an invoice from Owner/Agent. The obligation to pay fines and costs assessed against Owner/Agent may be in addition to any assessed directly against Resident.

Repairs and alterations

Make sure your lease contains a repairs and alterations clause that prohibits residents from making any substantial changes to the apartment without your permission:

> Resident shall make a written request to Owner/Agent regarding any repairs, decorations or alterations contemplated. Except as provided by law, no repairs, decorating or alterations shall be done by Resident without Owner/Agent's prior written consent. This includes, but is not limited to, painting, wallpapering, and changing locks. Resident may not make any alterations to cable or telephone inside wiring (such as may occur when changing telecommunications providers or adding phone lines) without prior written consent of the Owner/Agent. The consent request regarding proposed alterations to inside wiring shall include the name, address, and telephone number of any new telecommunications providers. Resident shall hold Owner/Agent harmless and indemnify Owner/Agent as to any mechanic's lien recordation or proceeding caused by Resident. Resident agrees to pay all costs resulting from the alteration and agrees to pay to the Owner/Agent any costs associated with restoring the inside wiring to the condition at the time of move-in, except for reasonable wear and tear.

Acceptance of premises

Leases typically include a provision stating that the resident has inspected the unit and finds the premises to be in a livable condition:

> Resident has inspected the premises, furnishings and equipment, and has found them to be satisfactory. All plumbing, heating and electrical systems are operative and deemed satisfactory.

The acceptance of premises provision along with the care, cleaning, and maintenance provision, covered next, establish the baseline condition of the rental unit at the time of resident's move-in and her responsibility to return the unit in the same condition (except for ordinary wear and tear) when she moves out. This enables you to charge the resident for damages that have occurred during the interim. (See Chapter 11 for more about inspecting the premises with the resident.)

Care, cleaning, and maintenance

Immediately following the acceptance of premises, include a statement enumerating the resident's obligations and duties in caring for, cleaning, and maintaining the rental unit:

> Except as prohibited by law, Resident agrees:
>
> (a) to keep the premises as clean and sanitary as their condition permits and to dispose of all rubbish, garbage and other waste, in a clean and sanitary manner, unless Owner/Agent has expressly agreed otherwise in writing in an addendum to this Agreement;
>
> (b) to properly use and operate all electrical, gas and plumbing fixtures and keep them as clean and sanitary as their condition permits;
>
> (c) to keep the premises and furniture, furnishings and appliances, and fixtures, which are rented for Resident's exclusive use, in good order and condition;
>
> (d) not to willfully or wantonly destroy, deface, damage, impair or remove any part of the structure or dwelling unit or the facilities, equipment, or appurtenances thereto or to permit any person on the premises, to do any such thing;
>
> (e) to occupy the premises as a residence, utilizing portions thereof for living, sleeping, cooking or dining purposes only which were respectively designed or intended to be used for such purposes.

(f) to leave the premises in the same condition as it was received, subject to normal wear and tear, as its condition permits.

(g) to return the premises, upon move-out to the same level of cleanliness it was in at the inception of the tenancy.

(h) to pay Owner/Agent for costs to repair, replace or rebuild any portion of the premises damaged by the Resident, Resident's guests or invitees.

(i) to promptly advise Owner/Agent of any items requiring repair, such as light switches or dripping faucets. Resident shall make repair requests as soon after the defect is noted as is practical.

Landscaping

The sample lease contains the following Landscaping provision:

> Resident ❏ is ❏ is not (check one) responsible for the upkeep of the yard and maintenance of the landscaping, including watering, mowing, weeding and clipping, or ☐ please see attached Addendum.

If the resident isn't responsible for landscaping, we recommend omitting this provision for simplicity.

Smoke detection device

As the property owner, you're responsible for fire safety. A smoke detection device provision can help you share that responsibility with your resident by making the resident responsible for testing and the smoke detector(s) in her unit and reporting any malfunction:

> The premises are equipped with a functioning smoke detection device(s), and Resident shall be responsible for testing the device weekly and immediately reporting any problems, maintenance or need for repairs to Owner/Agent. If battery operated, Resident is responsible for changing the detector's battery as necessary. Resident may not disable, disconnect or remove the detector. Owner/Agent shall have a right to enter the premises to check and maintain the smoke detection device as provided by law.

Making the resident responsible for testing the smoke detector(s) and reporting any malfunction is a win-win — it takes some of the burden off you and reduces the necessity of your disturbing the resident to perform the required tests.

Carbon monoxide detection device

The sample contract includes a carbon monoxide detection device provision that shares responsibility for testing and maintaining the device with the resident:

> If the premises are equipped with a functioning carbon monoxide detection device(s), Resident shall be responsible for testing the device weekly and immediately reporting any problems, maintenance or need for repairs to Owner/Agent. If battery operated, Resident is responsible for changing the detector's battery as necessary. Resident may not disable, disconnect or remove the detector. Owner/Agent shall have a right to enter the premises to check and maintain the carbon monoxide detection device as provided by law.

Carbon monoxide detection devices are generally required only in rental properties that use gas furnaces or that have wood-burning fireplaces or wood stoves or an attached enclosed garage or even rental properties with tuck-under parking or open carports with living space directly above where the cars will be parked. This means that if your units are all electric and don't have an attached garage, they probably don't require carbon monoxide detectors. However, residents sometimes use space heaters, some of which burn fuel (for example, kerosene or propane). You may want to include a provision in your lease that prohibits fuel-burning space heaters or allows only electric space heaters. If you allow fuel-burning space heaters, include a provision that in order to use such a heater, the resident must install and maintain a carbon monoxide detector.

Renters insurance

To transfer liability for any damages suffered by the resident (such as losses from theft or fires), make sure your lease contains a renters insurance provision:

> Resident's property is not insured by Owner/Agent. Resident is not a co-insured and is expressly excluded from coverage under any insurance policy held by Owner/Agent which is now in effect or becomes effective during the term of this Agreement. (CHECK ONE BOX)
>
> ❑ Resident is required to maintain renters insurance throughout the duration of the tenancy as specified in the attached Renters Insurance Addendum. Resident must provide proof of such insurance to the Owner/Agent within 30 days of the inception of the tenancy. Failure to comply with this requirement is a material violation of the Rental/Lease Agreement.
>
> ❑ Resident is encouraged but not required to obtain renters insurance.

Waiver of breach

The waiver of breach clause notifies the resident that any failure on your part to require strict compliance with any lease provision on any occasion doesn't prohibit you from requiring strict compliance with a lease provision in the future. For example, if you slack off and don't enforce the provision to have the resident pay her rent by a certain date, that doesn't set a legal precedent that gives residents the right to make late payments. The sample lease contains the following language:

> The waiver by either party of any breach shall not be construed to be a continuing waiver of any subsequent breach. The receipt by Owner/Agent of the rent with the knowledge of any violation of a covenant or condition of this agreement shall not be deemed a waiver of such breach. No waiver by either party of the provisions herein shall be deemed to have been made unless expressed in writing and signed by all parties to this Agreement.

Consider revising the language to make it easier for residents to understand. Here's one option from a lease provided by the US Department of Housing and Urban Development (HUD):

> The failure of the Owner/Agent to insist upon the strict performance of the terms, covenants, agreements and conditions herein contained, or any of them, shall not constitute or be construed as a waiver or relinquishment of the Owner/Agent's right thereafter to enforce any such term, covenant, agreement, or condition, but the same shall continue in full force and effect.

Joint and several liability

The joint and several liability provision makes all residents named on the lease collectively *(jointly)* responsible and each resident *(severally)* fully responsible for honoring the lease terms. For example, if one of three roommates named in the lease punches a hole in the wall, they're all responsible (jointly) to cover the damage. Each resident is also individually (severally) responsible for the total cost of the damage, so if you can track down only one of the residents, you can file a claim against her to pay the entire cost of the damages. She can then file a claim against the roommate who damaged the wall to collect the damages she paid.

Here's the joint and several liability provision from the sample lease:

> The undersigned Resident(s), whether or not in actual possession of the premises, are jointly and severally liable for all obligations under this Agreement and shall indemnify Owner/Agent for liability arising prior to the return of possession to the Owner/Agent for personal injuries or

property damage caused or permitted by Resident(s), their guests, and invitees. This does not waive "Owner/Agent's duty of care" to prevent personal injury or property damage where that duty is imposed by law.

Entry

The covenant of quiet enjoyment prohibits you from entering a resident's premises whenever you want, but state statutes and the entry provision in the lease allow you to enter residents' apartments under certain conditions and after providing sufficient notice:

> STATE law allows Owner/Agent or his/her employee(s) to enter the premises for certain purposes during normal business hours. The Owner/Agent will provide written notice to the Resident prior to the entry of the dwelling unit whenever required by state law. (California Civil Code Section 1954.) Resident's noncompliance with Owner/Agent's lawful request for entry is a material breach of this Agreement that may be cause for immediate termination as provided herein and by law.

To determine your rights and obligations related to entering a resident's premises, check your state's residential rental laws. Some state laws specify when landlords may legally enter rental units, even in the absence of a lease provision allowing such entry. Situations in which you're permitted to enter the premises include the following:

- ✔ You asked and the resident gave you permission to enter.

- ✔ You give the resident reasonable notice and enter the rental unit for a business purpose permitted by state law, such as to inspect the rental unit, perform necessary maintenance or repairs, or show the property to a prospective renter or buyer.

- ✔ You're responding to what you have good reason to believe is an emergency that threatens life or property.

Subletting and assignment

Every lease and rental agreement should include a provision that prohibits subletting and assigning:

- ✔ **Subletting:** Renting the unit to another person who's not named on the lease. The trouble with subletting is that the person who moves in has no contractual obligation to you under the lease, so you have no legal recourse to enforce the lease terms against that person.

- ✔ **Assigning:** Signing the rights and obligations of the lease over to someone else. The trouble with assigning is that it gives you no opportunity to screen the person who moves in.

The subletting and assignment provision in the sample lease is this:

> No portion of the premises shall be sublet nor this Agreement assigned. Any attempted subletting or assignment by Resident shall, at the election of Owner/Agent, be an irremediable breach of this Agreement and cause for immediate termination as provided herein and by law.

Instead of allowing subletting or assigning of the lease, you should terminate your lease with the existing resident and sign a new lease or rental agreement with the replacement renter, only after carefully screening and approving the replacement. See Chapter 19 for details.

Breach of lease

Whenever you set rules, you need to establish a way to enforce them. In a lease, you spell out the potential consequences — what action you may take if the resident doesn't abide by the terms of the lease:

> In the event that Resident breaches this Lease Agreement, Owner/ Agent shall be allowed at Owner/Agent's discretion, but not by way of limitation, to exercise any or all remedies provided Owner/Agent by <u>STATE</u> <u>STATUTE REFERENCE</u>. Damages Owner/Agent "may recover" include the worth at the time of the award of the amount by which the unpaid rent for the balance of the term after the time of award, or for any shorter period of time specified in the Lease Agreement, exceeds the amount of such rental loss for the same period that the Resident proves could be reasonably avoided.

Consider replacing this breach of lease clause with provisions that are more inclusive, clear, and specific. Here are some suggestions:

✔ **Make the resident responsible for breaches caused by household members and guests:**

Violations of the terms or conditions of this Lease Agreement by any of Resident's household, guests, invitees, or licensees shall be considered a breach by Resident. When Resident is more than one person, a breach by one resident shall be considered a breach by all residents.

✔ **Specify how you will notify resident of breach:**

In the event of such breach, Owner/Agent shall deliver a written notice to the Resident in breach specifying the acts and omissions constituting the breach. The Lease Agreement shall terminate and the Resident shall surrender possession as provided in the notice subject to the following:

(a) If the breach can be remedied by repairs, the payment of damages, or otherwise, and the Resident adequately remedies the breach prior to the date specified in the notice, the Lease shall continue in full force and effect;

(b) If substantially the same act or omission that constituted a prior breach of which notice was given recurs within six (6) months, the landlord may terminate the Lease Agreement upon at least five (5) days' written notice specifying the act(s) or omission(s) constituting the breach and the date of the termination of the Lease Agreement.

✔ **Indicate whether, how, and how much rent and security deposit may be refunded:**

If the Lease Agreement is terminated pursuant to this section, Owner/Agent shall return all unearned prepaid rent and any amount of the security deposit recoverable by the Resident.

However, if the breach by the Resident is nonpayment of rent, the Owner/Agent shall serve Resident with a seven (7) day written notice of termination, whereupon the Resident must pay the unpaid rent in full or surrender possession of the premises.

✔ **State under what conditions termination may be accelerated:**

Furthermore, the Lease Agreement shall be terminated with three (3) days' notice if the Resident has committed a substantial violation of the Lease Agreement or applicable law that materially affects health and safety, and the violation is not cured prior to the expiration of the three-day notice period.

Sale of property

The landlord's right to sell the property is a standard provision that allows the landlord to sell the property without affecting the resident's lease obligations. In essence, this provision allows you to sign your rights and obligations under the lease to the new owner:

In the event of the sale or refinance of the property: If Owner/Agent presents to Resident a "Resident's Certification of Terms - Estoppel Certification," or other similar Estoppel Certification form, Resident agrees to execute and deliver the certificate acknowledging that this Agreement is unmodified and in full force and effect, or in full force and effect as modified with the consent of Owner/Agent, and stating the modifications, within ten (10) days of written notice. Failure to comply shall be deemed Resident's acknowledgement that the certificate as submitted by Owner/Agent is true and correct and may be relied upon by any lender or purchaser.

Notice

All 50 states have a version of *Megan's Law* — legislation that, in part, may require you to include a notice indicating where residents can look up information about local registered sex offenders. The sample lease contains the following notice:

> Pursuant to Section 290.46 of the California Penal Code, information about specified registered sex offenders is made available to the public via an Internet Web site maintained by the Department of Justice at www.meganslaw.ca.gov. Depending on an offender's criminal history, this information will include either the address at which the offender resides or the community of residence and ZIP Code in which he or she resides.

Addenda

Your lease agreement is likely to include certain attachments, commonly referred to as *addenda*. The addenda provision provides a checklist of addenda that are incorporated into the lease agreement:

> By initialing as provided below, Resident(s) acknowledge receipt of the following applicable addenda (as checked), copies of which are attached hereto and are incorporated as part of this Agreement.

❑ Asbestos Addendum (Form 17.1)

❑ Political Signs Addendum (Form 39.0)

❑ Bedbug Addendum (Form 36.0)

❑ Pool Rules Addendum (Form 15.0)

❑ CC&Rs Addendum (Form 2.9)

❑ Proposition 65 Brochure (Form PROP65BROCHURE)

❑ Carbon Monoxide Detector (Form 27.1)

❑ Renters Insurance Addendum (Form 12.0-MF)

❑ Day Care Addendum (Form 28.0)

❑ Resident Policies Addendum (Form 17.0)

❑ Furniture Inventory (Form 16.1)

❑ Satellite Dish and Antenna Addendum (Form 2.5)

❑ Grilling Addendum (Form 35.0)

❑ Smoke Detector Addendum (Form 27.0)

❑ Guarantee of Rental/Lease Agreement (Form 41.0)

❑ Smoking Policy Addendum (Form 34.0)

❑ Lead-Based Paint Addendum (Form LEAD1)

❑ Unlawful Activity Addendum (Form 2.4)

❑ Mold Notification Addendum (Form 2.7)

❑ Waterbed Addendum (Form 14.0)

❑ Move-In/Move-Out Itemized Statement (Form 16.0)

❑ Pest Control Notice Addendum (Form 2.6)

❑ Pet Addendum (Form 13.0)

❑ Other _____

Resident(s) initials here: _____

To obtain copies of many of these addenda, visit www.dummies.com/go/ landlordlegalkit and click on the Lease folder.

Entire agreement

The entire agreement clause indicates that the agreement is limited to the lease terms and any addenda attached to the lease:

> This Agreement, which includes all attachments referred to above, constitutes the entire Agreement between the parties and cannot be modified except in writing and signed by all parties, except as permitted by applicable law. Neither Owner/Agent, nor any agent or employee of Owner/ Agent has made any representations or promises other than those set forth herein.

The entire agreement clause gives you added protection in the event that a resident claims you and she agreed to something outside of the written lease agreement.

Credit report

The credit report provision grants you the right to report late- or nonpayment of rent and other financial obligations to credit reporting agencies and authorizes you and your agent (for example, a collection agency) to obtain the resident's credit report in order to help collect past due payments:

> A negative credit report reflecting on your credit history may be submitted to a credit reporting agency if you fail to fulfill the terms of your credit obligations. Resident expressly authorizes Owner/Agent (including a collection agency) to obtain Resident's consumer credit report, which Owner/Agent may use if attempting to collect past due rent payments, late fees, or other charges from Resident, both during the term of the Agreement and thereafter.

Attorney's fees

To allow you to add attorney's fees to a judgment to enforce the lease provisions, add a clause to your lease agreement such as this:

> If any legal action or proceeding is brought by either party to enforce any part of this Agreement, the prevailing party shall recover, in addition to all other relief, reasonable attorney's fees and court costs, unless one of the following two boxes is checked:
>
> ❑ the prevailing party shall recover, in addition to all other relief, attorney's fees not to exceed $AMOUNT, plus court costs.
>
> Or
>
> ❑ each party shall be responsible for their own attorney's fees and court costs.

Selecting the right option for you is very important and one that should be done only after consulting your landlord-tenant attorney. In many parts of the country, attorneys that represent residents actually charge higher legal fees than the attorneys that specialize in representing landlords.

The problem is that *if* you, the landlord, lose a case against the resident through some technicality, the resident will be able to collect. In contrast, when a resident is evicted and fees are added to the judgment, a landlord may or may not actually collect all of the judgment and the fees and costs that he is due.

Therefore, if you're in an area where there are concerns about very high legal fees for resident rights attorneys, we advise that you select the option that limits the amount of possible out-of-pocket amounts. If you don't want to have to deal with the issue, then you can use the clause about each party being responsible for their own legal fees and costs.

Signatures

Every contract contains a signature section that all parties to the agreement must sign and date, as in the following example:

> The undersigned Resident(s) acknowledge(s) having read and understood the foregoing, and receipt of a duplicate original.
>
> RESIDENT 1
>
> Sign: _____
>
> Print: _____
>
> Date: _____

RESIDENT 2

Sign: _____

Print: _____

Date: _____

RESIDENT 3

Sign: _____

Print: _____

Date: _____

RESIDENT 4

Sign: _____

Print: _____

Date: _____

OWNER/AGENT

Sign: _____

Print: _____

Date: _____

Have all residents sign and date the contract. The more residents you have responsible for honoring the lease terms, including paying the rent on time, the more people you can hold accountable in court in the event of any breach of contract.

Considering Additional Provisions

Depending on state and local law and the rights and obligations you want to include in the contract, consider other provisions commonly found in leases and rental agreements, as presented in the following sections.

Delay of possession

Consider a delay of possession clause that protects you when situations beyond your control prevent the new resident from moving in on the scheduled day. Here's an example:

> Resident expressly agrees that if by any reason of the premises being unready for occupancy Resident is unable to enter and occupy the premises, Landlord shall not be liable to Resident in damages, but shall abate the rent for the period in which the Resident is unable to occupy the premises.

This provision establishes that unavailability of the leased premises on the scheduled move-in date doesn't justify cancellation of the lease by the resident, but rather entitles the resident to a rent set-off for the time the unit was unavailable for occupancy.

Delivery of notices

Consider adding a provision that all notices between landlord and resident must be in writing and defines when such notices are deemed as received by either party:

> Resident shall deliver any notice under this Lease Agreement or applicable STATE law in writing and by hand or by mail to the address provided for the payment of rent. Notice shall not be considered delivered until Owner/Agent's receipt of notice.

> Owner/Agent shall deliver any notice in writing to the Resident and notice shall be considered delivered when mailed to the leased premises or the Resident's last known mailing address or hand delivered or placed in Resident's mailbox. When Resident is more than one person, notice to one resident shall be sufficient to notify all.

Be sure to check with your landlord-tenant attorney for the applicable state law for your rental property as it pertains to what constitutes the proper procedures to follow in serving legal notices. Chapter 11 discusses an alternative to certified mail when you serve legal notices and/or communicate with your residents and need to be able to prove the document was mailed.

Note that the mailing provision for receipt of notices differs for landlord and resident: For the landlord, the notice from the resident is effective only upon actual receipt, while it's effective for the resident when the landlord mails it.

Pets

Landlords may legally prohibit pets of any kind, or may limit the type of pets that are allowed in the apartment, for example, allowing small birds or mammals, such as hamsters, while prohibiting dogs or cats. Here's a sample pets provision:

> No animal, fowl, fish, reptile, and/or pet of any kind shall be kept on or about the premises, for any amount of time, without obtaining the prior written consent and meeting the requirements of the Owner/Agent. Such consent, if granted, shall be revocable at the Owner/Agent's option upon giving a 30-day written notice. In the event laws are passed or permission is granted to have a pet, an additional deposit in the amount of $<u>AMOUNT</u> shall be required along with the signing of the Owner/Agent's Pet Addendum. The resident also agrees to carry insurance deemed appropriate by the Owner/Agent to cover possible liability and damages that may be caused by such animals.

Landlords may not prohibit service or comfort animals required by disabled residents according to fair housing laws (see Chapter 5). Landlords are legally permitted to impose rules for pets and service/comfort animals, such as those requiring residents to control their pet's behavior (for example, to protect other residents' quiet enjoyment and prevent dangerous behavior, and to clean up after them). Here's an example of a provision that allows service animals:

> A disabled resident may have a service or companion animal to provide fair use and enjoyment of the property, with permission of the Owner/Agent. The resident is responsible to clean up after the animal, to control the behavior of the animal and to pay for any damage caused by the service animal to the apartment, building or grounds beyond reasonable wear and tear. The service animal must meet local and state laws for vaccinations.

No illegal use

You may think that every lease has an implied agreement that the resident won't commit any illegal acts, but you actually have to spell it out in the contract:

> Resident shall not commit or allow illegal acts or omissions upon the leased premises or in any common area. Upon obtaining knowledge of any illegal activity upon the leased premises, Resident agrees to immediately inform Owner/Agent and law enforcement authorities. Resident shall bear responsibility for any and all illegal acts and omissions upon

the leased premises by Resident or any of Resident's household, guests, invitees, or licensees for any illegal act or omission upon the leased premises — whether known or unknown to Resident and shall be considered in breach of this Lease Agreement.

This clause enables you to prohibit illegal acts anywhere on your property and retain the right to evict residents when they or anyone related to them is convicted of violating this provision.

Notice of injuries

To enable you to notify your insurance provider of any injury claims in a timely manner, so they can be investigated and resolved promptly, include a notice of injuries clause, such as this:

Resident shall notify Owner/Agent no later than five (5) days after any injury or damage to Resident or Resident's household, guests, invitees and/or licensees, or any personal property, suffered in the leased premises or in any common area. Failure to provide such notice shall be considered a breach of this Lease.

Delay in repairs

To prevent breach of contract for instances when you can't complete repairs due to no fault of your own, the delay in repairs clause offers you some protection:

Any delays in repairs to be made by Owner/Agent beyond the Owner/Agent's control have no effect on the Resident's obligations under this Lease Agreement.

This provision is intended to prevent the resident from terminating the lease by claiming that you failed to make ordinary and necessary repairs when "reasons beyond Landlord's control" prevented you from doing so.

Notice of absence from premises

Every lease agreement should include a notice of absence from premises clause so that the resident has a way to notify the landlord of planned absences from the premises, while stipulating that during those absences, the resident is still obligated to honor the terms of the lease:

Resident shall provide written notice to Owner/Agent of any plans to be absent from premises for more than seven (7) consecutive days. If such absences are to be routine, Resident specifies expected frequency and duration of such absences here:

_____

_____

Resident expressly agrees and understands that during such absences, with or without notice, Resident shall honor all terms of this Lease Agreement, including the requirement to make timely rent payment.

Abandonment

Consider including in your lease a clause that allows you to retake control of the property in the event of an unnotified absence of more than a specified number of days (typically seven):

Absence of Resident from the leased premises for a period of more than seven (7) consecutive days without prior notice to the Owner/Agent, while rent or other money owed remain unpaid, is considered a breach of this Lease Agreement, and property shall be considered abandoned. Owner/Agent may immediately or any time thereafter enter and re-take the leased premises as provided by applicable STATE law and terminate this Lease without notice to Resident.

Materiality of application to rent

Your lease should include a provision that gives you the right to terminate the lease if you discover any inaccuracies in information that the resident supplied for screening purposes:

This lease is granted only on condition of the truth and accuracy of representations made by the Resident on the Application to Rent and in related documents and information. Such representations are material to the grant of this lease. Any misrepresentation by Resident on the Application to Rent or in any documents attached to or submitted with said application is considered a breach of this Lease Agreement.

For more about the application and screening process, see Chapter 7.

Remedies not exclusive

To acknowledge rights and remedies that may exist beyond the provisions in this lease, include a remedies not exclusive clause, such as this:

> The remedies and rights contained in and conveyed by this Lease Agreement are cumulative, and are not exclusive of other rights, remedies and benefits allowed by applicable <u>STATE</u> law.

Here, the lease specifies that rights and remedies may be available in state law that supplement those provided in the lease. The word *cumulative* gives you all the remedies and rights that are available according to the lease terms, as well as those provided by law.

Destruction of premises

You probably hate to think of the possibility of your property being destroyed in a fire, flood, or storm, but you need to prepare for these possibilities and stipulate the residents' rights in the event of such catastrophes:

> If the premises become destroyed for any cause beyond Owner/Agent's control so that Resident's use is seriously impaired, then this Lease Agreement shall cease and terminate as the date of such destruction, and Resident shall pay rent up to the time of such damage or destruction, or Owner/Agent shall refund any portion of unearned prepaid rent. If the leased premises or a portion of thereof becomes damaged for any cause beyond the Owner/Agent's control, but is repairable within a reasonable time, then this Lease Agreement remains in force and Owner/Agent shall, within said reasonable time, restore said premises or portion thereof to substantially the same condition prior to damage, and Owner/Agent shall abate rent in proportion to Resident's impaired use of the whole of said premises.

If such unusual circumstances occur, you should consult with your landlord-tenant attorney. Also, if just a portion of the premises is unusable (such as a 100-square-foot bedroom in a 2,000-square-foot, four-bedroom rental home), the abatement of total rent based on the portion that is unusable can make sense. But if the 100 square feet of that same rental home is the kitchen, the rental home could be argued to be uninhabitable.

Understanding the implied warranty of habitability

Every residential lease and rental agreement has an *implied warranty of habitability* requiring that the landlord maintain livable conditions — heat when it's cold, running water, a reasonable amount of hot water, gas and electricity where applicable, and so on. The warranty is implied, so it doesn't need to be stated in the lease or rental agreement.

Breach of this warranty gives the resident the right to withhold or escrow (set aside) rent payments in full or in part until habitability is restored. In some more serious cases, the breach of this covenant allows the resident to terminate the lease on the grounds of constructive eviction, seek damages against the landlord, and, in extreme cases, cause termination of the landlord's right to do business.

The failure of equipment in the apartment, such as the breakdown of a necessary utility — heat or water supply, for example — are obvious habitability shortcomings that the landlord must fix. In general, landlords are legally required to restore these services within a "reasonable" time period and at their expense.

Eminent domain

Eminent domain refers to the power of the state to seize private property without the owner's consent, often for the construction of public facilities, highways, and railroads. This provision is also typical of the way the subject is handled in real estate leases:

> In the event that the leased premises are taken by eminent domain, this Lease Agreement shall terminate on the date said premises are taken, and the rent shall be prorated to said date.

Governing law

Nearly every contract specifies that the laws of a certain jurisdiction govern the agreement:

> The statutory and case law of the State of <u>STATE</u> governs this Lease.

The laws that govern the lease influence the way the courts interpret the language in the contract and resolve any disputes. Two types of law govern leases in any jurisdiction:

- ✔ **Statutory law:** Laws that legislatures decide to adopt.
- ✔ **Case law (common law):** Laws established by judges in the process of resolving disputes.

To find out how to research federal, state, and local laws, see Chapter 2.

Chapter 10

Establishing a Security Deposit Policy

. . . .

In This Chapter

▶ Brushing up on legal restrictions regarding security deposits

▶ Settling on a security deposit amount to charge residents

▶ Telling the difference between damage and deterioration

▶ Giving back some or all of the security deposit to the resident

. . . .

*A*s a landlord, you probably want to charge a new resident a security deposit in addition to the first month's rent. A *security deposit* is a lump sum that a resident usually pays up-front to protect the landlord in the event that the resident fails to pay rent, damages the property, or causes the landlord to suffer some other financial loss. Laws, primarily state statutes supplemented by city ordinances, govern the maximum amount you're permitted to charge for a security deposit, how the deposit is to be managed during the course of the tenancy, the types of losses you're permitted to deduct, and how and when you must return any unused portion of the security deposit to the resident. Some states and cities also require that the money be deposited in an interest-bearing account and that any interest earned be paid to the resident.

As you may know or expect, the most common landlord-resident disputes involve security deposits. Disagreements over the amount of the security deposit and costs deducted for cleaning and repairs at the end of the tenancy top the list. Disputes also arise over when the landlord returns the security deposit and whether the resident is owed any interest on the amount of money the landlord gets to hold (usually for a year or longer).

In this chapter, we describe the legal and practical considerations of security deposit administration and provide guidance on how to avoid the most common disputes with residents regarding security deposits. You also find out how to distinguish ordinary wear and tear from damage and provide residents with an itemization form that properly accounts for any interest earned and costs deducted from the security deposit.

Defining the Legal Uses of Security Deposits

Some unsavory landlords treat security deposits as another source of income that's theirs for the taking. In the eyes of the law, however, a security deposit is actually the resident's money that the landlord holds in trust for the duration of the lease. Most states restrict landlord use of security deposits to only three or four purposes, including the following:

- ✔ Compensation for unpaid rent
- ✔ To repair damage to the rental unit, excluding ordinary wear and tear, caused by the resident or members of his household or guests
- ✔ To restore or replace property in the unit, such as furniture and furnishings or other items of personal property (including keys) according to terms of the lease, excluding ordinary wear and tear (refer to the later section, "Exempting Ordinary Wear and Tear" that explains exactly what *ordinary wear and tear* is)
- ✔ To clean the rental unit, so it's as clean as it was when the residents moved in
- ✔ To recover any portion of the security deposit used by the resident as payment for the last month's rent

Landlords can withhold from the security deposit only amounts that are reasonably necessary to remedy these damages.

The law of security deposits prohibits a landlord from making a security deposit nonrefundable or claiming in the rental contract that a security deposit is nonrefundable. As landlord, you must use security deposits only to cover actual financial damages and refund any amount remaining of the security deposit to the resident. In my (Laurry) experience, courts are especially suspicious of landlords' attempts to retain security deposits, except for the purpose of repairing significant damage to the residential rental unit. Similarly, landlords who use a different term for deposits that are made for the purposes intended to be covered by a security deposit, or withhold the return of a security deposit beyond the statutory term specified, are likely to incur the court's wrath, and result in damages assessed against the landlord or its managing agent.

The California Civil Code defines what a security deposit

Although you must always comply with the specific state and local laws concerning security deposits that apply to your rental property, the California Civil Code provides a generally applicable definition of security deposits and their purposes and uses and is helpful to illustrate how most security deposit laws are written. The California Civil Code states the following about security deposits:

As used in this section, *security* means any payment, fee, deposit or charge, including, but not limited to, any payment, fee, deposit, or charge . . . that is imposed at the beginning of the tenancy to be used to reimburse the landlord for costs associated with processing a new resident or that is imposed as an advance payment of rent, used or to be used for any purpose, including, but not limited to, any of the following:

(1) The compensation of a landlord for a resident's default in the payment of rent.

(2) The repair of damages to the premises, exclusive of ordinary wear and tear, caused by the resident or by a guest or licensee of the resident.

(3) The cleaning of the premises upon termination of the tenancy necessary to return the unit to the same level of cleanliness it was in at the inception of the tenancy. The amendments to this paragraph enacted by the act adding this sentence shall apply only to tenancies for which the resident's right to occupy begins after January 1, 2003.

(4) To remedy future defaults by the resident in any obligation under the rental agreement to restore, replace, or return personal property or appurtenances, exclusive of ordinary wear and tear, if the security deposit is authorized to be applied thereto by the rental agreement. (Civil Code Sections 1950.5(b)(1)-(4) [as of January 1, 2006]).

Deciding How Much to Charge as a Security Deposit

Many states don't limit the amount that may be charged as a security deposit, which means that for legal purposes, as is the case with setting rents, landlords can charge as much as they want. Other states impose strict limits on security deposits — usually not more than twice the amount of the monthly rent.

For guidance on how to track down state statutes regarding security deposits, visit www.dummies.com/go/landlordlegalkit and click on the Legal Resources folder.

Here are a few common strategies for deciding how much to charge for a security deposit:

✔ **Charge the maximum amount allowed or double the monthly rent.** A high security deposit protects you from any loss and encourages residents to respect the property. Another option is to charge the maximum amount only in high-risk situations; for example, if a new resident has a history of bad credit, negative landlord references, or prior evictions.

An exorbitant security deposit is a marketing disincentive that may hurt your occupancy rate, especially if a lot of rental units are sitting vacant in your neighborhood.

✔ **Charge higher rent as the alternative to a maximum security deposit.** Residents may prefer to pay more rent rather than a high security deposit. Doing so also benefits you because you get to keep the rent.

✔ **Increase the security deposit for furnished rental units.** By furnishing the unit, you increase your exposure to risk, because more items can get damaged, so charging a higher security deposit is reasonable.

Keep in mind that your prospective residents will be required to write some substantial checks to become comfortable in their new residential rental units. In addition to the check for the first month's rent and the security deposit, residents may incur the costs of moving, setting up Internet and cable TV accounts, and buying new furnishings and cleaning supplies. Setting a security deposit amount with your renters' other financial obligations in mind is a useful way to establish a solid, customer-friendly relationship. Another option is to collect the security deposit in installments; if rent is due on the first, consider making installments due in the middle of the month.

Some landlords believe that, because senior renters are less likely to cause damage than others, reducing their security deposit is sensible. Common sense suggests that these landlords are correct; the fair housing law, on the other hand, would probably consider this difference in treatment to be illegal discrimination, most likely because of its differential impact upon familial status. Note, however, that some states may, by statute, allow this disparity.

Setting separate deposits for pets

Many of the most popular pets are notorious for damaging rental units. Dogs may chew carpeting and furniture and scratch floors and trim. Unless they're declawed, cats often turn any vertical surface into a scratching post and tear up rugs. Dogs and cats often track dirt or litter around the apartment and may leave carpets infested with fleas. And most creatures leave a lingering odor in their wake. Because pets often cause damage, you may want to consider charging a separate deposit or increased rental fee to every household that has a pet and perhaps even a per-pet fee.

To protect yourself from potential losses from pet damage, you have several options:

- **Charge a separate, refundable pet deposit.** You can use some or all of the deposit to cover the costs of any damages caused by the pet or extra cleaning required because of the pet and return the remainder to the resident.

- **Charge a higher security deposit for renters who have pets.** A two-tiered security deposit policy charges one amount for renters without pets and another for residents who own pets. Theoretically, that should prevent arguments over whether a certain item of damage is attributable to the pet or some other source.

- **Require that residents get renters insurance that includes coverage for pet damages and liability.** Or you may charge a pet deposit and offer a discount on the deposit if the resident has renters insurance.

- **Charge a separate, nonrefundable pet deposit or fee.** Some landlords charge a pet deposit, sometimes camouflaged as *pet rent* in the lease or rental agreement, because they reasonably think that pets routinely cause damage. We strongly discourage this practice, even if it's legal in your area, because it too often results in disagreements.

Check state statutes and city ordinances before charging nonrefundable deposits. Some states, including California, specifically prohibit landlords from charging any fee or deposit that's not refundable. Other states, including Arizona, Nevada, Washington, Florida, and Georgia, allow landlords to collect nonrefundable fees, including pet deposits and cleaning fees.

Of course, you always have the option to prohibit pets altogether for a number of reasons — because they may cause damage, make too much noise, inconvenience other residents, or pose a safety risk. However, excluding pet owners excludes about 75 percent of all renters, which means that pet owners will automatically reject a "no-pets" property as a prospective resident, irrespective of its competitive pricing, amenities package, or other distinguishing characteristics. So, decide if you want to target pet lovers or tenants that are seeking pet-free housing.

Fair housing laws are absolutely clear about service animals: they're not pets, which means that they're not subject to such restrictions as pet deposits. However, the owner of the service animal is liable for any *damages* caused by the animal, such as teeth marks on trim, carpet torn by the animal's digging, urine or feces, hair or fur, flea infestations, and so on.

Avoiding the temptation to charge last month's rent

Some landlords collect last month's rent up-front and then use it as a supplementary security deposit, just in case the security deposit doesn't completely cover the costs of cleaning and repairs.

We strongly discourage you from collecting last month's rent as the outset of the tenancy for several reasons, including the following:

✔ Many states prohibit using the last month's rent for anything other than the last month's rent. You can't use the money to pay any cleaning or repair costs.

✔ Residents don't like the idea of a landlord holding their money for the duration of the lease (or longer). After all, it's *their* money.

✔ Collecting last month's rent in advance is likely to drive away any prospective renters.

If, near the end of the lease, a resident forgets that he had already paid last month's rent when he moved in and pays it again, refund the second payment immediately, especially if you operate in a state that requires last month's rent be used for its intended purpose.

The better approach is to collect monthly rents — including the final month's — when they come due, relying on the security deposit to cover any unpaid rent or other losses.

Exempting Ordinary Wear and Tear

Rental units, indeed all living spaces, gradually wear out from human use. Carpeting becomes worn, floors get scuffed, paint fades, wallpaper peels, metal rusts, and wood gets warped. This kind of natural deterioration falls within the definition of *ordinary wear and tear*: deterioration that occurs over time through normal usage, not as a result of negligence, carelessness, or abuse.

The difference between ordinary wear and tear and damage has puzzled landlords and infuriated residents for decades. In the following sections, we shed light on the differences between damage and ordinary wear and tear and explain how to use move-in and move-out checklists to assess damages.

Distinguishing damage from ordinary wear and tear

Among other things, security deposits allow the landlord to recover costs of physical damages to the premises caused by the resident or the resident's family or guests. To help you identify damage and exclude ordinary wear and tear, Table 10-1 compares the differences between the two.

Table 10-1	Ordinary Wear and Tear versus Damage
Ordinary Wear and Tear (Landlord's Responsibility)	*Damage or Excessive Filth (Resident's Responsibility)*
Smudges on walls, near light switches	Crayon marks on walls or ceilings
Minor marks on walls or doors	Large marks on or holes in walls or doors
A few small tack or nail holes	Numerous nail holes that require patching and/or painting
Faded, peeling, or cracked paint	Completely dirty or scuffed painted walls
Carpet worn thin from normal use	Carpet ripped or pulled up
Carpet with moderate dirt or spots	Carpet stained by spills or pets
Carpet or curtains faded by the sun	Carpet or curtains with cigarette burns
Moderately dirty miniblinds	Bent or missing miniblinds
Doors sticking from humidity	Broken hinges or doorframes
Drywall cracks from settling	Holes punched in walls or through doors
Peeling wallpaper	Wallpaper torn or cut
Scuffed flooring	Scratched or gouged flooring
Water stains in shower enclosure	Cracked shower enclosure
Loose railing	Railing missing or torn away from wall
Dirty screens and windows	Missing windows or screens, torn screens, or broken windows

Assessing damage with move-in and move-out checklists

You can easily determine the difference between the condition of a rental unit before and after residents lived in it by completing a move-in and a move-out checklist, as we explain in Chapters 11 and 20. A key benefit of such checklists is that they clearly illustrate on paper any damages that the resident is responsible for, which helps avert future security deposit disputes.

The move-in checklist establishes the baseline for the comparison at move-out. Is the apartment clean? Do the appliances work? Is the kitchen spotless? How about the bathroom, the tub, shower, and sink? Are the closet doors on-track and operating correctly? What about any unrepaired previous damages, such as the condition of the hardwood flooring, the on-again/off-again washing machine, or the carpeting?

The move-out checklist records the condition of the same items immediately after the residents move out. With the two lists in hand, you're ready to identify damages, which the resident pays for, and ordinary wear-and-tear, which is on your tab.

Complete the move-in and move-out checklists with the resident, so you can resolve any disagreements prior to repairs and cleaning. Take before and after photographs, and have the resident sign off on both the move-in and move-out checklist. If disputes arise later over the portion of the security deposit that's returned to the resident, these checklists, along with an itemized statement and receipts for any repairs and cleaning, should be sufficient to convince the resident that the charges are reasonable.

You're usually not allowed to charge the total replacement cost; courts typically require that landlords account for depreciation of items, such as carpets, countertops, doors, and so forth. For example, suppose the rental unit has carpeting with a 15-year rating (it's supposed to last for 15 years before you need to replace it). The carpet was installed five years before the current resident moved in, and the current resident lived in the unit for three years. The resident's cat shredded the carpet in several areas, and it needs to be replaced. You can't charge the resident for the full cost of the replacement carpeting. You need to figure that you have about 50 percent of the carpet's life expectancy, so charge the resident 50 percent the cost of the new carpeting.

Safeguarding and Returning Security Deposits

As soon as possible after a resident moves out, complete any repairs and cleaning that the resident is responsible for paying, subtract the costs for those services from the security deposit, and return the remainder to the resident. If your state or city requires landlords to hold security deposits in trust and pay residents interest, then be sure to add the statutory (or legally required) interest to the security deposit amount prior to deducting any repair and cleaning costs.

Returning security deposits to residents should be as simple as that, but because security deposit issues are at the center of so many disputes, you need to be very careful in your security deposit accounting and documentation. In the following sections, we explain the intricacies of managing security deposits and what you need to do to document your handling of security deposits.

State laws govern how and when security deposits are returned. Every state imposes legal requirements upon the time limit for their return. Visit www.dummies.com/go/landlordlegalkit and click on the Legal Resources folder for guidance in how to track down statutes that govern security deposit management in your state.

Mismanagement, misappropriation of funds, or sloppy accounting involving security deposits may result in stiff penalties. In some states, courts are allowed to award *treble* (common legal word that literally means *triple*) damages up to three times the security deposit, along with court costs and the resident's attorney fees.

Holding security deposits in a separate account

Some states require landlords to hold security deposits in a separate bank account, commonly referred to as a *trust account*. States that require segregating security deposits in trust accounts apparently share renters' concerns that their funds might not be available when they move out. Maintaining a single trust account with all of your residents' security deposits, separately recorded, is sufficient.

Regardless of whether your state or municipality has such a requirement, we recommend that you follow this practice in order to avoid disputes with residents and provide yourself with extra legal protection. By depositing the funds in your security deposit account, you acknowledge that the money belongs to the resident subject to deductions for any damages or unpaid rent. In addition, you avoid the temptation to use the security deposit for anything other than its intended use.

When you collect the security deposit, have the resident make out a separate check payable to the security deposit account, not to you or your business, so the security deposit doesn't intermingle with your finances. If you charge last month's rent, don't place it in the same account as the security deposit.

Keeping receipts for repairs and cleaning

As you complete repairs and cleaning after a resident moves out, keep the receipts as documentation of how much you paid for each service. Make sure each receipt has the following information:

- ✔ Date on which work was performed
- ✔ Description of the work performed
- ✔ Indication of who performed the work
- ✔ The rental unit address and number or letter
- ✔ Indication of who's responsible for covering the cost — resident or landlord

Attach all receipts to the move-in/move-out checklists form and store it in the resident's file folder.

Completing the security deposit itemization form

After you've inspected the rental unit and determined the proper charges, you need to prepare the Security Deposit Itemization Form. Complete this form and give the vacating resident a check for any balance due within your state's maximum time guidelines. Most states allow rental property owners 14 to 30 days to complete the accounting, but several states have no specific legal deadline. Make sure you don't wait until the last minute because the consequences in most states are severe, including forfeiting your rights to any deductions and paying punitive damages.

Visit www.dummies.com/go/landlordlegalkit and click on the Security Deposit folder to access a template for a Security Deposit Itemization form.

When listing charges on your Security Deposit Itemization Form, take out your digital camera or video recorder and take the following steps to carefully document repairs and associated costs:

1. **State the item that's damaged.**

   List all damaged flooring, window coverings, fixtures, appliances, and pieces of furniture separately.

2. **Note the specific location of the damage.**

   Document the room and which wall, ceiling, or corner of the room the damage is located. Use compass directions, if possible.

3. **Comment on the type and extent of the damage.**

   Be sure to describe the damage in detail by using appropriate adjectives, such as *filthy, substantial, excessive, minor, scratched, stained, soiled, ripped, cracked, broken, inoperative, missing, burned,* or *chipped.*

4. **Note the type and extent of repair done.**

   Describe the repair using words such as *spackle, patch, paint, steam clean, deodorize,* or *refinish.* Indicate if an item is so damaged that it has to be replaced and, if so, why. Indicating the item's age is helpful, especially if it was new when the resident first occupied the rental unit, and its life span was supposed to exceed the length of the tenancy.

5. **Document the cost of the repair or replacement.**

   List exactly how much you spent or plan to spend based on a third-party estimate. Include copies of receipts whenever possible.

Be specific. For example, if you merely indicate "Pet damage — $100" on the Security Deposit Itemization Form, you're likely to be challenged. However, if you provide details like "Steam cleaned carpeting in living room to remove extensive pet urine stains — $100" and include your actual receipt, you greatly improve your chances of winning if the matter gets to court. (In fact, maybe you won't even be challenged in the first place.)

Don't deduct from the security deposit unpaid rent that the resident withheld for good reason, such as the landlord failing to respond to a maintenance request regarding something that made the rental unit uninhabitable for a certain amount of time. If you're unsure why a resident hasn't paid the rent, find out before deducting it from the security deposit.

Dealing with unknown costs

If you won't know the final charges and deductions from the resident's deposit before your state's deadline for the accounting and/or return of the deposit balance, send the resident a written itemized accounting of the charges you *do* know and an estimated time that you expect to have the final charges. As soon as you know the costs, send the final accounting and any security deposit refund as soon as possible, as we explain in the next section.

Don't withhold the entire deposit if you know the undetermined items are likely to be much less than the balance of the deposit. In those instances, conservatively estimate the potential remaining charges and refund the balance of funds, along with your explanation letter, by the deadline. Most judges consider this move a good faith effort and won't penalize you if the matter ultimately ends up in court.

Some rental property owners give all vacating residents a *pricing chart* with a list of costs for different services or damaged items. These owners believe pricing charts minimize disputes because the charges are predetermined and are given to the residents in advance. They argue that the residents will see how expensive repairs are and will take care of some of the work on their own. This method has some logic, but it also poses potential problems because prices frequently change, and most courts insist on actual charges, not estimates. Also, many items can't possibly have preset prices for repair because different contractors may charge different amounts. Rest assured that a resident wouldn't pay up if your actual charge turns out to be much higher than the preset charge indicated on your pricing chart. But if the resident challenges your deductions and your actual invoice shows you paid less than what you charged the resident, you had better have your checkbook ready.

Adding statutory interest to security deposit calculations

Some states require landlords to pay interest on security deposits held in trust, although the methods of calculation vary widely. Here are some examples of these variations:

- ✔ The rate of interest to be paid on the accounts
- ✔ When the interest is to be paid
- ✔ Required notification by landlords to their residents regarding the above

Some cities impose their own requirements for interest on security deposits, even when their states don't.

Delivering the security deposit refund and itemization form

Send the security deposit itemization form and refund, if any, as soon as you're sure of the final charges. Residents need this money, and the longer they wait, the more impatient and upset they become — and the more likely they are to challenge your charges. Of course, you need to make sure your maintenance personnel have been through the entire unit carefully and found all resident damage beyond ordinary wear and tear. (In theory, you can always seek reimbursement for items discovered after you refund the deposit, but your chances of collecting in such cases are slim.)

Some residents want to personally pick up the deposit as soon as possible, whereas others don't even tell you where they can be reached. Generally, you should mail the Security Deposit Itemization Form to the address provided by your resident on the Resident's Notice of Intent to Vacate Rental Unit. If you don't have your vacating resident's forwarding address, send the form to his last known address, which may be your own rental unit. Perhaps he's forwarding his mail to a new address; if not, the check will be returned to you.

Residents, particularly roommates or married couples in the midst of a separation or divorce, may fight among themselves over the security deposit. Legally, the deposit belongs equally to all residents who signed the rental contract, unless otherwise agreed in writing. If you arbitrarily split the check between the residents, you can find yourself liable to the other residents.

In multi-resident situations where you have a court order or a written agreement or instructions signed by all the residents, always handle the deposit as directed. If you don't have a court order or a written agreement or instructions, follow these steps for paying out the security deposit:

1. **Make your deposit refund check payable jointly to all the adult residents.**

2. **Prepare a mailing that includes the refund check for one of the residents with a copy of the check to the others or put all former residents' names on the check.**

   Leave it up to the residents to handle the check's endorsement.

3. **Mail copies of your Security Deposit Itemization Form to each of the residents at his respective forwarding address.**

If your Security Deposit Itemization Form and refund check are returned undeliverable, be sure to save the returned envelope in case the former resident claims you never sent the legally required accounting. Many states have very severe penalties for improper deductions or failure to provide the security deposit accounting in a timely manner. Check with your state laws to determine the proper disposition of the resident's uncashed deposit refund check. Some states now allow electronic refund of the deposit if the parties have agreed on the use of such a process.

Be sure you're able to prove that you've met the legal requirements in terms of returning the deposit in a timely manner. Otherwise, the small claims courts may rule against you, because as a major player in the rental housing business, you're held to a higher standard of record-keeping.

You can send the security deposit itemization form and refund check via certified mail (as required by some states) to prove the date you sent it. However, if that isn't the required method of return, it's much more cost effective to go to the post office and ask for a *certificate of mailing,* which records the date you sent the check (and doesn't require the recipient's signature for delivery).

Collecting damages and unpaid rent in excess of a security deposit

As a landlord, you're probably going to encounter a time when a resident's security deposit isn't sufficient to cover the unpaid rent and the damage caused by the resident. Unless legally prohibited, allocate the deposit to first cover the damage and then cover the unpaid rent because it makes sense to apply the deposit to items that are more difficult to prove in court.

Say you're holding a $500 security deposit from a resident when he vacates, owing $350 in delinquent rent. When you inspect his unit, however, you find $400 in damage beyond ordinary wear and tear. The total of the rent owed and the damages done is $750, but the deposit is only $500. What should you do? First, apply $400 of the $500 deposit to cover the damage, and then allocate the remaining $100 toward the unpaid rent. You can then pursue the $250 delinquent rent balance with your rent collection ledgers and records as evidence to clearly prove this amount is owed. Unless prohibited by state law, you can apply rent payments toward the most recently accrued outstanding rent. Thus, if you have done an eviction and have a money judgment for rent up to the time of judgment, you can apply the rent payment to rent that accrued between the judgment and the time of move-out, which might not be part of your money judgment, depending on the court's rules.

Be sure to always record the actual costs for damages, even if you don't intend to pursue the resident for the balance owed. This way, you can prove your expenses in court if necessary.

In most states, even if your lawful deductions exceed the departing resident's security deposit charges, you must provide the resident with a full accounting of the damages. You must do so even if you file a small claims lawsuit for the balance due. So be sure to always follow the required procedures for the accounting of the deposit.

Handling security deposit disputes

No matter how fair and reasonable you are with your security deposit deductions, sooner or later you're bound to have a former resident challenge them. Even if your deductions were proper and you're sure you're right, going to court over this matter may cost you more than the deduction amount in legal fees. Often, the actual disagreement is over a relatively small amount of money.

For example, you may have deducted $100 for painting touch up, but your former resident may believe that the charge should be $50. So you're arguing over a mere $50 difference. Explore possible negotiations to resolve the matter before going to court. If you're sure that your charges were fair, always maintain that in your discussions with your former resident, even if you want to see whether a settlement is a possibility.

If you charge your residents for damage to the rental unit, you need evidence to back up your claim in case they dispute the damage. Digital photos or videotape of the damage can be effective tools to resolve disputes with residents or prove your position in court. In fact, many courts now have video monitors that you can use to show the judge or jury your evidence. Just be sure you have possession of the unit or have given proper legal notice before entering it to videotape. (See Chapter 16 for more about resident privacy rights.)

Chapter 11

Moving in a New Resident

. . . .

In This Chapter

▶ Agreeing on a move-in date

▶ Handling preliminaries prior to move-in

▶ Conducting the pre-move-in inspection with a new resident

▶ Protecting yourself with good recordkeeping

▶ Deciding the best way to communicate with residents

. . . .

An important way you can protect yourself against lawsuits and legally enforce the lease terms starts when you move a resident into her new home. To cover all the bases, you need to agree on a move-in date, review the rules with the resident, have her sign all agreements, and conduct a pre-move-in inspection of the premises.

This chapter outlines the important steps to start your landlord-resident relationship on the right legal foot. Here we explain how to protect yourself legally by keeping detailed records of your interactions with each resident and how to choose communications methods that provide clear documentation of those interactions. By following our guidance in this chapter, you're much less likely to run into disagreements and legal trouble with residents in the future. If you do, we explain what you need to do to pursue your rights and protect your interests in court.

 Moving is very stressful for most people. If your new resident has a bad move-in experience, this feeling can last for months or even stay on her mind throughout the tenancy. The timing of the orientation is critical. Move-in day has a great deal of activity, and your resident's mind is preoccupied. Her furniture is waiting to be unloaded, helpful friends and relatives are anxious to begin their tasks, and she has difficulty focusing on the details of her lease and the rules of occupancy. Try to schedule the brief orientation meeting at a less hectic time — usually before move-in day — so she can focus on her obligations and your expectations as you explain them.

Agreeing on the Move-In Date

When you inform your prospective resident that you've approved her rental application, you need to determine a mutually agreeable move-in date. You may have discussed this date during your initial telephone conversation or when you showed the property, but be sure to raise the subject again to guarantee you're in agreement.

After you approve new residents, some suddenly postpone setting the move-in date. They may do so because they're still obligated under a lease or 30-day notice at another rental property and don't want to double pay. Unless you're willing to suffer rent loss that you won't recover, insist that the resident begin paying rent to you on the originally scheduled move-in date. The time for your new resident to negotiate the move-in date was *before* you approved her. *Remember:* A delay may be considered reasonable as an accommodation, if it's requested because of a disability.

Residents often request to move the weekend before the start of their lease date in order to provide adequate time to complete the move and secure help. Owners often allow early occupancy if the unit is ready and even forego the day or two of rent as a goodwill gesture. Doing so can start your new resident off with a positive feeling, but we caution you to ask your new resident to provide proof that both utilities and insurance coverage are in place as of the date of actual physical occupancy.

In some situations, your rental unit may not be available on the agreed move-in date. Perhaps the prior residents didn't vacate when they said they would, maybe the unit was in much worse condition than you anticipated, or perhaps you just weren't able to complete the required prep work in time. If the unit won't be available as promised, communicate with your new resident immediately. Often, a new resident can adjust her move-in date as long as you give her reasonable notice. If she can't adjust the date, try to work out another arrangement.

Don't allow new residents to move just a few items into the rental unit prior to your preoccupancy meeting. As soon as those items are placed in the rental unit, the residency begins. If you have to cancel the rental for any reason, you have to go through a formal legal eviction that can take several weeks.

Meeting with a New Resident Prior to Move-In

After you and your resident decide on a move-in date — but a few days *before* the resident actually moves in and takes possession of the unit — you need to meet to deal with some technicalities, including inspecting the property and signing the inspection checklist, signing the lease or rental agreement, collecting money, and handing over the keys. (If the resident can't meet with you prior to moving in, then you need to have your meeting on move-in day, but prior to the time that the resident moves her possessions into the unit.)

Meeting with your new resident *before* her move-in date is important to ensure complete agreement on the terms and conditions of the rental. You want to make sure that there are no surprises with extra persons or pets or that your tenant thinks that you're paying her utilities. Although misunderstandings can always occur later in the tenancy, your chances of having a smooth landlord-tenant relationship can be greatly improved with this pre-move-in meeting to go over everything that one last time. The following sections walk you through each step of the pre-move-in process.

Although the rental property should be in rent-ready condition before you show it to rental prospects, it can get dirty or dusty quickly if there's any delay between showing the property and moving in the new residents. So before meeting with your resident prior to move-in, make a final visit to the unit to make sure there aren't any surprises when move-in day arrives.

Establishing your policies and rules

As an extension of the lease agreement, we recommend that you establish policies and rules that spell out your expectations for resident behavior. Make sure your residents know that these rules and policies are regulations that are legally enforceable and part of your rental contract, not optional guidelines. In the following sections, we guide you through the process of writing and then reviewing them with new residents.

Drafting your policies and rules

One of the easiest ways to write policies and rules is to start with an existing document and then modify it to suit your needs. Visit www.dummies.com/go/landlordlegalkit and click on the Move-in folder for a complete sample Policies and Rules document, as shown in Figure 11-1.

Your policies, rules, and regulations are separate from your rental contract, which an attorney drafts in legal language. The rules you draft should be expressed in a more informal and conversational tone. Use clear language that's neither harsh nor demeaning. Because your rules and regulations are an extension of your lease, have your lawyer quickly read them. Casual tone and language can put a softer spin on the document but may make the rules more susceptible to misinterpretation and more difficult to enforce and can even lead to a fair housing discrimination complaint.

Policies and Rules

We are proud of this property and we hope that your living experience here will be pleasant and comfortable. The support and cooperation of you, as our tenant, is necessary for us to maintain our high standards.

This is your personal copy of our Policies and Rules. Please read it carefully as it is an integral part of your rental agreement. When you sign your rental agreement, you agree to abide by the policies and rules for this rental property, and they are considered legally binding provisions of your rental agreement. If you have any questions, please contact us and we will be glad to help.

This document is an addendum and is part of the Lease or Rental Agreement, dated _____ , by and between _____, "Owner," and _____ "Tenant", for the premises located at: _____ .

New policies and rules or amendments to this document may be adopted by Owner upon giving thirty (30) days written notice to tenant.

Guests – Tenant is responsible for their own proper conduct and that of all guests, including the responsibility for understanding and observing all policies and rules.

Noise – While the Premises are well constructed, they are not completely soundproof and reasonable consideration for neighbors is important. Either inside or outside of the Premises, no tenant or their guest shall use, or allow to be used, any sound emitting device at a sound level that may annoy, disturb or otherwise interfere with the rights, comforts or conveniences of other tenants or neighbors. Particular care must be taken between the hours of 9 p.m. and 9 a.m.

Parking – No vehicle belonging to a Tenant shall be parked in such a manner as to impede passage in the street or to prevent access to the property. Tenant shall only use assigned and designated parking spaces. Tenant shall ensure that all posted handicap, fire zones or other no parking areas remain clear of vehicles at all times. Vehicles parked in unauthorized areas or in another tenant's designated parking space may be towed away at the vehicle owner's expense. Vehicles may not be backed in and repairs and maintenance of any sort are not allowed on the premises. All vehicles must be currently registered and in operative condition. No trucks, commercial vehicles, recreational vehicles, motorcycles, bicycles, boats, or trailers are allowed anywhere on the Premises without advance written approval of the Owner. All vehicles must be parked properly between the lines of the parking space. Tenant shall ensure that their guests abide by all of these parking policies and rules.

Form courtesy of Robert S. Griswold

Figure 11-1:
The beginning of a Policies and Rules form.

As you draft your policies and rules, keep these guidelines in mind to follow:

- ✔ **Frame your policies and rules in a positive way.** Review the rules with several of your friends and colleagues to find better ways to say the same thing. Be clear, direct, and firm, yet not condescending. And watch out for the *no index,* which happens when many of your rules are too blunt and negative, such as "No glass in the pool area," "No storage on your balcony," and "No riding skateboards on the grounds." Although each of these rules is reasonable and important for the safe and efficient operation of your property, you can say the same things in more positive language. For example, instead of saying, "No riding bikes on the grounds," you can say, "Please walk your bikes in common areas." Or instead of saying, "No glass in the pool area," you can say, "We gladly allow beverages by the pool in unbreakable containers." Phrasing the rules in a positive tone and minimizing the no index makes the rules — and you — seem friendlier to your resident.

- ✔ **Verify that your policies and rules are reasonable and enforceable.** Your rules must not discriminate against any member of a protected class. The term *protected class* refers to the federal antidiscrimination laws that protect groups of people because of race, color, sex, national origin, religion, handicap, and familial status, and by some state statutes that add to the list of protected classes. (See Chapter 5 for more about the protected classes.)

✔ **Avoid any reference to children, unless it's related to certain health and safety issues.** For example, you can have a rule that states, "Persons under 14 must be accompanied by an adult while using the spa," because legitimate safety concerns exist regarding unattended children in spas. But a rule that says, "Children aren't allowed to leave bicycles in the common area" is inappropriate because it singles out children and implies that adults can leave bikes in the common area if they want. A better way to handle this issue is to use wording that isn't age-specific, such as, "Bicycles aren't allowed to be left in the common area by anyone." Or an even more generic wording would be "Personal property should not be left unattended in the common area." With this verbiage, the rule applies to everyone and doesn't discriminate based on familial status or age.

✔ **At least every six months, review and modify your policies and rules, according to situations you encounter.** Remember that you don't want to alienate a resident by harassing her with rules or controlling her day-to-day life. Just because one resident demonstrates poor judgment doesn't necessarily mean it's time to create a new rule.

Whenever you revise your policies and rules, be sure to have an attorney or fair housing expert review the proposed changes. If you're an onsite manager, be sure your owner or supervisor has approved any rule changes in advance too. Then when informing your residents of the change, you should include the date of the revision and distribute two copies of the rules to every unit, along with instructions that all residents in the unit who are named on the lease sign one copy and return it to you. Remind residents that these rules supersede any prior versions.

Going over your policies and rules with your new resident

When you meet with a new resident, give her a copy of your policies and rules, allow her time to read them, and then ask whether she has any questions or concerns. If your resident doesn't understand a rule, clarify it for her. Then ask for her signature, which indicates she has received and understands the rules and regulations and agrees to abide by them.

All people named on the lease must sign your policies and rules to indicate that they recognize their obligation to comply with the rules.

Reviewing and signing legal documents

Residents and property owners alike are usually aware of all the required legal paperwork involved in residential renting. And although sifting through all that legalese isn't fun for anyone, doing so is important. Property owners and residents each have specific legal rights and responsibilities that are outlined in these documents, and being aware of what you're agreeing to — and being sure your residents know what they're agreeing to — is crucial.

The next several sections list and describe the documents you need to go over with your new residents and have them sign.

Lease or rental contract

Be sure your resident understands that when she signs your lease or month-to-month rental agreement she's entering into a business contract that has significant rights and responsibilities for both parties. Before your resident signs the rental contract (or any rental contract addenda), carefully and methodically review each clause. (See Chapter 9 for guidance on creating a lease or rental agreement.)

Certain clauses in the rental contract are so important that you should have the resident initial them to indicate that she's read them and understands and agrees with her rights and responsibilities. For example, the resident should initial the clause concerning the need for her to obtain her own renter's insurance policy to protect her property and cover her for liability claims.

Never give a resident the keys to the property before she's signed your required legal documents. When you give her the keys, you create an "oral" landlord-resident relationship, which can make it very difficult and expensive to regain possession of your rental unit if the resident disagrees with the terms in your lease and refuses to sign it. Before you hand over the keys, have every adult occupant sign all rental documents. (See "Taking security measures with a unit," later in this chapter, for details.)

Environmental disclosure forms

If you haven't already done so, be sure to give your new resident copies of the required legal and environmental disclosure forms, plus the Environmental Protection Agency (EPA) pamphlet for lead-based paint hazards, which is also required under federal law for most properties built before 1978. (Turn to Chapter 14 for more info on disclosure of these hazards.)

Mold addendum

Mold is a common term for a variety of fungus types found virtually everywhere in the environment — both indoors and outdoors. Blaming elevated mold levels for alleged health problems caused by exposure to certain mold spores, which are often called *toxic mold,* is a fairly recent phenomenon. Such claims are very controversial, and currently, no federal regulations exist regarding permissible exposure limits or building tolerance standards for mold.

To minimize the possibility of mold concerns at your property, give your resident a Mold Notification Addendum to educate her about how she can help prevent mold. (Turn to Chapter 14 for a sample Mold Notification Addendum and additional guidance on how to handle the issue of toxic mold.)

Smoke detector agreement

Inform your new resident of the importance of smoke detectors. You may even want to create a Smoke Detector Agreement to ensure that your resident fully understands the importance of this vital safety equipment and realizes that she must make sure the smoke detectors remain in place, operate properly, and have electrical or battery power. (See Chapter 13 for more about the importance of smoke detectors and other fire-safety equipment and to check out a sample Smoke Detector Agreement.)

Animal agreement

If you allow pets and your new resident has pets, you need to have her complete and sign an Animal Agreement, as shown in Figure 11-2. This document outlines your rules regarding your resident's animals. Please note that service animals for disabled residents aren't considered to be pets, but still require prior written permission to be housed on the premises.

Visit www.dummies.com/go/landlordlegalkit and click on the Move-in folder for a sample Animal Agreement.

A good animal policy clearly stipulates exactly which animals are acceptable as pets at your rental property. It may just be semantics, but you don't want to get to court and have your residents argue that the large iguana that damaged your rental unit isn't subject to your rules because it's not their "pet." We recommend broadening your rules from merely "pets" to "animals in general."

After the initial move-in, residents may be tempted to take advantage of your policy and bring in additional animals or pets. Residents often have heartwarming stories about how they've added new animals to the mix, but you need to retain control over the numbers, types, and sizes of the pet animals on your property. One way to do so is to meet and photograph the animal so there's no doubt as to what you've approved. Remember that small puppies can grow into large dogs, so make sure your policies anticipate the animal at its *adult* size. Also, note that smaller isn't always better. Some small breeds are noisier than their larger counterparts. Pets tend to be as responsible as the residents who care for them, control them, and pick up after them.

Keep current photos of all animals living on your property in the individual files of their owners. This practice may seem unnecessary, but no matter how large your security deposit is or how strict your rules are, animals have the potential to cause significant damage. Determining the source of the problem can be difficult if you can't accurately identify the guilty animal and its owner. Having a photo can also help if the original animal passes and the "replacement animal" doesn't meet your limitations.

Animal Agreement

This document is an addendum and is part of the Lease or Rental Agreement, dated _____,

by and between _____, "Owner/Agent",

and _____ "Tenant",

for the premises located at: _____.

In consideration of their mutual promises, Owner/Agent and Tenant agree as follows:

1. The Lease/Rental Agreement provides that without Owner/Agent's prior written consent, no animals whatsoever shall be allowed in or about the premises. Tenant shall not keep or feed stray animals in their rental unit or anywhere on the grounds. Tenant may not allow an animal to be in his rental unit or on the premises even temporarily. Tenant must advise his guests of this policy prohibiting animals or secure advance approval from the Owner/Agent.

2. Tenant desires to keep the following described animal (see attached photo), herein after referred to as "Pet", and represents it is a domesticated dog, cat, bird, fish, or _____. Said Pet is: Breed: _____; Size (current and adult height/weight): _____; Color _____. Tenant represents to Owner/Agent that said Pet is not vicious, and has not bitten, attacked, harmed, or menaced anyone in the past.

3. Tenant agrees to comply with all applicable ordinances, regulations and laws governing pets. If the Pet is a cat, it must be neutered and veterinary proof is required. Tenant must provide and maintain an appropriate litter box and not dispose of litter in the toilets. If the Pet is a bird, it shall not be let out of the cage. If the Pet is fish, the water container shall not exceed _____ gallons and will be placed in a safe location in the rental unit. Pet shall not be fed directly on carpet or any floor covering in the rental unit. Tenant shall prevent any fleas or other infestation of the rental unit or other property of Owner. Tenant shall not permit, and represents that Pet will not cause any damage, discomfort, annoyance, nuisance or in any way inconvenience, or cause complaints from, any other Tenant.

4. Tenant acknowledges and agrees that Owner/Agent may, at any time and in Owner/Agent's sole and absolute discretion, revoke its consent by giving Tenant written thirty (30) day notice, if Owner/Agent receives complaints from neighbors or other residents about Pet, or if Owner/Agent, in Owner/Agent's sole discretion, determines that Pet has disturbed the rights, comfort, convenience, or safety of neighbors or other tenants. Tenant shall permanently remove Pet from Owner's property upon Owner/Agent's written notice that consent is revoked.

5. If any rule or provision of this Animal Agreement is violated, Owner/Agent shall have the right to demand removal of Pet from the community upon three (3) day written notice. Any refusal by Tenant to comply with such demand shall be deemed to be a material breach of the Lease or Rental Agreement, in which event Owner/Agent shall be entitled to all the rights and remedies set forth in the Lease or Rental Agreement for violations thereof, including, but not limited to, eviction, damages, and attorney's fees.

6. Tenant shall be strictly liable for the entire amount of any wrongful death, or injury to the person or property of others, caused by Pet, and Tenant shall indemnify Owner/Agent for all costs resulting from same, including, but not limited to, litigation costs and attorney's fees.

7. Tenant agrees that Pet will not be permitted outside Tenant's unit unless restrained by a leash, cage, or other appropriate animal restraint. Tenant shall not tie Pet to any object outside the rental unit or premises. The Tenant agrees to promptly clean up after Pet, if necessary. Pet shall be allowed or walked only in the exterior area(s) designated by the Owner/Agent. Tenant shall not permit Pet in swimming pool areas, laundry rooms, management offices, clubrooms, playgrounds, other recreation facilities, and other dwelling units.

Date	Owner/Agent	Date	Tenant
		Date	Tenant

Figure 11-2:
A sample
Animal
Agreement.

Form courtesy of Robert S. Griswold

Pythons and piglets and goats, oh my!

In managing rental properties over the years, I (Robert) have seen just about every type of pet you can imagine. I once took over management of a small rental property where the owner allowed the residents to have pets. I wasn't too concerned until it became obvious that the prior management company didn't have any limitations. I soon found out that we had everything from the usual dogs and cats to a large Burmese python and a potbellied pig. One resident even had two goats on his patio. Strictly define exactly which animals are acceptable on your property, or you may be in for a big surprise. Refer to Chapter 5 for a discussion on service animals, which aren't considered pets.

Transferring the utilities to the resident

With the high cost of utilities, you need to be certain that you and your residents are on the same page regarding who's financially responsible for the rental unit's utility charges. Residents usually aren't very eager to begin paying for utilities, so be sure your rules and regulations clearly require your new resident to immediately contact the utility companies and put the utilities that are her responsibility in her name.

The best way to avoid paying for the resident's utilities is to provide contact information for all utilities at the resident orientation meeting and then require your new resident to contact the utility companies and establish the bills in her name while in your presence. You may also be able to handle the utility issues online, including verification that the resident has taken responsibility as of the move-in date.

Contact the utility companies in advance and find out how much notice they need to switch utilities over or turn them on and whether they're open for business on the weekends. You don't want a situation in which a resident moves in on Saturday, the water is turned off, and nobody can get in touch with the water company until the following Monday.

Another way to make sure your new resident handles this matter promptly is to confirm that she's transferred the utilities to her name prior to giving her the mailbox key. If they have contacted the utility company in advance of their projected move-in as you required, then it shouldn't be a problem in delaying their receipt of their mail. However, if push comes to shove, we don't suggest you hold their mailbox key hostage, as interfering with the US Mail could be construed as a crime.

In many states, landlords are required to disclose whether residents are financially responsible for any utility services outside of the rental unit. For example, exterior common area lighting may be connected to a rental unit, or a common area natural gas grill may be connected to a resident's gas meter. In some states, landlords must give residents an appropriate rent credit for the common area utilities they help pay. Check the laws in your area and be sure to disclose this kind of information if you're so required.

Collecting the rent and security deposit

During your pre-move-in meeting (and before the resident has the keys to the unit), be sure to collect the first month's rent and the security deposit. Payment may be in the form of a cashier's check or a money order but not a personal check (after all, you have no way of knowing whether it'll clear). Be sure to give your resident a receipt for payment, and also let her know whether your rent collection policy allows her to pay her future rent payments with a personal check.

Although cash is legal tender, have a firm policy *against* accepting cash unless doing so is absolutely necessary. Regularly collecting cash for your rents can make you a target for crime, and a surprising amount of counterfeit currency is floating around these days. You wouldn't want to have your bank tell you that your deposit is being reduced because some of the cash you deposited wasn't legitimate. Residents often move in on the weekends and in the evenings, so you don't want to have cash on you or at your home until you can get to the bank. Of course, if someone assists you in your rent collections, that person is also at risk (not to mention the fact that cash is harder to keep track of, and your assistant may be tempted to skim off some of it for her own needs).

Prior to handing over the keys to your new resident and allowing her to take possession, you need to insist on having full payment in hand through *good funds* (as opposed to *insufficient funds,* where a person writes a check and doesn't have the money to cover it in her account). Although most landlords guarantee the receipt of good funds by a bank cashier's check, or a money order or (as a last resort for reasons indicated above) cash, many landlords aren't aware that both cashier's checks and money orders can be stopped. So be sure to immediately deposit any cashier's checks or money orders you receive. Financial institutions and convenience stores allow the purchaser to stop payment because these financial instruments can be lost or stolen. However, bank cashier's checks and money orders are superior to personal checks because they do represent good funds and won't be returned to you because of a lack of money to cover them.

If, despite our strong advice, your resident persuades you to accept a personal check, then at least don't give her access to the property until you've verified with her bank that the check will be honored. Your best bet is to take the check to the resident's bank and cash it or at least have it certified. If the bank certifies the check, it's guaranteeing that the resident has sufficient funds available, and the bank will actually put a hold on the funds. Of course, cashing the check is the only sure way to collect your funds, because a devious resident can always stop payment on even a certified personal check.

Check scanners are now available from some financial institutions for a fee (or without charge for their larger customers). These devices can process personal checks by scanning the micro-encoding on the bottom of the check and essentially making a bank deposit remotely. You can cut down on the processing time of a check and know immediately whether it's good simply by using one of these scanners. New technology is becoming more readily available, such as taking a photo of the check with your smartphone.

Inspecting the property with your resident

The number one source of landlord-resident disputes is the disposition of the resident's security deposit. You can avoid many of these potential problems by conducting a pre-move-in inspection with your new resident and completing and signing an inspection checklist.

The following sections provide you with a sample inspection checklist, lead you through the process of completing and signing the inspection checklist, and provide some additional suggestions on how to avoid potential future problems.

Completing and signing the inspection checklist

Your inspection checklist is just as important as your rental contract. By using an inspection checklist at the time of both move-in and move-out, you can avoid many potential misunderstandings and disagreements. The purpose of the inspection isn't to find all the items you or your maintenance person forgot to check; you should've already verified that the unit meets your high standards. The purpose of the move-in inspection is to clearly demonstrate to the resident's satisfaction that the unit is in good condition except for any noted items and to establish the baseline condition should any damage be noted when the resident vacates.

Online you can find a sample Move-In/Move-Out checklist from the California Apartment Association. To access this document, visit www.dummies.com/go/landlordlegalkit and click on the Move-in folder. The first column of the checklist is where you note the unit's condition before the resident moves in. The last two columns are for use when the resident moves out and you inspect the unit with her again (see Chapter 20 for more information on the move-out process).

To conduct your inspection and lead the new resident through the process of completing the form properly, make sure you do the following:

✔ **Physically walk through the rental unit with your new resident and guide her through the inspection form.** Let the resident tell you what she observes, especially any problems that are unsatisfactory, and make sure the description of any damage or concern is clearly worded.

Whenever possible, have the resident fill out the checklist legibly in her own handwriting. If a dispute arises later that finds its way into small claims court, the credibility of the form will be stronger if the resident was the one who completed it.

If doing this walk-through with your resident isn't possible, then you should complete the move-in/move-out inspection checklist on your own and ask that all adult occupants review and sign the form as soon as possible upon move-in. Inform the resident that you'll be glad to deliver her mailbox key after you have the approved form in hand. While you can't hold it hostage if your tenant needs to get their mail, the mail-box key is a very useful tool in motivating a resident to promptly review and approve the inspection checklist.

✔ **Note the condition of every item in every room.** Indicate each item's condition — new, excellent, very good, dirty, scratched, broken, and so on — but also include details, such as writing "the built-in timer doesn't work" rather than just saying that the oven is "broken." That way your resident understands that the oven does in fact work and knows she won't be held responsible for this specific item upon move-out. If you comment only on dirty or damaged items, a court may conclude that you didn't inspect or forgot to record the condition of an item that you're now claiming that the resident damaged. You may think everyone knows and agrees that all items without any notation are in satisfactory condition, but the resident will likely tell the court that the item was at least some-what dirty or damaged and that you shouldn't be able to collect for it.

Always note the conditions of the carpets, floor coverings, window coverings, walls, and ceilings because they're often the most common areas of dispute with residents upon move-out. Although you shouldn't charge residents for ordinary wear and tear, they should pay for the damage if they destroy the carpet. Indicate the carpet's age and whether it's been professionally cleaned as part of your rental turnover process. When a resident leaves after only six months and has destroyed the carpet, you can guarantee she'll remember the carpet as old, dirty, and threadbare. The resident's selective memory won't recall that the carpet was actually brand new, or at least in very good condition, and professionally cleaned upon her move-in.

✔ **Note any items that need to be fixed.** If you discover any problems during your inspection walk-through, note them on the inspection form and take steps to have them corrected, unless the corrections aren't economically feasible. For example, you may have a hairline crack along the edge of the bathroom countertop. If you determine refinishing or replacing the countertop is too costly, just note the condition on the inspection form so that your resident isn't erroneously charged upon move-out.

Be sure your inspection checklist reflects any repairs or improvements made after the initial walk-through inspection. For example, if you and your resident note on the form that the bathroom door doesn't lock properly, you should then have that item repaired, necessitating an update to the inspection form to be initialed by your resident.

✔ **Note any and all mildew, mold, pest, or rodent problems.** These issues require immediate attention, because they make the property *uninhabitable* and give the resident the legal grounds to break the contract, seek a rent reduction, or even subject you to expensive penalties. See Chapter 12 for more about your obligation to maintain habitable residences.

✔ **Sign the inspection checklist and have your new resident sign it.** Without signatures, a court may not allow the inspection checklist as evidence.

✔ **Give your resident a copy of the completed and signed checklist for her records.** That way the resident can review her own copy when she moves out if there are charges.

Your resident may discover that an item doesn't work only after move-in when she tries to use it, so you need to be flexible. For example, the oven may have tested in working order, but when the resident initially used it, it doesn't properly heat. The showerhead may have tested well for temperature and pressure, but the resident finds both to fluctuate when put to normal use. Encourage your new resident to inform you within seven days or so if something's not working, so you can quickly address any issues that are your responsibility.

When properly completed and signed, an inspection checklist documents the resident's acceptance of the property's condition at move-in and serves as a baseline for the entire tenancy. If the resident withholds rent or tries to break the lease by claiming the unit needs substantial repairs, you can prove the unit's condition at move-in by referring to the checklist. And when the resident moves out, you're able to clearly note the items that were damaged or weren't left clean so that you can charge the maximum allowed under your state or local laws before returning the remainder of the security deposit.

Taking photos or a video

To avoid disputes over security deposits, record the rental unit's condition before the resident moves in using photos and/or video. In addition to your inspection checklist (see the next section), you'll have some visual evidence to help refresh the resident's memory or to show the court if the matter ends up there.

If you use a video camera, be sure to get the resident on video stating the date and time, if she's cooperative. If your resident isn't present, bring a copy of that day's newspaper and include it in your recording. With photography, be sure to include a caption or descriptions with all photos and provide a running, detailed narrative with the recording. If your camera has a date-stamp feature, enable it.

Orienting a new resident to appliances and utility shut-offs

When your resident moves in, don't assume she knows everything about the property. Take a few minutes after your walk-through with the resident to do the following:

✓ **Provide your resident with the appliance manuals or at least copies of the basic operating instructions.** These manuals get lost over the years, but many manufacturers have manuals online that you can download and print.

✓ **If you have natural gas appliances or gas heat, instruct your resident to contact the local utility company if she has any questions or concerns.** This step is particularly important if she detects the foul smell commonly associated with a gas leak or has any concerns or questions about proper operation of the appliances. The resident should also contact the utility company or your maintenance person if she needs to relight a pilot light.

✓ **Tell your resident where the utilities are and how to shut them off.** Utilities may need to be shut off because of severe weather, a water leak, an electrical short, or fire on the property. If you have a serious storm or earthquake, your resident needs to be able to immediately turn off the natural gas supply as well.

Providing an informational letter

The key to success in managing rental properties, avoiding lawsuits, and giving yourself legal leverage to enforce policies is to provide residents the information they need to govern their own behavior. Give all new residents either a resident handbook or a Resident Information Letter, such as the one in Figure 11-3, that outlines all of your policies and procedures that are too detailed to include in your rental contract.

Tenant Information Letter

Tenant Name(s) _____
Rental Unit Address _____

Dear _____,

We are very pleased that you have selected our property to be your home. We hope that you enjoy living here and would like to share some additional information that will explain what you can expect from us and what we will be asking from you:

1. Owner/Manager:

2. Rent Collection:

3. Notice to End Tenancy:

4. Security Deposits:

5. New or Departing Roommates:

6. Move-in/Move-out Inspection Checklist:

7. Maintenance and Repair Requests:

Figure 11-3:
Resident
Information
Letter.

Form courtesy of Robert S. Griswold

You can visit www.dummies.com/go/landlordlegalkit and click on the Move-in folder for a sample Resident Information Letter. You can also attach details on the proper operation and care of appliances, plus other important info your resident needs to know about the rental unit.

Customize your resident handbook or information letter to present the rules you've implemented for each rental property, as explained in the earlier section, "Establishing your policies and rules." Although this information should be customized for each property, here are some of the basic items to include

- ✔ Property manager name and contact number
- ✔ Procedures to follow in case of an emergency
- ✔ Rent collection information, including when rent is due, how and where payment is to be made, and how late fees and other charges are calculated and handled
- ✔ Requirements for ending the tenancy, including the notice requirement

✔ Procedures for the return of the security deposit

✔ Handling of new or departing roommates

✔ Proper procedures for requesting maintenance and repairs (include a service request form, as explained in Chapter 12)

✔ Reminder to check and test smoke and carbon monoxide detectors

✔ Reminder to immediately contact the landlord or the manager if water intrusion/leaks or any sign of mold/mildew is present

✔ Lockout procedure and fees (consider charging residents $20 for a lockout during reasonable hours, say Monday through Friday from 9 a.m. to 6 p.m., and $40 for a lockout during nonworking hours — nights and weekends)

✔ Charges for lost keys, entry cards, or gate or garage door openers

✔ Renter's insurance requirements

✔ Guest occupancy policy

✔ Annual interior unit inspection walk-through policy, if any

✔ Utility shut-off locations, including a separate diagram for the individual unit and information on how to shut off the utilities

✔ Essential appliance information, such as what not to place in a garbage disposal and how to keep refrigerator coils clean

✔ Trash collection and recycling program information

✔ Parking policies

✔ Property rules and policies

✔ Community association or homeowners' association rules and policies

Many residents misplace this information when they need it most during the tenancy, so many professional rental owners and property managers use the Internet to improve the efficiency of managing their properties. You can put the majority of this information online in an electronic resident handbook that you can update as necessary. The advent of social media has brought the option to landlords of having a website for multiple properties or even specific websites for each of their rental properties. You may be tech savvy yourself or you may turn to someone who can create an online presence for you in a very cost-effective manner. But be sure that you keep your content fresh and current.

Remember that having this information online may be efficient and handy, but it's not in lieu of giving your resident actual physical copies of all items upon move-in. You should also give your residents in writing any changes to the

resident handbook, and, as required by law, provide in writing any changes in legal terms or policies and rules and then get the signature of each person on the rental agreement to ensure they received the updated version.

Taking security measures with a unit

Dispensing the keys is a very serious issue that has significant liability for landlords and managers. Not securing the rental unit's extra keys can allow access to a resident's rental unit, potentially leading to theft or crimes involving serious bodily injury. If you fail to follow reasonable security measures or let keys fall into the wrong hands due to your carelessness, you could be held legally liable for any property loss, medical bills and other economic claims, such as pain and suffering or mental anguish. Master keys and duplicates require careful handling and should be stored only in a locked metal key cabinet or safe.

In addition, make sure doors, windows, and locks are in working order and up to the local industry standard. Include an entry lock set and a sturdy deadbolt with at least a $^{13}/_{16}$-inch throw on all solid-core, exterior entry doors. Provide peepholes on the main or primary exterior entry door as well.

Some states have laws specifically requiring rental property owners to provide window locks. Whether legally required or not, we recommend you provide locks for all windows that can be opened. Install window locks on upper-level windows as a safety device and as a way of minimizing the chance that young, unsupervised children may fall from an open window.

Changing the locks between residents is extremely important. Prior residents may have retained copies of the keys and may return to steal or commit some other crime. You can purchase and install an entirely new lock or have your maintenance person or a locksmith rekey the existing lock. If you have several rental units, substitute the existing lock set with a spare lock set. Keep several extra locksets in inventory so you can rotate locks between units upon turnover. Have your new resident sign a statement indicating she's aware that the locks have been changed or rekeyed since the prior resident vacated. Then give her a copy of the locksmith receipt for her records.

If you have a master key system for your rental properties, be extremely careful with it. Don't keep any extra copies or loan the master key to anyone whom you don't trust implicitly. Although locksmiths are required by law to have written authorization prior to duplicating a key marked "Do not duplicate," remember that an individual who wants a copy of your key to commit a crime isn't likely concerned about breaking the law by illegally copying the key.

Changing locks between residents: Why it's important

As the host of a live weekly radio show on real estate for more than 14 years, I (Robert) was often amazed at some of the stories I heard from callers. I'll never forget the call I received from a resident in a small multi-unit rental property who was shocked to find out that another resident had a key to his unit.

Apparently, one of the residents had loaned his key to a family member who got confused and inadvertently entered my caller's rental unit. When the caller confronted the landlord, he wasn't very concerned and didn't understand the resident's concern. He stated that he always used the same locks on all units so that he didn't have to carry around extra keys. Lesson: Make sure all your locks are uniquely keyed!

Keeping Detailed Resident Records

You need to be able to immediately access important written records, and one way of doing that is to have an organized filing system to ensure you don't waste time searching aimlessly for a lost or misplaced document. You should always keep the original signed documents in your files because you'll need them should you ever have to go to court. You can provide your resident with either copies, or you may want to have multiple sets of originally signed documents. The best way to accomplish this goal is to set up a new resident folder for each resident at the time of her move-in that includes the following:

- ✔ Resident contact and information form
- ✔ Rental application
- ✔ Rental application verification form
- ✔ Credit report
- ✔ Other reference information, including criminal background report, if any
- ✔ Holding deposit agreement and receipt, if applicable
- ✔ Signed rental contract
- ✔ Lead-based paint disclosure form
- ✔ Smoke detector agreement
- ✔ Any other addenda to the lease or rental agreement

✒ A move-in/move-out inspection checklist

✒ Photos or DVDs of the unit, taken at move-in

Set up a file folder for each of your rental properties with individual files for each resident. Turn to this file throughout the tenancy, adding to it all new documents such as rent increases, notices of entry, maintenance requests, and correspondence. Keep resident files for four years after the resident vacates. And remember that your resident's file contains personal information such as Social Security numbers, credit reports, and bank account numbers. With the concerns about identity theft, you want to always protect these files as if the information were your own and store the files in a locked cabinet. After four years, destroy old files properly — by shredding or burning them.

Choosing a Reliable Means of Communication

Communication is key in avoiding misunderstandings and disagreements with residents. Proof of your communication with residents is essential in defending yourself and pursuing your legal rights in court. So choose your means of communication wisely.

If you need to deliver an important notice to a resident, we recommend that you go old school — hand deliver the documents directly to your tenant's door. You should also send a copy using traditional mail to have it delivered with a return receipt requested slip, so you have proof that your notice was delivered. Keep a copy of the notice you sent along with your receipt from the post office to show the date and time you sent the notice. Personal service of all important notices, then also mailing with a return receipt requested slip, include the following:

✒ Late rent payment

✒ Lease termination

✒ Inspection/repair requiring entry to premises

✒ Warning of lease term violation

✒ Notice of right to reclaim abandoned property

✒ Change in rules and regulations

✒ Extension of lease

✒ Security deposit disposition

The legal acceptability of electronic notices

According to two laws, electronic communication is equivalent to printed communication in business transactions, including landlord-resident interactions:

✔ The Uniform Electronic Transactions Act (UETA) provides a legal framework for the acceptability of electronic signatures and records in government and business transactions. Forty-seven states, the District of Columbia, Puerto Rico, and the Virgin Islands have adopted the UETA. As of this writing, Illinois, New York, and Washington haven't adopted the UETA but have their own statutes governing electronic transactions.

✔ The Electronic Signatures in Global and National Commerce Act (ESIGN) is a federal law that allows the use of electronic signatures and records in interstate and foreign commerce.

Even though electronic communication and agreements are considered legally binding, we recommend that you continue to deliver printed notices by personal delivery or via traditional mail for any situations in which you need to establish a record of communication. Email and text messages tend to get lost or deleted over time, and residents may deny ever having received them.

For less important notices and communication, calling the resident on the telephone or sending an email or text message is sufficient. These less formal means of communication are suitable in the following situations:

✔ To remind a resident of the need to access the premises on a certain date and time when you already notified the resident in print

✔ To alert residents of criminal activity in the area that they need to be aware of

✔ To let residents know of any services that may be temporarily unavailable, such as a workout room being closed for renovations

✔ To remind them that their rent will increase per previously agreed lease escalation terms

When a new resident moves in, describe your preferred means of communication and ask the resident for her preferred means of informal communication. Some residents may prefer to receive text-message notifications, whereas others may not even have a mobile device or service that allows text messaging. Just make sure you can prove this communication took place.

Using phone calls or texts for less important communication is fine, but remember that if you ever need to prove you had specific conversation or text message exchange, then you'll need to have hard copies in writing to use in court. Therefore, we suggest that you send a letter or an email documenting the verbal or text communication and place a hard copy in the tenant file.

Part III

Recognizing Your Responsibilities and Liabilities

Crime and Drug-Free Housing Addendum

This document is an addendum and is part of the Lease or Rental Agreement, dated _____,

by and between _____, "Owner/Agent",

and _____ "Tenant",

for the Premises located at: _____.

In consideration of the execution or renewal of a lease of the Premises identified in the Lease or Rental Agreement, Management and Lessee agree as follows:

1. Lessee, any member of Lessee's household, or a guest or other person under the Lessee's control shall not engage in criminal activity, including drug-related criminal activity, on or near said Premises. "Drug-related criminal activity" means the illegal manufacture, sale, distribution, use, or possession with intent to manufacture, sell, distribute, or use a controlled substance (as defined in section 102 of the Controlled Substance Act (21 U.S.C. 802)).

2. Lessee, any member of Lessee's household, or a guest or other person under Lessee's control shall not engage in any act intended to facilitate criminal activity, including drug-related criminal activity, on or near said Premises.

3. Lessee or members of the household will not permit the Premises to be used for, or to facilitate criminal activity, including drug-related criminal activity, regardless of whether the individual engaging in such activity is a member of the household or a guest.

4. Lessee or members of the household will not engage in the manufacture, sale, or distribution of illegal drugs at any location, whether on or near said Premises or otherwise.

One of your primary legal obligations to residents is to provide them with habitable housing, ensuring all essential items are in good repair. To find out more about your duty to repair, visit www.dummies.com/extras/landlordlegalkit.

In this part . . .

✔ Fulfill your legal obligation to maintain habitable premises by performing regular maintenance and responding to resident requests for repairs.

✔ Recognize and correct safety issues to protect your residents and your property and reduce personal injury claims.

✔ Address the health risks posed by environmental hazards, including asbestos, lead paint, toxic mold, rodents, and bugs.

✔ Team up with local law enforcement to fight crime and limit your exposure to liability for crimes committed on your property.

✔ Know under what conditions you're allowed to enter a resident's unit, when you need permission, and when you must notify the resident.

✔ Resolve common problems with residents without having to take legal action.

Chapter 12

Repairing and Maintaining the Premises

....

In This Chapter

▶ Providing habitable dwellings

▶ Holding residents accountable for their legal obligations

▶ Making maintenance and repair top priorities

▶ Taking action when residents withhold rent over maintenance issues

▶ Watching your back when hiring contractors

....

*U*ntil the late 1960s, renters routinely signed leases that required them to do their own apartment repairs and maintenance. Landlords could lease units as-is, delivering only the physical space with no regard for the apartment's condition. In the absence of fraud or misrepresentation, residents had no recourse and were bound by the lease contract to pay rent, even if their landlords were in violation of state laws or local housing codes.

Beginning in the early 1970s, however, state legislatures started to take aggressive measures to remedy this problem by adopting laws requiring landlords to ensure the habitability of their residential rentals.

This chapter spells out your duties to provide and maintain the habitability of your residential rental properties, including your obligation to perform necessary repairs, and outlines the legal consequences for noncompliance.

Honoring Your Duty to Maintain Habitable Housing

When a landlord leases residential property to a renter, the implied warranty of *habitability* requires that the premises be *fit to live in*. The warranty is implied in every written or oral residential lease, and any lease provision that attempts to limit or waive the warranty is contrary to public policy and therefore void. During the term of the rental contract, the landlord must also perform routine maintenance work and make repairs that are necessary to maintain the apartment's habitability. However, you, the landlord, aren't responsible for repairing damage caused by the resident or the resident's guests, children, and/or pets.

In the following sections, we describe the factors that contribute to habitability, explore state and local codes, explain your obligation to prevent nuisances and protect children, and look at the potential penalties for noncompliance.

Defining habitable

A good way to define *habitable* and *fit* is to review the characteristics of a habitable apartment. Every state has its own list of baseline qualities that make a residential rental property habitable. Most of these lists include the following:

- Waterproofing and weather protection of roofs and exterior walls, including unbroken windows and doors

- Plumbing, gas facilities, and functional heating facilities that conform to applicable law in effect at the time of installation and that are in good working order

- Running water and reasonable amounts of hot water available at all times and connected to a sewage disposal system that meets code

- An electrical system, including lighting, wiring, and equipment, in good working order

- Common areas that are clean and sanitary and free from debris, filth, rubbish, garbage, rodents, and vermin

- Extermination in response to the infestation of rodents or vermin throughout residential premises

- Floors, stairways, railings, and adequate trash receptacles in good repair

- Compliance with all applicable building, housing, and health codes that would constitute conditions hazardous to a resident's life, health, or safety

In addition, residential rental property must have all of the following equipment:

- A working toilet, wash basin, and bathtub or shower. The toilet and bathtub/shower must be in a room that is ventilated and that allows for privacy.

- A kitchen with a sink that can't be made of an absorbent material (for example, wood).

✔ Natural lighting in every room through windows or skylights. Unless there is a ventilation fan, the windows must be able to open at least halfway.

✔ Safe fire or emergency exits leading to a street or hallway. Stairs, hallways, and exits must be kept litter free. Storage areas, garages, and basements must be kept free of combustible materials.

✔ Operable deadbolt locks on the main entry doors of rental units and operable locking or security devices on windows.

✔ Working smoke detectors in all units of multi-unit buildings, such as duplexes and apartment complexes. Apartment complexes also must have smoke detectors in common stairwells and carbon monoxide detectors in units with gas appliances or attached garages.

Every state has its own definition and list of what makes a residential rental property habitable, so you should read your state statute for details. Landlord.com has an excellent summary for each state along with links you can click to read the statute in its entirety. Check out the summaries at `www.landlord.com/state-habitability-statutes-by-state.htm`.

Not all defects in a property rise to the level of making a dwelling uninhabitable. Worn carpeting, leaky faucets, and peeling wallpaper are certainly repairs you and your resident want attended to, but they don't require urgent action, and they don't give residents the legal grounds to withhold rent payments or terminate the lease.

Adhering to local codes

You must also adhere to local building and health codes that impact the habitability of a property. Building and health codes cover a wide range of issues and may including the following:

✔ Number and placement of smoke detectors and carbon monoxide detectors

✔ Insect screen requirements for any opening that can be used for ventilation

✔ Amount of support required for upper floor decks

✔ Lot grading to prevent accumulation of stagnant water

✔ Hall and stairway lighting

✔ Storage beneath stairways (whether storage is allowed and if so under what conditions)

✔ Number of square feet of floor space required for each resident

We strongly encourage you to be familiar with the general requirements of your local building and health codes and be alert for any changes brought to your attention through your local NAA affiliate or IREM. Codes for existing buildings often require that the building comply with the codes at the time of construction, not with current building codes. Health and safety ordinances, on the other hand, tend to be susceptible to change.

Preventing and eliminating nuisances

The *covenant of quiet enjoyment* (see Chapter 9) is a promise to residents that you'll protect the residents' right to undisturbed use of the rental property. A *nuisance* is anything that a reasonable person would consider to be offensive or seriously annoying, in violation of the covenant of quiet enjoyment, including the following:

- ✔ Foul odors
- ✔ Intrusive neighbors (or landlords)
- ✔ Loud noise or music
- ✔ Solicitors
- ✔ Smoke, particularly tobacco and marijuana smoke
- ✔ Vibrations from nearby machinery

You have an obligation to your residents to prevent nuisances and eliminate any nuisances that you become aware of. If a resident informs you of a nuisance and you fail to take action to correct the situation, the resident may take legal action against the person causing the nuisance, against you, or against both of you. (See "Suffering the consequences of falling short," later in this chapter, for more about legal recourses a resident may pursue if you don't correct a nuisance situation.)

If a resident reports a nuisance or you become aware of it on your own, respond quickly by taking the following steps:

1. **Investigate the alleged nuisance to determine if you consider it annoying or offensive.**

   Any investigation or report from law enforcement or a impartial governmental agency or even a neutral tenant can also be helpful in understanding and documenting the nuisance.

2. **If the nuisance is between residents, encourage them to settle their differences themselves.**

   If they can, skip to the last step.

3. **If possible, contact the source of the nuisance in person, inform him about the problem, and instruct him on what to do to correct his actions or the situation.**

4. **If the nuisance continues, deliver a warning letter to the source of the nuisance informing him of the problem and letting him know the corrective action he must take immediately.**

   (See Chapter 17 for a sample letter of warning.)

5. **If the nuisance still continues, file for an injunction to make the person stop the action or correct the nuisance situation.**

   An *injunction* is a court order requiring an individual to take specific action to minimize the negative effect of his conduct on the plaintiff, up to and including an outright prohibition on the negative action. The courts use this extraordinary remedy in special cases when monetary damages can't compensate the violation of the plaintiff's property rights. The nuisance must be substantial and continuous. Failure to comply with a notice of an injunction is punishable by being held in contempt of court.

6. **If the injunction fails to have the desired effect, and a resident is the source of the nuisance, you may need to evict the resident, as we explain in Chapter 19.**

7. **Write a letter to the resident who complained of the nuisance thanking him for reporting it and informing them that you took appropriate action to eliminate the nuisance and the outcome.**

   Keep a copy for the resident files.

Dealing with smoking

Some states now include tobacco smoke in their statutes, defining it as a private nuisance. Utah, for example, defines secondhand smoke as a nuisance if it infiltrates any residential unit more than once a week for at least two consecutive weeks and interferes with the neighbor's "comfortable enjoyment of life or property." Unless the affected neighbor waives the right to sue for the smoking nuisance, he may sue the smoker directly and may also sue the landlord if the smoker is a renter. And in California, the state's Air Resources Board considers secondhand smoke to be a "toxic contaminant."

Secondhand smoke is increasingly a subject of nuisance complaints. Until recently, if apartment residents suffered from their neighbors' cigarette smoke, moving out was the only option. The situation is changing, however, and nonsmokers are beginning to exercise their legal rights. Take any complaints seriously or you could be named in a lawsuit.

To reduce public nuisance claims based on tobacco smoking, establish your rental property as a nonsmoking facility. Tobacco smokers aren't members of a protected class; that is, the Fair Housing Act doesn't prohibit discrimination against smokers, but focus on the activity rather than the person. You may even consider including your property's nonsmoking status in your advertising.

Distinguishing between three types of nuisance

In the eyes of the law, a nuisance can be either public, private, or attractive:

✔ **Public nuisance:** Something that offends or annoys the surrounding community or is likely to negatively affect the community's health, safety, comfort, or convenience. Examples of public nuisances include a manufacturing plant that produces a foul odor, prostitution, failure to obey leash laws, and blocking off streets or sidewalks.

✔ **Private nuisance:** Anything that interferes with an individual's right to the quiet enjoyment of his property, including property he's renting. Examples of private nuisances include loud noises, smoke or dust, foul odors, and vibration from nearby machinery.

✔ **Attractive nuisance:** A dangerous object, condition, or structure that's tempting for children. Examples of attractive nuisances include unsecured swimming pools or construction sites, abandoned vehicles, refrigerators left outside with the doors on, high-voltage power lines or equipment, and deep holes or trenches. (Technically speaking, an attractive nuisance is a type of private nuisance.) For more about attractive nuisances, see "Protecting children," later in this chapter.

Dealing with excessive noise on a state and local level

Regardless of whether your state or local municipality has specific noise ordinances, take seriously any complaints from residents about excessive noise. You're still responsible, as landlord, to help protect your residents' right to quiet enjoyment of their property. However, any noise ordinances give you and your residents more legal ammunition in the fight against excessively loud sounds.

California, New Jersey, and other states and local municipalities have taken action to fix the problem of excessive noise in residential areas, including apartment buildings. The California Noise Control Act recognizes that levels of noise can impact health and well-being. The Act, which became effective in 1973, gave cities and communities the power to establish noise ordinances and enforce them, in order to "prohibit unnecessary, annoying intrusive or dangerous noise." In response, city ordinances often restrict loud sounds that may be heard through common walls, ceilings, or floors.

Protecting children

Toddlers and young children seem to be captivated by dangerous things — electrical outlets, water, dials, things that heat and glow, ladders, large appliances, and even cavelike structures that many adults would find scary. Their tendency to put themselves in harm's way is the reason for *attractive nuisance laws*, which are intended to protect children from their own curiosity.

An *attractive nuisance* is an object, structure, or condition that's both dangerous and inviting or intriguing to youngsters. Attractive nuisance laws can hold apartment owners responsible if a child is injured by an *artificial condition* on the property and these five conditions are met:

- The owner knows, or ought to know, that children are likely to trespass on the property.

- The property's condition has the potential to cause death or serious bodily harm to children.

- The children involved are too young or inexperienced to understand the risk presented by the condition.

- The benefit of maintaining the condition or the cost of remedying the condition is minimal, compared to the risk to children.

- The owner fails to take reasonable measures to eliminate the danger posed by the condition.

Swimming pools, which are appealing and potentially dangerous to children, have been the focus of many attractive-nuisance lawsuits. Courts have held landowners liable even if the children clearly haven't been invited onto the property and the landlord had fenced the pool area but didn't securely gate it.

Even structures designed for children can be dangerous to them. Recent cases have involved skateboard ramps, trampolines, jungle gyms, play sets, and tree houses, which are considered to be classified as attractive nuisances, particularly if they're accessible to children younger or less experienced than their intended users. This means you need to be aware of the potential and unique health and safety factors presented by these features of your rental property. It doesn't mean you refuse or discourage prospective residents with children from living at your rental property, as such a practice could be construed as familial discrimination. Nor should you implement overly prohibitive age-related rules

Suffering the consequences of falling short

When landlords fail to maintain habitable and nuisance-free rental properties and fail to remedy serious issues raised by residents, several consequences may follow. However, for you to be held legally liable and for residents to have a right to take recourse, the following five conditions must be met:

- The issue makes the resident's premise uninhabitable or a significant threat to the resident's life, health, or safety.

- The resident notified you of the issue.

- Neither the resident nor the resident's guest, child, or pet caused the damage. (If one of them caused the damage, then the resident is responsible for fixing it or paying for it to be fixed.)

✔ The resident gave you or your agent access to the premises to perform the repair. Residents can't demand that you repair damages if they substantially interfere with your ability to perform the repair, such as preventing an electrician from entering the unit to fix faulty wiring.

✔ You failed to remedy the situation in a reasonable amount of time. (What's *reasonable* varies according to several factors, including how the residents are affected and the state and local statutes, but two to four weeks are typical. Of course, if the heating goes out in the middle of a frigid winter day, reasonable may mean immediate attention is required.)

Generally, residents have the legal right to take any of the following actions:

✔ **Withhold or escrow some or all rent until the repair is made.** In some areas, residents must obtain permission from the courts to withhold or escrow rent, and the amount withheld may be limited.

✔ **Hire an outside contractor to make the repair and deduct the costs from future rent payment(s).** Residents should only use qualified and licensed personnel plus provide copies of any bids or estimates and written proof of payment for a reasonable amount to complete the work.

✔ **Personally repair and deduct the repair costs from future rent payments.** Residents shouldn't attempt to do the work themselves (or a relative or friend) unless they're qualified and properly licensed, if required, to do the specific work needed.

✔ **Sue for damages from the date of the landlord's knowledge of the breach of the warranty of habitability.** The measure of damages is generally the difference between the value of the rented premises in its uninhabitable condition and its fair market rental value.

✔ **Sue to force the landlord to make repairs by obtaining a court order requiring the landlord to make the repairs.** Note, however, that courts are unlikely to use this option because it involves costly court supervision to ensure the repairs have been made. A variation of this remedy allows the landlord and resident to agree that the resident may repair the damage or hire a contractor to perform repairs and subtract the cost of repairs from future rent payments.

✔ **Move out and terminate the lease.** If the premises are truly uninhabitable, the resident has the right to move out temporarily or permanently based on the grounds of *constructive eviction* — by failing to provide residents with a habitable dwelling, you essentially evicted them, breaking the lease or rental agreement. Furthermore, the resident may sue for money damages for the landlord's breaking the lease and may also recover for emotional and physical stress and discomfort.

One of the rarely mentioned costs of a landlord's failure to provide habitable housing is a decline in occupancy. As residents move out in response to substandard living conditions, occupancy and revenue from rent payments drop. Keeping your rental units and common areas in good repair is a good business decision.

Residents in properties regulated by the New York City Housing Authority (NYCHA) may make a claim for breach of the warranty of habitability even if they fail to serve a notice of claim on the NYCHA before raising the claim, as long as they seek only a rent set off and not a money judgment. Residents who want a money judgment from the NYCHA must serve the city with a notice of claim for damages.

 If the failure to provide habitable living conditions violates state or local building or health codes and inspectors verify the violation, they may require you to fix the problem and pay additional fines or penalties.

Informing Residents of Their Legal Obligation to Maintain Their Units

As landlord, your repair and maintenance obligations ensure that your rental units and common areas are habitable and fully compliant with local codes. But legislators don't hold you solely responsible for the cost of maintaining your rental property and keeping it in good repair. Residents have duties to maintain their units and pay for any damage (beyond normal wear and tear) that they or their guests cause.

These sections explain resident responsibilities and expand on what you're allowed to do legally to recoup the cost you incur for repairing any damage a resident or one of his guests causes.

Knowing your residents' responsibilities

Residents are required by law to maintain the habitability of their apartments. They're required to take reasonable care of the rental unit and common areas and keep them in good condition. Residents must repair or pay for the repair of any damages that they or their guests, children, or pets cause.

Just as state statutes list landlords' responsibilities in maintaining a habitable rental property, they list resident responsibilities, which typically include the following:

✔ Comply with state and local building, health, and housing codes imposed upon residents.

✔ Keep the premises reasonably clean, safe, and sanitary as the condition of the unit permits.

- Use and operate gas, electrical, plumbing, sanitary, heating, ventilating, air conditioning, elevators, and other fixtures and facilities properly; for example:

    - Don't overload electrical outlets.

    - Don't flush large, foreign objects down the toilet.

    - Don't allow any gas or electrical appliance or plumbing fixture to become filthy.

- Dispose of trash and garbage in a clean and sanitary manner.

- Don't destroy, damage, or deface the premises, or allow anyone else to do so.

- Don't remove any part of the structure, dwelling unit, facilities, equipment or *appurtenances* (such as fences, signs, irrigation ditches, and rights of way) or allow anyone else to do so.

- Use the premises as a place to live and use the rooms for their intended purposes, such as using the bedroom as a bedroom and not as a kitchen.

- Notify the landlord when deadbolt locks and window locks and other security features aren't working.

- Notify the landlord when a condition arises that makes the premises uninhabitable or is likely to result in the premises becoming uninhabitable.

- Immediately alert the landlord if the smoke detector or carbon monoxide detector isn't operating properly.

Print out the list of resident responsibilities for your state and include them in the information packet you present to all new residents. Better yet, go over the list with them and ask whether they have any questions. (See Chapter 11 for more about moving in a new resident.)

Be careful about permitting residents to perform even minor repairs. Few residents are licensed carpenters, plumbers, or electricians. They may buy second- or third-rate fixtures to replace higher quality fixtures that came with the apartment. We recommend that you require all residents to inform you of any repair or maintenance issues and obtain your written approval before moving forward. This approach gives you oversight and input into how the repairs are performed.

Seeking damages when residents fall short

When residents fail to honor their legal duties in maintaining the premises, you have several options, depending on the rules and regulations in effect in your area:

✔ Send the resident a notice describing the problem and giving the resident a specific date by which the repairs or maintenance must be performed. (The number of days varies according to state and local statutes.)

✔ Perform the repairs or hire a contractor to perform the repairs and then present the resident with an itemized bill requesting payment by a specific date.

✔ Initiate eviction proceedings if the resident fails to perform repairs or compensate you for repairs you performed or paid for. (Refer to Chapter 19.)

Make sure your rental contract has a provision that holds residents responsible for any damages caused by negligence or misuse of the rental property by the resident or the resident's guests, children, or pets. Such a clause enables you to pursue remedies in small claims or general court proceedings.

Putting a Proactive and Responsive Maintenance and Repair System in Place

The single best (and perhaps only) way to limit your exposure to claims of failing to maintain habitable premises is to develop a *responsive maintenance and repair system* — a system that's proactive in keeping your property in tip-top condition and responds quickly and effectively to resident requests for repairs.

Implementing an effective system begins before a resident moves into an apartment. Carefully inspect the condition of the apartment, including the plumbing, electrical outlets and fixtures, heating and air conditioning, and each piece of equipment in the unit, including smoke and carbon monoxide detectors, the stove, refrigerator, icemaker, washer, and dryer, to ensure that everything is in proper working order. Use the move-in checklist provided in Chapter 11 to ensure a thorough inspection of the premises and everything in it. Correct any and all defects in the property to bring it up to move-in condition.

When your rental property, including common areas, is in good repair, keep it that way by setting up a proactive and responsive maintenance and repair program. In the following sections, we explain how to put together such a system.

Recognizing the benefits of a proactive and responsive system

Lousy landlords tend to see only the costs of maintenance and repairs. Successful landlords see the many benefits, which include the following:

- ✔ **Lower costs for preventive maintenance than for repairs:** Replacing a roof when it begins to show significant wear is less expensive than replacing it when it starts to leak and then having to replace drywall, carpeting, and flooring and compensating residents for their personal belongings damaged by the leak.

- ✔ **Higher occupancy:** Being responsive to your residents' needs enhances resident retention and your reputation among prospective renters. Higher and more stable occupancy saves you time and money in marketing and advertising and moving residents in and out.

- ✔ **Higher rent:** By providing top-quality residences and common areas, you can justify charging higher rent, and residents who recognize quality in product and service are usually willing to pay extra for it. (If a court decides that a residence you own is uninhabitable, it may order you to drop the rent as part of the judgment.)

- ✔ **Better clientele:** Better properties attract better clientele who are willing to pay more in rent and are more likely to take better care of their units.

- ✔ **Less exposure to risks of legal action:** By keeping your rental property in good repair and free of hazardous conditions, you limit your exposure to legal risks and other recourse residents may seek in several ways, including the following:

  - Proper maintenance and responsive repairs reduce threats to the life, health, and safety of residents, reducing the frequency of potentially costly accidents and other mishaps.

  - Residents have no or fewer legal grounds for withholding rent.

  - Positive relations with residents makes them more willing to resolve issues directly with you rather than hauling you into court.

  - In the event that a resident does file a claim against you, you have better grounds for your defense, especially if you keep impeccable maintenance and repair records. Being able to show a good track record as a landlord goes a long way in proving to a judge that you're not a slumlord. Even better is proof that you responded quickly and reasonably to the resident's request for repairs.

Maintenance costs and repairs are significantly less than the sticker price when you account for the tax deductions you can take for those costs. For every $100 worth of repairs, you may find yourself paying $70 or less after accounting for deductions.

Establishing a policy and setting goals

Base your maintenance and repair program on a policy of complying with applicable code requirements, ensuring the habitability of apartments throughout each resident's stay, and keeping your resident's happy (make customer satisfaction a top priority). At a minimum, set the following two goals:

- Maintain rental units and common areas to habitable standards as set forth in state statutes and local municipal health and building codes.

- Respond within a reasonable period of time consistent with the nature and urgency of the request.

Better yet, set specific, measurable goals, that exceed minimum requirements:

- Maintain properties in their best condition possible.

- Attend immediately to urgent issues that affect the habitability of a rental unit, including heating and air-conditioning failure, roof or plumbing leaks, locks that don't work, hazardous conditions, and inoperable smoke detectors, carbon monoxide detectors, and fire alarms.

- Respond within 48 business hours to any resident request for non-urgent maintenance or repair, such as fixing a leaky faucet or a torn screen. (State and local regulations may give you more time, but to keep your residents happy, we recommend responding within 48 hours.) If you can't complete the repair within 48 hours, let the resident know when to expect the repair and the reason for the delay. (See "Responding to residents' maintenance requests," later in this chapter, for details.)

- Inspect all rental units once a year and whenever a resident moves in or out if all applicable laws allow such entry. (Some states such as California, don't have laws that specifically allow a landlord to enter a rental unit on an annual or other periodic basis for purposes of an inspection to determine condition. Although federal housing subsidy programs do clearly require the landlord and the tenant to agree to an independent third-party inspection [usually by a local housing authority] on an annual basis as a requirement to receive the financial assistance.)

- Inspect all common areas every quarter unless an area requires more or less frequent inspections. For example, a pool may require daily maintenance in the summer and little or no maintenance for the rest of the year.

- Solicit resident feedback twice a year regarding any health or safety issues that need to be addressed.

Make sure that you and your workforce never make a promise that you can't or won't keep. Many landlords tend to fall into the "overpromise, under-deliver trap," which provides short-term satisfaction for their residents that is shattered when the promise, however reasonable it seems at the time, turns out actually to be, from the resident's perspective, a lie.

Conducting regular maintenance and repair inspections

We recommend that you inspect all rental units once a year and whenever a resident moves in or out, as explained in the previous section. You can use the move-in checklist from Chapter 11 to conduct these inspections.

In addition, inspect the exterior of all units and all common areas for any maintenance and repair issues, including the following:

- Roof wear or damage
- Significant cracks or raised sections in sidewalks or parking areas
- Loose or missing handrails in stairways
- Standing water that may develop into a health or safety hazard
- Lighting
- Fire alarms, fire extinguishers, and fire hoses
- Dangerous or hazardous conditions, such as sink holes, exposed electrical wiring, and abandoned cars or appliances

 Enlist residents in your efforts to properly maintain the property. Every six months during their tenancies, distribute a blank inspection form to your residents and ask that a resident in each unit complete the form and return it to you. (See the next section for a sample form.) Follow up to remedy any deficiencies they report. You may also want to post notices in common areas requesting that residents report any health or safety issues they notice, along with phone number to call.

Responding to residents' maintenance requests

Even with an aggressive maintenance and repair program, things break and wear out. To maintain resident satisfaction, you need a system that enables residents to submit maintenance requests and then respond to those requests effectively and in a timely manner.

Here we provide a maintenance request form that residents can use to submit requests for repairs, explain how to respond when you receive a request, and provide guidance on how to use feedback from residents to improve your maintenance and repair system.

Drafting a resident's maintenance request form

Making sure that your residents have plenty of opportunities to let you know about any maintenance and repair needs they discover during their tenancy is good business. Whenever possible, when you have contact with your residents, either orally or in writing, check to see if they have any repair requests.

When a resident moves in, provide the resident with a maintenance request form, such as the one shown in Figure 12-1, and make these forms available in your rental office and on your website (if you have a website). For a copy of the sample Maintenance Request Form, visit www.dummies.com/go/ landlordlegalkit and click on the Maintenance folder.

Make sure your Maintenance Request Form contains the following information:

- Date the maintenance request is being submitted

- Resident's name, address, and unit number

- Home, work, and/or cell phone number (you may also want to include a space for an email address)

- A description of the service requested

- The most convenient time for the resident to have the service performed

- Authorization to enter the premises if nobody's home (have the resident sign if possible, as some states require permission except in an emergency)

- Name of the person on your staff who received the request

- Indication that the work has been completed and by whom or that the work hasn't been completed, a reason why, whether professional assistance is required and why, and a date when the service will be completed

- Indication of whether the cost for the repair is to be charged to the resident

- The reason for the charge and the amount

- Any additional comments

- Place for you or the staff member who received the request to date and sign it

Resident's Maintenance Request

_____   Maintenance Request Number _____
Date

_____
Name

_____
Street address   Unit number, if any

_____
City/state/zip code

_____
Home phone   Work or alternate phone

_____
Email

Service Requested (Describe very specifically):
_____
_____
_____
_____
_____

Best time to perform service (Day and time):
_____

Authorization: Owner/Agent/Service personnel are authorized to enter rental unit if Resident is not present unless specific instructions have been given in advance to the contrary.

_____
Signature of Resident

If verbal approval received, given by:_____. Received by: _____

Report of action taken
____ Completed, by_____ (Upon completion- describe problem/work done/materials used)
_____
____ Unable to complete on _____, because _____
____ Outside professional assistance required, because _____
____ Will return to complete on _____
____ Resident has been notified of delay and agreed to allow repair on _____

Charge cost to Resident: ____ Yes   ____ No   If Yes, Reason _____
_____

Comments: _____
_____
_____

Received: _____   _____
             Date   Owner/Agent

Figure 12-1:
Sample
Mainte-
nance
Request
form.

Form courtesy of Robert S. Griswold

If you have a website, consider creating a maintenance request form that residents can complete and submit online for their convenience. Email is also an excellent way to receive and respond to your residents. Be sure to keep hard copies in the tenant's files as evidence to support you in case there is ever a claim that you failed to properly maintain the premises or respond in a timely manner.

Responding to maintenance requests

In the best of all possible worlds, landlords would respond immediately to maintenance requests, but such quick response isn't always realistic. We recommend responding to urgent matters immediately and to non-urgent matters within 48 business hours. If you can't perform the repair within 48 hours (for example, no contractor is available or you need to order a part), call the resident to let them know when he can expect the repair to be completed and the reason for the delay.

Follow up with a letter, such as the Notice of Intent to Enter Rental Unit shown in Figure 12-2, so you have documented proof that you kept the resident informed. For a copy of the sample Notice of Intent to Enter Rental Unit, visit www.dummies.com/go/landlordlegalkit and click on the Maintenance folder.

Notice of Intent to Enter Rental Unit

Date _____

Name _____

Street address _____

City/state/zip code

This notice is to inform all persons in the above Premises that on the _____ day of _____, 20 ___, beginning approximately between the hour of _____ am/pm and until _____ am/pm, the Owner, Owner's agent or Owner's employees or representatives, will enter the Premises for the following reason:

_____ To perform or arrange for the following repairs or improvements:
_____
_____
_____

_____ To show the premises to:

    _____ a prospective resident

    _____ a prospective or actual purchaser or lender

    _____ workers or contractors regarding the above repair or improvement

_____ Other: _____
_____
_____

Naturally, you are welcome to be present. Please notify us if you have any questions or if the date or times is inconvenient.

Sincerely,

_____
Owner/Manager

Figure 12-2:
Notice of
Intent to
Enter Rental
Unit.

Form courtesy of Robert S. Griswold

The importance of documenting repairs

Documentation of complaints is a necessary aspect of a good repair and maintenance program. Failure to ensure that site personnel strictly document these requests can have entirely unexpected consequences. Here's an example from my own experience:

Residents who were members of a minority class claimed that their management company responded to minorities' maintenance requests after all requests from non-minority residents were processed and completed. They brought a claim for damages against the management company for the delay and the alleged racial basis. At trial they offered testimony from other minorities who verified and actually documented his discrimination claim. Testimony from the principal of the defendant management company didn't dispute the argument. Indeed, the response was essentially this: "We actually don't know how we process work orders. We don't log them in or document when they've been handled. And we really can't testify about when any of the plaintiff's requests were handled. We try to handle them according to the seriousness of the problem. We're good at maintenance, though, and I'm sure we don't intend to discriminate." The jury, not surprisingly, found for the minority claimants and awarded them substantial money damages.

Using maintenance requests to perfect your system

Knowledge is power. Consider creating a database to log all maintenance requests, and then use the database to produce reports that shed light on areas that could use improvement. For each record in the database, you may want to include the following information:

- Date maintenance request received
- Date of service
- Resident name
- Resident address
- Resident apartment number
- Room where repair was needed
- Type of repair (plumbing, HVAC, smoke detector, and so on)
- Repair performed
- Repair cost
- Name of contractor or staff member who performed the repair
- Replacement fixtures, parts, or appliances
- Warranty expiration date for any new parts, fixtures, or appliances

A database gives you a wealth of information that you can easily search and use to improve your maintenance and repair system, defend against any claims of neglect, and even save costs. Here are examples of a few specific ways to use such a database to your benefit:

✔ Identify products, such as refrigerators or electric ranges that are prone to failure

✔ Quickly determine whether a part, fixture, or appliance is still under warranty

✔ Check to see whether your response time (the period of time between receiving a request and providing the requested service) is improving or getting worse

✔ Determine whether your repair costs are rising or falling

✔ See which contractors are best based on cost and how long comparable repairs last (whether contractors need to be called back)

Dealing with Residents Who Withhold Rent

Many states and some cities allow renters to withhold rent payments when their apartments are uninhabitable, conditioned upon their willingness to escrow their rent payments — that is, deposit the amount of the rent with a court, housing authority, or other neutral third party, until the apartment is returned to a habitable condition.

If a resident withholds rent, you have several options depending on whether the area in which you operate allows rent withholding and whether the resident has valid legal grounds for withholding rent (see "Suffering the consequences of falling short," earlier in this chapter for conditions that may justify rent withholding):

✔ If the resident has good reason to withhold the rent, fix the problem and inform the resident that the problem has been fixed. If you can't make the resident's rental unit habitable in a reasonable amount of time, consider offering to move the resident into another unit until repairs can be made.

Although some claims may seem frivolous or appear to be attempts to avoid paying rent, try to resolve the claim informally, either personally or through mediation or arbitration, in order to avoid the added costs of legal proceedings and additional damages the court may decide to award the resident. Refer to Chapter 17 for more assistance, including more information about how mediation and arbitration work.

✔ If state and local statutes don't specifically allow rent withholding, inform the resident that withholding the rent is illegal. Try to work out a mutually beneficial solution that meets your needs and the needs of your resident. If you can't reach an agreement and the resident continues to withhold rent, you can evict him for breach of the lease or rental agreement.

✔ If the resident withholds rent because of your failure to repair damages caused by the resident or his children, guests, or pets, inform the resident of his legal obligations to maintain the property. Give him a list of obligations from the state's statutes and then allow him a reasonable amount of time to repair the damage and resume payments. (You may offer to make the repairs and charge the cost to the resident.) If he continues to withhold rent, you may need to initiate eviction proceedings, as explained in Chapter 19.

✔ If the resident withholds rent even though he hasn't met the conditions that legally justify rent withholding, inform him of his rights and obligations under the law. For example, if the resident didn't notify you of certain damage or didn't allow a reasonable time to complete the repairs, let him know that you weren't given a reasonable opportunity to fix the problem and that he must continue to pay rent. Let the resident know that you will complete the repairs as soon as possible and within the period of time allowed by law (or sooner).

If you're in the wrong, as a gesture of good faith, you may want to consider accepting reduced rent payments for any months that the property was uninhabitable or substandard. If the courts became involved, they may order such a rent reduction.

Keep a paper trail. Note dates and times of conversations (in person or over the phone) you had with the residents, copies of any email or text messages, and copies of any written correspondence. If you reach an agreement with the tenant, put it in writing, sign it, and have the resident sign it. Place all documentation in the resident's file.

Exploring Contractor-Related Legal Issues

Although you may perform most maintenance and repairs yourself or have maintenance personnel to handle most of these duties for you, some maintenance and repairs require the expertise of a licensed contractor, such as an electrician or plumber. Whenever you hire someone to work for you, you're taking on a legal risk. The contractor may sue you for anything from nonpayment to unsafe conditions that resulted in a costly accident. Before hiring a contractor, know the legal risks and take steps to minimize those risks, as we explain in the following sections.

Hiring licensed, bonded, and insured contractors

Whenever you need an outside contractor to perform maintenance or repairs or to install products, make sure that your contractor is licensed (if your state or municipality licenses contractors) and is bonded and insured:

✔ **Licensed:** A *licensed* contractor has training in the field and usually must prove a certain level of expertise to a state licensing board. In many states, in order to be licensed, a contractor must also be bonded and insured. Most, but not all, states and many local municipalities require that building contractors be licensed. If you operate in a state that licenses building contractors, you can find a link to your state's licensing board(s) at www. nascla.org/licensing_information.

✔ **Bonded:** A *bonded* contractor's work is guaranteed by a third party (the issuer of the bond). If the contractor fails to perform the work, performs substandard work, fails to obtain a required building permit, fails to pay subcontractors, or conducts other behavior that could potentially make you liable for the costs, you can file a claim with the bond issuer for compensation. To find out whether a contractor is bonded, asked for the name and contact information for the bond issuer and the contractor's bond number. Call the bond issuer to verify that the contractor is bonded and to make sure the bond amount is sufficient for covering the cost of the project.

✔ **Insured:** Contractor insurance shifts the costs of any accidents to the contractor's insurance company instead of making you or your insurance company responsible. To ensure that the contractor has the proper insurance:

- Have the contractor add you as an *additional insured* to his general liability policy.

- Ask to see the contractor's current certificate of insurance and then contact the insurance company to verify and to check whether the contractor will have adequate general liability coverage for the complexity and riskiness of the work involved.

- Make sure that the written contract that you execute with the contractor specifically requires that the contractor has sufficient general liability insurance in effect at the inception of the work and throughout its duration, and that the contractor's insurance is primary in the event of a claim.

Be aware of e-cigarettes

Electronic or e-cigarettes are relatively new, but they're already an evolving alternative to tobacco cigarettes. Because they're so new, researchers don't know much how e-cigarettes affect the user's health or the risk of second-hand exposure to the vapor. (E-cigarettes are also called *electronic nicotine delivery systems (ENDS) or personal vaporizers.*)

Some jurisdictions, such as New York City, have passed laws banning them indoors. We expect much more legislation on them in the future. As a landlord, you may want to simply regulate e-cigs the same way as tobacco cigarettes, but you also need to be aware of this issue and implement policies and rules that comply with the evolving laws and regulations.

Insuring uninsured workers

Damages and injuries are, unfortunately, fairly common in the rental housing industry, particularly when site personnel do the work, simply because common repairs and maintenance occur frequently. Make sure that you have sufficient general liability and worker's compensation insurance to cover the cost of potential instances of accidents, injuries, and negligence claims. These policies protect against payments as the result of bodily injury, property damage, medical expenses, libel, slander, the cost of defending lawsuits, and settlement bonds or judgments required during an appeal procedure.

Consult with your insurance professional, but remember that worker's compensation coverage is important even if you don't have employees because most state laws make you as the property owner responsible should the contractor you hire not have coverage or their coverage is insufficient.

Getting warranties to cover the work

Another inevitability in the apartment business is the fact that, even when landlords get background information and recommendations about contractors, sometimes the work is substandard. Reputable contractors, plumbers, and electricians provide ironclad warranties for service and will return to the property to fix any problems that arise, and do the work for free within a reasonable time, usually one year after the work was completed.

Nonetheless, getting a warranty for contracted work that covers both material defects and coverage against workmanship errors is good practice. Contractors must be willing to be held liable for all the work they do, including the materials they use, excluding any materials supplied by you, the landlord.

If a contractor is bonded, you have additional protection against substandard or incomplete work. (See the earlier section, "Hiring licensed, bonded, and insured contractors," for details.)

Chapter 13

Minimizing Injuries from Potentially Dangerous Conditions

In This Chapter

▶ Taking preventive measures to help residents avoid accidents and injuries

▶ Conducting a safety assessment of your rental property

▶ Recognizing the high costs of noncompliance

As a rental property owner, you have a legal duty to keep rental units and common areas in a reasonably safe condition. Of course, you must adhere to all state and local building, safety, and health codes, as Chapter 12 explains, but you should take additional safety measures to minimize the likelihood of accidents and injuries.

This chapter describes preventive measures you can take to protect your residents' safety, explains how to keep on top of safety issues by conducting regular safety inspections and encouraging residents to promptly report potential and actual safety issues, and helps you evaluate your legal liability for keeping rental units and common areas in safe condition.

Preventing Injuries in Rental Units and Common Areas

Though you can't guarantee and be responsible for ensuring your residents' safety, you need to make sure that the rental units and common areas are reasonably safe for their intended use at the time your resident moves in and throughout the tenancy. (A reasonable person would arrive at the conclusion of what is reasonable.) The following sections highlight products and tactics you can use to keep your rental unit safe for its residents.

Using materials safer than standard glass

Rental units typically contain shower enclosures and windows made of glass or another transparent material. Units may also have entryway doors, sliding patio doors, or even closet doors made entirely or partially of glass or a glass-like material.

Whenever you replace shower doors, sliding glass doors, glass entry doors, glass closet doors, or any window in the kitchen or bathroom, we strongly encourage you to make sure your supplier and/or installer provides you with a safer alternative to standard glass, such as one of the following options:

- ✔ **Tempered glass:** Tempered glass is a type of safety glass that's four to five times stronger than standard glass and is manufactured by a special process so that when it breaks, it crumbles into small, granular pieces with relatively smooth edges. All new glass shower enclosures and doors are made of tempered glass. Shelves inside refrigerators are also typically made of tempered glass.

  Tempered glass is often required by code, but even if it isn't, the cost isn't much more but the safety factor is significantly improved. You may want to make this a standard part of the scope of your improvements when you look to renovate or upgrade your rental unit.

  Tempered glass is often labeled with a small decal in the corner, but not always. If you're unsure, consult with a professional glass installer or general contractor who's knowledgeable about glass.

- ✔ **Laminated glass:** Laminated glass consists of two panels of tempered glass held together by a vinyl layer between them. When the glass breaks, it crumbles into granular pieces that stick to vinyl instead of flying out all over the place.

- ✔ **Acrylic:** Acrylic (often marketed as Plexiglas, Lucite, Acrylite, and other brand names) is a clear or translucent plastic that's much lighter than glass and tends not to shatter when broken. Even if the acrylic does shatter, the shards aren't as likely as glass to cause cuts.

On the other hand, standard (nontempered) glass is hazardous in two ways:

- ✔ **Standard glass isn't very strong.** Any moderate force can break through standard glass of a standard thickness, including the force of a baseball or golf ball, a hand, or a head.

- ✔ **When standard glass breaks, it splinters into dangerous, jagged shards.** Broken glass is a common source of serious cuts.

As long as your property's glass windows and doors are in good condition, you're not required to replace them because they're grandfathered in under the building code that was in effect at the time the property was constructed. However, you should be aware of this safety issue.

If you have furnished rental units, don't purchase or rent any furniture containing nontempered glass. Most major national furniture rental companies don't even offer products with nontempered glass, but some low-end suppliers still import products with nontempered glass, which can be very dangerous when used in a rental property.

Using safe cords (or no cords) for window coverings

Another way that you can prevent injury and even death in your rental units is to utilize miniblinds, vertical blinds, and shades with safe cords or no cords.

The Consumer Product Safety Commission (CPSC) has identified window coverings with cords as one of the top five hidden hazards in homes. An estimated 1 billion (yes, *billion*) miniblinds, vertical blinds, or shades are in use in the United States, and children ranging from 7 months to 10 years old have suffered strangulation deaths or injuries when the window covering cord became wrapped around their necks. These cords also pose a danger to pets.

Here are some options you may want to consider for protecting residents' children and pets:

- ✔ Warn residents of the risk and inform them of actions they can take to prevent accidents to children and pets.

- ✔ Replace unsafe corded window coverings with safer corded coverings or with no-cord options immediately or whenever you need to replace the window coverings for other reasons. (You're under no legal obligation to replace window coverings, but safer options prevent accidents and lawsuits.)

  If a resident requests that corded window coverings be removed from the rental property, replace the window coverings at your cost or share the cost with the resident. You may let residents install their own window coverings at their expense.

- ✔ Take other methods to secure the cords, so they're less accessible to young children and pets. These methods are often included in the packaging with new window coverings and should be installed if they're available. Or, if you have older window coverings already installed, you can purchase cord cleats and spring tension devices that help secure the cords and reduce the risk.

For more information on window cord safety, including free retrofit kits for many corded window covering products, go to the Window Covering Safety Council website at www.windowcoverings.org.

Securing swimming pools, spas, and hot tubs

Among the most desirable amenities for a rental home or multi-unit apartment community are swimming pools, spas, and hot tubs. But these amenities can create safety problems for landlords and property managers. Be sure to check your local building code requirements regarding enclosure fencing, pool covers, pool alarms, and self-closing gates that can minimize accessibility risks by children or others who shouldn't be unattended near or in any of these amenities.

State and local health departments and similar agencies also have strict guidelines about additional required safety equipment, plus proper water maintenance and testing/reporting procedures that you need to follow and document. You also need to post the required signage and provide rules or lease clauses that remind your residents about the unique dangers associated with these amenities. These dangers include the need for constant adult supervision and safe practices, such as no glass and no running or diving. Of course, the most secure fence, gate, or additional safety feature won't protect a child (or anyone who can't swim) if the person is left unattended inside a pool or spa enclosure.

Being in compliance with the Virginia Graeme Baker Pool and Spa Safety Act

The seven-year-old granddaughter of former Secretary of State James Baker III, Virginia Graeme Baker, tragically drowned in a swimming pool in 2002 when she was trapped underwater by the suction of a spa drain despite the efforts of two adults to rescue her.

The federal act named after her requires that, effective December 19, 2008, all swimming pool and spa drain covers available for purchase in the United States meet specific performance standards that prevent this type of tragedy. Furthermore, public swimming pools, wading pools, spas, and hot tubs must meet these requirements as well.

A multifamily apartment building would be considered a public facility, while a single-family rental home likely wouldn't, because private pools, spas, and hot tubs built before the effective date aren't required to comply with this federal law. Nonetheless, we strongly urge all landlords and property managers to immediately contact a professional pool/spa maintenance company and verify that all their swimming pools, wading pools, spas, and hot tubs fully comply. This company can also advise as to any state or local requirements about pools, including the regular safety checks of all systems and drains.

In addition to fencing and adult supervision, many jurisdictions require additional safety measures, including pool/spa safety nets or covers, self-closing gates or sliding glass doors, pool/spa water alarms, gate alarms, and door alarms for all doors from the rental units or common area facilities that have direct access to the swimming pool.

Ensuring security of construction sites

When you hire a contractor, the contractor is supposed to secure the construction site, but as the property owner, you could become the target of a lawsuit for any injuries that your residents suffer due to contractor neglect, a resident's carelessness, or a combination of the two. To protect yourself, supervise your contractor. On the construction site make sure the contractor and construction workers take these precautions:

- ✔ **Fence off and clearly mark any hazardous construction areas.** Deep holes, stacks of wood, bricks, or other building supplies, unattended power tools or heavy machinery, hazardous materials, and other conditions can pose a risk to children.

- ✔ **Make sure nothing can fall outside the construction area.** Be especially careful when working on scaffolding, or on ladders, or on a roof.

- ✔ **Cordon off any areas where delivery trucks or site vehicles travel to or from the site.** The construction company may need to secure entrances and exits so as not to inconvenience residents.

- ✔ **Erect barriers around or cover any holes that someone could fall into.** You may also need to barricade stairwells to prevent anyone from climbing the stairs and falling from an area under construction.

- ✔ **Keep a close eye on the worksite and any tools or other equipment.** Fences aren't always effective in keeping people out, especially children.

- ✔ **Lock up or remove any potentially dangerous tools or machinery when the site is left unattended.** This includes any power cords, hoses, or supply lines generators, and air compressors.

Warn all residents in writing, not giving any special attention to those who have children, whenever you're planning a construction project that may require their increased vigilance.

Improving exterior lighting

Exterior lighting is required to improve security on your rental property, as we explain in Chapter 15, but lighting is also important for making your property reasonably safe to prevent injuries. A poorly lit parking lot could prevent a motorist from seeing one of your residents walking across the parking lot. A dimly lit stairwell increases the risk that a resident will trip and fall. To improve exterior lighting, take the following measures:

- ✔ Replace any burned-out bulbs immediately.

- ✔ Regularly inspect the lighting in walkways, stairwells, entryways, and parking areas, and install additional external light fixtures, where needed.

- ✔ Encourage residents to let you know of any areas they think require additional lighting, and attend to any issues they call to your attention.

Preventing injuries from pets

As we explain Chapter 11, we don't recommend a no-pets policy, because it will negatively impact your marketing success. However, we do recommend that you have a policy that prohibits certain animals and allows others on the condition that the resident follow certain rules and the animal behaves itself. You may be held liable for any injury caused by an animal on your rental property if you knew that the animal posed a danger to residents and their guests and failed to take reasonable precautions to prevent injury.

To prevent injuries from pets, we recommend that you take the following measures:

- ✔ Require in your rental contract that residents obtain your approval before bringing any new pets or other animals into their rental unit or common areas.

- ✔ Permit only appropriate domestic pets, such as dogs, cats, hamsters, guinea pigs, gerbils, fish, and certain birds that may be suitable for an urban setting. Farm animals may be allowed in rural settings.

- ✔ Specify a size limit based on the expected adult size of the animal. Limiting animals to 30 or 40 pounds can keep out many of the most dangerous animals.

- ✔ Remember that assistive animals for the disabled aren't considered pets and aren't controlled by pet restrictions. However, you may require that the exceptions to the rules be reasonable on a case-by-case basis.

Focusing on fire safety

Fire safety is a critical issue for rental owners. Fire can spread quickly and fully engulf an entire room, rental unit, or home in a matter of minutes. Fire also produces poisonous gases and smoke that are disorienting and deadly.

Fire inspections are conducted regularly in most areas; when your property is inspected, you will receive written notification of any deficiencies. You must remedy these items immediately, and you must contact the appropriate officials in writing to acknowledge that you've corrected the items and to request a follow-up inspection. Be sure to obtain written confirmation that all items have been satisfactorily corrected.

In the following sections, we provide additional guidance on how to prevent fires and reduce fire damage, injuries, and fatalities.

Addressing fire hazards

The best way to ensure fire safety is to prevent fires from occurring in the first place. Educate residents about major fire hazards in the home and encourage them to follow recommended safety precautions. Here are the top five home fire hazards:

- ✔ Cooking-related fires, including leaving a stove unattended, allowing grease to build up in ovens or on stovetops, using a stove or oven to heat the premises, or getting flammable items too close to burners

- ✔ Heating-related fires, including placing flammable items (furniture, bedding, towels, or window covers) on or too close to baseboard or portable heaters, using an extension cord with a portable heater, or leaving a fireplace fire unattended

- ✔ Smoking and related hazards, such as leaving lighters or matches within a child's reach

- ✔ Burning candles or halogen lamps

- ✔ Outdoor grilling on patios, on balconies, or too close to the building

Ask your local fire department for any educational materials you can distribute to residents about fire hazards and provide tips to prevent fires. Your insurance carrier may also conduct inspections and provide lists of safety issues or suggestions.

Providing and maintaining fire extinguishers

In some areas, rental owners are required by law to provide fire extinguishers and to properly inspect and service or recharge them upon resident turnover. A multipurpose dry chemical fire extinguisher can be a valuable and effective tool to quickly extinguish a small fire. If not required by law, evaluate your potential liability if the fire extinguisher is defective, used improperly, or unsuitably maintained. If someone gets hurt because the fire extinguisher you provided wasn't working properly when she needed it, you can be held liable. Fortunately, local fire departments are often willing to offer your residents instruction on the proper use of extinguishers.

Installing and maintaining smoke detectors

Fires are always serious, but the most dangerous ones are those that start while the residents are asleep, which is a primary reason that all states require rental owners to install smoke detectors in all rental units. We strongly recommend installing smoke detectors in or near kitchens, in or near all rental unit hallways and exit routes or preferably just inside and in all sleeping areas in compliance with applicable local building or fire codes and the alarm manufacturer's specifications. If you don't know your local requirements, contact your local fire department or building inspection agency for the exact specifications.

Always inspect and test the smoke detector according to the manufacturer's instructions upon resident turnover. If a fire hurts a resident because the smoke detector wasn't working properly when she moved in, she can sue you. So be sure to keep written records of your inspection and testing of the smoke detector and have your resident initial her rental contract or Smoke Detector Agreement (check out Chapter 11 for more on this document) indicating that the smoke detector was tested in her presence and that she can perform her own tests.

Address all resident requests for smoke detector inspections and repairs. Note such requests in your maintenance log, along with the date that the smoke detector was repaired or replaced. If the resident is present, have her sign to acknowledge that the smoke detector now works properly. Smoke detector complaints are always a top priority requiring immediate attention, so keep new smoke detectors on hand. Some states or local government entities are phasing in requirements for smoke detectors that have a ten-year, nonremovable battery, so check with your local fire department to see if there are plans to institute such changes.

Giving residents a fire evacuation plan

Work with your local fire department to develop an evacuation plan for your property. See if you can get written permission from residents to provide written notification to authorities of any rental units occupied by residents with children or others who may require assistance in an emergency, or suggest to residents that they notify the authorities themselves. You want to provide written instructions to all residents on evacuation plans and encourage them to develop their own evacuation plan, along with a place where family members or roommates should meet after evacuating the building.

Preparing for natural disasters

Every region in the United States experiences its own set of challenges from Mother Nature, so make sure that you and your residents are prepared for whatever natural disaster may be possible at your property. Every state and many local jurisdictions have emergency preparedness offices that can provide information and tips to help you and your residents take the appropriate steps now, before an emergency happens. You can find contact information for these offices in your local telephone directory.

The Federal Emergency Management Agency (FEMA) has useful resources available online to identify and assess your risk for hazards that can affect you. Its website (www.fema.gov) even has a Hazard Information and Awareness section that allows you to see exactly what natural disasters or hazards have previously occurred in your area.

In many parts of the country, snow and ice accumulation can create dangerous conditions. Many states and local municipalities have laws requiring owners to remove snow and ice from walkways or driveways; others don't. Regardless of the legal requirements, we recommend that you clear stairways, walkways, and driveways promptly.

Identifying Potentially Dangerous Conditions

You can't address safety hazards unless you know about them. In the following sections, we explain two ways to identify potentially dangerous conditions: by having residents notify you of any safety concerns and by conducting regular safety inspections.

Encouraging residents to report safety concerns

Your residents may notice a safety hazard before you do, so encourage them to report any potential or actual safety concerns immediately. Consider posting a sign in common areas that includes an email address and a phone number to call. You may also want to remind residents every six months by sending them a form they can complete and submit to report any health or safety concerns they notice.

You can't monitor your rental property 24/7, so enlist the help of your residents, respond promptly to any concerns they raise, and thank them for helping you keep your property reasonably safe. By expressing your dedication to resident safety, you're likely to improve your retention rate in addition to preventing costly accidents and lawsuits.

Conducting regular safety inspections

Don't rely solely on residents to report safety issues they notice. If there is no legal prohibition against it, be proactive by conducting regular safety inspections, as we explain here.

Inspecting rental units

Whenever a resident moves out, inspect the property for any of the following signs of a potential safety hazard:

- Blackened, scorched, or loose outlets or light fixtures, which may indicate an electrical problem
- Damaged carpet or uneven floors that could trip residents
- Loose stairs or handrails
- Smoke detectors and carbon monoxide detectors that don't work
- Fire extinguishers that have lost their charge
- Extinguished pilot lights in gas appliances, including furnace, water heater, and gas range
- Broken glass or loose materials that could cause cuts, punctures, or other injuries
- Overly hot water that could scald residents, especially children, the disabled, and older adults
- Standard outlets in bathrooms and around the kitchen sink that really should have ground fault interrupters to protect against electric shock

We reiterate: Enlist the support of residents in keeping your rental property safe. Encourage them to notify you immediately of any safety issues that arise within their rental units or anywhere on the property.

Inspecting common areas

At least annually, inspect your property to identify potential safety issues. Here are some areas to focus on:

- Inadequate lighting or burned-out lights
- Sick, dying, or damaged trees or tree limbs or limbs close to power lines
- Stairwells and railings (check all railings to see whether they're loose)
- Uneven pavement or sidewalks due to cracks, expansion, or settling
- Deep holes or depressions in the ground

- Fences and gates, especially around any swimming pool, spa, or hot tub

- Cracked tiles or other defects around the pool, spa, or hot tub

- Flammable materials, such as boxes or stacks of newspapers on patios or on or under stairs

- Windows without insect screens, window locks, or other devices to prevent someone from coming in

- Decks or patios pulling away from the building

- Smoke alarms, fire alarms, fire extinguishers, or fire hoses, if any

- Smell of natural gas, which may indicate a gas leak

- Breaker boxes for any burned or scorched surfaces that may indicate electrical problems

- Exposed wires that may cause electric shock or electrocution

Evaluating Your Legal Liability

You have an obligation to protect anyone who enters the property legally, including residents, their visitors, and tradespeople, against an unreasonable risk of injury because of the design, construction, or condition of the property. The reason: You, the landlord, and possibly your property manager, have control of the property, whereas others on the premises don't. Currently, principles of negligence tend to hold landlords liable for damages when the landlord's failure to use reasonable care results in risk of harm to others.

In the following sections, we describe several things you can do or not do that may make you legally liable for damages or personal injuries that occur at your rental property and make you aware of the damages you may be ordered to pay if you're found liable.

Knowing when you're liable

When someone files a claim against a landlord for injuries, the courts look at the actions the landlord did or failed to do that allegedly caused the injuries. Courts often look for four things to determine whether and to what degree the landlord's actions or inaction contributed to the damages suffered by the injured party.

Negligence

You, as the landlord, are considered to be legally negligent if they, or their agents (for example, property managers) fail to complete timely repairs, conduct routine inspections, or perform necessary maintenance work. Although state negligence laws affecting landlords vary, landlords are generally held liable for negligence if they willfully fail to maintain the property in a habitable condition by performing basic maintenance or correcting dangerous conditions they knew or should have known would create a risk of injury to their residents and visitors. (For more about your liability to maintain habitability, see Chapter 12.)

A landlord's failure to regularly inspect equipment such as electrical units and water heaters as required by law is obviously negligent. Bottom line: You're responsible for upkeep of your properties and maintaining they're in a safe, function condition or risk liability for negligence.

Failure to maintain or repair

The legal principle of premises liability means that certain areas of a multi-family property, such as common hallways and stairs, are considered to be under the control of the landlord. Equally important, you'll be held liable absent such a duty to repair if you negligently make repairs that turn out to be dangerous.

Slip and fall is a good example of premises liability. The term is shorthand for a personal injury case in which a person slips or trips and falls, and is injured on someone else's property. If these cases occur on a rental premises, the property's landlord can be held legally responsible if there was a dangerous condition that wasn't addressed properly in a timely manner.

Premises liability cases are based on claims of dangerous conditions such as torn carpeting, poor lighting, narrow, uneven, or slippery stairs, or a wet floor inside an apartment building that can cause someone to slip and suffer injury from the fall. Other causes of slip and fall injuries are broken or uneven public walkways or rain, ice, snow, or hidden hazards, such as a pothole in the parking lot. You may be liable for damages when victims sustain injury as the result of the slip and fall.

Plaintiffs injured in a slip and fall must prove the following:

- ✔ The cause of the accident was a dangerous condition.
- ✔ The landlord had control over the dangerous condition.
- ✔ The landlord knew, or should have known, that the dangerous condition existed and negligently failed to correct it.
- ✔ The dangerous condition presented an unreasonable risk to someone on the property.
- ✔ The condition existed for a sufficient amount of time that the landlord should have corrected it.
- ✔ The condition must have been something that the injured party shouldn't have anticipated, a requirement implying that people can't be expected to avoid dangers unless they're aware of those dangers.

Violation of a health, safety, or building code

You, the landlord, can be sued for negligence for violating a statute or a building code intended to protect residents' health or safety. For example, building codes often specify locations where handrails and other similar features must be installed. If a resident or a visitor falls on a stairway without required handrails, and the lack of the handrail caused the injuries, the landlord may be held responsible for damages as a result of the violation.

Reckless or intentional acts

Landlords can be held liable for reckless or intentional acts:

- *Reckless* means extremely careless behavior regarding an obvious problem. An example of a landlord's recklessness is failure to correct a dangerous defect, such as a malfunction in the property's electrical system that has existed for several months and eventually causes extensive fire damage to several apartments.
- *Intentional* means action taken deliberately to cause harm to a person; for example, an apartment manager who verbally abuses a resident, leading to mental suffering, medical bills, and lost wages. Intentionally harmful acts in the rental industry are infrequent, but they do occur.

Damages for these extreme kinds of conduct are often substantial and may include punitive damages, as the nearby sidebar defines.

Considering potential damages

Money damages are most often assessed against landlords because of successful claims of negligence, which typically involves landlords' failure to maintain habitable conditions for their residents or failure to perform necessary maintenance or correct dangerous conditions that pose injury risks.

Avoiding the sting of punitive damages

Punitive damages are judgments in excess of the amount of money required to compensate the victim for actual damages, such as medical bills and lost wages. Courts may award punitive damages to victims of reckless or intentional acts in order to punish the landlord and send a strong message to other landlords that such behavior won't be tolerated.

In many states, insurance doesn't cover punitive damages; the landlord must pay them personally. To avoid the sting of punitive damages, avoid taking any deliberate action to harm a resident and do your best to address any safety issues immediately.

A finding of negligence requires the judge or jury to conclude that the behavior of the landlord or the landlord's agents was unreasonable under the circumstances, that is, that the defendant owed a "duty of due care" to the injured person, and *breached* (violated) that duty, which resulted in the plaintiff's injury. Whether the defendant breached the duty of due care to the plaintiff requires that the judge or jury conclude that:

- ✔ The defendant had control over the dangerous condition or situation, and failed to maintain or repair the problem.

- ✔ The injury resulting from the dangerous condition was foreseeable to a reasonable person in the landlord's position.

- ✔ Fixing or resolving the dangerous condition wouldn't have been unreasonably expensive.

- ✔ The dangerous condition was likely to cause serious damage or injury.

Splitting the cost of negligence

If the courts decide that your negligence contributed to someone's loss, you're not necessarily responsible for paying 100 percent of the damages. Most states have adopted a *comparative negligence test* in which the relative percentages of negligence by the plaintiff and the defendant are used to determine the plaintiff's damage recovery. In other words, if the judge or jury decides the landlord was at fault, they then decide whether the plaintiff's own carelessness contributed to the accident. If so, they then decide the percentage of fault of each party. For example, if the total damages are $50,000 but the plaintiff is found to be 20 percent contributory negligent, the damage award is $40,000.

Only a few states allow contributory negligence defenses. *Contributory negligence*, a principle of common law, means that if a person is injured in part because of her own negligence — that is, her negligence contributed to the injury or its severity — the injured person can't collect *any* damages from someone whose negligence supposedly caused the injury. This principle prevents a badly injured person who's only slightly negligent from collecting any damages against a very negligent defendant, which is why most states don't allow the contributory negligence defense.

Chapter 14

Preventing and Eliminating Hazardous Environmental Conditions

....

In This Chapter

▶ Addressing any air quality issues

▶ Tackling the legalities of lead paint and toxic mold

▶ Preparing for the possibility of pest infestations

▶ Protecting residents from exposure to hazardous wastes

▶ Shielding yourself legally and financially

....

Part of your legal responsibility to residents involves preventing and eliminating environmental hazards and disclosing when such hazards exist. We define *environmental hazard* as anything that could potentially adversely affect a person's health. Here are the environmental hazards we cover in this chapter:

✔ Asbestos

✔ Carbon monoxide

✔ Formaldehyde

✔ Radon

✔ Lead paint

✔ Toxic mold

✔ Pests, including rats, mice, roaches, spiders, mosquitoes, and bedbugs

In this chapter, we provide guidance on how to prevent and eliminate these environmental hazards, evaluate your liability, and reduce your exposure to legal action resulting from neglect or failure to disclose an environmental hazard.

Clearing the Air Your Residents Breathe

Several of the most common environmental hazards are airborne — asbestos, carbon monoxide, formaldehyde, and radon. In the following sections, we describe each hazard along with ways to eliminate or reduce the hazard and how you can protect your residents and lessen your liability.

Go to the source. These environmental hazards emanate from a source. The most effective solutions are those that attack the problem closest to the source.

Asbestos

Asbestos is a naturally occurring fibrous mineral that's very strong and heat-resistant. Because of its strength and flame-retardant nature, from the 1940s to around 1981, the construction industry used it in all sorts of building materials and applications. Any building, including homes and rental properties, especially those built prior to 1981 may contain numerous products containing asbestos, including acoustic ceilings, vinyl flooring and tile backings, flooring *mastic* (a type of adhesive), insulation, wall and ceiling panels, carpet padding, roofing and siding, pipe and duct insulation, patching and spackling compounds, and furnaces.

Do *not* assume that a property built or remodeled after 1981 is free of materials containing asbestos.

According to the American Lung Association, if you suspect that you have materials containing asbestos in your rental property, do the following:

- **Leave it alone.** Disturbing the asbestos will make more fibers airborne and increase exposure for you and your tenants. Be sure to warn the tenants not to disturb these materials and have them notify you immediately if these materials are damaged in any way.

  Some asbestos materials are *friable,* meaning they crumble into small particles or fibers. Materials containing asbestos may also crumble easily if mishandled. Even if the material was originally intact, asbestos may be released into the air if the material is sawed, scraped, sanded, or subjected to other mechanical processes.

- **Have it tested.** Unless the material is labeled as containing asbestos, you may not be able to tell whether it does just by looking at it. Call a certified asbestos-removal service to have the material tested and obtain professional advice on whether to have it repaired or removed. If the material is in good shape and likely to remain undisturbed, it may not pose a significant risk.

✔ **Have it repaired or removed, if advised to do so.** To reduce the hazard, professionals may repair or remove the asbestos:

- Repair usually involves either sealing or covering the asbestos material. Sealing is also commonly referred to as *encapsulation* and involves coating materials so that the asbestos can't be released. Encapsulation is only effective for undamaged asbestos-containing material. If materials are soft, crumbly, or otherwise damaged, sealing isn't appropriate, and the substances should be removed by a qualified professional.

- Removing asbestos-containing materials is an expensive and hazardous process to be completed only by trained personnel using special tools and techniques, and should be a last resort. Hire a licensed contractor who specializes in removing asbestos-containing materials, because improper removal can increase the health risks to the workers, yourself, and your future tenants.

  Unauthorized removal of asbestos may be illegal. Punishment may include hundreds of thousands of dollars in fines and perhaps time in prison.

Check with your local and state officials for any disclosure requirements they may require. Some states and municipalities insist asbestos materials be disclosed to tenants, along with a warning not to disturb them.

If your rental property was built prior to 1981, you also need to comply with Occupational Safety and Health Administration (OSHA) asbestos regulations for any of your employees or contractors you hire. Visit www.osha.gov for more information. Refer to the nearby sidebar for additional information.

The lowdown on asbestos

The federal Occupational Safety and Health Administration (OSHA) has developed regulations that apply to any building constructed prior to 1981. These buildings are presumed to have asbestos unless a certified asbestos expert inspects the property and verifies that it's free of asbestos.

Exposure to asbestos can lead to an increased risk of lung cancer; *mesothelioma,* a cancer of the lining of the chest and the abdominal cavity; and *asbestosis,* a condition in which the lungs become scarred with fibrous tissue.

No known safe exposure level to asbestos exists. However, when the asbestos is intact and can't become airborne, exposure to it isn't a problem. Smokers who inhale exposed asbestos fibers have a greater risk of developing lung cancer than nonsmokers. Although most people who get asbestosis have usually been exposed to high levels of asbestos for a long time, even a short but significant exposure can cause harm. The symptoms of asbestos-related diseases don't usually appear until about 20 to 30 years after the first exposure to asbestos.

Carbon monoxide

Carbon monoxide (CO) is a colorless, odorless, and poisonous gas produced when fuel burns incompletely, and it can build up in a rental unit in mere hours. If the leak occurs when the tenants are asleep, they can easily lose consciousness, suffer a serious injury, or die before noticing anything's wrong.

The following items all produce carbon monoxide:

- Fireplaces
- Gas appliances
- Gas or kerosene space heaters
- Gas-powered generators
- Gas water heaters
- Natural gas and oil furnaces
- Wood-burning stoves

When these items are working properly, carbon monoxide is safely vented to the chimney or another venting system. If they aren't vented properly, then carbon monoxide can build up within a rental unit.

To protect residents and limit your liability, take the following precautions:

- Follow all state and local building, health, and safety codes regarding the use of items that emit carbon monoxide and the use of carbon monoxide detectors.

- Install carbon monoxide detectors in all units that contain items or are in close proximity of sources that produce carbon monoxide, regardless of whether you're required to do so by law. Some jurisdictions have specific rules about the required location, so make sure you know what is legally required for your rental properties. In some states, garages are a mandatory location, but we believe you should automatically include a carbon monoxide detector in any enclosed garage even if it's not legally required.

Carbon monoxide detectors are now readily available. These devices are either hard-wired (some with a battery backup) or battery operated and emit a loud sound when an unsafe level of CO is detected. Currently, more than 25 states require carbon monoxide detectors in certain residential buildings, and soon the requirement will likely be mandatory in most states just as smoke detectors are legally required.

- If units have gas furnaces, water heaters, fireplaces, or wood-burning stoves, have chimneys or vents professionally inspected and cleaned regularly (assuming your residents will allow entry and full access during their tenancy).

> ✔ Have any gas furnaces and water heaters inspected for carbon-monoxide leaks prior to new residents moving in. You may also want to see if your tenants will allow periodic inspections too.
>
> ✔ Prohibit the use of gas or kerosene space heaters, which are a common source of carbon-monoxide poisoning, as well as fires.
>
> ✔ Educate tenants on the dangers of carbon monoxide, and stress the importance of not using gas or kerosene space heaters in the unit.
>
> ✔ Respond immediately to any tenant complaints about possible carbon monoxide poisoning.

Formaldehyde

Formaldehyde is a chemical with a pungent odor that's commonly used in building materials and household products and produced by combustion and certain other natural processes. According to the Environmental Protection Agency (EPA), the most significant sources of formaldehyde in dwellings are pressed wood products, including "particleboard (used as subflooring and shelving and in cabinetry and furniture); hardwood plywood paneling (used for decorative wall covering and used in cabinets and furniture); and medium density fiberboard (used for drawer fronts, cabinets, and furniture tops)." Other sources include smoking, unvented gas stoves or kerosene space heaters, adhesives, and paints and other coating products.

Formaldehyde is a human *carcinogen* (cancer-causing agent) and in concentrations above 100 parts per billion (ppb), it can cause eye, nose, and throat irritation, nausea, headaches, coughing, and difficulty breathing. It may also worsen allergy and asthma conditions.

Government health agencies haven't established a safe concentration of formaldehyde. Formaldehyde concentrations in outside air (fresh air) range from 3 ppb in rural areas up to 20 ppb in urban areas and around power plants, incinerators, and manufacturing plants. Indoors, concentrations are generally higher; one survey reported concentrations ranging "from below the limit of detections to 3.68 ppm (3,680 ppb)." The Centers for Disease Control (CDC) ranks formaldehyde concentrations for manufactured housing on a scale of 1 to 1,000 with 10 is considered low, 100 moderate, and 1,000 high. (Formaldehyde released from building materials generally decreases over time.)

To protect residents from the health risks that formaldehyde poses and to reduce your exposure to legal action, take the following measures:

> ✔ If you suspect high levels of formaldehyde in a building or a resident reports that the rental unit is making him ill, have the air professionally tested by sending an air sample to a certified lab.

Search the Internet for "formaldehyde test kit" to find services that mail you everything you need to collect an air sample and mail it in to the lab for testing.

✔ Use exterior-grade pressed wood products for inside repairs and upgrades, for example, if you need to replace the subflooring. (Exterior-grade products contain phenol, not urea resins, which emit less formaldehyde.) Before purchasing building materials, including cabinets, check about their formaldehyde content, and choose products with no or less formaldehyde.

✔ Educate residents on what they can do to reduce formaldehyde concentrations in their rental units:

• Maintain moderate temperatures and reduce humidity. (Heat and humidity increase the rate at which formaldehyde is released from products.)

• Increase ventilation, especially after repairs and upgrades that use products containing formaldehyde and whenever new furniture is brought into the unit.

Your rental property may not be the primary source of formaldehyde in the air. The source may be furniture the resident moved into the unit.

Radon

Radon, a radioactive gas, is a human carcinogen that the EPA cites as the second leading cause of lung cancer in the United States and that claims 20,000 lives annually. Found in soil and rock in all parts of the country, radon is formed as a byproduct of the natural decay of the radioactive materials radium and uranium. Radon gas is invisible; it has no odor or taste. However, most radon found in buildings poses no direct threat to human life because the concentration is generally below the minimum safe level.

Although currently no federal requirements exist regarding disclosure or even testing for radon gas, it's a potentially serious health issue and one that's receiving more attention. Be aware of radon levels in your rental units and check with local authorities for more information about the prevalence of radon and appropriate precautions you should take to avoid radon exposure. (Florida and New Jersey have been particularly aggressive in addressing the radon problem.) Be sure to check with your local authorities for any specific disclosure requirements and always test if you discover that radon levels are high in your area.

Although radon may be found in all types of homes and buildings throughout the United States, it's more likely to occur in certain areas of the country and in the lower levels of tightly sealed, energy-efficient buildings, where insulation limits the flow of air from the inside to the outside and ventilation is poor. (Search the Internet for "EPA Radon Map" to view a map that shows the areas of the United States at highest risk for elevated radon concentrations.)

Assessing and Limiting Your Liability for Lead Paint and Toxic Mold

Lead paint and toxic mold are the two most prevalent and serious environmental hazards in residential housing. In the following sections, we provide guidance on your obligation to disclose any existence of lead paint or toxic mold in or on your rental property and your responsibilities in protecting residents from exposure to these toxic substances.

Lead paint

The federal Residential Lead-Based Paint Hazard Reduction Act of 1992 covers all dwellings built before 1978 and requires rental housing owners or their property managers to notify tenants that the property may have lead-based paint. Testing for lead-based paint or removal isn't currently required under federal law, but to comply with federal, state, and local laws, you must do the following:

- Obey any state or local lead hazard reduction laws, some of which require testing and careful maintenance or removal of lead paint.

- Disclose known lead-based paint hazards on your property.

Most rental property owners use a Lead-Based Paint Disclosure form (see Figure 14-1) to ensure they've complied with the Residential Lead-Based Paint Hazard Reduction Act of 1992. Access this form by visiting www.dummies.com/go/landlordlegalkit and clicking on the Hazardous Conditions folder, print it online at www.epa.gov/lead/pubs/lesr_eng.pdf, or contact the National Lead Information Center (NLIC) at 800-424-5323 for a copy.

- Provide residents with an information pamphlet from the EPA titled "Protect Your Family from Lead in Your Home." You can get this pamphlet online at www.epa.gov/lead/pubs/leadpdfe.pdf in both English and Spanish. The pamphlet is also available in other languages (namely Arabic, Russian, Somali, and Vietnamese) at www.epa.gov/lead/pubs/leadprot.htm. A few states (including California and Massachusetts) have their own pamphlets on lead-based paint hazards that the EPA has authorized for distribution in lieu of the EPA pamphlet.

Whichever pamphlet you provide your residents, keep a copy of the disclosure form signed and dated by the residents. You must keep this written record of compliance with the disclosure requirements on hand and readily available for review for a minimum of three years in case of an investigation or audit.

Figure 14-1:
Sample
lead-based
paint
disclosure
form.

> **Disclosure of Information on Lead-Based Paint and/or Lead-Based Paint Hazards**
>
> **Lead Warning Statement**
> *Housing built before 1978 may contain lead-based paint. Lead from paint, paint chips, and dust can pose health hazards if not managed properly. Lead exposure is especially harmful to young children and pregnant women. Before renting pre-1978 housing, lessors must disclose the presence of known lead-based paint and/or lead-based paint hazards in the dwelling. Lessees must also receive a federally approved pamphlet on lead poisoning prevention.*
>
> **Lessor's Disclosure**
> (a) Presence of lead-based paint and/or lead-based paint hazards (check (i) or (ii) below):
>
> (i) _____   Known lead-based paint and/or lead-based paint hazards are present in the housing (explain).
>
> _____
>
> _____
>
> (ii) _____   Lessor has no knowledge of lead-based paint and/or lead-based paint hazards in the housing.
>
> (b) Records and reports available to the lessor (check (i) or (ii) below):
>
> (i) _____   Lessor has provided the lessee with all available records and reports pertaining to lead-based paint and/or lead-based paint hazards in the housing (list documents below).
>
> _____
>
> _____
>
> (ii) _____   Lessor has no reports or records pertaining to lead-based paint and/or lead-based paint hazards in the housing.
>
> **Lessee's Acknowledgment** (initial)
> (c) _____   Lessee has received copies of all information listed above.
> (d) _____   Lessee has received the pamphlet *Protect Your Family from Lead in Your Home.*
>
> **Agent's Acknowledgment** (initial)
> (e) _____   Agent has informed the lessor of the lessor's obligations under 42 U.S.C. 4852(d) and is aware of his/her responsibility to ensure compliance.
>
> **Certification of Accuracy**
> The following parties have reviewed the information above and certify, to the best of their knowledge, that the information they have provided is true and accurate.
>
> | | | | |
> |---|---|---|---|
> | Lessor | Date | Lessor | Date |
> | Lessee | Date | Lessee | Date |
> | Agent | Date | Agent | Date |

Form courtesy of US Environmental Protection Agency

All housing constructed after January 1, 1978, along with rentals that meet any of the following conditions are exempt from federal lead-based paint disclosure regulations:

✔ Housing for the elderly or persons with disabilities (unless any child under 6 is living there or is expected to live there)

✔ Short-term rentals of 100 days or fewer

✔ The rental of an individual bedroom or similar room in a residential home

✔ Certain university housing, such as dormitory housing or rentals in sorority or fraternity houses

✔ Zero bedroom units, such as studios, lofts, or efficiencies

✔ Housing that has been inspected and certified as lead-free by a state-accredited lead inspector (meaning the complete absence of lead-based paint, not just encapsulated)

Contact the EPA or your state health and environmental agency for specific information. If you're advised that your property is exempt, be sure to receive written verification before ceasing to follow the federal requirements.

Don't try to remove lead paint yourself. Scraping or sanding the lead paint releases it into the air and surrounding area, making it much more hazardous. Painting over the paint merely masks the underlying problem. If your property has lead-based paint, hire a licensed contractor to inspect its condition and advise you on measures to take. The contractor may seal the paint or use special processes to remove it.

Rental property owners or managers who fail to follow the federal regulations for lead-based paint can face significant fines. To enforce these regulations, the federal Housing and Urban Development (HUD) agency and the EPA are working together to investigate complaints from residents who believe they may have been exposed to lead-based paint. If a resident doesn't receive the required EPA or approved state information pamphlet or the disclosure statement, the owner or property manager may be subject to one or more of the following penalties:

- ✔ A notice of noncompliance
- ✔ A civil monetary penalty of up to $11,000 per violation for willful and continuing noncompliance
- ✔ An order to pay the injured tenant up to three times his actual damages
- ✔ A criminal fine of up to $11,000 per violation

Recently, the EPA and HUD began aggressively enforcing these regulations and levied significant and well publicized fines against rental property owners and managers who haven't complied with the law. Government testers have been known to pose as prospective residents, and federal agents have scoured leasing and maintenance records looking for evidence that property owners or managers knew or should have known about the existence of lead-based paint hazards on their property. This is *not* an area where you want to tempt fate. Make sure you comply with this law and keep the required documentation on file in an easily retrievable location for at least three years.

For more information about lead paint, review the extensive resources available from the EPA and the National Lead Information Center (NLIC) by visiting www.epa.gov/lead or by calling 800-424-5323.

Toxic mold

Mold is the common term for a variety of fungi commonly found in nature. Mold is everywhere, but not all of it is toxic to everyone. However, the effect of toxic mold on health has become an increasing concern for rental property owners and managers.

According to the EPA, toxic mold has the potential to cause health problems for some persons who have asthma or are allergic to certain types of mold. For these individuals, contact with specific molds can cause allergic responses such as sneezing, runny nose, red eyes, and skin rash. But toxic mold can also irritate the eyes, skin, nose, throat, and lungs of people without allergies. Symptoms other than these reactions aren't commonly reported as a result of mold inhalation.

Inspect your rental unit for mold and mildew carefully before the tenant moves in and have it removed. Also, eliminate the source of any moisture that may encourage the growth of mold and mildew. Common problems that give rise to mold and mildew are leaks and poor ventilation, especially inside bath and shower enclosures.

Getting to know the Renovation, Repair, and Painting Rule

In 2011, the EPA began enforcing the Renovation, Repair, and Painting Rule (RRP Rule). It requires contractors who conduct renovation work in residential buildings built before 1978 to be a "lead-safe certified firm" and follow specific work practices to prevent lead dust contamination. The program aims to reduce the amount of lead dust created during renovation, repair, and painting of rental units and common areas and affects renovation contractors, maintenance workers in the rental housing industry, and painters and employees of other specialty trades. These workers must attend EPA-approved courses taught by a government-approved trainer.

Some of the requirements outlined in the RRP Rule include distributing information to building occupants to notify them of the work being conducted, obtaining written certification from the adult occupant that the information has been received, posting signs defining the work area, isolating the work area by closing windows and doors, and covering ducts or other openings that can't be sealed with plastic sheeting. The specific lead dust reduction practices also include covering the floor with plastic or similar material, negatively pressurizing the work space, storing daily waste under containment that prevents the release of dust, disposing of the waste in a sealed bag approved by the EPA,

and placing all waste in a lined container and disposing of it at an EPA-approved site. You can find further information concerning lead-safe work practices at `www.epa.gov/lead/pubs/renovation.htm`.

Note: The RRP Rule typically doesn't apply to minor maintenance or repair activities (such as patching holes) where less than 6 square feet of lead-based paint is disturbed in a room or where less than 20 square feet of lead-based paint is disturbed on the exterior, but this doesn't include window replacement, demolition, or prohibited practices.

When the RRP Rule applies, renovators (which could be you or your maintenance workers if you have received the required training and are EPA-certified as previously discussed and handle such renovation projects in-house rather than using unaffiliated licensed and certified contractors) are required before starting any work to provide all tenants with a copy of the EPAs "The Lead-safe Certified Guide to Renovate Right" pamphlet. This pamphlet is available in English and Spanish in several formats at `www2.epa.gov/lead/renovate-right-important-lead-hazard-information-families-child-care-providers-and-schools`.

Provide new residents with a copy of your mold notification addendum. A sample Mold Notification Addendum is shown in Figure 14-2. To access the sample Mold Notification Addendum, visit www.dummies.com/go/landlordlegalkit and click on the Hazardous Conditions folder.

MOLD NOTIFICATION ADDENDUM

Page_____
of Agreement

This document is an Addendum and is part of the Rental/Lease Agreement, dated _____ between
_____(Date)_____ (Owner/Agent) and
_____
(Name of Owner/Agent)
_____ (Resident) for the
(List all Residents as listed on the Rental/Lease Agreement)

premises located at _____, Unit # (if applicable) _____
(Street Address)
_____ , CA _____.
(City) *(Zip)*

It is our goal to maintain the highest quality living environment for our Residents. The Owner/Agent has inspected the unit prior to lease and knows of no damp or wet building materials and knows of no mold or mildew contamination. Resident is hereby notified that mold, however, can grow if the premises are not properly maintained or ventilated. If moisture is allowed to accumulate in the unit, it can cause mildew and mold to grow. It is important that Residents regularly allow air to circulate in the apartment. It is also important that Residents keep the interior of the unit clean and that they promptly notify the Owner/Agent of any leaks, moisture problems, and/or mold growth.

Resident agrees to maintain the premises in a manner that prevents the occurrence of an infestation of mold or mildew in the premises. Resident agrees to uphold this responsibility in part by complying with the following list of responsibilities:

1. Resident agrees to keep the unit free of dirt and debris that can harbor mold.

2. Resident agrees to immediately report to the Owner/Agent any water intrusion, such as plumbing leaks, drips, or "sweating" pipes.

3. Resident agrees to notify owner of overflows from bathroom, kitchen, or unit laundry facilities, especially in cases where the overflow may have permeated walls or cabinets.

4. Resident agrees to report to the Owner/Agent any significant mold growth on surfaces inside the premises.

5. Resident agrees to allow the Owner/Agent to enter the unit to inspect and make necessary repairs.

6. Resident agrees to use bathroom fans while showering or bathing and to report to the Owner/Agent any non-working fan.

7. Resident agrees to use exhaust fans whenever cooking, dishwashing, or cleaning.

8. Resident agrees to use all reasonable care to close all windows and other openings in the premises to prevent outdoor water from penetrating into the interior unit.

9. Resident agrees to clean and dry any visible moisture on windows, walls, and other surfaces, including personal property, as soon as reasonably possible. (Note: Mold can grow on damp surfaces within 24 to 48 hours.)

10. Resident agrees to notify the Owner/Agent of any problems with the air conditioning or heating systems that are discovered by the Resident.

11. Resident agrees to indemnify and hold harmless the Owner/Agent from any actions, claims, losses, damages, and expenses, including, but not limited to, attorneys' fees that the Owner/Agent may sustain or incur as a result of the negligence of the Resident or any guest or other person living in, occupying, or using the premises.

The undersigned Resident(s) acknowledge(s) having read and understood the foregoing.

_____   _____   _____   _____
Date   *Resident*   *Date*   *Resident*

_____   _____   _____   _____
Date   *Resident*   *Date*   *Resident*

_____   _____
Date   *Owner/Agent*

Figure 14-2:
Sample
Mold
Notification
Addendum.

Form courtesy of CAA

If, despite their best efforts, your tenants suspect any issues of elevated moisture or smell or see any mildew or mold, they should notify you immediately. You must take claims of visible mold seriously, possibly by arranging for a maintenance person or contractor to investigate. Follow the EPA guidelines regarding mold removal (available at `www.epa.gov/mold`) and consult with experts if the problem is severe and persistent. In such cases, use qualified professionals and carefully document all communication to minimize the prospect of being sued by your tenants.

For more information about mold and how to minimize or get rid of it, check out the following resources:

- ✔ "Guidelines on Assessment and Remediation of Fungi in Indoor Environments": This document, published by New York City's Department of Health and Mental Hygiene, is widely considered to be the first comprehensive document to establish best practices for mold assessment and remediation. You can find it online at `www.nyc.gov/html/doh/html/environmental/moldrpt1.shtml`.

- ✔ "A Brief Guide to Mold, Moisture, and Your Home": This publication, produced by the EPA, is an excellent resource for both rental property owners and tenants. It's available at no charge from the EPA at `www.epa.gov/mold/publications.html`.

Informing and protecting residents during repairs and renovations

Whenever you're planning a major renovation that's likely to kick up a lot of dust, inform residents who live nearby about your plans, the possible risks of exposure to airborne substances, any safety concerns, and precautions that you and your contractors will take to protect the residents' health and safety. Let them know if they need to avoid the area under construction or any alternate routes they need to take to access their units.

Make sure your maintenance staff or the contractors you hire follow the required precautions (such as those required for the RRP Rule that we discuss in the nearby sidebar) to reduce or eliminate resident exposure to airborne substances. For example, for lead paint removal, work areas may need to be enclosed in plastic sheets of a certain thickness with negative pressure exhaust ventilation to create a vacuum that limits exposure to airborne lead or other toxic particles. Precautions vary according to the nature of the hazard and the type of work performed, but you should only retain companies with maintenance or renovation personnel that are trained and have extensive experience doing the specific type of work under similar circumstances. Remember they may also need to be certified as required by the EPA for certain work.

Preventing and Exterminating Pests

As we explain in Chapter 12, landlords and property managers are required by law to provide and maintain habitable housing. In many areas of the country, maintaining habitable housing includes the responsibility to provide living areas that have none of the following critters:

✔ **Rats or mice:** Rats and mice pose a health hazard to residents and are known to spread more than 35 diseases to humans.

✔ **Cockroaches:** Cockroaches not only pose a health hazard to humans, but they can also damage personal items, including electronic gadgets, and cause anxiety, sleep deprivation, and emotional distress.

✔ **Bedbugs:** Bedbugs aren't known to carry any diseases to humans, but they often cause severe emotional distress for anyone who lives with them and for landlords and property managers who have to deal with the public relations nightmare when word gets out that the property has bedbugs. For additional information, visit www.epa.gov/bedbugs.

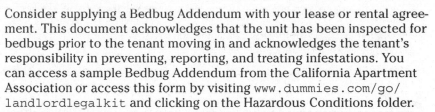

Consider supplying a Bedbug Addendum with your lease or rental agreement. This document acknowledges that the unit has been inspected for bedbugs prior to the tenant moving in and acknowledges the tenant's responsibility in preventing, reporting, and treating infestations. You can access a sample Bedbug Addendum from the California Apartment Association or access this form by visiting www.dummies.com/go/landlordlegalkit and clicking on the Hazardous Conditions folder.

✔ **Termites:** Although termites don't pose a direct health risk to humans, the damage they cause to floors, walls, and cabinets may create entrances for rats, mice, and roaches, and if the termites cause structural damage, that can lead to accidents and injuries.

✔ **Fleas:** Properties that allow pets are likely to become infested with fleas, especially if the owners don't apply flea treatments. Fleas generally don't pose a huge health hazard to humans, but fleabites cause intense itching, which often leads to scratching, which may cause infection.

✔ **Ants:** Ants are more of an embarrassing nuisance than a health hazard, but most residents don't want to share their walls, floors, and countertops with ants.

Losing sleep over bedbugs

In my (Laurry's) experience, bedbug infestation is an *extremely* hazardous environmental condition that potentially impacts the habitability of not only the individual identified apartment unit but also many of the apartments in a large property.

Here's a typical scenario: A resident of a 314-unit rental property calls the manager to report suspected bedbugs in his apartment, which is on the second floor of the building. The manager immediately contacts a professional exterminator and sets up an appointment to enter the unit to determine whether bedbugs are present. The manager notifies the resident by telephone and by a typewritten message delivered to his apartment of the date and time of the inspection. The inspection confirms that the unit is infested, and that an immediate extermination is required in order to prevent the spread of bedbugs to other units in the building.

The manager again notifies the resident as above; the written notification advises the resident to pack up his clothing and bedding in bags and to take additional measures to provide the exterminator with unimpeded access to the entire apartment. The resident fails to comply with the instructions and prevents the exterminator from entering the apartment. The same process is repeated, but by the time the exterminator gains access to the unit and provides the necessary services, 11 days have passed since the resident initially notified the manager. By this time, six units above the resident's apartment on the third floor, and eight units on the ground floor of the building have become infested. Of the 15 units, including the initial apartment, four residents, claiming their apartments are uninhabitable, move out of the building, and two of them, justifiably enraged, share their experiences in detail on the Internet, specifically identifying the property, the resident manager, the owner, and the management company with their postings.

To keep these and other pests at bay, implement a two-pronged attack consisting of prevention and extermination:

- ✔ **Prevention:** Caulk all cracks around the windows, foundations, drains, and pipes that may allow pests to enter the unit. Proper maintenance may help prevent infestations in the first place and contain them to certain units.

- ✔ **Extermination:** Hire a professional exterminator to inspect your property, deal with any existing issues, and then follow up on a regular schedule to ensure that your property and all rental units remain pest-free.

Prior to providing the initial treatment, the exterminator must notify the landlord or property manager and all residents and indicate the pesticides that will be used. Keep your copy of the notice and provide a copy to every future resident the treatments may affect.

If you encounter bedbugs at your property and want to get rid of them, be prepared for the process to take some time and require a fair amount of patience — as well as sizeable expense. The good news is that you don't have to rely solely on pesticides. Instead you can turn to an integrated pest management program that combines chemical and nonchemical treatments (such as applying excessive heat over an extended period of time). But don't attempt this heat treatment on your own! Call a professional or someone with specific training in this technique.

Check state and local laws regarding conditions in the history of the property that you're required to disclose to prospective residents. More and more states and local municipalities are beginning to require disclosure of pest infestation, particularly for occurrences of bedbugs.

Preventing and Eliminating Hazardous Waste

As a landlord of residential property, you probably don't need to be very concerned about hazardous wastes. This is more of a concern for commercial property owners who rent to businesses that need to dispose of hazardous wastes, such as dry cleaners, auto repair shops, print shops, and manufacturing plants. However, as a residential landlord, you still need to be concerned about residents pouring used car oil down sewers or drains, tossing old batteries in trash receptacles, or storing hazardous materials in their apartment that could leak or otherwise affect other residents.

In the following sections, we provide guidance on how to determine whether a substance is a hazardous waste, identify common sources of such wastes, educate residents on proper disposal, and figure out who's responsible for removing the hazardous waste.

Determining whether something is a hazardous waste

According to the EPA, "*Hazardous waste* is waste that is dangerous or potentially harmful to our health or the environment. Hazardous wastes can be liquids, solids, gases, or sludge [mixtures of liquid and solids]. They can be discarded commercial products, like cleaning fluids or pesticides, or the byproducts of manufacturing processes." Common consumer products that are or contain hazardous wastes are the following:

✔ Paints, stains, and solvents

✔ Cleaning solutions

- Motor oil, transmission fluid, and antifreeze
- Batteries
- Herbicides, insecticides, and pesticides
- Fluorescent light bulbs
- Electronic devices, including computers, TVs, and smart phones
- Pharmaceuticals
- Most flammable products, including gasoline, kerosene, and propane

If you're unsure whether a substance qualifies as a hazardous waste, use the Definition of Solid Waste (DSW) Decision Tool to make your determination. Visit www.epa.gov/osw/hazard/dsw/tool.htm for the tool and instructions on how to use it.

Identifying common sources of hazardous wastes

Hazardous wastes may contaminate your property from the outside in or the inside out, so you need to know what the most common sources are and then monitor them vigilantly. In the following sections, we name the most common sources of hazardous wastes, provide examples, and offer guidance on what you can do to prevent or correct contamination.

Neighboring businesses

Manufacturing plants, dry cleaners, gas stations, car washes, sewage treatment plants, landfills, print shops, labs, medical facilities, cosmetic manufacturers, chemical plants, and other businesses mostly in the manufacturing sector are common sources of hazardous wastes. Wastes may contaminate your property, so keep an eye on neighboring businesses and contact your local environmental or health agency if you have any concerns. (The EPA tries to outsource enforcement to state, county, and local agencies.)

Contractors and maintenance workers

Careless contractors and maintenance workers may spill or improperly dispose of paints, solvents, cleaning solutions, and other hazardous materials, which is another reason to keep an eye on contractors and maintenance staff. Train your maintenance staff on the proper disposal of hazardous materials. (See the later section, "Educating residents and staff on proper use and disposal of hazardous substances," for details.)

Residents

To address potential issues with residents improperly disposing of hazardous materials, focus on two areas: what they can pour down the drain and what they can dump in the trash. Monitoring either of these two disposal methods is nearly impossible, so encourage recycling and green living and educate residents on proper disposal methods, as explained in the later section "Educating residents and staff on proper use and disposal of hazardous substances."

Meth labs

A very serious and growing problem in residential rental properties is methamphetamine contamination from residents who use their units or portions of their units to produce the illegal drug methamphetamine. Any residential property used for producing methamphetamine may have extensive contamination. If you suspect methamphetamine contamination, call your local law enforcement agency to inspect the property and secure the premises.

Officers will call a county or local health officer who will inspect the property. If the property is found to be contaminated with methamphetamine, law enforcement or the health officer will usually call in a contractor to remove any containers with chemicals and any equipment used in the production process, but trace elements of chemicals may remain in tubs, sinks and drains, in carpeting and in cabinets, on walls, in the ventilation system, and on shelves and other surfaces. Call a contractor who's certified in eliminating methamphetamine contamination to perform the cleanup. Law enforcement officers or the health officer who performed the inspection may have names and contact information for local cleanup services.

Educating residents and staff on proper use and disposal of hazardous substances

Dealing effectively with hazardous wastes usually involves educating consumers and getting everyone in a community, including business owners, government agencies, and environmental groups, to cooperate. You can do your part to encourage residents and staff to adopt environmentally friendly practices and by educating them on how to reduce and dispose of hazardous substances. Here are a few suggestions:

- Provide residents and staff with information about local toxic waste collection sites — locations and hours. (Some communities sponsor *tox-drops* one or two times a year, where local residents can drop off toxic products and electronic equipment.)

- Inform residents on what they should recycle, place in the trash, and never place in the trash. You may want to put signs on trash receptacles indicating what not to place in the receptacle.

✔ Purchase nontoxic or less toxic products for use in cleaning, repairing, and maintaining your rental property.

✔ Encourage residents to use nontoxic or less toxic products, when possible.

✔ Instruct residents and staff to use only the recommended amounts of product (or less). Using excessive amounts of cleaning solution, for example, places that much more of it into the environment.

✔ Encourage recycling.

Figuring out who's legally liable for the cleanup

To determine which party is liable for cleaning up a hazardous waste, courts typically look to the party responsible for introducing that waste to the property. If the landlord or one of his agents caused the mess, he's responsible for the cleanup. If the resident or resident's child or guest caused the mess, then the resident is responsible for the cleanup, regardless of whether the hazardous waste is inside or outside the rental unit.

If a third-party, such as a delivery truck or delivery person, introduces the hazardous waste, determining whether the landlord or resident is liable becomes more challenging. If the waste is inside the rental unit, the landlord is likely to pin it on the resident. If it's outside the rental unit, the landlord is more likely to be responsible. However, in either case, the landlord or the resident may take legal action against the third party to collect any damages, including any cleanup costs incurred.

Chapter 15

Protecting Residents and Workers from Criminal Acts

....

....

Crime is a fact of life for everyone, including rental property owners and residents. Residents need to act prudently, but as a landlord, you must take an active role in implementing policies and security measures for the safety of your residents and their guests. Even if your property is located next door to the local police station in the safest neighborhood in town, you still need to implement proper building security measures and team up with residents and local law enforcement to fight crime.

In this chapter, we provide guidance on how to tighten security of your rental property and your business, deal with criminal acts (typically theft and assault) that occur despite your best efforts, and communicate honestly with current and prospective residents about safety and security on your property.

Eyeing Your Obligations and Legal Liability

As landlord, you probably know that you have responsibilities to not only protect residents from crime but also work with residents and local law enforcement personnel to identify and stop criminal activity occurring on your property. You may wonder what those responsibilities entail and what measures you must take to fulfill those responsibilities.

You've come to the right place. These sections explain what your obligations are in general and how to find out specifically what the law requires you to do in your state or municipality. As a word of caution, we also let you know the possible legal and financial consequences of failing to do your part to protect residents from crime and to stop criminal activity occurring on your property that you know about.

Knowing your responsibilities

Regardless of whether your state or municipality has specific requirements to secure your rental property, you need to take reasonable measures to protect residents and deal with any criminal activity. *Reasonable measures* include providing doors and windows that residents can lock and latch from the inside and providing sufficient lighting in parking areas, walkways, and hallways at night (see "Attending to security essentials," later in this chapter, for more measures you must take).

In addition to establishing these essential security procedures, you may need to strengthen them if your rental property is in a high-crime area or if state or local codes require you to do so. For example, in some areas, you may be legally required to equip standard entry doors for every unit with a peephole or install additional security lighting or alarms. Contact your local property association or state or local housing authority to find out about any specific security measures you're required to implement to protect residents from crime. (See "Taking Practical Security Measures," for more about steps you can take to protect residents from crime.)

Grasping the potential costs of lax security

Failure to perform your due diligence in protecting residents from crime is potentially very costly legally and in other ways. Here's an itemized list of the costs you could incur by failing to implement reasonable security features and those required by law:

- ✔ Attorney fees and court costs if a resident files a lawsuit against you for loss or damage resulting from criminal activity on your property.

- ✔ Damages a judge orders you to pay a resident for property loss, personal injury, and possibly even emotional distress.

- ✔ Decreased occupancy and rent collections as your property develops a reputation as being a dangerous place to live and demand for your rental units drops.

- ✔ Higher repair and maintenance costs for any vandalism and other damage done to your property caused by commission of a crime.

- ✔ Forfeiture of your rental property to the state. See the nearby sidebar for more details.

A stiff price to pay

In Minnesota, where I (Laurry) practice law, landlords and residents are both held accountable for not committing or allowing unlawful activities on the premises. (Many other states have this same statute.) The statute requires language in every rental contract (lease or rental agreement) stating that the landlord and resident agree that neither will allow any of the following crimes on the premises or in the common area or curtilage (land) of the premises:

✔ Unlawful possession of controlled substances

✔ Prostitution or related activity

✔ Unlawful use or possession of a firearm

✔ Possession of stolen property

✔ Manufacturing, selling or buying, giving away, bartering, delivering, exchanging, or distributing a controlled substance

If a resident breaches this agreement (and the police aren't involved), the landlord has the right but isn't obligated to evict the resident. If a resident breaches the agreement and is arrested, and if the police notify the landlord of the crime, then within 15 days of receiving notice, the landlord must file for eviction of the tenant or ask the county attorney to do so. If the landlord doesn't file for eviction or ask the county attorney to do so, and the resident is arrested again for committing the same crime on the same property, the landlord can end up losing her property to the state.

Increasingly, judges are finding that landlords are legally liable for any losses or personal injuries residents suffer at the hands of a third-party criminal, and the awards are often huge. Make security a top priority.

Taking Practical Security Measures

As a landlord, you probably want to know specific steps you can take to secure your rental property and protect residents from crime. In the following sections, we explore several options for you to consider.

Turning to a crime prevention program

Although you can't directly control the amount of crime in your rental property neighborhood, you can be proactive. A great way to take the initiative in fighting crime is to join or start a crime prevention program in your neighborhood or within your rental community. Check with your local police department and neighborhood association to see what programs are available in your area.

One of the best crime prevention programs for rental property owners is available through most local law enforcement departments. The Crime Free Multi-Housing Program (www.crime-free-association.org/multi-housing.htm) unites rental property owners, local law enforcement, and residents in an effort to fight crime and raise the local standard of living. Trainers certified with the nonprofit International Crime Free Association teach owners and managers how to help keep illegal activity out of their rental properties. This training is comprehensive and covers applicant screening techniques, proper preparation of rental contracts, warning signs of drug activity, crisis resolution, and ongoing management responsibilities. Residents receive instruction on how to identify criminal and suspicious behaviors, and they're strongly encouraged to take responsibility to prevent crime from occurring.

After the training is complete and you demonstrate that you're screening prospective residents, evicting problem ones, and using a Crime and Drug-Free Housing Addendum, your property can be certified as a Crime Free Multi-Housing Community. After certification, you can display signs at the entrances to your rental property to alert any prospective residents that your property doesn't tolerate any criminal or drug-related activity.

Figure 15-1 shows what a sample Crime and Drug-Free Housing Addendum looks like. To access a copy that you can print, visit www.dummies.com/go/landlordlegalkit and click the Risk Management folder.

Take the time to know the names of law enforcement officers who patrol your neighborhood. Share their names and telephone numbers with your employees and residents and encourage them to talk with and cooperate with those officers.

Taking necessary security precautions

One of the best ways to keep crime from occurring at your rental property is to make security a top priority. Although you can't guarantee that your property is safe, you should do what you can to increase the likelihood that residents don't encounter problems. The following sections cover some security issues worth considering, for your property's safety and your residents' well-being.

One of the best ways to secure your rental property is to screen applicants carefully, as Chapter 8 explains. In addition to credit checks and references from previous landlords, criminal histories are especially important.

Crime and Drug-Free Housing Addendum

This document is an addendum and is part of the Lease or Rental Agreement, dated _____,

by and between _____, "Owner/Agent",

and _____ "Tenant",

for the Premises located at: _____.

In consideration of the execution or renewal of a lease of the Premises identified in the Lease or Rental Agreement, Management and Lessee agree as follows:

1. Lessee, any member of Lessee's household, or a guest or other person under the Lessee's control shall not engage in criminal activity, including drug-related criminal activity, on or near said Premises. "Drug-related criminal activity" means the illegal manufacture, sale, distribution, use, or possession with intent to manufacture, sell, distribute, or use a controlled substance (as defined in section 102 of the Controlled Substance Act (21 U.S.C. 802)).

2. Lessee, any member of Lessee's household, or a guest or other person under Lessee's control shall not engage in any act intended to facilitate criminal activity, including drug-related criminal activity, on or near said Premises.

3. Lessee or members of the household will not permit the Premises to be used for, or to facilitate criminal activity, including drug-related criminal activity, regardless of whether the individual engaging in such activity is a member of the household or a guest.

4. Lessee or members of the household will not engage in the manufacture, sale, or distribution of illegal drugs at any location, whether on or near said Premises or otherwise.

5. Lessee, any member of Lessee's household, or a guest or other person under Lessee's control, shall not engage in acts of violence or discharge firearms on or near said Premises.

6. Violation of any of the above provisions shall be a material violation of the Lease or Rental Agreement and good cause for termination of tenancy. A single violation of any of the provisions of this addendum shall be deemed a serious violation and a material noncompliance with the Lease or Rental Agreement. It is understood and agreed that a single violation shall be good cause for termination of the Lease or Rental Agreement. Unless otherwise provided by law, proof of violation shall not require criminal conviction, but shall be by a preponderance of the evidence.

7. In case of conflict between the provisions of this addendum and any other provisions of the Lease or Rental Agreement, the provisions of the addendum shall govern.

_____   _____   _____   _____
Date   Owner/Agent   Date   Tenant

_____   _____
                                                  Date   Tenant

Figure 15-1: Crime and Drug-Free Housing Addendum.

Form courtesy of Robert S. Griswold

Securing doors and windows in rental units

Start by making sure that any way to enter the rental unit (door or window) can be locked or latched from inside the unit. To secure doors and windows, do the following:

- ✓ **Equip every standard, solid-core entry door for every unit with a locking doorknob and deadbolt (preferably with minimum 1-inch throws or even longer).** Some areas require a keyless deadbolt for added security when residents are home. (For details about securing keys and re-keying locks, see "Maintaining control over locks and keys," later in this chapter.)

- ✓ **Equip every sliding entry door with a security bar.** A *security bar* typically is a wooden rod approximately the diameter of a broom handle that a resident can place in the track between the sliding door and the door jamb that prevents the door from sliding open. Sliding doors should also have pins in the overhead frame that prevent the door from being lifted out.

- ✓ **Keep all the doors to the common areas of the building locked.** If any building locks are broken, fix them immediately. Give a set of keys to all exterior locks to local police personnel so that the officers on your beat can gain access to the building during routine patrols.

- ✓ **Make sure all windows have latches that residents can use to lock windows from inside.** Newer windows will have these built in, but you need to buy them for older windows. Pins that go through the window frame or doweling in the window track can be used to secure a window in a slightly open position to provide air flow but not wide enough to allow access.

- ✓ **Install peepholes in rental unit entry doors.** Residents should be able to see visitors before opening their doors. (State or local codes may require peepholes.)

In addition to keys and/or access-control systems, use standard security devices such as deadbolts and locking passage sets. All wood entry doors should be solid core and have wide-angle peepholes or door viewers. Window locks and safety pins for all sliding glass doors, or even simple wood doweling for window tracks, are valuable security devices. Make sure your resident initials on her move-in checklist (refer to Chapter 11) that all these security devices are operative and that she knows to contact you immediately if any locks or security devices are inoperative. Repair any broken locks or security devices immediately upon notification.

Make sure that all common area building entries have a clearly marked street address and that all apartments have clearly marked apartment numbers on their doors. This makes it easy for you, your residents, and local law enforcement to communicate regarding where illegal activities are taking place.

Lighting up parking lots, hallways, and other areas

Effective outdoor lighting has many benefits to dissuading crime. Proper lighting can serve as a deterrent to vandalism and other crime while illuminating your building walkways and the common areas to help prevent risks to residents and guests. The right lighting plan can also beautify your building and improve your property's curb appeal. Just remember that lighting is effective only if it's operative, properly located, and has the right type of fixture and light bulb for the intended purpose.

When lighting your rental property, keep these tips in mind:

- **Install appropriate lighting.** Make sure the lighting is sufficient to fully illuminate key areas, including parking lots and entryways.

  Avoid going overboard. Too much lighting may irritate a resident whose bedroom is 20 feet from the 5,000-watt bulb that illuminates the parking area.

- **Keep fixtures clean and clear.** External light fixtures get dirty over time or become littered inside with dead bugs. If the fixture has a cover over the light bulb, that cover can become cloudy over time. Keeping the fixtures clean and clear ensures that they cast the maximum amount of light.

- **Replace any exterior lighting on clock timers with photocells that automatically detect darkness.** This keeps your property well lit and eliminates the need to constantly adjust timers to accommodate changes in daylight hours over the course of every year. Plus, photocells turn on the exterior lights on dark, stormy days. You can easily inspect and test your lights during the day by blocking the photocell sensors with tape to simulate darkness.

- **Establish a regular schedule for inspecting the common area exterior lighting and immediately repair broken fixtures and replace any burned-out bulbs.** The best time for inspecting and testing your lights is at night, when you can see that all fixtures are working properly and providing sufficient illumination in the correct locations. Proper lighting in parking lots is very important because many residents routinely use parking areas after dark. Be sure to ask your residents to notify you of any inoperative lighting, and log your lighting inspections, repairs, and bulb replacements in your maintenance records.

Overgrown shrubs and other landscaping may provide hiding places for criminals and conceal criminal activity, so keep shrubs and other landscaping trimmed and restrict access to unused or dead spaces. For example, you may want to install a plywood barrier blocking off the space under the first floor stairs to prevent it from being used by dealers and their customers. Consider walling off or fencing off stairwells, spaces under porches, small alcoves, or the space under the stairs.

Being vigilant and keeping residents posted

Part of your duty is being vigilant and warning your residents about criminal activity in the area, so they can protect themselves and perhaps even assist in deterring crime. To stay abreast of any criminal activity in or around your rental property, do the following:

- **Keep in touch with local law enforcement.** If they send out notices of criminal activity in the area, sign up to receive them. (See "Turning to a crime prevention program," earlier in this chapter for additional guidance on teaming up with local law enforcement.)

- **Engage with residents.** By establishing casual relationships with residents and conversing with them every so often, you're likely to hear about any concerns they have regarding their safety.

- **Watch for signs of criminal activity.** Some signs are more obvious than others. For example, if someone is vandalizing the property, you or a member of your staff is likely to notice it immediately. On the other hand, you may not notice increased traffic around a certain resident's unit that may be a sign of drug dealing unless you're actively watching for it.

- **Inform residents of any criminal activity in the area and tell them what they can do to protect themselves.** By cautioning residents of criminal activity in the area, you're likely to make them more diligent in protecting themselves. For example, they may be more likely to lock their doors and latch their windows. They're also likely to become more vigilant, at least for a while, thus becoming another crime deterrent.

Educating and connecting residents

Although you can be held legally liable for losses or personal injuries that your residents suffer as a result of a crime, you can shift much of the burden of protecting residents to them by educating them and encouraging residents to get to know one another. Close-knit communities are much less susceptible to crime. In the following sections, we explain various ways to encourage and equip residents to protect themselves and one another.

Providing guidance on crime prevention

Residents may not know the measures they need to take to protect themselves, so provide them with some guidance. Here are a few precautions to pass along to residents:

- Lock all doors and latch all windows prior to leaving your unit, even if you're just stepping out for a moment.

- Use the security bar and door pins to secure sliding entry doors from the inside.

✔ Use the deadbolt lock to secure the entry door whether you're in your unit or leaving it.

✔ When someone knocks on your door or rings the doorbell, look through the peephole, if available, to check who the person is before opening the door. A security chain that attaches the door to the door jamb isn't very secure, but it's better than nothing.

✔ Keep window coverings closed at night and whenever the unit is left vacant.

✔ Put some lights, televisions, and radios on timers during the day and at night when the unit is vacant, to make people think someone is home.

✔ Record all serial numbers of any valuable devices, including televisions, sound systems, computers, and game consoles, to help police identify any stolen goods.

Contact local law enforcement to see whether they have crime-prevention booklets or tip sheets that you can distribute to residents. If they don't, you can find such items online. For example, the National Crime Prevention Council offers a free checklist with advice and suggestions to help residents evaluate the current safety features of their units and building and tips on getting to know the neighbors. To access the tip sheet, visit www.ncpc.org/resources/files.

Paying attention to resident questions and concerns about security issues

When a resident directly inquires about safety or security at your property, always provide an honest answer and inform her of any recent confirmed serious or violent criminal incidents. Of course, you obviously can't disclose what you don't know, but if a resident asks a question or expresses a concern about safety or security and you don't know the answer, obtain the answer, if possible, and pass it along to the resident or refer the resident to local law enforcement for more information. If you do have knowledge of bodily injury or other serious incidents on your property, discuss with your attorney the options on disclosure. Refer applicants or residents to local law enforcement for information on such incidents that have occurred off-site.

Implement any reasonable security measures a resident requests. If a resident makes a reasonable security request and you fail to provide it, you may be held liable for any loss or personal injury the resident or resident's children or guests suffer as a result.

Encouraging residents to report suspicious activity

The more eyes you have watching your property, the more likely you're going to find out about any criminal activity on the premises. Ask residents to report any crimes or suspicious activity to local law enforcement and to share their observations with neighbors.

Discourage residents from becoming vigilantes. The only weapon they should use in their crime-fighting efforts is a telephone to call local law enforcement.

Encouraging residents to connect with one another

As mentioned previously, close-knit communities are less susceptible to crime, because community members know who should and shouldn't be in the area, they watch each other's back, and they share information. Of course, you can't force residents to establish personal relationships with one another, but you can encourage and facilitate the bonding process. Here are a couple suggestions:

- ✔ Form a crime-watch group and invite residents to become a part of it. See "Turning to a crime prevention program," earlier in this chapter, for details.

- ✔ Sponsor get-togethers, such as a once-a-month breakfast or picnics in the spring, summer, or fall.

- ✔ Organize competitions, such as volleyball or basketball tournaments, or a chili cook-off.

Tightening security

If your rental property is in a high-crime area or increased security is standard for rental properties in your area, you may need to beef up security with one or more of the following:

- ✔ **Fences and gates:** To limit access to a large rental complex, you may want to fence in the property and install gates at all entrances, providing access only to residents and their guests. Fences and gates are a huge expense, regardless of whether gates are electronic or require security personnel to turn away unauthorized visitors.

- ✔ **Security personnel:** If you need to have security personnel guard and monitor the property, you have several options to consider, including the following:

  - • A standing guard service to provide around-the-clock protection

  - • A drive-through and property lock-up service that makes a predetermined number of random checks of the premises each evening (either by vehicle or on foot) and includes the securing of common area facilities

- • A part-time guard with a staggered schedule to deter criminals by keeping them guessing

- • A law-enforcement officer who offers off-duty security services (if the law-enforcement agency allows it)

✔ **Security cameras:** Security cameras deter crime and help identify suspects and gather evidence. They're relatively unobtrusive for residents, but they can be costly to purchase and service, and monitor, and you need procedures in place to store the video recordings.

✔ **Security systems:** Security systems aren't common in rental units, but that may change as technology improves and costs drop for wireless security systems. If you're operating in a high-crime area or a resident has experienced a break-in, consider working with the resident to explore solutions and perhaps share the costs of added security.

Securing Your Business

As a landlord and rental property owner, you're a business owner, and you have certain legal obligations to secure your business and oversee operations in a way that further protects residents from crime and protects any employees you hired.

To do so, you want to provide guidance on how to keep resident records and master and duplicate keys from falling into the wrong hands, to screen employees and monitor their behavior, and to protect employees from residents.

Safeguarding the rental office and resident records

Your rental office has a lot of sensitive information. To ensure that this information doesn't get in the wrong hands, you want to make sure your rental office and resident records are secure and protected.

Resident records contain a great deal of information that identity thieves can use to commit crimes. Most resident records contain the person's name, address, contact information, and Social Security and driver's license numbers, and may contain bank account and credit card numbers. If this information falls into the wrong hands and results in identity theft, and it did so due to your carelessness, a resident could sue you for any damages, including the emotional distress often caused by identity theft.

To limit your liability, we encourage you to take the following measures to secure resident records:

✔ If you store files electronically,

- Use encryption software and password protection to deter unauthorized access.

- Install virus protection and a firewall and keep them updated and running whenever the computer is on.

- Use a desktop computer located in a secure location. Avoid storing resident information on laptops or other portable devices that are easy to steal. (If you must store them on a portable device, lock the device with a secure password.)

✔ Never release information about a resident without her written permission except pursuant to a subpoena.

✔ Before discarding any paperwork that contains a resident's personal information, shred it.

✔ Retain as few documents as possible containing a resident's Social Security or driver's license number.

✔ Include as little personal information as possible when corresponding with a resident, especially when doing so electronically (email or texting).

✔ Destroy all resident records after the required number of years has passed for keeping those records (usually no more than four years after the tenancy has ended).

Maintaining control over locks and keys

Master keys or duplicate keys that fall into the wrong hands make it easy for the criminal element to break into rental units, so take the following precautions to limit access to these keys:

✔ Avoid using a *master key* — a key that opens all locks. One lost key can require you to rekey an entire property.

✔ Keep all duplicate keys in a locked metal key cabinet or key safe that is securely affixed and can't be removed.

✔ Don't label them duplicate keys with the residents' addresses or unit numbers; rather, code them so that if they become lost or stolen, they can't be used easily.

✔ If a resident reports a lost or missing key, change or rekey the lock instead of just giving her a duplicate key, unless she's sure the key is irretrievably lost and can't be traced back to the rental unit. Charge the resident a reasonable fee to cover your costs of getting a new key made.

✔ Don't give contractors a key to a resident's unit. Arrange to have some-one let the contractor in.

✔ Change or rekey a unit's entry locks prior to a new resident moving in. A prior resident may have returned the right number of keys, but could have made extras.

✔ If you use a keycard system, as we explain in the nearby sidebar, disable any lost or stolen keycards.

If a resident wants to rekey or change a lock, make sure she provides you with a duplicate key so that you can enter the unit to resolve emergencies and make agreed-upon repairs. If you find an added or changed lock, verbally explain your policy and request a copy of the key. If the resident doesn't want to give you a copy of the new key, send a polite but firm letter informing her of your policy and indicate that failure to provide access could result in respon-sibility for damages, or even eviction. Ultimately, you may need to consider eviction if you aren't able to obtain a copy of the key.

Using keycard systems

I (Robert) have personally installed keycard systems with great success. *Keycards* are the size of a credit card and contain a small microchip that provides a unique identification number that's almost impossible to forge.

More sophisticated keycard and other access-control systems are now available and are regularly used in hotels and motels. When com-bined with full-perimeter fencing, keycard sys-tems can be effective in controlling access, as long as your residents cooperate and don't let anyone follow them in. Originally these systems weren't cost-effective unless you owned a larger rental property, but in the last decade or so, costs have dropped considerably, making them affordable for many smaller properties.

You can install keycard readers at all access control points on the property, such as vehicle and pedestrian gates, as well as common area facilities. Another great feature of keycards is that, with the use of an ATM-type station, they can store monetary value and be used for laun-dry machines, tennis court lights, or any other amenity that you want to charge for or control.

Screening potential employees

Because your employees will have close contact with your residents, make sure you screen all candidates before hiring them. You can't solely rely on a résumé, an interview, and a list of references when making hiring decisions. You must focus on more in-depth screening, including mandatory criminal background checks, especially for any employee who will have access to money, keys, or any occupied rental units. If you choose to conduct your own background checks on employees, pay particular attention to work and residence history.

Conducting criminal background checks is also important because of the minimal day-to-day supervision in many positions, the rental housing industry and building maintenance trades have historically been relatively easy areas for individuals with poor work history, alcohol or substance abuse problems, and serious criminal convictions to find employment. But many managers and maintenance personnel are in a position of trust; they often assist in the collection of rent and of cash from coin-operated laundry equipment, have regular resident contact, and have ready access to building equipment and supplies and the rental units. Therefore, the liability for a landlord who fails to properly screen employees or contractors is very high.

In Minnesota, for example, the law requires that rental property owners run background checks on prospective building managers. If the manager has been convicted of a serious crime (such as murder, rape, or stalking), the owner may not hire the manager or must discharge the manager if the manager has already been hired. The law was named after Kari Koskinen, a woman murdered by her building manager. The manager had a previous criminal record that wasn't disclosed to her or the property owner.

The employment screening process is much more difficult than resident screening because of the numerous state and federal laws protecting applicants for employment. These laws make it difficult for the small rental owner to meet all the legal requirements of hiring. If you own just a few properties, you may want to consider using a professional outside employment firm to locate and screen prospective employees.

Be sure to check with an employment law specialist before initiating a pre-employment screening policy to ensure your application procedures meet all legal requirements and to help you avoid federal law pitfalls. For example, a job applicant's credit history can be important if the employee will be handling money. Yet the federal Fair Credit Reporting Act (FCRA) covers employee background checks, and several mandatory disclosures are required. Also, the Americans with Disabilities Act (ADA) severely restricts an employer's ability to seek information about an applicant's medical history. The applicant or employee can volunteer information, but you can't ask questions concerning physical limitations, mental illness, prior workers' compensation claims, lost time due to illness or injury, or prior drug and alcohol addictions. Be very careful; employers who violate the FCRA or ADA regulations may suffer significant penalties.

The following sections describe the process of pre-employment screening of prospective employees and explain the convenience of working with an employment-screening firm.

Explaining the process

Focus your pre-employment screening on education, job history, and personal references, plus a criminal background search and a drug/alcohol screening. Follow these simple steps up-front for the pre-employment screening:

1. **Have each prospective employee complete an employment application that lists her education, experience, and references, and have her specifically authorize your right to investigate the provided information.**

   If you're hiring an employee who'll live on-site, require that she complete a separate rental application and rental contract, and be sure to include any other adult occupants, just as you would if this were a non-employee rental.

2. **Prescreen your prospective employee on the phone.**

   Describe the job requirements, hours, and compensation. Then discuss the applicant's current employment status. Review her qualifications, skills, and experience; reconfirm her interest in the position with the proposed work schedule and compensation.

3. **If there seems to be mutual interest, schedule an in-person interview and a tour of the rental property.**

Hiring an employment-screening firm

The ever-changing and more restrictive employment-screening regulations are creating a strong demand for employment-screening firms. We recommend using these firms, particularly those that specialize in the rental housing industry, whenever possible, especially if you own a smaller rental property.

Be wary of employment-screening firms that claim to be able to conduct a single national criminal database search. Not all states offer statewide searches, and the data is often inaccurate or dated in those states that do. Also, the statewide data typically only includes felony records, not serious misdemeanors, so the most thorough information must still be gathered on a county-by-county basis. Though the ability to conduct comprehensive employment screening is improving, the reality is that federal, state, and county law enforcement bureaus have outdated systems and don't always share information with one another.

We recommend specifying that you want your employment-screening firm of choice to conduct a criminal background check in every county where your prospective employee lived, attended school, and worked. This type of check costs more up-front, but it's a good investment that pays dividends and offers peace of mind in the long run.

Keeping tabs on employee behavior

Having employees increases your liability, particularly when it comes to violence and sexual harassment. Keep your eyes and ears open so you don't miss the following danger signs:

- ✔ Although it doesn't happen often, be careful if you ever have any indication that your employees display abusive tendencies, make threats, or show any signs of violent or disruptive behavior. You aren't always liable if one of your employees threatens or harms someone, but workplace violence is a concern throughout the country, and rental housing employees are often in positions of authority, with access to personal information and rental units. Watch for any signs of threats, illegal drug possession, or the illegal possession and/or use of weapons. If you become aware of any of these signs or if you find out about prior attacks or convictions for violent crimes, immediately contact your employment law specialist for advice on the proper response, which may include a written warning or the employee's immediate termination.

- ✔ Sexual harassment claims by residents against managers, other employees, or contractors (or even other residents) are a growing concern for rental property owners. You need to have a clear, firm, written, zero-tolerance policy against sexual harassment, and you must promptly and fairly investigate any complaints. Cases of employee or contractor misconduct have been a problem for years. However, recent litigation against owners is making this matter even scarier in cases where one resident accuses another resident of sexual harassment and alleges that the owner or manager either condoned such actions or failed to take proper steps to address the concerns. This territory is dangerous, so don't jump to conclusions; balancing the need for a prompt and accurate investigation against the rights of the accused individuals can be difficult. Immediately contact your attorney for advice when you're told about any sexual harassment allegations.

Dealing with Troublesome Residents

Despite impeccable resident screening, sometime in your career, you're likely to rent to people who cause trouble and disturb and possibly even harm their neighbors. As landlord, one of your responsibilities is to curb criminal behavior, perhaps even to the point of having a resident evicted. If you know of criminal activity occurring on your property, and you fail to take action to have it stopped, then other residents may try to hold you accountable for any damages they suffer as a result.

In the following sections, we provide guidance on how to respond to criminal behavior in general and, more specifically, how to deal with domestic conflict and situations involving illegal drugs.

Responding to general criminal behavior

Whenever you become aware of any criminal behavior occurring on or near your property, you need to take action. Of course, your response depends on the seriousness of the crime, the degree of danger it poses to you and others, and other factors, but your options generally boil down to the following (listed in escalating severity):

✔ **Discuss the situation with the resident.** If you're dealing with a petty crime, such as disturbing the peace or public intoxication, you may want to discuss the situation with the resident first, express your expectations, and perhaps even issue a verbal warning along with possible consequences if the behavior continues. (Log the date and time of your encounter and write down what happened in the resident's file, or send the resident a letter confirming the conversation so you have a record of it.)

✔ **Issue a written warning.** If a verbal warning doesn't achieve the desired results, issue a written warning or a notice to perform covenant or quit and keep a copy of it in the resident's file. A written warning or covenant notice serves as documented proof that the resident had ample opportunity to correct a problem if you have to eventually evict the resident.

✔ **Call law enforcement.** When danger to persons or property appears imminent or you see a serious crime, such as assault or theft, in progress, call 911 immediately. You may also want to contact law enforcement if you tried to curb the behavior yourself but were unsuccessful. Getting local law enforcement involved sends a signal that the resident's behavior is unacceptable and that you won't tolerate it. This very credible verification of a police report can also be excellent evidence should legal action such as a restraining order or an eviction become necessary.

✔ **Encourage the resident to leave.** If residents pose a risk to your property or their neighbors, you may need to ask them to leave.

Consider offering incentives to encourage the residents to leave voluntarily and avoid potentially costly legal action. Incentives may include letting the resident out of the lease with no repercussions, refunding the security deposit and covering the costs of cleaning and repairs yourself, and even offering to cover a portion of the costs to relocate. Be sure any such agreement is in writing and money is only paid after the resident has completely vacated the premises. You shouldn't have to reward a resident for bad behavior, but if you want them gone badly enough and have reason to believe that evicting them would cost even more in time, money, and aggravation, these incentives may be a small cost to pay.

✔ **Evict the resident.** Violation of the terms of the rental contract justifies eviction. Refer to Chapter 19 for more discussion on eviction.

Whatever action you take in response to a person's bad behavior, if that behavior puts other residents or their property at risk, notify them in writing of the risk and what you're doing to address it. If you fail to warn residents, and something bad happens to them, the law may hold you responsible.

Handling domestic issues

Couples (or any combination of two or more individuals) who rent units together and have domestic disputes provide a tough challenge for rental property owners. As with disputes between neighbors or roommates, you need to avoid getting involved. You lack the authority to side with one party or the other, so stay neutral, encourage the couple to resolve their problems themselves, and continue treating all parties fairly and equally.

Unfortunately, some disagreements between residents involve domestic violence, and you may receive a request from one occupant to change the locks or remove one of the other residents from the lease. Don't agree to any such changes, regardless of the strength of the resident's argument, without first seeking legal advice and obtaining a copy of a restraining order or other appropriate documentation from the requesting resident.

In some circumstances you may be able to avoid an argument about changing the locks because the other party may be willing to voluntarily leave or allow the changing of the locks. But to cover yourself, even if the other party is cooperative or isn't disputing the matter, insist on a verifiable letter or agreement documenting the other party's consent. Be careful not to discriminate against the victim of domestic violence by evicting her, especially if the perpetrator is no longer in the rental unit and doesn't return to the property.

Some state laws allow victims of domestic violence to give notice and breach their lease without penalty upon presentation of either a court order or a police report.

The Violence Against Women Act (VAWA) of 2005 prohibits public housing agencies and rental properties that accept Housing Choice Vouchers from denying an applicant because she's been a victim of domestic violence or stalking. Nearly 30 states have passed legislation protecting women in similar situations, so check with local legal counsel if you run into one. Interestingly, VAWA protection has recently been confirmed to apply to men who are victims of domestic violence.

Dealing with druggies and dealers

The possession, use, and sale of illegal drugs is a common problem for landlords, especially in large apartment complexes. No matter the size of your rental unit, you must take action to discourage any activities involving illegal drugs, particularly drug dealing, or you risk the forfeiture of your rental property.

Larger properties often have a diverse resident demographic, including some groups who are statistically more likely to use drugs. The common areas of the buildings usually offer unoccupied or unused spaces, where transactions can occur unobserved. And when the availability of illegal drugs at an apartment complex becomes generally known, the problem can easily become widespread.

The best way to deal with drug users and dealers is to make your rental property a place where drug-related activities are prohibited and where such activities can be more easily detected. You can prohibit drug-related activities by enforcing the terms spelled out in your rental contract and any crime- and drug-free amendments to that agreement. To discourage drug use and sales, take the precautions we describe earlier in this chapter in the section "Taking necessary security precautions."

Being Truthful about Safety and Security

Although touting your rental property as a safe and secure place for residents can be an effective marketing technique, avoid inadvertently increasing your liability. This problem arises when you represent or even imply that your property is safer and more secure than competing properties. If you make these kinds of claims, your security had better live up to your statements.

In reality, no rental property is immune from crime. Crime can and does happen virtually everywhere, despite your best efforts and those of residents and law enforcement.

Don't use the words *safe, secure, security,* or any variations thereof in your advertising, phone conversations, or vacancy showings, because if your resident ever becomes a crime victim, she'll certainly claim that your ads or comments gave her the expectation of security. Be sure that prospective residents understand that neither you nor law enforcement officials can guarantee any level of safety for them, their family and guests, or their personal possessions or vehicles. When discussing any building features, speak generically without embellishment. For example, if you happen to have an alarm device in your rental unit, don't refer to it as a "security protection system" or imply that the resident's safety is assured because of this or any other building feature. Simply state the fact that the rental unit is equipped with an alarm.

Test any alarm and demonstrate the proper use of all security hardware and devices in the presence of your residents. Then have them sign an acknowledgment. Remind your residents in writing to test these devices because they can fail or malfunction, and to call immediately for repairs or replacement.

Some landlords put disclaimers in their rental contracts that say the owner isn't responsible if a resident suffers damage or an injury, regardless of the cause. Because they have this disclaimer in place, owners get careless and slow in responding to resident complaints about lighting or window latches that don't work. But what these owners don't realize is that these disclaimers are almost certainly unenforceable. Many states have laws that invalidate such broad clauses because the disclaimers attempt to shift the owner's duty to properly maintain the premises to the resident. However, informing residents of the following within your rental contract language is a good idea:

- ✔ You don't promise security beyond the essentials of door locks, window latches, and external lighting.

- ✔ The residents acknowledge that you don't and can't guarantee the safety or security of them, their family, or their guests.

- ✔ You don't guarantee the effectiveness or operability of security devices.

- ✔ The resident should have renter's insurance (see Chapter 9).

See your local legal counsel for assistance preparing the proper language and documentation.

Chapter 16

Understanding Resident Privacy and Your Right to Enter the Premises

*T*he maxim "A man's home is his castle," which dates back to Roman times, has become a set of legal principles that are generally known as the castle doctrine. The *castle doctrine* provides that people's dwellings, and often any legally occupied area such as a vehicle or office, are places where they have certain protections and immunities, including the right to use force to defend against an intruder.

When applied to the residential rental housing industry, the law presents a conflict between the rental property owner and resident rights. Although the property belongs to the owner, as long as the resident resides in that property, it's the resident's castle.

In this chapter, we explore the legal interests of owners and renters and explain how you can maintain your ownership rights without violating your residents' right to undisturbed use of the property. In addition, we provide guidance on how to protect a resident's personal information and avoid harassment claims.

Balancing Owner and Renter Rights

As the owner, when you lease a rental unit to a resident, you give that resident possession of the unit for as long as he resides in it. For the duration of the residency, your access to the unit is limited by various laws and covenants, stated or implied, that boil down to the following:

- The resident's right to enjoy the unit undisturbed significantly limits your right to enter the premises. You don't have the right to enter at any time you choose or for any reason that crosses your mind. To find out about acceptable reasons to enter a residence, see "Looking into state statutes," later in this chapter.

- Only in cases of actual emergency, when you have no opportunity to provide advance notice, do you have the absolute right to enter the unit.

- In the absence of an emergency, you must give reasonable notice and enter only during reasonable hours. For more about what "reasonable notice" means, see "Exercising Your Right to Enter a Residence," later in this chapter.

- By contract (lease or rental agreement), you may be able to extend your right to enter the premises to other circumstances. However, state statutes may disallow such exceptions to the rules even if a resident signs the agreement.

In the following sections, we explain the law, provide guidance on state statutes, and suggest wording to add to your lease or rental agreement to protect your right to enter a unit.

Exploring the influence of contract and property law

The laws governing the relationships between landlords and residents have evolved over several centuries, primarily from the following two branches of law:

- **Contract law:** Rules that govern the rights and obligations of two or more parties who enter into an agreement. Contract law is most evident in the lease or rental agreement that delineates the rights and obligations of the landlord and resident.

- **Property law:** Rules that govern ownership and rental of *real property* (land and buildings) and *personal property* (anything that can be easily moved into or out of real property).

The law of real property historically has emphasized ownership rights, giving landlords authority to enter their residents' premises. Over time, however, the mingling of property and contract law has reduced these rights, recognizing that, for legal purposes, the landlord has contractually given possession of the rental unit to the resident for the duration of the lease.

Honoring the implied covenant of quiet enjoyment and warranty of habitability

The evolution of contract and property law has resulted in some lease terms that are *implied* (assumed to be included), even if they're not actually written down — in every residential lease. Two of these implied terms come into play in determining when a landlord has the right to enter a resident's dwelling:

✔ **The implied covenant of quiet enjoyment** guarantees renters the right to the undisturbed use of the property. This right restricts landlord access to the rental unit to certain times and for certain reasons and requires that in most cases, the landlord provide reasonable notice prior to entry. Residents also have a duty to one another to honor the covenant. (See Chapter 9 for more about the implied covenant of quiet enjoyment.)

✔ **The implied warranty of habitability** requires landlords to provide their residents with dwellings that are safe, sanitary, and operational. (See Chapter 12 for more about the implied warranty of habitability.)

As landlord, you must balance the covenant of quiet enjoyment with the warranty of habitability. Although residents have the right to undisturbed use of the rental unit, you have an obligation to maintain habitability, which may require gaining access to the unit for inspections, maintenance, and repairs. To honor both of these implied terms, give residents advance notice that you need to enter the premises and, if possible, get their permission to do so. See "Giving residents advanced notice and getting permission," later in this chapter, for details.

Looking into state statutes

The implied covenant of quiet enjoyment is open to wide interpretation. To narrow its scope, many state legislatures have developed their own statutes that provide acceptable reasons for landlords to enter rental units. These reasons usually fall into two groups — those that require reasonable notice and those that don't, as we explain in the following sections.

Breaching the implied warranty of habitability: What it can cost you

Housing codes were established to ensure the habitability of residential places. In many states, the *breach* (a legal term meaning *breaking*) of this warranty may result in the resident's right to withhold or escrow rent payments (deposit funds with the court) until habitability is restored. In more serious cases, the breach of this warranty may allow the resident to terminate the lease on the grounds of *constructive eviction* (in laymen's terms, when a landlord acts in such a way that significantly interferes with the tenant's use and enjoyment of the property), seek damages against you, the landlord, and, in extreme cases, cause termination of your right to do business as a landlord.

For guidance on how to track down your state's statutes that govern the landlord-resident relationship, visit www.dummies.com/go/landlordegalkit and click the Legal Resources folder.

State statutes may also restrict your right as a landlord to enter the premises to business hours (or *reasonable hours,* which usually means 9 a.m. to 6 p.m. on weekdays and 10 a.m. to 3 pm on weekends). State statutes may also include additional language about how much advanced notice is required and how notices are to be delivered. See "Giving residents advanced notice and getting permission," later in this chapter for details.

If your state has no statutes regarding a landlord's right to enter an occupied rented rental unit, then contract and case law come into play. In the event of a lawsuit, the courts will look at the lease and legal precedents to arrive at a decision.

Acceptable reasons to enter a residence without notice

In a few situations, depending on your state law, you don't need to provide a resident with advance notice of your need to enter the residence:

- ✔ To respond to an emergency, such as when you become aware of a problem that risks injury to life or property — for example, a fire or a broken water pipe

- ✔ When a resident has abandoned or surrendered the premises

- ✔ To respond to a court order, such as a resident refuses entry to repair known health and safety issues in the rental unit

- ✔ When the resident gives verbal permission at the time of the request

Acceptable reasons to enter a residence with reasonable notice

The law typically permits you to enter the premises for any of the following reasons, after providing the resident reasonable notice (see "Giving a resident reasonable notice" later in this chapter for more information):

- ✔ To inspect for or make necessary repairs or alterations and to supply necessary or agreed services.

- ✔ To check for problems during a resident's extended absence. Your lease may require residents to notify you when they plan to be away from their apartments for several days or longer. But even without such a provision, if you become aware that a resident has been absent for a long time, you need to be able to enter the apartment to make sure that utilities, such as electricity and water, aren't being wasted.

- ✔ To inspect smoke detectors or make an annual inspection in government-funded housing.

- ✔ To show the property to a prospective renter, buyer, or lender, or when you have good reason to suspect that the current resident has abandoned the premises.

Stating your right to enter the premises in your rental contract

If you want the right to enter the resident's rental unit in nonemergency situations, such as to show the unit to prospective residents if state law allows, add a specific provision to the lease that allows you to enter under limited and reasonable circumstances and only after providing adequate notice. Here's an example:

> "Landlord shall have the right to enter the leased premises at all reasonable times for the purpose of inspecting the same and/or showing the same to prospective Residents or purchasers, and to make such reasonable repairs and alterations as may be deemed necessary by Landlord for the preservation of the leased premises or the building and to remove any alterations, additions, fixtures, and any other objects which may be affixed or erected in violation of the terms of this Lease. Landlord shall give reasonable notice of intent to enter premises except in the case of an emergency. Furthermore, Landlord retains a Landlord's lien on all personal property placed upon the premises to secure the payment of rent and any damages to the leased premises."

Don't try to take away a resident's right by including such a clause as "Landlord may enter the premises at any time and for any reason without giving prior notice to the Resident," because judges won't look favorably upon contracts that attempt to take away an individual's legal right to privacy. Nor will they look kindly upon landlords who attempt to do so.

Exercising Your Right to Enter an Occupied Residence

As the owner and landlord of a rental property, you have a right to enter a resident's apartment in certain situations, but whether, when, why, and how you exercise that right are crucial to keeping you out of legal trouble. In the following sections, we recommend a low-key approach designed to keep you and your residents happy. We also explain how to give appropriate notice, what to do when a resident refuses to give you access, and what to expect if you're found guilty of violating a resident's right to undisturbed use of the property.

Building rapport with residents

Knowing and obeying the laws that govern the landlord-resident relationship are important. You and your residents share an interest in maintaining and improving the physical condition of the rental unit, which is much more attractive than the flip side where you and the residents don't.

As a result, you want to strive to establish landlord-resident relationships based on courtesy and respect, rather than on strict application of the law. Collaborate with your residents to find a balance between their right to undisturbed use of the property and your right of entry — a fair and reasonable agreement that enables you to effectively serve their needs. Demonstrating your commitment to helping your residents by being courteous, maintaining the grounds, responding quickly to maintenance calls, and resolving any issues that arise goes a long way toward maintaining cooperation.

Smart landlords realize that establishing and maintaining positive relationships with their residents is key to resident retention. Residents who continue to live in their apartments after their leases expire, often agreeing to rent increases, is good business. Re-renting vacant units involves expenses associated with losing rents (you can't collect rent on unrented units), advertising, and making sure the unit is rent-ready. You can't recover these costs. Consequently, you're well advised to notify your residents of any intention to enter the premises, provide a reason for the need, and reach a mutually acceptable agreement about the specific time of entry.

Entering a residence only when necessary

Even though you have a right to enter a resident's dwelling under certain conditions, don't abuse that right. Knocking on doors to check in and trying to check out the condition of the unit and what's going on inside when the resident cracks open the door is a violation of privacy, regardless of your intention. As long as residents pay their rent and comply with the other terms of their lease, you need to back off and give them space to live their lives and enjoy the premises they're paying you to use. In any event, enter only for legitimate business reasons. (Refer to the earlier section, "Acceptable reasons to enter a residence without notice" for specific reasons that you can enter without notice.)

Respecting resident privacy and personal space not only makes sense legally but it's also a wise approach to doing business. Nobody likes a snoopy, intrusive landlord or property manager. If you earn such a reputation, current residents will move out and spread the word to anyone who'll listen. They'll also probably post their opinions online.

Giving residents advanced notice and getting permission

Unless you're responding to an emergency or a resident has abandoned or surrendered the rental unit, you're required to provide reasonable notice of your need to enter the premises. We also strongly recommend that you obtain the resident's permission to enter the premises, although doing so isn't always possible. In the following sections, we explain what "reasonable notice" means and discuss the possibility of getting permission.

The best practice is to respect your residents' right to privacy by seeking a mutually convenient date and time to enter while providing as much notice as possible, except in emergency situations.

Giving a resident "reasonable notice"

State laws typically spell out what "reasonable notice" means in terms of the following factors:

✔ **Time:** In most states, "reasonable notice" means you have to deliver the notice to the resident at least 24 or 48 hours prior to entering the premises. Other states leave "reasonable notice" open to interpretation, but in practice, 24- to 48-hour notice is usually sufficient.

✔ **Method of delivery:** Some state statutes specify that notices must be in writing and require certain methods of delivery, such as in person, slipped under the residence door, via mail, email, or fax, and so on. If your state allows mail delivery of notices, it may also specify how many days in advance the notice must be mailed in order to meet the time requirement. In some states, providing oral notice is acceptable.

Even if your state doesn't require written notice, we recommend that you do so to rebut any claim by the resident that notice wasn't provided. Keep a copy of the notice and record the method of delivery and the date and time it was delivered. Consider following up with a courtesy phone call to the resident the day before to remind him.

✔ **Details:** State statutes may specify the details required in the notice, including your reason for needing to enter the premises, who will be entering the premises, and the date and approximate time you or your agent plan to enter the premises. Refer to Chapter 12 for a sample notice.

For guidance on how to track down state statutes that define "reasonable notice" in your state, visit www.dummies.com/go/landlordlegalkit and click on the Legal Resources folder.

Getting permission, when possible

The law permits you to enter a resident's unit without notice, if the resident gives you permission to do so. If you need to do so only occasionally, such as to make a repair, in many instances all that's required is a telephone call and a short conversation about the time of entry. On the other hand, if the repair is complicated or likely to require extended time, the better approach would be to talk with the resident to arrive at acceptable dates and times for entry, and to prepare the agreement in writing for his signature.

Be polite. Asking for permission is an opportunity for you to build rapport with your clientele. Just imagine how angry a resident would probably get if she received 24-hour notice the day before she's expecting relatives to drop by for a visit! Consider making a courtesy call a few days prior to the day you plan to enter the residence, and then sending an email a day or two prior to entry, according to the state statute.

Responding to a resident's unreasonable refusal to let you enter

Occasionally, a resident refuses to give you access to his dwelling, even after receiving adequate notice of a legitimate business reason for the entry. If the resident's refusal is reasonable (for example, she works at home and has an important conference call scheduled for that day), you should strongly consider honoring the refusal. Simply reschedule for another time.

If the refusal is unreasonable and the resident won't cooperate on setting a convenient date and time for you to enter the premises, the law allows you to enter, as long as you do so peaceably and behave professionally after you enter.

Don't try to force your way into a resident's living space. If a resident refuses repeatedly to cooperate with you, you may need to decide whether you want to keep that resident. If you have reason to suspect a resident may let you enter but cause other problems (such as falsely accusing you of assault or stealing), bring another person along to act as a witness regarding your entry and subsequent actions.

Counting the potential costs of abusing your right to enter

Abusing your right to enter a resident's dwelling is potentially very costly. Violations pose significant legal risks, including expensive lawsuits and money judgments based upon claims of invasion of privacy, breach of the implied covenant of quiet enjoyment, infliction of emotional distress, and liability for trespass.

A judge may also decide that your actions constitute *constructive eviction* — compelling a resident to leave without giving notice. Constructive eviction is grounds to unilaterally release the resident from the lease agreement with no further obligations.

Honoring Additional Resident Rights: Do's and Don'ts

Resident rights extend beyond the doors of their dwellings and beyond the confines of the rental property. You also need to respect and protect any personal data you collect about residents, avoid the temptation to contact your resident at work (unless service of notice at work must be attempted by state law if service at the unit is unsuccessful), and be very careful not to spread rumors about a resident that may negatively affect his ability to pursue future opportunities in housing, employment, and so on.

The following sections highlight several resident rights you need to be aware of and explain how you can respect and protect each right.

Do ease up on overnight guest restrictions

Landlords frequently limit overnight guests, such as allowing a guest for no more than ten days in any six-month period and requiring written approval for longer stays for no more than 14 days. Landlords do this to keep long-term guests from gaining the status of full-fledged residents who haven't been screened or approved, who haven't signed the lease or rental agreement, and consequently aren't legally responsible for complying with the lease terms.

Some landlords can be overly suspicious about residents' guests, even going to the extreme of requiring residents to register guests who may be staying for only a day or two. Remember that your goal as a landlord is to be continually aware of the need for resident retention. Placing undue scrutiny upon your residents and their guests can not only impede your retention goals but also be considered an invasion of privacy.

Don't release information about a resident

As landlord, you collect sensitive personal data about residents. You know where residents work, how much they earn, their credit history, the timeliness of their rent payments, and much more. Because you have so much information about residents, people who need that information are likely to ask you for it. And if you're a people pleaser, you may be tempted to share that information. Resist the temptation. Don't release information about a resident unless one of the following is true:

- ✔ The resident has given you permission, in writing, to release specific types of information. Keep in mind that this situation is exceptional. Renters — and therefore, landlords — consider a resident's personal and business matters to be confidential. On occasion, a resident will direct the landlord, typically in the resident's absence, to release information to a third party, such as a forwarding address.

- ✔ Another landlord asks you to share the resident's rental payment history or market rent.

- ✔ The request is from a law enforcement officer or public safety agent who needs the information for official purposes. For this type of request, you may decide that your policy is to require a subpoena.

- ✔ The information requested is already publicly available.

- ✔ The information is needed in the event of an emergency.

If you choose to release information about a resident, stick to the facts and make sure the facts are accurate. Communicating information that is incorrect or based on guesswork, if discovered to be wrong, is likely to result in legal action by the resident.

The most common situation is a request from a tenant's prospective landlord about timely rent payments and performance of other rental obligations, such as unit upkeep, interactions with other residents, or legal actions.

The safest course is not to release such information. A relatively safe course is to make sure your communication is entirely factual and specifically limited to the tenant's rental history, including any eviction proceedings.

If you have employees, establish a policy and communicate it clearly to your staff that you, as landlord, are solely responsible for providing information to outsiders about your residents. People who seek potentially damaging information, including gossip, are likely to contact your rental office and connect with various personnel who may be tempted to talk about residents' personal lives, hearsay about their objectionable behavior at the property, or similar subjects that would be considered private. Actions that may be invasions of privacy are likely to result in unfavorable legal action; your duty as a landlord is to prevent them.

Don't call or visit a resident at work

Your residents' rights to privacy extend to their workplace. Use your common sense about contacting them during their workday. If, for example, you need to schedule a time to make repairs to a unit, make the necessary contact when the resident isn't at work. Consider using emails or texts for quick contact. If you're unsuccessful, consider the most appropriate time to call the resident at work.

Never make a personal visit to your resident at work. Such visits are deemed harassment and can get you into legal trouble unless you're serving a notice pursuant to state law requirements. If you can't get in touch with a resident by calling his personal phone number, then call the work number and leave a brief message with your name and telephone number. Omit any details about the reason(s) for your call.

Don't be snoopy

Like most people, landlords are naturally curious. You may wonder what your residents are up to and who their guests are. Being curious is okay, and monitoring what's going on is part of your job securing the safety of all your residents, but don't go overboard. Grilling the guests, peeking in windows, and conducting surveillance to see what your residents and guests are up to are likely a violation of a resident's right to privacy and expose you to potentially costly lawsuits.

A resident's dwelling is his home and his castle. As long as he pays his rent, gets along with his neighbors, and takes relatively good care of your property, honor his privacy. Imagine how you would feel if someone were snooping on you.

Don't ostracize a resident you don't like

If you've had a terrible experience with a resident, you may feel obligated to warn your friends and colleagues. Don't do it. Going out of your way to tarnish someone's reputation, even if what you say is true, is likely to trigger a lawsuit accusing you of libel.

We recommend that you lay the terrible experience to rest and be grateful that the person has moved on. If another landlord or property manager calls to ask about your former resident and you feel compelled to share what you know, limit the scope of your answers to verifiable facts, such as rent payment history, verified complaints filed by other residents, law enforcement reports, and any eviction actions taken against the resident. Of course, if an eviction has occurred, making sure that a money judgment is filed and recorded in the public records can help future landlords to discover that your former resident was a problem. Typically, evictions that only involve regaining the possession of your rental unit (and there is no money judgment) won't be reflected on credit reports.

Chapter 17

Resolving Landlord-Resident Disputes

*A*lthough the proper resident screening and selection techniques greatly improve your success in picking good residents, you're sure to come across a problem resident or two. Some residents avoid paying rent, disturb the neighbors, damage property, or keep a growing collection of broken-down cars on the front lawn or in the driveway. Whatever the issue, you need to resolve it or, if that's not possible, get rid of the resident.

This chapter gives advice for handling some common resident problems and suggests valuable alternatives to eviction. It also prepares you for some scenarios you may encounter so you know right away how to deal with them.

Settling the Most Common Problems

The level of response you take toward a problem resident depends on how severe the problem is and how frequently it occurs. Some issues — including nonpayment of rent, additional occupants not on the rental contract, noise, and unsupervised children — are breaches of the rental contract. If, after one or more written warnings, the resident doesn't correct the problem, you need to take legal action to remove the resident.

Documentation is critical whenever you have a problem with a resident. Even minor problems are worth documenting because, over time, they may add up or increase in severity. If you need to evict a resident, you must have written documentation of the problem's history, because you'll likely have the burden of proof if you end up in court. Refer to Chapter 8 for how to keep detailed records.

These sections highlight several of the more common problems you may experience with your residents and how to handle them.

Late-, partial-, or nonpayment of rent

One of the toughest issues you'll encounter as a landlord is how to deal with a resident who consistently pays her rent late or, even worse, doesn't pay her rent at all. In other respects, the resident may not create any problems, but she just can't seem to comply with the contract's payment requirements.

Whenever a resident's rent payment is late, clearly inform her in writing that she has breached the rental contract. If you fail to enforce timely rent payment obligations or your late charges, the resident can later argue that you've waived your rights to insist on compliance with the contract's rent payment provisions or to collect future late charges. Inform the resident in writing that chronic late payments are grounds for eviction, even if you're not necessarily willing to go that route just yet. (See Chapter 7 for additional details on how to handle late-, partial-, and nonpayment.)

The strength of the rental market is usually the most important factor to consider when deciding whether to evict a resident. If it's a renter's market and you know that finding another resident will be difficult, you may be willing to be more flexible in handling rent payment issues. Be sure that you document the start and end of a change in policy so that you can show that you apply policies equally without regard to a resident's protected class.

Additional occupants

Residents frequently abuse the guest policy by having additional occupants in their rental units for extended periods. But you may have trouble determining the difference between a temporary guest and a new live-in occupant. Be sure that you have specific guest policies as part of your rental agreement or policies and procedures. If you suspect your resident has added another occupant, talk to the resident to find out what's going on. Point out your guest policy, but be sure to get her story before jumping to conclusions. This practice is sound not only because it's considerate but also because you need to avoid claims of discrimination, particularly if the additional occupant is a child.

In the case of children (where custody is an issue), we suggest you add them to the lease or rental agreement because they really aren't guests but family members. Because legally they're minors, they don't need to complete a rental application or go through your prospective resident screening process, as adults would. If the addition of the child causes the household to exceed your occupancy, have a written policy for handling the situation differently from the addition of an adult.

If your resident doesn't comply with your guest policy, immediately send her a Lease or Rental Agreement Violation Letter indicating that the additional occupant must be formally added to the rental contract as a resident or a notice to perform covenant or quit will be served. (All new adult occupants must complete a rental application, go through the resident screening process, and sign the rental contract if approved.) If the resident fails to cooperate, you may need to take legal action. This problem is serious. I (Laurry) am working with a developer/management company that specializes in low-income apartments. The agencies that fund this product type are vigorous about auditing occupancy, including unapproved persons living in these properties. If the situation isn't addressed promptly, the financing can be in danger.

For a sample Lease or Rental Agreement Violation Letter, go to `www.dummies.com/go/landlordlegalkit` and click on the Rental Contract folder.

A common guest policy in the rental housing industry is to allow guests to stay in the unit for up to 14 consecutive days. But savvy residents just ask their guests to leave for a day or two and then return. Although tough to enforce, we suggest modifying your guest policy to limit visits to a total of no more than 14 days in any six-month time frame. You should uniformly enforce this policy to the best of your ability to avoid allegations of discrimination.

Proving occupancy can be difficult. The receipt of mail or the presence of a vehicle on the property for excessive periods of time is often solid proof. Local law enforcement and your mail carrier can be of great assistance here.

Be careful when determining whether an additional occupant is a rental contract or guest policy violation if the individual may qualify under fair housing law as a *caregiver,* which is a disability accommodation. Typically, a caregiver isn't on the rental contract, isn't responsible for rent payment, and often can be a family member. You can screen her for behavior issues but not for credit because a caregiver isn't responsible for rent. Don't have caregivers sign the lease; instead, have them enter into a caregiver agreement that indicates they're living on-site only for the purpose of performing assistance services and that they agree to follow your policies, except that they're exempt from any senior housing age restrictions. Seek the advice of legal counsel if you have any questions.

Inappropriate noise level

Unreasonable or excessive noise is likely the most common complaint that landlords and property managers receive from residents. Downplaying the seriousness of the issue is easy, especially if you live across town. But unreasonable or excessive noise is a nuisance by law in most areas. You don't want a few noise complaints to spiral into a resident taking official action against you or refusing to pay her rent because of her "loss of quiet enjoyment" of the property, as explained in the nearby sidebar. Many jurisdictions have noise ordinances, and some allow action such as fines or violation notices to be taken against you as well as your resident. Residents may also find that their local small claims court is willing to give them a healthy rent credit for their loss of sleep!

You usually hear about a noisy resident from one of the resident's neighbors. The neighbor may or may not have already made her concerns known directly to the noisy resident. If she has and the noise continues unabated (or she isn't willing to take any action), then, as a first step, you should contact the resident, explain that there's been an anonymous complaint, and inform the resident that you expect her to live quietly with her neighbors. Confirming the substance of your conversation in a follow-up letter to the noisy resident is wise, and be sure to file it in their resident file in case further action is needed.

If the unacceptable noise continues, tell the complaining residents that they can always contact law enforcement and file an official complaint as soon as the noise level becomes a problem. Then they should let you know that they've done so.

Have a policy that requires all resident complaints regarding neighbors — especially noise — to be in writing. Neighbors usually don't want to go to court to testify; they just want you to quickly solve the problem and allow them to keep their anonymity. But if the noisy resident disputes the charges, the courts are usually reluctant to accept your unsubstantiated testimony. A report from law enforcement and a written complaint made simultaneously by a neighbor carry a lot of weight. If residents don't send you a written complaint, write them and state that you're still waiting for them to document the problem, that you can't do much without their cooperation, and that you'll recount what you understand they told you and correct any mistakes in a responsive letter. If residents fail to provide a written complaint, this confirmation letter at least has some value. Although it would be hearsay and inadmissible to prove that the noise occurred, it may be admitted in court to show that management received complaints.

Honoring the mutual covenant of quiet enjoyment

Multifamily living is often a lot like living in a college dormitory, where residents conduct their daily activities in close proximity to others. Residents' recreation can be noisy, and noise permeates thin apartment walls. Because renters relax at different times, the noise is likely to disrupt other residents whose schedules aren't in sync. Unfortunately, even long-time renters can forget or disregard this reality.

Landlords have turned to lawyers to help them respond effectively to noise complaints, and attorneys have responded with a duty known as the *mutual covenant of quiet enjoyment* — a promise, *assumed to be included* in every residential rental contract, that grants the right of undisturbed use of the property to every resident and prohibits residents from disturbing one another. As landlord, you guarantee every resident's right to quiet enjoyment of the premises.

Although rent increases and eviction proceedings are the sources of most landlord-resident disputes, you need to be receptive to disturbance complaints, as well, particularly because they're subject to your guarantee of quiet enjoyment. If you're having difficulty explaining the covenant of quiet enjoyment to a resident, compare it to the *golden rule*: Treat others as you would like others to treat you. Every resident is entitled to quiet enjoyment during her apartment residency, and consequently owes quiet enjoyment to every other resident.

Unsupervised children

Under federal law, with the exception of the limited number of HUD-certified senior housing properties, you must accept children at your rental property. Unfortunately, one of the toughest dilemmas you'll face is dealing with a resident's unsupervised child on the grounds of your property. If you don't do anything and the child gets hurt or hurts someone else, you may be sued for failing to take reasonable action. But if you don't handle the matter properly, the resident may claim that you're discriminating against families with children. In this case, you need to be able to prove that you acted reasonably and consistently.

If you become aware of an unsupervised child at your property who is in a potentially dangerous situation, immediately contact the parent or caretaker or, if the situation is serious, and you balance the risk between possible personal injury with possible civil rights violations, escort the child home to her parent(s). Also send a letter to your residents warning them of the seriousness of the matter. If the written notice isn't effective, you can always call the police or social services while advising your residents, in writing, that an eviction may be warranted. As with all communication with your tenants, be sure to keep copies. Diplomacy is essential here, because nothing can hit a nerve as quickly as someone accusing a child of misbehaving.

You can expect age- and activity-appropriate supervision of children, but that doesn't mean constant observation from close proximity. Adults will get distracted even when watching very young children. But you can address any health and safety issues to make your rental property reasonably safe for persons of all ages, and you must address lease violations for the disturbance of other residents. If your residents fail to properly supervise their children and the children damage your property, don't just talk to the children about the problem. Immediately contact the residents and officially advise them of the health and safety issues or lease violations, stressing the fact that they're responsible for the actions of all household members and guests and that disturbances or property damage by residents of any age are unacceptable. Communicate in writing or provide a letter confirming your conversation. This kind of action is usually sufficient, but if the damage is severe or continues, notify the residents in writing, bill them for the damage, and warn them that any continued problems will result in eviction.

Consulting Your Attorney for Advice

When you're unsure of how to handle a difficult situation with a resident, consider consulting an attorney for advice prior to taking any action that could possibly weaken your case if the matter eventually ends up in litigation. Anything you do, say, or write could be used against you in court, so having an attorney on your side to help you avoid legal pitfalls is a good idea.

Involve your attorney early in the process by requesting her input when you're developing your rental contract and any other legal documents. All too often, landlords call their attorneys only when problems arise, often when it's too late for the attorney to do much good. You may also find that the laws have changed and that the way you always handled a certain situation in the past is no longer the proper or legally accepted way. The cost for consulting an attorney to prevent problems is considerably less than the cost of a lawsuit, regardless of whether you win or lose. Refer to Chapter 2 for more information about using and hiring an attorney.

Resolving Problems without Eviction

When serious problems arise with a resident, your first impulse may be to evict the resident and find a replacement. After all, a resident who doesn't pay or who damages your property or disturbs her neighbors can drag you down and perhaps even taint your reputation as a landlord.

However, evictions are expensive and emotionally draining. They can also be costly in terms of lost rent, legal fees, property damage, and turnover expenses. And they can earn a negative reputation for your rental property with good residents in the area. Always consider the costs of any decision you make — in dollars, in reputation, and in resident relationships. Evaluate each situation carefully and turn to eviction only as a last resort.

In the following sections, we introduce several alternatives to eviction, starting with talking with the resident and escalating to the point of getting the resident to leave voluntarily.

Document any conversations you have or agreements you reach in writing, and make sure both you and all residents sign and get a copy of any written agreements. You may send a letter to the resident reaffirming your agreement or type a one-page report that includes the resident's name, the date and time you met, what you discussed, and what you agreed to. Place a copy of the report or letter in the resident's file.

Hashing it out: Listening and talking

Communication is an important tool in solving problems and resolving disputes, and it doesn't always need to come in the form of a warning letter or eviction notice. For mild to moderate first-time offenses, consider taking a nonconfrontational approach by following these guidelines:

- **Avoid the urge to blame the resident.** The fact that the problem involves the resident doesn't necessarily mean that the resident is the problem.

- **Don't try to interpret the resident's motivation.** You don't know why the resident did something wrong or failed to do what she was supposed to do unless you ask and she tells you.

- **Ask questions when appropriate.** If a resident missed a rent payment, the reason may matter. For example, if the resident had to deal with a family crisis, the situation may be temporary and nothing for you to worry about. On the other hand, if you find out that the resident lost her job, you need to know how she plans to pay the rent.

  Don't ask questions when the answers don't matter. For example, if a resident habitually exceeds the speed limit when driving through the apartment complex, any reason why she's doing so doesn't matter. She's endangering the lives of the other residents, and it needs to stop.

- **Approach the issue as a problem that you need help solving.** Separate the problem from the resident and enlist the resident's help in solving it. You may say something like, "Hi, Wendy. Some of the neighbors have complained about loud music coming from your apartment. As the owner, I have to make sure everyone can enjoy their property. Can you think of any ways to listen to the music without disturbing the neighbors?" This opens the discussion to possible solutions, such as repositioning the speakers, turning down the bass, wearing wireless headphones, and so on. If you simply tell the resident to turn down her music, you're more likely to put her on the defensive.

✔ **Stick to the facts.** Don't make sweeping generalizations, such as "You never pay the rent on time," unless they're true, because the resident can easily dispute such a statement. Instead, say something along the lines of "In six of the past seven months, I received your rent payment five days or more after the due date." A statement such as this is much more difficult to dispute, because you're telling what you experienced, not what you assume the resident did.

Be fair and friendly, but firm. Listen more than you talk and do your best to understand the situation from the resident's perspective, but the bottom line is that you need to be satisfied with the outcome. If you're dealing with a resident who's unwilling to cooperate, you may need to apply some pressure, possibly even to the point of evicting the resident.

Bringing in a mediator

If you're unable to reach an agreement by dealing directly with a resident, you have three ways to settle the disagreement:

✔ *Litigation* involves filing a claim with a court to have a judge or jury determine whether a party's legal right(s) have been violated by the failure of the other party to honor her obligation(s) as agreed to in a legally binding contract, such as a lease. (See "Taking a resident to small-claims court," later in this chapter, for details.)

✔ *Mediation* is an opportunity for both parties to settle their differences informally with the assistance of an objective third party. Although litigation involves rights and obligations and determining who's right and who's wrong, the goal of mediation is to arrive at a resolution that serves the needs of both parties to their mutual satisfaction. Mediation is typically less expensive than litigation. When done successfully, everyone wins.

✔ *Arbitration* is a cross between litigation and mediation. Like litigation, arbitration calls on an objective third party to determine who's right and who's wrong and award any damages to the injured party. Like mediation, the case is handled outside the legal system. Arbitration may be legally binding or not, depending on what the parties agree to prior to the hearing. If the parties agree to nonbinding arbitration and one party isn't satisfied with the ruling, she's free to file a legal claim, seeking a resolution through litigation.

Many organizations offer both mediation and arbitration services, so if mediation doesn't resolve the issue, you can always try arbitration. Check with your local bar association for referrals.

These sections help you determine whether a disagreement is suitable for mediation and offer guidance on how to find a good mediator.

Entering mediation with the right mindset

By the time parties enter mediation, they're usually very emotional. Each party thinks she's right and the other party is wrong. That's okay. Mediators are trained to deal with emotions. In fact, while litigation discourages participants from expressing emotion and relies solely on evidence to prove one's case, mediation encourages participants to express their emotions, so the mediator can help the parties discover and deal with the issues that are at the root of those emotions. As many mediators point out, the real issues that must be dealt with are often hurt feelings.

Mediation is usually most effective when parties enter into it with a positive attitude and with confidence that mediation will resolve the dispute. So, try your best to be positive and willing to let the mediator do her job. Be honest about how you feel and candid in answering any questions the mediator or the other party asks. Only by getting everything out in the open can you hope to reach a long-term solution.

Identifying disputes that can benefit from mediation

If you can't resolve a dispute with a resident you want to keep, then mediation is the preferred approach, because it's more likely (than litigation or arbitration) to lead to a long-term solution and less likely to embitter either party. Mediation is very useful for resolving civil disputes, such as those involving contracts.

If a resident's violation of the lease terms is so egregious or persistent that you want to remove the resident, then forget about mediation. Try to get the resident to move out voluntarily and, if that isn't an option or doesn't work, file a legal claim to have the resident evicted. Mediation can't help when either party is uncooperative or at least open to the possibility of arriving at a solution. (For more about getting a resident to move out voluntarily, check out the section, "Encouraging a voluntary move-out" later in this Chapter. Refer to Chapter 19 for more about eviction.)

Finding a qualified mediator

If you and your resident are open to the idea having a mediator help you resolve your dispute, the next order of business is to find a qualified mediator. Start by contacting your local affiliate of the National Apartment Association (NAA), community center, or bar association. Many cities and towns, especially the larger ones, have mediation centers that can handle most types of disputes for free or for a modest fee. You can also track down private-practice mediators (often called *neutrals*) through various associations or directories online, including the following:

- ✔ www.nafcm.org (NAFCM stands for the National Association for Community Mediation)
- ✔ www.mediate.com

- www.jamsadr.com (JAMS stands for the Judicial Arbitration and Mediation Services; ADR stands for the Alternative Dispute Resolution)
- www.adr.org
- www.judicatewest.com

Writing a warning letter

For serious or minor but persistent infractions, consider sending the resident a warning letter that includes the following:

- The resident's name, address, and unit number
- The date
- A clear statement of why you're sending this letter
- Any history of what's been done or not done to resolve the issue up to this point
- A clear statement of the desired outcome (for example, timely rent payments, assurances that all residents, including children will follow your rules, removing an old refrigerator from the porch, and so on)
- A deadline for correcting the problem or dealing with the issue
- A statement of the consequences of failing to address the issue to your satisfaction
- Your contact information

Hand-deliver the warning letter or mail it at a US Post Office with a certificate of mailing, so you have proof that the letter was delivered. You can also use certified mail, return receipt requested if the resident will sign for the letter. But our experience is that the more savvy the resident, the less likely it is that they will accept the letter. So just going to the US Post Office and sending the letter through regular mail but getting a certificate of mailing is not only more economical but still provides that proof you will need in court as well as actually being much more likely to actually be received (and read) by your resident. Always keep a copy of all communications (and the certificate of mailing or return receipt) in your files.

For more serious infractions, consider giving the resident an ultimatum via a legal notice, such as a Pay Rent or Quit notice or Perform Covenant (Cure Breach) or Quit notice, as explained in Chapter 19. A Pay Rent or Quit notice tells the resident to pay the rent within so many days (typically three to ten) or move out.

Taking a resident to small-claims court

Whenever you have a dispute with a resident that the two of you can't resolve, consider taking the matter to small-claims or municipal court. Small-claims courts are typically funded through tax dollars, so court costs are minimal. The jurisdictional limits for these courts range from $2,000 to $15,000, but the majority are $5,000 or less. Consult with your local court for its limits.

Prior to the date of the hearing, gather all your evidence, which should be easy if you have a folder for your resident that includes documentation of all your transactions and interactions. Your evidence is likely to include the following items:

- ✔ Your testimony and credibility

- ✔ Written contracts (such as the lease and your policies and procedures)

- ✔ Photographs

- ✔ Written correspondence (letters, email, text messages)

- ✔ Documentation of any oral communication (in person or over the phone)

- ✔ Witness testimony (either in person or a written statement signed by the witness and notarized)

- ✔ Documentation of steps you've taken to mitigate any damages you're claiming (for example, evidence that you tried to rent the apartment after the resident abandoned the unit to minimize the lost rent)

Prepare a timeline that traces the history of the matter you're bringing to court, so you have it clear in your mind and can present events in chronological order. You should also clearly label each document that supports a portion of your testimony in sequential chronological order so it's easy for the court (and even your resident) to follow your presentation. The court has to decide based on often conflicting testimony so make sure you are prepared and organized and are able to articulate your position on the issues while providing documents that support your version of the facts. A clear, consistent story of exactly what happened improves your credibility.

Encouraging a voluntary move-out

If a resident commits a criminal act or a serious breach of your rental contract, your only option is to get the resident to move out. You can do it forcefully through eviction or by giving the resident one or more incentives for moving out voluntarily. Eviction is a long, costly, and frustrating process, so we strongly recommend that you do your best to get the resident to move out voluntarily by offering one or more of the following incentives:

- **Termination of the rental contract without penalty:** You and the resident sign a mutual termination agreement, as explained in Chapter 19, and your resident is off the hook for any rent due after she moves out.

- **Refund of the entire security deposit:** You agree to return the entire security deposit to the resident, even if the unit has suffered damages or the resident still owes some rent.

- **Cash:** For residents who don't have the money to move out, you may want to offer to pay their moving expenses or hand them cash as soon as they move out of the unit, return the keys, and sign the mutual termination agreement.

Return the security deposit or pay a cash incentive only after the resident moves out and returns the keys. Residents who are strapped for cash may spend the money on something other than moving expenses and then claim that they have no resources to move out. In addition, as soon as the residents move out, change the locks.

If the resident refuses to move out voluntarily, eviction may be your only remaining option. Refer to Chapter 19 for details.

Avoiding Retaliation

Most states prohibit landlords from retaliating against residents for taking action to protect their rights. For example, you're not allowed to terminate a resident's lease, increase the rent, deny services (such as use of the pool or laundry room or cutting off their free wi-fi), or punish the resident in other ways if a resident does any of the following:

- Withholds a portion of rent payments to compel you to perform a repair that's your responsibility

- Reports an unhealthy condition to the local health inspector

- Organizes residents to protest against a new policy you're trying to enforce

- The resident accuses you of discriminating against her

Retaliating against residents is a bad business practice regardless of whether your state deems it illegal. If a resident takes action against you for a legitimate reason, find out what the resident wants and do your best to meet her needs. If you think the resident is being unreasonable, then explain why you disagree and do your best to resolve the issue in a way that addresses your mutual interests. If that doesn't work, then mediation, arbitration, or litigation may be necessary.

Part IV

Changing and Ending Leases

Tenant's Notice of Intent to Vacate Rental Unit

_____

Date

Owner/Manager

_____

Street Address

_____

City, State, Zip code

Dear _____,

This is to notify you that the undersigned tenants, _____,
hereby give you written notice of intent to vacate the rental unit at _____
on _____.

We understand that our Lease or Rental Agreement requires a minimum of _____ days notice before we move. This Tenant's
Notice of Intent to Vacate Rental Unit actually provides _____ days notice. We understand that we are responsible for paying
rent through, the earlier of: 1) the end of the current lease term; 2) the end of the required notice period per the Lease or Rental
Agreement; or 3) until another tenant approved by the Owner/Agent has moved in or begun paying rent.

In accordance with our Lease or Rental Agreement, we agree to allow the Owner/Agent reasonable access with advance notice in
order to show our rental unit to prospective renters or workmen and contractors.

Sincerely,

_____

Tenant

_____

Tenant

_____

Tenant

In this part, we discuss situations in which you need to change or end a lease or rental agreement and perhaps even evict a resident. To find out how to retain good residents, visit www.dummies.com/extras/landlordlegalkit.

In this part . . .

✔ Modify a lease or rental agreement or create a new one when a resident adds a roommate.

✔ Protect your legal rights when residents want to sublet a rental unit or assign their lease to someone.

✔ End a lease by not renewing it, by agreeing with the resident to terminate it, or by terminating it for breach of contract.

✔ Terminate a rental agreement with or without cause.

✔ Evict residents who give you trouble.

✔ Follow the proper procedure for moving a resident out in order to protect yourself against future legal claims.

Chapter 18

Handling Cotenancies, Sublets, Assignments, and Guests

- -

In This Chapter

▶ Steering clear of legal issues involving roommates and guests

▶ Recognizing the legal obligations of cotentants

▶ Understanding what subleases and assignments are

- -

As much as you may wish that the residents you screen and approve will honor the lease agreement, you need to accept the fact that residents often need to move out prematurely, part with old roommates, and take on new roommates and houseguests. As renters, residents usually have the legal rights, to some extent, to take any of these actions. As a landlord, however, you need some control over who moves out and who moves in, so you don't end up with violent, destructive, or deadbeat renters you never had the opportunity to screen. Likewise, you must have some control over the behaviors of visitors and guests in order to protect your property and your residents' rights.

Of course, you can use your lease or rental agreement to strictly enforce the terms of the lease and prevent residents from taking on new roommates, subletting or assigning the lease to another renter, or housing a long-term guest, but sometimes, being flexible is best for both your resident and your business.

In this chapter, we help you navigate the tricky situations that often arise when nonresidents enter the picture. We not only explain how to protect your legal rights but also point out your options and help you weigh their pros and cons.

Recognizing Legal Issues Involving Nonresidents

Residents (commonly referred to as *tenants*) are people who've signed your lease or rental agreement promising to abide by the terms of the agreement. Everyone else is a *nonresident* — a guest or a roommate who has no legal protections or obligations under the lease or rental agreement. Although you have little to no say about whom your residents invite over, you and your residents have legal rights and responsibilities with respect to nonresidents, including the following:

- Residents are liable for the behavior of their family members, *invitees* (guests), and *licensees* (people they choose to contract with, for example as roommates). A clause in your lease or rental agreement should state that any violation of the agreement caused by the resident or anyone she has over is a breach of the contract (see Chapter 9).

- If a nonresident causes damage or harm and you fail to take appropriate action, you could be held liable for any harm that the person causes to someone on your property and for any personal property damage or loss.

- As landlord, you have the right to limit the number of days a guest is allowed to visit, but you need to specify it in the lease. For example, you may want to allow overnight guests to stay up to 14 days in a six-month period without your written permission.

  Remain flexible with residents' girlfriends/boyfriends, who may be overnight guests far more than 14 days in a six-month period. But remember that from a fair housing perspective you need to have the same policies for all residents.

- As landlord, you have the right and obligation to determine who resides in a rental unit. After all, you must do your best to protect other residents and guests from harm and from property damage and loss. (See Chapter 15 for more about protecting residents and their guests from criminal acts.)

- If a nonresident stays for a certain length of time, moves her possessions into a rental unit (or to a residence with your knowledge) that person may become a tenant or lodger in the eyes of the law, even though the person isn't named on the lease. However, without the person's signature on a lease or rental agreement, you may have a difficult time enforcing the agreement or evicting the person without evicting the resident, as well.

  Inform your residents of the risks of letting someone live with them who's not on the lease or rental agreement. If the law deems the person a tenant, the resident may have a very difficult time getting the person to move out later and your ability to evict the person is compromised.

When does a houseguest become a resident?

As Benjamin Franklin once said, "Guests, like fish, begin to smell after three days." However, an adult resident may have a guest for far longer than three days, which gives rise to the following questions:

> When does a houseguest become a resident?

> When does a houseguest need to start paying rent?

If an adult houseguest moves his possessions into the rental unit or starts paying rent, the houseguest becomes a resident and must have his name added to the lease or rental agreement. If the houseguest has simply been staying with the resident, then residency depends on how long he has been living in the unit. Generally speaking, after about 14 days, a houseguest can be determined to be a resident and should have his name added to the lease, so he is responsible to start paying rent (and pay a security deposit if the amount of the deposit varies depending on the number of residents). The state or municipality in which you operate may specify a different period of time — typically 30 or 60 days.

Of course, if a resident has a significant other who sleeps over regularly, you probably don't want to force the resident to add this person to the lease. Strict enforcement of such a policy would likely cause some residents to move out before or after the lease term expires.

In the following sections, we discuss the importance of transitioning long-term visitors into residents and the one exception to the rule — New York's Roommate Law.

Don't add anyone to the lease until you've screened and approved the person, as we explain in Chapter 8.

Understanding cotenancy and why it matters

Whenever someone moves into one of your rental units for a long-term stay, establish cotenancy as soon as possible (assuming you've screened and approved the person) by having him sign the lease or rental agreement. In most cases, you'll want to draft a new lease and have all residents sign it, in order to increase the rent to cover the new resident. If you're not increasing the rent, you can simply have the new resident sign and date the existing lease.

Establishing cotenancy is important, because it makes the new resident legally responsible for adhering to the lease terms jointly (together with the other residents) and severally (each resident). (For more about joint and several liability, see Chapter 9.)

When all residents sign the lease to establish a cotenancy, you have the power to take legal action against any and all of those residents when any one of them breaches the lease or rental agreement by

- Not paying the rent on time
- Failing to maintain the rental property
- Disturbing the neighbors
- Bringing in a new roommate without your approval
- Bringing a pet into a no-pets unit
- Smoking in a nonsmoking unit
- Committing criminal acts
- Not adhering to other lease terms

Noting New York's Roommate Law

If you rent property in New York state, residents may be allowed to bring in a roommate, in certain situations, without your approval. As stated in New York's Roommate Law (New York Real Property Law (R.P.L.) § 235 (F)), which states in part:

> 3. Any lease or rental agreement for residential premises entered into by one tenant shall be construed to permit occupancy by the tenant, immediate family of the tenant, one additional occupant, and dependent children of the occupant provided that the tenant or the tenant's spouse occupies the premises as his primary residence.

> 4. Any lease or rental agreement for residential premises entered into by two or more tenants shall be construed to permit occupancy by tenants, immediate family of tenants, occupants and dependent children of occupants; provided that the total number of tenants and occupants, excluding occupants' dependent children, does not exceed the number of tenants specified in the current lease or rental agreement, and that at least one tenant or a tenants' spouse occupies the premises as his primary residence.

In other words, if a resident is the only person on the lease, he can have a roommate. If two or more residents are on the lease, they can have a roommate as long as the total number of people in the unit doesn't exceed the maximum number of people the lease specifies (excluding the resident's dependent children).

However, the law does allow landlords to "restrict occupancy in order to comply with federal, state, or local laws, regulations, ordinances or codes," so if a roommate's not on the lease, you can take legal action to have the roommate removed.

Dealing with Common Cotenant Issues

Cotenancy often results in unique situations. For example, a resident's inability to pay his share of the rent may result in late-, partial-, or nonpayment. Likewise if the cotenants have a dispute and one of them moves out, the remaining residents may have trouble paying the rent and finding a replacement roommate. Cotenants may even expect you to resolve their disputes. And you may encounter problems when a resident takes on a troublesome roommate without getting your approval. The following sections offer some advice on how to handle these and other cotentant issues.

Deciding who pays the rent

How your residents choose to divide the rent between them isn't your decision, and accommodating your residents by accepting multiple payments can cause administrative nightmares. Doing so can also lead a roommate to erroneously believe that he's not responsible for the entire rent. You're better off having a firm policy of requiring one payment source (either check, money order, or electronic payment) for the entire month's rent. This practice offers more than just administrative convenience. Legally, each roommate in your rental property is *jointly and severally* liable for all rental contract obligations, meaning that if one skips out, the others owe you the entire amount.

Encourage your residents to let the delinquent roommate know that they're all on the hook until the balance is paid. After all, your residents are in a better position to track down their elusive roommate than you are.

Don't accept partial rent payments from two or more cotentants. You may not receive all the payments at the same time or for the proper amount. When you call the residents, some of them may say that they paid their share and that you need to track down one of the other residents. Make it easier on yourself by requiring a single rent payment from all of the cotentants in a unit.

Raising the rent and security deposit

If one of your residents brings in a new roommate, you may want to raise the rent to cover the added expenses you're likely to pay and to lower your exposure to risk. After all, the more people living in a rental unit, the greater the wear and tear on the apartment and common areas and the greater your exposure to risk. An additional resident may also take up another parking space and increase your cost of landlord-paid utilities and other operating expenses.

To avoid misunderstandings about the cost for an extra roommate, include a clear statement in your lease or your policies and procedures document regarding the maximum number of occupants and specify how much each additional occupant (up to the maximum) will raise the monthly rent. Your security deposit policy (see Chapter 10) should also include a statement of the amount of the security deposit required for each additional roommate. Requiring an additional security deposit provides you with leverage to compel the new resident to comply with the lease terms. Be sure to check with a local fair housing expert to make sure that increasing rent or the security deposit per occupant isn't considered discrimination of the basis of a familial status violation.

Taking a hands-off approach to cotenant disputes

When cotentants try to get you involved in their disputes, we have one word of advice: *Don't!* Instead, tell the residents to work out their differences among themselves. Remind them that they're responsible as a group for complying with the lease agreement. If you get involved, you're likely to find yourself in a no-win situation in which one or all cotentants turn against *you*.

Unless a resident has a restraining order against a cotenant, don't change the locks or take any other action to prevent a cotenant from entering the rental unit. If you're concerned that a resident will be harmed by his roommate, consult with local law enforcement or other relevant agencies and let your resident know what actions he can take legally to protect himself. If you're dealing with a tense situation, call 911 and let law enforcement handle it.

In domestic violence situations that are disrupting your other residents, you may be tempted to evict the victim as well as the perpetrator in order to rid yourself of the problem. Be careful. In some states, including Rhode Island, evicting a victim of domestic violence is illegal or restricted to limited fact situations.

Terminating a cotenant's lease

When a cotentant needs or wants to leave before the lease term expires, you need to ensure that you continue to receive rent payments from the remaining residents, decide what to do with the departing resident's share of the security deposit, determine whether you should terminate the existing lease, and if you will then sign a new lease with the remaining residents, which may include a new resident as discussed in the next section.

How a cotenant's departure plays out varies depending on whether he signed a lease or month-to-month rental agreement, whether he has found a suitable replacement, whether you want the remaining residents to stay, and other factors. When a cotentant leaves or gives you written notice of his plans to move out, keep the following information in mind:

✔ If the cotentant signed a month-to-month rental agreement, he should give you a written 30-days' notice prior to leaving, which gives the other residents and you 30 days to find a suitable replacement. Regardless of whether you find a suitable replacement, the departing resident will no longer be responsible for any rent beyond that 30-day period if he moves out by the expiration of the notice.

✔ If a cotentant breaks the lease by leaving prior to the expiration of the lease term, you have the option to terminate the lease with the others and evict them, if necessary. If they're good renters, keep them and give them time to find a replacement. If they're not good renters, the breach of the lease by one resident gives you the opportunity to get rid of them all.

✔ Although the departing resident is responsible for any unpaid rent, courts expect you to do what's possible to mitigate (lessen) the damages (any lost rent or reimbursement of advertising that you claim the residents owe you). For example, if the departing resident finds a replacement, you need to accept the replacement or have a good reason to reject him. If the departing resident and his cotentants can't find a suitable replacement, and they can't or won't pay the rent in full, you need to advertise the unit and find new residents.

✔ As soon as a suitable replacement is found or you decide to evict the residents, terminate the existing lease, as we explain in Chapter 19, so a departing resident can't come back and claim that he never really intended to leave.

Deciding Whether to Allow Subleases or Assignments

A resident may approach you and request the right to assign or sublet his interest in the rental unit.

✔ If you allow an *assignment,* the new resident takes over all aspects of the original resident's rental contract, and you can take legal action directly against the new resident if that ever becomes necessary. In effect, the assignment of a lease substitutes another person for the original resident, including all the legal obligations for which the original resident was responsible.

Of course, you would only consider allowing a departing resident to assign his rental contract after following your normal applicant screening process and determining the proposed new resident is qualified.

✔ *Subleases* are a relationship solely between your resident and the new resident. You can't directly sue the new resident for unpaid rent or damage to the property; all you can do is go after the original resident. In the sublease situation, the sublessee has no obligations, legal or otherwise, to you. Your legal relationship continues only with the resident.

Residents usually only request the right to assign or sublet when they must suddenly relocate for personal or professional reasons. Typically, rental contracts prohibit subleases because you want to have a direct relationship with the occupant. Therefore, having a provision in your lease that absolutely prevents subleasing is extremely important. Assignments are superior to subleases because they give you the opportunity to screen and approve the new resident's application and create a legally binding landlord-resident relationship.

Subleases needlessly complicate the landlord-resident relationship and prevent you from directly taking legal action against the occupant of your premises. Doing so erodes your ability to respond to situations in which the new occupant is violating lease terms, such as disturbing neighbors or not following policies and rules for parking or the proper use of the common area pool or spa. If the proposed occupant meets all your rental criteria, propose terminating the current rental contract and entering into a new one with him.

Chapter 19

Revising and Terminating Rental Contracts

. . . .

In This Chapter

▶ Modifying a rental contract

▶ Recognizing various ways to end a rental contract

▶ Evicting residents as a last resort

. . . .

*W*hen you and one of your residents sign a rental contract (known either as a lease or rental agreement), you're both obligated to abide by its terms. However, you can change the terms of the contract unilaterally at certain times, as well as whenever you and the resident agree to a change. In addition, both you and your resident have the power to terminate the contract for certain reasons, by giving the other party reasonable advanced notice.

This chapter focuses on the intricacies of altering and terminating rental contracts. You find out how to modify the terms of a contract, how you or your resident can terminate a contract without breaching it, and how to follow legal eviction procedures when a resident just doesn't work out.

Changing the Rental Contract Terms

When you and your resident sign a rental contract, neither party can change the terms of the contract except in the following situations:

- ✔ You and your resident have a month-to-month rental contract, and you've given the resident notice of the change as required by your state. (Most states require a minimum 30-day notice.)

- ✔ The fixed-term contract has expired, and the resident is willing to renew it with the modified terms. In other words, you and resident agree to sign a new contract when the current one expires.

- ✔ You and your resident mutually agree to the proposed change(s).

If your rental property is subject to rent regulation, be extra careful when raising the rent. For more about setting rents, informing residents of rent increases, and dealing with rent regulation, see Chapter 7.

When you're ready to change the rental contract, you can do so in any of the following ways:

- ✔ **Edit the existing contract.** If the changes are minor, you can edit the contract by crossing out or adding language and then signing (or initially) and dating each change and having your resident sign (or initial) and date each change.

- ✔ **Attach an amendment or addendum to the existing agreement.** An *amendment* is any change to the original contract. An *addendum* is an addition to the original contract. Make sure the edits or changes are typewritten or otherwise legible.

You can find several addendums to the rental contract by visiting www. dummies.com/go/landlordlegalkit.com and clicking on the Rental Contract folder. You and your resident must sign and date the amendment or addendum to show that you both agree to the changes.

- ✔ **Create a new rental contract.** If your resident is renewing the rental contract or your changes are substantial, consider creating an entirely new contract that you both sign and date. Write on the original contract "Canceled on" followed by the date, and then sign and have your resident sign to acknowledge the cancellation. (You may also use a Mutual Termination of Lease or Rental Agreement form, as explained in the next section, to document the cancellation.) Make sure the cancellation date is the same as the date of the new contract. (Keep a copy of the original and new contracts.)

Don't blindside your resident with changes to the rental contract. We recommend calling the resident (or meeting her in person) to discuss the proposed changes and then following up with a written notice. Deliver the written notice as required by state law. States typically require a minimum 30-day notice in writing delivered in person or by mail. Check with your attorney or your local affiliate of the National Apartment Association (NAA) to find out the requirements for your area.

Terminating a Rental Contract

Landlords and residents often have many good reasons to terminate a rental contract. For example, a resident may get married or buy a house and need to move to a new dwelling, or you may need to terminate your contract with a resident who fails to pay rent or abide by other lease terms.

As landlord, you need to know when you and the resident have the right to terminate your rental contract and the proper procedure you must follow to terminate the contract without legal repercussions. The rules for terminating a rental contract vary according to its type: lease or rental agreement. The following sections fill you in on the details, so you can avoid unnecessary legal risks. We also explain under what circumstances that you and your resident can terminate a lease or rental agreement and provide you with the forms required to give proper notice.

Terminating a lease

You can terminate a lease in any of the following three ways:

- Let the lease expire and don't renew it.
- Mutually agree with your resident to end the lease.
- Require that the resident move out for breach of contract.

In the following sections, we explain each option.

Serving a Notice of Nonrenewal

You can terminate a fixed-term lease at the end of the term for any reason or no reason at all by serving the resident with a Notice of Nonrenewal of Lease, as shown in Figure 19-1. For a copy of this form, visit www.dummies.com/go/landlordlegalkit.com and click on the Rental Contract folder.

Some states don't require landlords to serve residents with a notice of non-renewal. However, if your lease requires the resident to give you advanced notice of her intent to move out, most courts interpret that duty to be reciprocal, and you have to give the resident a notice of nonrenewal if you decide not to renew the lease.

Notice of Nonrenewal of Lease

Date: _____

Premises: _____

Tenant: _____

Landlord: _____

Landlord's Address: _____

As TENANT [*Name*] _____ of the above-referenced PREMISES, you are hereby notified that LANDLORD [*Name*] _____ has elected <u>not</u> to renew the lease of the PREMISES which will expire on the ____ day of _____ 20____.

Accordingly, TENANT [*Name*] _____ s further notified that:

1. TENANT must vacate the PREMISES on or before said lease expiration date.

2. If TENANT does not vacate the premises on or before said lease expiration date, under [*State*] _____ law TENANT will be liable for additional rent of $_____ per day; or _____ times the daily rental rate for each day tenant stays beyond said expiration date.

3. All rent must be paid. The security deposit is <u>not</u> a substitute for the last month's rent or any other month's rent.

LANDLORD:

_____
Signature of landlord or authorized representative

Figure 19-1:
Notice of
Nonrenewal
of Lease.

Form courtesy of IREM

Even if a notice isn't legally required, informing the resident in writing 30 to 60 days in advance that the lease won't be renewed is wise. Doing so gives residents time to decide whether they want to stay or move. If they decide to move, it gives them time to find new accommodations.

Mutually agreeing to terminate the lease

Lease termination can be a useful strategy to avoid the hassle and expense of court proceedings because some renters just aren't good candidates for multifamily housing. They make too much noise, don't pay rent on time, trash the premises, or violate occupancy standards, perhaps by having long-term guests in violation of your lease.

If a resident just isn't working out for you, and you can't resolve the problem using techniques like we explain in Chapter 17, consider the possibility of terminating the lease. Meet with your resident and discuss the desirability of ending the lease without further obligation on either party. If your resident agrees, sign and have your resident sign a Mutual Termination of Lease Agreement, as shown in Figure 19-2. For a copy of this agreement, visit www.dummies.com/go/landlordlegalkit and click on the Rental Contract folder.

Mutual Termination of Lease or Rental Agreement

This Mutual Termination of Lease or Rental Agreement is made on _____, 20 _____,

and (check one)

_____ effective immediately;

_____ as of _____, 20 _____

terminates the Lease/Rental Agreement, dated _____, 20_____ between

_____ (Owner/Agent) and

_____ (Resident) for the

premises located at _____, Unit # _____ (if applicable)

(Street Address)

_____, _____ _____.

(City)   (State)   (Zip)

For valuable consideration, the Owner/Agent and the Resident agree:

1) The Owner/Agent and Resident agree they are bound by the terms of the Lease or Rental Agreement indicated above.

2) The Owner/Agent and Resident have mutually agreed to terminate the Lease or Rental Agreement effective as indicated above.

3) The Owner/Agent and Resident agree that all terms and conditions of the Lease or Rental Agreement indicated above are in full force and effect until the mutually agreed date of termination, including, but not limited to, all rent for said premises is due and payable up to and including the date of termination.

The undersigned parties acknowledge having read and understood the foregoing.

_____	_____	_____	_____
Date	Resident	Date	Resident
_____	_____	_____	_____
Date	Resident	Date	Resident
_____	_____	_____	_____
Date	Owner/Agent	Date	Owner/Agent

Figure 19-2:
Mutual
Termination
of Lease
or Rental
Agreement.

Form courtesy of Robert S. Griswold

Giving bad renters an incentive to move

I (Laurry) provide services to a company that develops and manages a portfolio of low-income housing properties. The incidence of rent delinquencies is, unfortunately, high. The owner files evictions in large numbers, but the court system in the states in which the owner operates are overwhelmed with these and similar landlord-tenant matters; the result is that the delinquent residents often continue to live, rent-free, in their apartments for several months before they can be evicted, which means that prospective renters who could pay rents in full and on time can't move into these properties.

We've put in place a program that forgives all past-due rent, avoids eviction, and pays residents who agree to participate a nominal sum to seek alternative housing, on condition that residents relocate within several days. The apartment units are in great demand and are quickly re-rented. The departing residents, who receive whatever remains of their security deposit, together with these small stipends, don't have an eviction on their records and are often successful in finding new housing. The strategy can be used to circumvent the formal evictions process for violations of other lease provisions as well.

In addition, some residents whose lease-violative behaviors or inability to pay rent timely simply shouldn't be living in rental housing. The availability of lease terminations can be a vehicle to conclude their leases without involving the court system and the costs associated therewith. The lease termination document is effectively a contract: the resident's consideration for the termination is giving up the right to continue renting the unit (and continuing to, for example, violate other residents' right to quiet enjoyment); the landlord's consideration can be a nominal stipend or discontinue eviction proceedings that have previously been brought.

Court proceedings to evict residents can be expensive. Proceeding by way of lease termination as an alternative allows the landlord to have a unit available for a prospect who will pay rent on time and/or observe the terms and conditions of the lease agreement, both of which are beneficial to the owner. Some landlords prefer to proceed with eviction proceedings solely for the purpose of ensuring that the defaulting resident will have an eviction on her record, so that a new prospective landlord will be warned that the resident is a bad business risk. The alternative is better.

Terminating the lease for breach of contract

You can terminate a lease prior to the date on which it ends only if the resident's behavior is criminal or constitutes a serious breach of the lease terms. If you have good reason to terminate the lease prior to its end date, you may need to serve the resident with a legal document first that gives the resident a chance to address the issue(s) that concern you, such as nonpayment of rent or damage to the unit. (See "Serving legal notices," later in this chapter, for details.)

If the resident fails to address the issue(s) by the specified date, then you can follow up with a termination notice, such as the notice shown in Figure 19-3. For a copy of this termination notice, go to www.dummies.com/go/ landlordlegalkit and click on the Rental Contract folder.

To: _____
  And all occupants
  [INSERT PROPERTY ADDRESS]

You are hereby notified that your lease agreement with [PROPERTY NAME] _____ is being terminated _____ days from receipt of this notice; the effective termination date being _____ _____.

The reason for said termination is:

  NON-PAYMENT OF RENT IN THE AMOUNT OF _____ DOLLARS
  ($_____) NOW DUE AND UNPAID, BEING THE RENT DUE FROM
  _____ TO _____.

You are hereby required to remove yourselves and personal belongings from and deliver the possession of said premises by returning all keys to the undersigned within _____ days or the undersigned will institute legal proceedings against you to receive possession of said premises.

The premises herein referred to are described as:

[INSERT PROPERTY NAME AND ADDRESS]

_____

_____

You have _____ days within which to discuss this proposed termination of tenancy with the manager. The _____-day period will begin on the earlier of: (a) the date the notice was hand delivered to the unit, or (b) the day after the mailing date of the notice (or if required by state law, served by a process server).

If you request the meeting, the manager agrees to discuss the proposed termination with you.

You have the right to defend this action in court.

_____
Name

_____   _____
Title   Date

Mailed USPC _____

Placed on Door _____

Process Server _____

Figure 19-3: Sample termination notice.

Form courtesy of Robert S. Griswold

Ending a rental agreement

Ending a rental agreement is much easier than terminating a lease, because a rental agreement is a month-to-month contract. In most states, you can terminate a rental agreement for any cause or without cause:

- ✔ **With cause:** If a resident's behavior constitutes a serious breach of contract, you can terminate the rental agreement immediately or by giving the resident only a few days' notice, depending on state and local laws. Follow the same procedures you would follow for ending a lease due to breach of contract (see the previous section, "Terminating the lease for breach of contract," for details).

- ✔ **Without cause:** Some states prohibit landlords from ending rental agreements without cause, so check the legal requirements for your state. If your state permits termination without cause, make sure you deliver the notice of nonrenewal at least 30 or 60 days prior to the termination date as required by state law.

State laws can be very specific about when, how, and in what form termination notices must be presented. Residential rental property that's subject to rent control may have additional requirements. Contact your local NAA affiliate to find out about state and local requirements.

Dealing with a resident's termination of the rental contract

Like landlords, residents generally are bound to honor the terms of a rental contract until the date on which it ends unless the resident and landlord mutually agree to terminate it, as explained earlier in "Mutually agreeing to terminate the lease." Residents also have the legal right to terminate a rental agreement if the landlord breaches the contract — typically by not maintaining the unit or by failing to secure the resident's right to quiet enjoyment of the property.

Residents may also terminate a lease or rental agreement under certain extenuating circumstances, including the following, depending on federal, state, and local laws:

- ✔ Death
- ✔ Bankruptcy
- ✔ Military service that requires relocation a certain number of miles from the rental unit
- ✔ Serious illness or the need for an elderly resident to move into a nursing home or assisted-living facility

✔ Resident is a victim of stalking, sexual assault, or domestic violence

✔ Landlord's breach of contract

If a resident buys or builds a house, she remains bound to the contract unless it contains a buy-or-build provision.

If a resident breaks the rental contract without good cause or without giving notice, she's responsible for paying rent until the contract expires (or the end of the month in the case of a rental agreement) or up to the day when a new resident moves in. However, you're obligated to help mitigate the damages caused by any lost rent. In other words, you need to do your best to find a suitable replacement as quickly as possible (usually within one to two months), so the departing resident isn't stuck paying three or four months' rent for a dwelling that she's no longer living in.

To discourage residents from terminating a lease prematurely without an acceptable reason, consider adding language to your rental contract that gives residents the option to pay an early termination fee. A termination fee covers lost rental income along with the costs of advertising the unit, processing applications, screening applicants, and processing paperwork for the new resident. You may deduct the termination fee from the security deposit.

You can add the language in the contract itself or use the Early Termination of Lease Term addendum shown in Figure 19-4. For a copy of this addendum, visit www.dummies.com/go/landlordlegalkit and click on the Rental Contract folder.

Requiring an intent to move out notice

Add a clause to your rental contract requiring residents to provide written notice at least 30 days prior to the date they plan to move out. Having the resident notify you in advance and in writing helps you avoid lawsuits from your current and new residents:

✔ If a resident merely tells you that she plans to move out on a particular date and fails to do so, she can deny that she told you, and you would have a difficult time proving she did. The resident would have a tough time disputing a written notice that includes the move-out date and her signature.

✔ If your new resident is ready to move in, but your current resident hasn't moved out on the agreed upon move-out date, you may need to pay storage fees and arrange temporary accommodations for your new resident. You may even lose your new resident if she decides to live elsewhere.

Addendum to Lease — Early Termination of Lease Term
(To be attached to Lease Agreement)

Tenant Name(s):_____

Apartment Community Name:_____

Lease Dates:_____

This Addendum, made this ____ day of _____, 201___, is attached to, and made a part of, that certain Apartment Lease Contract (the Lease) by and between _____ [Company name] and _____ [Tenant's name].

In consideration of the Lease and the mutual covenants contained herein, the parties agree as follows:

_____

EARLY TERMINATION OF LEASE TERM

During the initial term specified in Paragraph 1, a Lessee shall be entitled to terminate the lease by providing Landlord with written notice (as required in Paragraph 29) of not less than thirty (30) days (specifying a vacate date of the last day of a calendar month) and payment of an early termination fee equal to:

    a)   Two (2) months' rent if Lessee has fulfilled less than nine (9) months of the Lease term (as of the proposed vacate date), or

    b)   One (1) month's rent if Lessee has fulfilled at least nine (9) months of the Lease term (as of the proposed vacate date).

The Lease will be considered terminated upon receipt by Landlord of a proper written notice and payment (in the form of a cashier's check or money order) of the early termination fee and all rent and other charges (on or before the vacated date) due through the date of Lessee vacating the apartment. If Lessee fails to timely vacate, pay the early termination fee, or pay any other charges due through the date of vacating, the attempted early termination permitted by this paragraph shall be deemed void, and the other provisions of this Lease with respect to charges associated with a Lease break shall apply.

_____   _____
Tenant   Date

Figure 19-4:
Early Termination of Lease Term addendum.

DISCLAIMER: These sample forms and agreements are not endorsed by the Institute of Real Estate Management. They are presented for informational purposes only and should not be relied on for accuracy, completeness, or consistency with applicable law. The user is advised to check all applicable state and federal laws before using these forms, agreements, or parts thereof. Because certain forms have legal implications (e.g., management agreements, rental applications), it is recommended that downloaded versions of such forms should be reviewed with legal counsel prior to their use and that any modifications made by the user should also be reviewed by legal counsel.

Form courtesy of IREM

Provide residents with a Tenant's Notice of Intent to Vacate Rental Unit, as shown in Figure 19-5, to make it easy for them to provide the written notice you need. For a copy of this notice, head to www.dummies.com/go/landlordlegalkit and click on the Rental Contract folder.

Tenant's Notice of Intent to Vacate Rental Unit

Date _____

_____
Owner/Manager

_____
Street Address

_____
City, State, Zip code

Dear _____ ,

This is to notify you that the undersigned tenants, _____ ,
hereby give you written notice of intent to vacate the rental unit at _____
on _____ .

We understand that our Lease or Rental Agreement requires a minimum of _____ days notice before we move. This Tenant's
Notice of Intent to Vacate Rental Unit actually provides _____ days notice. We understand that we are responsible for paying
rent through, the earlier of: 1) the end of the current lease term; 2) the end of the required notice period per the Lease or Rental
Agreement, or 3) until another tenant approved by the Owner/Agent has moved in or begun paying rent.

In accordance with our Lease or Rental Agreement, we agree to allow the Owner/Agent reasonable access with advance notice in
order to show our rental unit to prospective renters or workmen and contractors

Sincerely,

_____
Tenant

_____
Tenant

_____
Tenant

Figure 19-5:
Tenant's
Notice of
Intent to
Vacate the
Rental Unit.

Form courtesy of Robert S. Griswold

Accepting rent after the lease ends

When a resident stays in a unit after the lease ends and continues to pay rent, the lease automatically renews (in a few states) or changes to a month-to-month rental agreement (in most states). You have several options for dealing with residents who choose to continue to live in a unit and pay rent after their lease expires:

- Continue to accept rent payments as part of a month-to-month rental agreement (in states where this occurs).

- Renew the lease for another year or let the lease automatically renew (in states where this occurs).

- Revise or attach an amendment to the existing lease (if you and your resident agree to the changes), sign and date the lease, and have your resident sign and date it.

- Terminate the lease and draw up a separate agreement that lets the resident stay in the unit and pay rent for a fixed number of days, weeks, or months (use the Mutual Termination of Lease or Rental Agreement form, as explained earlier in the section "Terminating a lease").

If you accept rent payments from a resident, you're creating an informal contract with the resident that allows her to live in the unit. If you want the resident to move out, try to get the resident to sign a Mutual Termination of Lease or Rental Agreement that specifies the date on which she must move out and don't accept rent for any period beyond that date. If the resident refuses to sign the agreement and move out, you may have to initiate eviction, as explained later in this chapter in the section "Evicting Troublesome Residents." If you agree to allow the resident to live in the unit beyond the expiration date of the mutual termination agreement, put your agreement in writing, and have your resident sign and date it before you accept payment for the extension.

Prorating rent

Ideally, you and your resident choose to terminate your agreement as of the first of the month (or the beginning of the next rental period), so you don't have to prorate rent. However, termination doesn't always occur on schedule. Ten days into the month, a resident may give her required 30-day intent to vacate notice and move out on the tenth of the following month (or on the 30th day per your calculations, which can vary depending on the length of month in question). You then have to prorate the rent for those extra days.

You can try to enforce a policy stating that residents must give their 30-day notice on the first of the month or pay the entire month's rent, but that's not always in your best interest. If your resident gives his 30-day notice 10 days into the rental period, and you use the security deposit to cover rent for the remaining 20 days of the following month, you may be guilty of misusing the security deposit. We recommend that you accept the resident's termination notice whenever she gives it and accept partial (prorated) rent for the last several days the resident remains in the unit before the notice expires.

Unless otherwise agreed, you normally uniformly apportion rent from day to day using a 30-day month. Divide your monthly rental rate by 30 to determine the daily rate and multiply your answer by the number of days in the partial rental period. (This formula applies to February as well.)

Evicting Troublesome Residents

Some residents just don't pay their rent; others violate the rules or are involved in criminal activities. In these situations, after you've explored your other options, you may have no other reasonable alternative but an eviction. The eviction process, which we explain in the following sections, can be intimidating and costly, but keep in mind that allowing the resident to stay only prolongs the problem.

The eviction process varies greatly from state to state, and many attorneys who specialize in representing rental property owners offer guidebooks that outline the specific legal steps for an eviction action in your area. Your local Institute of Real Estate Management (IREM) chapter or National Apartment Association (NAA) affiliate can provide attorney references. You can access contact information for both groups by heading to www.dummies.com/go/landlordlegalkit and clicking on the Resources folder.

Serving legal notices

To evict a resident, you need to follow the applicable law as well as the terms of the contract. Although the terminology varies from state to state, three basic types of legal notices are required, depending on the circumstances:

- **Pay Rent or Quit notices:** These notices are given to residents who haven't paid rent and require them to pay the rent or move out. Residents are typically allowed 3 to 10 days to pay in full, depending on the law in your state, but some jurisdictions allow up to 30 days. Be careful not to include late fees or other nonrent charges in your Pay Rent or Quit notice, because many courts will determine that the notice is overstated, and you may lose your case.

- **Cure or Quit (or Perform Covenant or Quit) notices:** This paperwork is given to residents who've violated terms or conditions of the rental contract. It gives residents a limited number of days (determined by state law) to cure the violation or vacate the premises; if they fail to do so, they're subject to an eviction action. The most common violations are an unauthorized pet or occupant or unpaid fees, such as late charges, returned check fees, or utility bills.

  Note that if your residents choose to quit or move-out within the number of days provided by the required legal notice, they're still obligated under all the terms of the existing lease or rental agreement. This isn't some tricky way for your residents to be relieved from their contractual obligations by simply not paying rent and then waiting for you to serve them a Pay Rent or Quit notice.

✔ **Notice to Quit or Unconditional Quit notices:** These documents are the most severe types of notices and require residents to vacate the premises without the opportunity to cure any deficiency. Most states discourage the use of these notices unless residents are conducting illegal activity, have repeatedly violated a significant term or condition of the rental contract, or have severely damaged the property.

Filing a formal eviction action

If your resident doesn't cure the violation or leave the property after receiving the appropriate legal notice, she isn't automatically evicted. Instead, you must begin a formal eviction process by following these steps:

1. **File the required forms with your local court and arrange to have the resident properly served with a summons and complaint.**

   The complaint is usually a preprinted form, and you can only seek unpaid rent and actual damages (such as court costs and attorney's fees). Many times, daily rental damages continue to accrue during the *pendency of the action* (the time between when you file and the court issues its decision), and they can be added to the judgment granted at the end of the court process.

   Serving a legal notice isn't simply a matter of mailing the notice or slipping it under the resident's door. You must have an authorized person attempt to physically deliver the legal notice to the resident face to face. If the notice can't be delivered directly to the resident, there are usually procedures for substitute service or posting and mailing pursuant to a court order. Every state has specific rules and procedures as to what exactly constitutes *proper legal service,* including who can serve notices, the method of delivery, the specific parties who can be legally served, and the amount of time the resident has to respond to the legal notice. Serving some legal notices (such as complaints) may not be simply a matter of mailing the notice. Check with your attorney for the requirements in your area.

2. **By law, a trial date is set, and your resident has a certain number of days to file an answer to your summons and complaint.**

   Residents usually either deny the allegations you've made in your eviction action or claim that they have an *affirmative defense* (a legal justification for their actions). The resident may deny your allegations, for example, if she has a canceled check showing that the rent was paid and your records are in error.

Frequently, residents know that they've materially breached their rental contracts and voluntarily leave the premises. Or sometimes residents settle with you out of court.

If your resident settles informally, you must officially dismiss your court eviction action because doing so is the proper way to treat your resident and it also preserves your reputation with the court. After all, courts have limited resources and don't respond well to parties who resolve their matter and fail to file a timely dismissal. Also, failing to dismiss an eviction action can result in a negative credit standing for your resident. Be sure that you put your informal settlement agreement in writing, with all residents acknowledging that they have given up the right to possess the premises.

3. **If your resident doesn't file an answer in a timely manner, the eviction action proceeds to court without the resident.**

   This scenario is known as an *uncontested eviction*. The court requires you to prove your case, but the resident isn't there to respond to or deny your charges. Typically, you can easily prevail in this situation, as long as you have good documentation.

4. **If your resident files an answer and appears at court, each party receives the opportunity to present its evidence before the court makes a ruling.**

   This scenario is known as a *contested eviction*. In the alternative, the parties can enter into a formal written settlement right before trial. Then the judge signs the settlement and it becomes a court order. If a settlement isn't reached, the parties proceed to present evidence in the courtroom. If you're prepared and credible, you can generally win. However, the courts can be very harsh if you've acted illegally or in a retaliatory or discriminatory manner toward the resident.

   You may also have to show that you've properly and promptly responded to any complaints by your resident during her tenancy, especially those that involve allegations of health and safety violations or uninhabitable conditions at your property. This is where your detailed keeping of all maintenance or service requests and written documentation showing all communications between you and the resident will be very helpful to your case.

   A resident may be able to argue that he's entitled to additional time to work out a payment plan for the unpaid rent or that she has a hardship that requires the court's leniency. Courts have been known to allow a resident an extension because of inclement weather, an appeal of the ruling, serious health issues, or other situations beyond the resident's control.

Some jurisdictions show extra leniency during the fall and winter holidays, so you may want to be more diligent to get your matter to court quickly if the holidays are approaching.

5. **If you win the eviction lawsuit, you must present the judgment to local law enforcement.**

Local law enforcement gives the resident one final notice before going to the rental unit and physically removing the resident (and in some states her possessions). Arrange to have someone meet the law enforcement officers at the property at the designated time, and be sure that you have a locksmith or a capable employee to be able to open the unit if the residents have changed the locks and to rekey the unit immediately after you receive legal possession of the unit.

Following the do's and don'ts of the eviction process

Although the eviction process is rather straightforward in most areas, you still want to ensure you don't do anything to jeopardize the proceedings. We can't guarantee that the process will run smoothly, but if you keep the following in mind, you can alleviate many headaches:

✔ **Do use an attorney.** The filing and serving of eviction actions are governed by very precise and detailed rules. The smallest mistake can result in delays or even the loss of your case on technicalities, regardless of the fact that the resident hasn't paid rent or has otherwise violated the rental contract.

✔ **Don't fail to properly respond to maintenance requests.** Even if you're in the middle of an eviction process with a resident, you're *always* responsible for properly maintaining the premises. If someone gets hurt because of your failure to keep the property in good condition, you can be sued. We recommend that you fix the problem immediately and worry about who is responsible later.

Residents and their attorneys are very sensitive to maintenance issues. Any failure to respond to a resident's request for maintenance can be used as a defense in the eviction action.

✔ **Don't get too emotionally involved in an eviction process and make an irrational decision that can be construed as a self-help eviction.** See the nearby sidebar for more about self-help eviction.

Avoiding self-help eviction

A *self-help* or *constructive eviction* is a situation in which the owner takes illegal actions to effectively force the resident to vacate the premises. Veteran rental property owners love to tell stories about the good old days when they could just change the locks or shut off the electricity or water to encourage a resident to immediately vacate the premises. But in today's reality, no states tolerate these aggressive tactics, regardless of how bad the resident behaves. In many states, even reducing or eliminating free services such as cable TV may be prohibited; the court may consider this move an illegal self-help measure, and the resident can sue for significant penalties.

To avoid ending up on the wrong side of a lawsuit, don't pursue vigilante justice. Follow legal eviction procedures and work through the courts and local law enforcement when you need to evict residents. The wheels of justice turn slowly, but taking matters into your own hands may result in serious (expensive) consequences.

Collecting judgments

When you win in court and your resident owes you for unpaid rent, damages, or legal fees and court costs, you've received a *money judgment* against the resident. But the judgment isn't worth much unless you're able to collect. If you know that the resident has a job or other unencumbered assets, in most states you can obtain a court order to garnish her salary or have local law enforcement seize her assets and sell them, with the net proceeds of the sale going to you.

The majority of problem residents aren't easy to locate, so your best bet may be to hire a licensed collection agency to attempt to locate the resident and collect your judgment. These agencies are usually paid on a contingency basis and receive a portion of the collected amount, typically ranging from one-third to one-half of the amount. Sometimes they add any out-of-pocket expenses (*hard costs*) of collection to the amount they retain. Although you may want to make your own efforts to enforce the judgment, remember that collection agency success rates and fees are often tied to the age of the bad debt. So the sooner you submit the judgment for collection, the easier it is for the agency to collect, lowering the fee you have to pay.

Your success in collecting judgments often depends on how hard you worked throughout the tenancy. The rental application typically contains valuable information for a collection agency, including the resident's Social Security Number (SSN) or Individual Taxpayer Identification Number (ITIN), prior addresses, current and prior employment information, banking and credit card account information, vehicle information, and emergency contact names and addresses or telephone numbers. If you require a resident to complete this application, you verify its accuracy, and you keep the info updated, then you have a great place to start hunting her down for collections.

Chapter 20

Moving a Resident Out

· ·

· ·

Moving a resident out sounds easy. You inspect the rental unit, deduct unpaid rent and the cost of any damages from the security deposit, refund the remaining amount to the resident, and you're done, right? Not exactly. In order to protect yourself legally and avoid later disagreements regarding the security deposit refund and other issues, you must prepare for your resident's move-out in advance and carefully follow a process that documents her exit.

We suggest that you start preparing for your residents' eventual move-out when they first move in. Yes, you read that correctly — when they move in. The Resident Information Letter (covered in more detail in Chapter 11) provides residents with the legal requirements of move-out, as well as your expectations for giving proper notice. You can use the Move-In/Move-Out Itemized Statement (also explained in Chapter 11), which you complete upon move-in to establish the unit's baseline condition, to evaluate the unit's condition on move-out, and to calculate the appropriate charges, if any.

In this chapter, we lead you through the process of moving a resident out of her rental unit. We encourage you to require written notice of your resident's move-out plans and provide the resident with an information letter designed to end your landlord-resident relationship on a positive note. We also lead you through the process of inspecting the rental unit and explain the steps to take when a resident abandons her rental unit without providing any notice.

Requiring Written Notice of Your Residents' Move-Out Plans

When they plan to move, most residents are likely to call to let you know, even if your rental contract contains a clause that requires written notice. Some residents may put their notices in writing by sending you simple one- or two-sentence letters or e-mail messages but omit important details. Although any type of written notice from a resident is usually legal, a proper notice provides the information you need to know and documentation of the resident's plans.

To be sure you're complying with the law in all regards, require your residents to submit a Tenant's Notice of Intent to Vacate Rental Unit, as shown in Figure 20-1.

Visit www.dummies.com/go/landlordlegalkit to access a version of the Tenant's Notice of Intent to Vacate Rental Unit online that you can print, fill out, and supply to your residents. You can find it in the Tenancy folder.

Tenant's Notice of Intent to Vacate Rental Unit

Date _____

Owner/Manager _____

Street Address _____

City, State, Zip code _____

Dear _____,

This is to notify you that the undersigned tenants, _____,
hereby give you written notice of intent to vacate the rental unit at _____
on _____.

We understand that our Lease or Rental Agreement requires a minimum of _____ days notice before we move. This Tenant's Notice of Intent to Vacate Rental Unit actually provides _____ days notice. We understand that we are responsible for paying rent through, the earlier of: 1) the end of the current lease term; 2) the end of the required notice period per the Lease or Rental Agreement; or 3) until another tenant approved by the Owner/Agent has moved in or begun paying rent.

In accordance with our Lease or Rental Agreement, we agree to allow the Owner/Agent reasonable access with advance notice in order to show our rental unit to prospective renters or workmen and contractors.

Sincerely,

_____
Tenant

_____
Tenant

_____
Tenant

Figure 20-1: Tenant's Notice of Intent to Vacate Rental Unit.

Form courtesy of Robert S. Griswold

Time is truly of the essence concerning your resident's move-out. Several states have deadlines for the accounting or return of the security deposit of only 14 or 15 days, and virtually *all* states require the security deposit accounting to be completed within 30 days. See Chapter 10 for more about managing and returning security deposits.

Often landlords and property managers receive less than the legally required notice or no notice at all. So how do you determine the resident's financial responsibility in such cases? Say the required notice is 30 days, and the resident gives you a written notice on the tenth of the month that she plans to vacate at the end of the current month. The resident must vacate as agreed, but she's responsible for the full rent through the required 30-day notice period. In such instances, you may have a legal obligation to re-rent the property to mitigate the resident's loss; however, in situations where only a few days remain in the required notice period, most courts don't expect you to re-rent the unit.

Providing Your Resident with a Move-Out Information Letter

A great way to improve the chances that a resident leaves your property in good condition is to communicate your expectations as soon as you discover that the resident is planning to move out. The Move-Out Information Letter (see Figure 20-2) thanks your residents for making your rental unit their home and provides them with the procedures for preparing the unit for the final move-out inspection. It also informs them of your policies and method of returning their security deposit after any legal deductions.

You can access a printable version of the Move-Out Information Letter by visiting `www.dummies.com/go/landlordlegalkit` and looking in the Move-out folder.

Although state law and your rental contract may contain information on the security deposit refund process, most residents appreciate receiving this information so they know what to expect without having to search for their rental contract while trying to pack.

The Move-Out Information Letter reminds residents that they can't apply their security deposit to the last month's rent and that it's only to be used as a contingency against any damages to the unit or for other lawful charges. If no portion of a resident's deposit is called "last month's rent," you aren't legally obliged to apply it in this way. Unless your rental contract uses this wording, don't allow your residents to try to apply their deposit toward their final month's rent or you may not have enough money on hand to cover any legally allowed charges. The only time that you apply the security deposit funds to rent is if unpaid rent is one of the damages you suffer, as the landlord, after the resident has vacated.

Figure 20-2:
This letter can help end the landlord-resident relationship on a positive note.

> **Move-Out Information Letter**
>
> Tenant Name(s) _____
> Rental Unit Address _____
>
> Dear _____,
>
> We are pleased that you selected our property for your home and hope that you enjoyed living here. While we are disappointed to lose you as a tenant, we wish you good luck in the future. We want your move-out to go smoothly and end our relationship on a positive note.
>
> Moving time is always chaotic and you have many things on your mind, including getting the maximum amount of your security deposit back. Contrary to some rental property owners, we want to be able to return your security deposit promptly and in full. Your security deposit is $_____. Note that your security deposit shall not be applied to your last month's rent as the deposit is to ensure the fulfillment of lease conditions and is to be used only as a contingency to be used to ensure the fulfillment of lease conditions according to the applicable law.
>
> This move-out letter describes how we expect your rental unit to be left and what our procedures are for returning your security deposit. Basically, we expect you to leave your rental unit in the same condition it was when you moved in, except for ordinary wear and tear that occurred during your tenancy. To refresh your memory, a copy of your signed Move-in/Move-out Inspection Checklist is attached reflecting the condition of the rental unit at the beginning of your tenancy. We will be using this same detailed checklist when we inspect your rental unit upon move-out and will deduct the cost of any necessary cleaning and the costs of repairs, not considered ordinary wear and tear, from your security deposit.
>
> To maximize your chances of a full and prompt refund, we suggest that you go through the Move-in/Move-out Inspection Checklist line-by-line and make sure that all items are clean and free from damage, except for ordinary wear and tear. All closets, cabinets, shelves, drawers, countertops, storage, refrigerator and exterior areas should be completely free of items. Feel free to check-off completed items right on this copy of the Move-in/Move-out Inspection Checklist, as we will use the original for your final inspection.
>
> Some of our tenants prefer to let professionals complete these items. You can contact your own professional or upon request we will be glad to refer you to our service providers so that you can focus on other issues of your move. You will work directly with the service provider on costs and payment terms knowing that you are working with someone that can prepare the unit for the walkthrough inspection. Call us if you would like contact information or for any questions as to the type of cleaning we expect.
>
> Please be sure to remove all personal possessions, including furniture, clothes, household items, food, plants, cleaning supplies and any bags of garbage or loose items that belong to you. Of course, please do not remove any appliances, fixtures or other items installed or attached to your rental unit unless you have our prior written approval.
>
> Please contact the appropriate companies and scheduled the disconnection or transfer of your phone, cable and utility services in your name. Also, cancel any newspaper subscriptions and provide the U.S. Postal Service with a change of address form.
>
> Please contact us once all of the conditions have been satisfied to arrange an inspection of your rental unit during daylight hours. To avoid being assessed a key replacement charge, please return all keys at the time you vacate.
>
> You have listed _____ as the move-out date in your notice. Please be reminded that you will be assessed holdover rent of $_____ per day for each partial or full day after the above move-out date that you remain in the rental unit or have possession of the keys. If you need to extend your tenancy for any reason, you must contact us immediately. An extension may not be available, so contact us as soon as possible. Please be prepared to provide your forwarding address where we may mail your security deposit.
>
> It is our policy to return all security deposits either in person or at an address you provide within _____ after you move out **and** return all keys. If any deductions are made for past due rent or other unpaid charges, for damages beyond ordinary wear and tear, or for failure to properly clean, an itemized explanation will be included with the security deposit accounting.
>
> If you have any questions, please contact us at _____. Thank you again for making our property your home. We have enjoyed serving you, and we hope that you will recommend our rental properties to your friends, family, and colleagues. Please let us know if we can provide you with a recommendation letter. Good luck!
>
> Sincerely,
>
> _____
> Owner/Manager

Form courtesy of Robert S. Griswold

If the vacating resident is a good one, ask whether you can provide her with a letter of recommendation. A positive reference can be very helpful to residents, whether they're moving to a new rental property or buying a home. This kind of offer is welcome and courteous and is one that most residents have never received from prior landlords. The bonus for you? Residents often work extra hard to make sure the rental unit is clean and undamaged to earn that recommendation.

Conducting the End-of-Lease Inspection

After your resident vacates your rental property, inspect it as soon as possible, preferably during daylight hours. Doing so allows you to determine what work you need to do to ready the property for a new resident and to assess any charges that you need to deduct from the former resident's security deposit.

A good way to motivate residents to comply with your move-out procedures is to remind them that they'll receive the full sum of their deposit (plus interest if required by statute) if they have paid all rent due and leave the rental unit in clean condition, with no damage beyond ordinary wear and tear. (For help in distinguishing damage from ordinary wear and tear, check out Chapter 10.)

To ensure the walk-through runs smoothly, you need to understand the process and how to handle the security deposit if you uncover damages. The following sections can help.

Thoroughly inspecting the property

Many landlords have been asked to perform the move-out inspection with some or all of the resident's possessions still in the rental property, only to discover that creative residents can hide damage very easily. If your resident asks you to inspect the property this way, politely decline and schedule the move-out inspection with your vacating resident just *after* she removes all her furnishings and personal items, turns in all her keys, and either disconnects the utilities or converts them to your name as the property owner. Most damage occurs when residents move their belongings in or out, so another plus for doing the inspection at this time is that you can make sure the resident doesn't do additional damage after the inspection while she's removing her possessions.

Unfortunately, you can't always arrange to do the inspection with your resident after she has actually moved out. In this case, conduct the move-out inspection as soon as possible and preferably with a witness present (or at least a digital still or video camera). If you wait too long to inspect the unit and then discover damage, the resident may claim that someone else must have caused the damage, and you may face an uphill battle in court.

We strongly recommend performing the final move-out inspection with the vacating resident present. Doing so resolves many of the issues that can later become contentious enough to end in small claims court. If you live in a state that allows the resident to be present when you're determining the proper security deposit deductions, consider doing that as well.

Residents have been known to show up for the walk-through, but deny that they know anything about the damaged items you find. Refer to your Move-In/Move-Out checklists. If the checklist clearly indicates that the item was in good condition when the residents moved in and is now damaged, their claim of innocence doesn't stand much of a chance. However, if the move-in remarks are blank or vague, you may have some problems justifying a deduction.

As the landlord, the courts hold you to a higher standard of record-keeping by the courts; they usually interpret any missing or vague documentation in favor of the residents.

Completing the move-out checklist

As you inspect the property, complete the move-out portion of the Move-In/Move-Out checklist that you started when the resident moved in. (See Chapter 11 for details on completing the move-in portion of the checklist.)

Indicate each item's condition — new, excellent, very good, dirty, scratched, broken, and so on — but also include explanatory details, such as writing "Hole in drywall two feet above the floor under the window on NE wall of SE bedroom" rather than just writing "Damaged drywall." The more specific you are about the damage and its location, the less likely the resident will dispute the damage later.

If possible, complete the checklist in the resident's presence and have her sign and date the checklist. If the resident is unavailable, have your witness sign and date the checklist.

Taking photos to document any damage

Regardless of whether you took photos or recorded video to document the condition of the rental unit prior to move-in, take photos or record video to document the rental unit's condition as you perform your move-out inspection.

Use your camera's date-stamp feature to include the date on all photos or video recordings. Although date stamps can be tampered with (changing the camera's setting to a phony date), the date stamp usually increases the evidence value of the photos or video recording. Or you can use the popular technique of taking a picture of the current daily newspaper. This can also be deceiving if someone want to back date an inspection, but certainly proves the inspection was no sooner than the publication date of the newspaper.

Recognizing common damage deductions

As you inspect the property for damage and complete the move-out checklist, don't overlook common damage deductions related to costs for

- Cleaning the unit to make it as clean as it was when the resident moved in
- Replacing damaged or missing items provided with the unit, including all keys, carpeting and flooring, furniture, appliances, light fixtures, and window and door screens
- Repainting the unit due to damage to the walls, ceiling, or paint (beyond tiny nicks and scratches)

Consider giving the resident the option of fixing any damage prior to moving out. Disputes often arise when landlords don't give residents advanced notice of deductions and one last chance to clean the unit and repair any damage. By giving the resident an opportunity to bring the unit up to move-in condition, you avoid any nasty surprises that could spark a dispute with the security deposit (refer to Chapter 10 for more information).

Reclaiming an abandoned rental unit

Occasionally, residents abandon your rental unit without notice. This discovery can be good news if you're taking legal action against the resident, because you're sure to save lost rent days and may be able to reduce your legal costs.

Each state has its own definition of abandonment, so make sure you comply with all state legal requirements before trying to determine that the rental unit is abandoned. The best way to know for sure is to contact the resident and have her give you a statement in writing relinquishing her rights to possession of the unit. Emailing as well as calling her place of employment when you suspect abandonment is a good idea. You can also check with the neighbors or reach out to the emergency-contact person on her rental application.

Have a policy in place requiring that your residents inform you if they plan to be absent from the unit for more than one or two weeks. Knowing that they haven't skipped town can be helpful in determining whether a property is abandoned or the resident is just away.

Consider giving the resident a legal notice in order to enter the unit if you suspect that the resident has abandoned your property. You can serve this notice by mailing a copy to your resident at the unit address and/or by posting the notice on the front door as required by your state law. After you're inside the unit, look for additional evidence, including removed furniture, clothing, and toiletries; stale, spoiled, or missing food; and absent pets. You can also send your resident a note or letter. If it's returned undeliverable or forwarded to a new address, it can be an indication your resident has abandoned the unit.

If you already have an eviction action under way, your legal counsel may suggest that you continue the legal process until you receive possession. This way you can minimize your potential liability in the event that the resident shows up later and claims the right to the rental unit. Or if no eviction action is in progress, be sure to serve the required legal notice of belief of abandonment. When you've met your state requirements, you can take possession of the unit and begin your turnover work to put it back on the rental market. The disadvantage to declaring abandonment is that you won't get a court judgment for possession or for money.

Part V
The Part of Tens

Visit www.dummies.com/extras/landlordlegalkit to find out about ten important laws that govern residential rentals and the landlord-resident relationship.

In this part . . .

- ✔ Discover ten ways to reduce your exposure to legal claims and defend yourself when such lawsuits are unavoidable.

- ✔ Focus on communicating with residents and getting all agreements in writing.

- ✔ Find out how to become a better landlord, so residents will be less likely to take legal action against you, and if they do, they'll have a tough time proving their case.

- ✔ Find an apartment or landlord association to obtain additional information and training.

Chapter 21

Ten Tips for Staying Out of Legal Trouble

In This Chapter
▶ Operating according to the highest ethical standards
▶ Selecting only the best applicants without discriminating illegally
▶ Getting all agreements in writing
▶ Keeping your property in good repair
▶ Using security deposits only for their intended purpose

Staying out of legal trouble is a lot less costly and aggravating than getting out of legal trouble. In this chapter, we present ten preventive measures that can help you avoid lawsuits and defend yourself when such lawsuits are unavoidable.

Acting beyond Reproach

Acting beyond reproach helps you steer clear of legal trouble in two ways:

✔ When you do the right thing, you earn respect, and people are less likely to file claims against people they respect and like.

✔ By always acting ethically, you establish a reputation of being fair and reasonable, which gives you credibility in the courtroom. A track record of cheating people out of money is likely to undermine your credibility in the courtroom.

Complying with the law is the bare minimum. To stay out of legal trouble, act ethically — above the law and beyond reproach. In other words, do the right thing, such as:

✔ Screen applicants using only those characteristics that matter, such as whether the evidence leads you to believe that the applicant will pay the rent on time, take care of the property, and get along with his neighbors.

✔ Treat residents with respect and consideration. Clear and timely communication is one of the most considerate things you can offer.

✔ Focus on customer satisfaction by putting the residents' needs before your own.

✔ Treat contractors, employees, and other personnel the way you would like to be treated.

✔ Work only with contractors, employees, and other personnel who operate ethically.

Screening Applicants Carefully

To avoid trouble, keep potential troublemakers out of your rental units. As much as you want to maintain 90 to 100 percent occupancy, you need to select the best applicants from the available pool.

Market and advertise strategically and aggressively to expand your pool of applicants and attract the type of residents you want (without breaking any fair housing laws). You can be more selective when you have more and better applicants from which to choose. Refer to Chapter 6 for more on advertising your property within the law.

Substandard renters can hurt your business in several ways:

✔ Through lost rent and the time and aggravation of collecting rent from residents who fail to pay in full and on time

✔ By damaging your property and increasing your maintenance and repair costs

✔ Through the loss of good residents, who understandably want to live next to good neighbors

✔ By introducing a criminal element to your property that increases your exposure to lawsuits

✔ Through the time and expense of getting the bad renters to leave, possibly through the drawn-out legal process of eviction

✔ By giving your rental property a bad reputation that keeps potentially good residents from applying

Keeping Abreast of Changing Laws

Laws are subject to change at all levels — federal, state, and local — and ignorance of the law is no excuse for breaking it. As landlord, you need to be aware of any new legislation that affects landlord responsibilities, resident rights, building codes, taxes, and so on.

One of the best ways to keep abreast of changing laws is to join a state or local apartment association that keeps its members posted of legislative updates. If you can't find a state or local apartment association, head to the National Apartment Association's website at `www.naahq.org` and search for an affiliate.

Writing a Solid Rental Contract

Your *rental contract* (a fixed-term lease or month-to-month rental agreement) establishes the resident's legal rights and obligations. Review your rental contract carefully and have a qualified local attorney review it to make sure the contract terms are clear, correct, and comprehensive, and that they comply with federal, state, and local laws. (See Chapter 9 for more about composing a rental contract.)

Contract terms need to be clear and written in proper legal language. A resident who violates the terms of a rental contract that are clearly presented in proper legal language will have a difficult time proving her case in court. If a term's wording is ambiguous or worded improperly, a resident could use it as a successful defense against a claim.

Have a local attorney who is experienced in drafting residential rental property agreements review your rental contract and any and all addendums to the contract along with your policies and rules.

Complying with Fair Housing Laws

As a landlord, you want to target your marketing and advertising to quality renters and then screen out any applicants that are likely to test your patience. You need to be selective, and nothing is wrong with doing so. However, you can't disqualify applicants or treat residents differently based on any of the following federally protected classes:

- Race
- Color
- Religion

- ✔ National origin
- ✔ Sex
- ✔ Familial status
- ✔ Disability

Your state or municipality may specify additional protected classes, including source of income, marital status, sexual orientation, and personal appearance, to name a few. For more about fair housing laws, see Chapters 5 and 6.

Maintaining Your Property

Poorly maintained property can lead to legal trouble in several ways, including the following:

- ✔ Stairs, walkways, and handrails in disrepair can lead to trips and falls and potential personal injury lawsuits.
- ✔ Failing to address issues that make a unit uninhabitable give the resident the right to break the lease or withhold a portion or all of the rent payment.
- ✔ Burned-out lights in parking lots, entryways, and other common areas increases the risk of injury and crime.
- ✔ Poorly maintained plumbing can cause health risks.
- ✔ Broken locks, screens, and windows make it easier for criminals to gain unauthorized access to rental units.

Conduct regular maintenance inspections (if legally allowed) and encourage residents to report maintenance or repair issues they notice. Attend to these items as quickly as possible, and thank residents for helping you maintain the property. Chapter 12 provides additional information about the importance of unit maintenance.

Keeping a Paper Trail

From the time a resident submits an application until the day she moves out, document all communications (written or spoken) in writing. Detailed documentation not only helps you defend yourself in court, but it also often convinces a resident not to file a legal claim in the first place. Many times, all you need to do to discourage a resident from filing a false claim against you is to present your evidence.

Keep a file for every resident that includes the following items:

- ✔ Signed rental application

- ✔ Your screening policy, which includes criteria you use to screen applicants

- ✔ Signed copies of the rental contract and other agreements, along with amendments and addenda to agreements

- ✔ A signed Move-In/Move-Out checklist that documents the condition of the property prior to the resident moving in and after the resident has moved out along with before and after photographs

- ✔ Maintenance records, including resident requests

- ✔ Incident reports

- ✔ Resident complaints and your responses

- ✔ All correspondence to and from the resident

- ✔ Record of all relevant spoken agreements

- ✔ All legal notices, including late-rent and termination notices

Following Legal Eviction Procedures

The eviction process is long, costly, and aggravating, so landlords sometimes perform *self-help* or *constructive* evictions. They turn off the heat, electricity, or water; change the locks on the unit; or harass the resident until she moves out "voluntarily." Self-help eviction is a breach of the rental contract on the grounds that the landlord interferes with the resident's quiet enjoyment of the property or makes the property uninhabitable. It gives the resident the right to move out without paying any additional rent. Courts even may award additional damages to the departing resident. When you need to evict a resident, follow the legal guidelines for doing so as Chapter 19 discusses.

Practicing a Reasonable, Legal Security Deposit Policy

Disagreement and confusion over security deposits are often at the root of disputes between landlords and residents, so establish and practice a security deposit policy that complies with state and local laws. Here's what we recommend:

✔ Charge a security deposit that's within any legal limit set by state or local statute or no more than one or two months' rent if your state and locality don't specify a limit.

✔ Place security deposits in a separate, interest-earning account that's used exclusively for security deposits, even if your state or city doesn't require separate deposits or accounts that accrue interest.

✔ Deduct only damages (beyond ordinary wear-and-tear), cleaning, and unpaid rent from the security deposit.

✔ Promptly return any unused portion of the security deposit to the resident, (along with any interest the money has earned if required, or if you do voluntarily) and an itemized statement showing what the deposit paid for.

State and local laws vary a great deal on the security deposit amount, whether it's refundable, whether it must be kept in a separate account, whether the account must be interest-bearing, and what it can be used for, so find out the rules that govern security deposits before establishing your policy. You may also want to talk with other landlords in the area to find out the standard practice in your area. Refer to Chapter 10 for more advice about security deposits.

Promising Less, Delivering More

Managing resident expectations helps keep them satisfied. If residents have high expectations that you can't or won't meet, they're going to be dissatisfied with what they get. For example, if you lead a resident to believe that you'll refund her security deposit in full as long as nothing's damaged when she moves out, and you deduct a cleaning fee from the damage deposit, the resident will understandably be confused and upset and may even take legal action against you.

Be especially careful when marketing and advertising your units. If you advertise a swimming pool that turns out to be more like a cesspool, your resident is likely to feel cheated.

Chapter 22

Ten (or So) Tips for Being a Better Landlord

In This Chapter

▶ Determining whether you have the right stuff to be a good landlord

▶ Building relationships with residents and with professionals in the industry

▶ Increasing your knowledge through training and certification

▶ Keeping up on repairs and maintenance issues

*B*eing a highly qualified landlord who is committed to customer satisfaction plays a big role in avoiding the legal pitfalls of managing residential rental properties. If you treat your residents with contempt, fail to address their needs, and are careless in screening residents and performing your other duties as a landlord, you're likely not to be respected by your tenants.

In this chapter, we encourage you and explain how to boost your credentials as a landlord and establish the positive personal and professional relationships that make success possible.

Assessing Your Landlord Readiness

Not everyone is cut out to be a landlord. In fact, even some landlords aren't cut out to be landlords. Before you choose to seek your fortune in the residential rental industry, take your pulse, and make sure you have the following:

✔ **A property manager or building supervisor or the desire and energy to be one:** If you don't have a property manager or at least a building supervisor, then you're it, and you can expect to receive text messages and phone calls at any time of the day or night demanding your immediate attention.

✔ **Knowledge of your and your residents' legal rights and obligations:** You must know and follow the rules and regulations that govern the residential rental industry so you're not tripped up by exasperating technicalities.

✔ **Attention to detail:** Specifically, you must craft a clear and detailed rental contract and other legal documents, carefully screen every applicant and roommate, enforce your rules consistently and fairly, and keep a written record of all relevant interactions you have with residents.

✔ **Patient persistence:** Regardless of how emotional or annoying a resident is, you must keep your cool while working toward the outcome you desire. Angry reactions, including retaliating against a resident, are likely to lead to legal battles and resident retaliation.

✔ **Assertiveness:** You need to tell your residents what you need and when you need it, enforce the terms of the lease and any additional policies and procedures, and be prepared to evict residents who are bad for business, regardless of how much you like or sympathize with them.

✔ **Cash-flow management skills:** Rental payments and bills don't always arrive on schedule. Rental payments tend to arrive on time or late, while bills blindside you at the most inopportune time. You need to be able to manage your cash flow, so you have at least as much money coming in as you do going out.

Maintaining Rapport with Residents

The best ways to maintain positive relationships with residents are to treat them fairly and respectfully and respond to their maintenance and other service requests promptly. In other words, focus on customer service. Satisfied residents rarely complain or file lawsuits and are more likely to pay their rent on time, take care of their rental units, and get along with their neighbors.

If possible, get to know a little about each of your residents on a personal level — without becoming intrusive. Consider inviting residents to a cookout and then mingle with the guests. You may engage in small talk and, if appropriate, ask questions to find out about any concerns they have regarding the property or their rental unit, how the property is being managed, or incidents you're unaware of. Landlords and residents are much less likely to get into bitter disputes and much more likely to settle their differences outside of the courtroom when they know, respect, and trust one another.

Establishing Professional Relationships

Networking is an excellent way to become a better landlord. Just be sure you network with the right people — other competent and dedicated landlords, property managers, bankers, attorneys, contractors, and so on. Meet regularly with professionals in your community who have a stake in the local residential rental market to talk shop. Discussing situations with colleagues often provides you with the very information you need to resolve a difficult issue.

Use your smartphone or computer to store the names and contact information for professionals in your industry who seem to be very good at what they do. Don't hesitate to call for assistance. Most of the best professionals are generous with their time and expertise, so don't hesitate in calling or emailing them for assistance. Be sure to give back to professionals who help you by referring potential clients or customers to them and assisting in any other ways you're able to.

Joining an Association

A great way to connect with colleagues is through your local landlord, apartment, or real estate investors association, such as the following:

- ✔ **National Apartment Association (NAA)** at `www.naahq.org`. Mouse over Join, click Find an Affiliate, and use the search page to track down state or local affiliates. Click an affiliate's link to visit its website and find out more about it.

- ✔ **Institute of Real Estate Management (IREM)** at `www.irem.org`. IREM is an affiliate of the National Association of Realtors and an international community of real estate managers dedicated to ethical business practices, maximizing the value of investment real estate, and promoting superior management through education and information sharing. To find a state or local chapter, visit IREM's website, click Chapter, click Find a Chapter, and use the resulting page to search for chapters in your state.

To broaden your search, use your favorite Internet engine to search for your state followed by "landlord association," "apartment association," or "real estate investor association." The search results are likely to include links to relevant groups. If you find a national association, its website probably contains a search feature to find local affiliates.

Don't merely join a landlord or apartment association. Attend meetings and educational offerings and use their resources to become a better landlord. After you develop a good feel for the association and its members, consider taking on a leadership role by becoming an officer or director or serving on a committee. Through leadership, you build your reputation and expand your network almost effortlessly.

Taking Landlord Training Courses

Several states and large cities offer free or low-cost landlord training programs that cover just about everything you need to know about screening, contracts, codes, exterior maintenance, property management, fire and safety inspections, eviction, and keeping crime out of your rental property. These training programs are valuable, especially in bringing you up to speed on the basics and on local ordinances and building codes. If you can't make it to class, at least try to find and read a state or local manual for landlords; many of these manuals are PDFs that you can read online or print. At the end of most of these manuals is a list of local resources for landlords and residents.

Most landlord, apartment, and real estate investor associations also offer continuing education programs in property ownership and management, marketing, maintenance, and other aspects of owning and managing residential rental property.

Getting Certified

To become more educated in property management and build your credentials as someone who's committed to excellence and is ethical, work toward becoming a certified manager. The Institute of Real Estate Management (IREM) offers three certifications for individuals:

- Certified Property Manager (CPM)
- Accredited Residential Manager (ARM)
- Accredited Commercial Managers (ACoM)

If you're planning to manage your rental properties yourself, we strongly recommend that you get certified. If you're in the market to hire a property manager, look for applicants with one or more of these certifications or accreditations. Check with your local NAA affiliate for their certifications.

Keeping Abreast of Legal Developments

Several governing bodies — federal, state, and local — enact and enforce legislation and regulations that affect residential rental properties and landlord and resident rights and obligations. If a law or regulation changes and you don't know about it, you're more likely to violate it and end up in legal trouble.

In Chapter 2, we show you how to conduct legal research on your own, but you typically research a legal topic only when you're dealing with a specific issue that you may have been able to avoid had you known the law in the first place. The two best ways to keep abreast of changes to laws and regulations is to have someone who's more qualified do it for you:

✔ **Attorney:** Many attorneys who specialize in serving landlords keep their clients informed of any changes they need to be aware of. If you have an attorney, ask him to keep you posted. It's as simple as broadcasting an email message to all of his clients.

✔ **Trade association:** National landlord or apartment associations and their local affiliates may post changes to laws or regulations on their website or inform registered members via email or text.

Being Proactive

Landlords come in three types: passive, reactive, and proactive. A passive landlord collects rent and does as little as is required to stay in business. A reactive landlord collects rent and addresses problems as they arise. To be a proactive landlord, you need to do the following:

✔ Inspect your rental property regularly for maintenance and repair issues, if allowed by law.

✔ Encourage residents to report maintenance and repair issues.

✔ Respond promptly and courteously to all resident requests and concerns.

✔ Work closely with local law enforcement to *prevent* crime rather than merely calling 911 when a crime occurs.

✔ Notify residents in writing in advance of anything you're planning to do that may inconvenience them or disturb their peaceful enjoyment of the property — timely and clear communication is essential.

✔ Stress the importance of customer service and satisfaction with any and all of the people who work for you.

Honing Your Communication Skills

Disputes often arise over misunderstandings rather than actual differences of opinion. By improving your communication skills, you can reduce the number and severity of misunderstandings between you and the people you interact with on a daily basis. Here are a few suggestions for refining communications with residents, employees, contractors, and others:

- ✔ Keep everyone in the loop. When people know what to expect, even if it's bad, they're more willing and able to accept it.

- ✔ Listen more than you speak and ask questions to clarify a situation before you make any statements. Reacting to what you assume happened or what you assume is a person's intended meaning is worse than saying nothing.

- ✔ Write clearly and succinctly. Visit www.plainlanguage.gov for guidance, and use spelling and grammar checker to clean up documents and even email and text messages before sending them.

- ✔ Speak with residents in person or over the phone about more complex and sensitive issues. Don't rely solely on email and text messages, which are often misinterpreted. After you resolve an issue, document it, sign and have your resident sign it if necessary, and file it in the resident's folder.

Hiring an Expert When Necessary

A landlord commonly wears many hats. One day you're an attorney, the next day you're a plumber or an accountant or even an electrician. That's fine, as long as you're competent and doing it yourself is financially wise; otherwise, hire a pro. A qualified professional in any given field can perform a task better, faster, and often for less money than a do-it-yourselfer.

When deciding whether to perform a task yourself, consider the costs, including the lost income you could be making by investing your time in more lucrative activities. Consider the fact that you can deduct the money you pay a professional from your gross profit, but you can't deduct the time you invest in a project. Also think about the potential risk: If you injure yourself on the job, who will pay your bills and lost wages and manage the property? In addition, if you don't do quality work, you may need to redo it or hire a professional to do it right, and you'll be responsible for any damages that occur due to the lack of quality the first time.

Index

G

H

• *M* •

• S •

About the Author

Laurence C. Harmon, President of Harmon *Law* LLC, specializes in real estate law and provides extensive teaching, market research, and consulting on subjects related to multifamily housing, marketing, and management, with concentration in federal and state fair housing law. He earned his bachelor's degree in history and marketing, cum laude, from Pomona College, Juris Doctorate (JD) with honors from the Stanford University School of Law, and the Certified Property Manager (CPM) designation from the Institute of Real Estate Management (IREM).

He has published textbooks and numerous articles on marketing residential rental properties and resident retention, including *Contemporary Apartment Marketing: Strategies and Applications* (IREM, 1994); *The Resident Retention Revolution* (IREM, 1995); *The Tenant Retention Solution* (IREM, 1996); and *Residential Marketing: The Science and the Magic* (IREM, 2007). He can be contacted at harmonlaw@outlook.com.

Robert S. Griswold, MBA, is the author of *Property Management Kit for Dummies* as well as the coauthor of *Real Estate Investing For Dummies* with Eric Tyson. He earned a bachelor's degree and two master's degrees in real estate and related fields from the University of Southern California's Marshall School of Business. His professional real estate management and investing credentials include the Counselor of Real Estate (CRE), CPM, Accredited Residential Manager (ARM), Certified Commercial Investment Member (CCIM), and Professional Community Association Manager (PCAM).

Robert is a hands-on property manager with more than 35 years of practical experience, having managed more than 800 properties representing more than 60,000 rental units. He owns and runs Griswold Real Estate Management, Inc., a property management firm with offices in southern California and southern Nevada. Visit www.griswoldremgmt.com.

Dedication

From Laurry: I dedicate this book to my wife — and constant inspiration! — Kathleen, with whom I recently celebrated the blessing of our 25th anniversary. She and I began our personal and professional partnership more than three decades ago, working together in property management, co-authoring four apartment marketing and leasing textbooks published by the Institute for Real Estate Management, and collaborating closely and lovingly on our various real estate and other challenging ventures ever since. My beloved family includes our daughter, Laura, and our sons, Jeremy, Collin, and Blair, as well as grandbabies Beatrice and Joe. My fondest love and gratitude to all of them!

Another blessing has been the continuing influence of the late Caroline Scoulas, our erstwhile IREM editor, who enthusiastically supported and challenged us during the preparation and pruning of the books we wrote during her tutelage. This book is very much a product of the mentoring Caroline so selflessly provided to us. We hope that it is worthy of her.

From Robert: I dedicate this book to God for blessing me with my wife Carol (of 32 years) and with my four incredible children — Sheri, Stephen, Kimberly, and Michael. I am sure grandkids aren't far away.

Author's Acknowledgments

This book was made possible through the efforts of some very fine people at John Wiley & Sons, Inc. Special thanks to acquisitions editor Erin Calligan Mooney for choosing us to write this book; to project editor and copy editor Chad Sievers for his guidance and for keeping everything on track and for ridding our prose of grammatical glitches, spelling snafus, and the occasional awkward phrase; to freelance technical writer, Joe Kraynak, for his assistance in presenting our information and insights in a clear, easily digestible format; and to technical editor Kathleen Belville, for fact-checking the manuscript and making sure our advice hit the mark.

Publisher's Acknowledgments

Acquisitions Editor: Erin Calligan Mooney

Development Editor/Contributor: Joe Kraynak

Project Editor: Chad R. Sievers

Copy Editor: Chad R. Sievers

Technical Editor: J. Kathleen Belville, Esq.

Art Coordinator: Alicia B. South

Project Coordinator: Patrick Redmond

Project Manager: Rick Graves

Cover Photos: ©iStockphoto.com/dem10